Triathletes in Motion

Marc Evans

Jane M. Cappaert, PhD

Human Kinetics

Library of Congress Cataloging-in-Publication Data

Evans, Marc, 1953-
 Triathletes in motion / Marc Evans, Jane Cappaert, PhD.
    pages cm
 Includes index.
 1. Triathlon--Training. I. Title.
 GV1060.73.E94 2014
 796.42'57--dc23

                          2013045504

ISBN-10: 1-4504-3220-4 (print)
ISBN-13: 978-1-4504-3220-7 (print)

The web addresses cited in this text were current as of February 2014, unless otherwise noted.

Acquisitions Editor: Tom Heine; **Project Consultant:** Kevin Bigley; **Developmental Editor:** Laura Pulliam; **Assistant Editors:** Elizabeth Evans; Jan Feeney; **Copyeditor:** John Wentworth; **Indexers:** Robert and Cynthia Swanson; **Graphic Designer:** Fred Starbird; **Graphic Artist:** Tara Welsch; **Cover Designer:** Keith Blomberg; **Photograph (cover):** Right and middle photos Ali Engin; left photo Fotolis Royalty Free; **Photographs (interior):** © Human Kinetics, unless otherwise noted; **Visual Production Assistant:** Joyce Brumfield; **Photo Production Manager:** Jason Allen; **Art Manager:** Kelly Hendren; **Associate Art Manager:** Alan L. Wilborn; **Illustrations:** © Human Kinetics, unless otherwise noted; **Printer:** Sheridan Books

Human Kinetics books are available at special discounts for bulk purchase. Special editions or book excerpts can also be created to specification. For details, contact the Special Sales Manager at Human Kinetics.

Printed in the United States of America   10 9 8 7 6 5 4 3 2 1

The paper in this book is certified under a sustainable forestry program.

Human Kinetics
Website: www.HumanKinetics.com

United States: Human Kinetics
P.O. Box 5076
Champaign, IL 61825-5076
800-747-4457
e-mail: humank@hkusa.com

Canada: Human Kinetics
475 Devonshire Road Unit 100
Windsor, ON N8Y 2L5
800-465-7301 (in Canada only)
e-mail: info@hkcanada.com

Europe: Human Kinetics
107 Bradford Road
Stanningley
Leeds LS28 6AT, United Kingdom
+44 (0) 113 255 5665
e-mail: hk@hkeurope.com

Australia: Human Kinetics
57A Price Avenue
Lower Mitcham, South Australia 5062
08 8372 0999
e-mail: info@hkaustralia.com

New Zealand: Human Kinetics
P.O. Box 80
Torrens Park, South Australia 5062
0800 222 062
e-mail: info@hknewzealand.com

E5785

Triathletes in Motion

Contents

Acknowledgments

After finishing and presenting the 150-page outline to my publisher, I asked Jane Cappaert to come on board—not to write the book per se but to validate the complete book and be a strategic collaborator. She did this with exceptional intelligence, expertise, and timeliness. I met Jane when I was the USA Triathlon head coach and at the Olympic Training Center in Colorado Springs in the early 1990s. Jane was the director of biomechanics for USA Swimming at the Center for Aquatic Research. Her published work and our discussions were influential for the Speedo contour and swim foil training paddles that I invented and patented with engineer Peter Cazalet. For my second book, *Endurance Athlete's Edge* (Human Kinetics), Jane confirmed the energy system and training methods I put forward. Her expertise in swimming biomechanics is based on her highly regarded published work as a researcher and scientist. During many conversations and edits of this manuscript, Jane was pivotal in facilitating my themes chapter by chapter. Her contributions to this book exceeded every expectation.

Kevin Bigley is one of the most knowledgeable physical therapists I have worked with. Kevin has an easygoing manner and a keen eye for movement assessment and function and exercise remedies. He thoroughly appreciates the importance of individual assessment. His experience in evaluating movement, musculoskeletal injury, and biomechanics and prescribing state-of-the-art exercise remedies is outstanding. Working through my original movement and assessment outlines, Kevin established the best approach for individual assessments that are a central part of this book.

Unique to this book are the sidebars by Chrissie Wellington, Dave Scott, Torbjorne Sindballe, Sarah Groff, and Mark Allen. They brought forth original and meaningful material. In every instance, they took on their uncompensated assignments earnestly and professionally.

No less important are the models for the techniques, tests, and exercises. I wanted photos of open-water ocean swimming, and world-record holder Karlyn Pipes (photographed by Dana Richardson) flawlessly demonstrated the techniques presented in the book. Professional athletes Ryan and Maia Ignatz were a picture-perfect combination for running images in the unique way I envisioned. Last, but not least, are the models for the movement and stability exercises and tests: Alison, Ariel, Carley, Cory, and Courtenay. I am grateful for their patient help and ability to take direction with such kindness.

From Human Kinetics Publishers, developmental editor Laura Pulliam and photographer Neil Bernstein were unbelievably supportive and professional; they deserve my most sincere thanks. Laura was professional and optimistic, and she demonstrated at every step that she understood how meaningful I wanted this book to be. Graphic designer Nancy Rasmus was outstanding as was graphic artist Tara Welsch, both helping make the text, exercise photos, and illustrations accessible. Finally, Consumer division director Jason Muzinic and acquisitions editor Tom Heine were on board early, and their overall comperehension and leadership is sincerely appreciated.

A project of this scale doesn't get done without a lot of quiet moments. It has taken literally thousands of hours. However, I have over the years thought a lot about whom and how to thank certain individuals. Now, at this moment, I know the best way to do that is individually and privately. Their encouragement, care, integrity, patience, friendship, and love have meant the world to me.

Make all of your movements in sport and life better than the last.

Marc Evans

Introduction

More than 30 years ago a unique career emerged. I became the first coach of triathlon. There were no established standards for training triathletes. Almost all knowledge was gained firsthand. Shaping my philosophies were several dog-eared textbooks on physiology, swimming technique, and science. I depended on those to help me form a basis for coaching triathletes.

Like the professional, Olympic, ITU, and Ironman triathlon coaches of today, I coached a team of pioneering elite triathletes in Northern California. The workouts were volume and intensity driven but had another attribute: competition among the triathletes. The training sessions were often long and intense and resulted in successful performances. Still, differences in race outcomes and overuse injuries for some meant more individual attention was needed.

From the beginning, technique has been my main interest in coaching. As a triathlon coach, I considered it essential to become equally skilled at teaching swimming, cycling, and running.

Because of this ideology, individual coaching made sense. Despite developing better ways to coach technique, I was missing something. The underlying limitations in functional movements were the way in which they affected technique and ultimately performance. Thousands of assessments and technique lessons have served as the research laboratory influencing the triathlon standards in this book.

Triathletes in Motion: Assessing Movement for World-Class Technique and Performance is about the foremost principle of training: individualization. This is the basis on which all other levels of training are constructed because no two athletes are alike. Training must be based on these four components: movement, mobility, stability, and technique. Your posture, movement (joint mobility and flexibility), core stability, and technique must be the functional foundations.

In this book you will progress through a series of tests and exercises using accurate, controlled, effortless, and smooth (ACES) movements and progressions. Ultimately, better functional movement improves skill and the innovative technique development system, body lines (body postures and positions), will teach you how to learn cutting-edge techniques in swimming, cycling, and running. Together, the Evans Assessment principle is a model where training is based upon a comprehensive and completely individualized evaluation of movement and stability and combines the development of technique.

Every assessment, test, exercise, and technique includes guidelines for evaluating, training, teaching, and developing more individualized training. With this book, you or a coach will evaluate your movement, stability, and technique, which is a paradigm shift in triathlon training and coaching. This new foundation makes your training program, workouts, and any coaching philosophy more relevant to you.

There are 30 years of examples in triathlon proving why *functional* movements are ideal. Champions such as Mark Allen, Natascha Badmann, Nicola Spirig, Javier Gomez, and Mirinda Carfrae all demonstrate this. Every one of these world and Olympic champion triathletes has functional mobility and stability where they matter most: in the local stabilizers of the pelvis. The run segment of triathlon reveals their graceful and powerful symmetry. Becoming a better triathlete embodies these and other characteristics, the functional foundations of training.

Triathletes in Motion begins with the principles of performance. These are the broader structures of training: balance and posture, flexibility, mobility, stability, nutrition, psychology, and management of intensity. You will learn how to make a preliminary self-test to get a glimpse at your functional movement, load transfer, and stability. More in-depth tests come in later chapters.

Chapter 2 establishes the physiological foundations of triathlon performance: maximal oxygen capacity ($\dot{V}O_2$max), lactic acid, economy, cardiac output and stroke volume, and the energy systems. More theories of training and coaching are also examined: fitness, movement, technique, optimization, overload, specificity, stimulus, interval, recovery, periodization, tapering, and warm-up.

Chapter 3 on posture begins the first stages of improving movement. One self-test and many exercise remedies are given for improving flexibility, joint mobility, and stability. These are organized by asymmetrical movements, and exercises are selected based on how you fared on the test. You will learn how to perform the exercises and progress by training the right number of sets and reps (ACES). This field test allows coaches to examine preliminary movements and stability and make specific recommendations.

In chapter 4, you will learn how to assess functional movement and stability even further. Even greater individualization is possible using a pass–fail (ACES) process for correcting movement. This chapter is essential reading for gauging and achieving normal movement and learning the exercises for improving movement and stability.

In chapter 5, core training is approached in a unique way—at the local stabilizing levels. Endurance athletes must be able to maintain stability locally (at the joint level) and transfer load efficiently from the pelvis for long periods. Unfortunately, many popular forms of core training miss the mark on this central aspect of training. Performed correctly, deeper core training will result in better stability, load transfer, technique, economy, and resistance to fatigue.

Chapters 6, 7, and 8 could be books unto themselves. You will explore theories and the best learning techniques in swimming, cycling, and running. We describe the mechanics and phases of movement and techniques as well as how to achieve postures and positions (body lines) during movement. Technique exercises and workouts complete each chapter and deliver the tools for learning and teaching better movements.

In triathlon, every movement makes a difference and affects performance. This book shows you how to do this better, one athlete at a time. Triathletes and coaches will develop unique training programs and teach techniques in many ways. However, each should be based on the foremost of all the principles: individualization.

You can shape better results from periodization models, training workouts, and innovative regimens of coaches. If you evaluate, correct, and train the areas identified with needs, you will establish a better foundation to build even better performance.

As a former coach and now an educator, I hope this book will help triathletes, coaches, and triathlon federations train more functionally, economically, effectively, and individually.

Marc Evans
Boulder County, Colorado

1 Foundations of Triathlon Performance

The principle that form follows function confirms that we must consider individuals in individual ways. This principle applies not only in terms of volume and intensity of training but in how triathletes move functionally, transfer load, and produce force. Every triathlete responds to training in a unique way, but one element common to all triathletes is the capacity for improvement. This is why assessment is necessary for improved performance, no matter what your current performance level. Only through accurate assessment can weaknesses be targeted and limitations in functional movement corrected. No training program, periodization plan, or intensity and volume–based system will work for every triathlete in the same way. If we rely on elite athlete performances as the basis for training and coaching, we might miss what differentiates those top triathletes from those who just miss the podium.

The economy, or efficiency, of the very best triathletes is built on fully functional movement at the joints, stability at the deeper levels of the core and pelvis, and muscles that function with the right amount of tension. Such triathletes compensate less and can maintain positions that stabilize posture while swimming, generate optimal forces while cycling, and uphold proper posture while running. All triathletes should assess for individual differences beginning with the mobility of joints, flexibility, and stability of muscles.

A triathlete training via intensity and volume–based workouts might indeed find this approach working, sometimes with great success. But how much better might outcomes be if the foundations of movement and stability were combined with optimal technique? The way that energy is transferred to the arms and legs is functionally interrelated, and improving this transfer can make for better posture and position when swimming, cycling, and running. Every triathlete is seeking just the right mix of mobility, flexibility, and stability that produces improved technique, economy, and capacity to reach best performances.

An important principle we'll discuss further in chapter 2 is the principle of individualization, which holds that training must be designed based on a triathlete's individual needs. Because we do not all respond to the same training in the same way, optimal training can never be generalized across triathletes. This of course presents challenges for coaches, who must strive to discover the precise and unique set of variables at play for each triathlete they coach. Similarly, as an individual triathlete you must avoid the temptation to train the way a friend trains just because he or she has achieved success. The pitfalls of this are obvious. Your friend's set of strengths and weaknesses is likely much different from your own. To adopt his or her training program without prior assessment could lead to diminished performance and increased injury risk. Training at the top level of triathlon is complicated. There are so many distinctions in movement and stability among triathletes, and each one of them influences how the triathlete should progress in his or her training. Our goal in this book is to help you determine, through assessment and technique development, the exact areas in which you need improvement, as well as the exact training progression that will yield optimal results for *you,* the individual triathlete. We do this by showing you how to assess on a case-by-case basis the functional movements and stability of your body regions and helping you to design a training program that promotes symmetric movement, efficient transfer and use of energy, and continuous advancement of technique.

Again, there cannot be one single training program, periodization plan, or workout system that works best for all triathletes. Yet many training and coaching programs are generic in their approach, with an entrenched emphasis on training and group workouts that are based on intensity and volume and provide little or no individualization. With all that we know today, training in the absence of periodic comprehensive individual assessment is unthinkable.

By *assessment* we mean much more than testing intensity for power, heart rate, and training-intensity zones. Individual triathletes move far different from one another, and all triathletes have limitations in functional movements, whether caused by muscle length, joint mobility, or core stability. Any of these limitations undoubtedly affects movement efficiency and deters development of optimal technique. Today's triathletes and coaches are learning, outsourcing, and moving toward an all-inclusive, or holistic, approach, becoming proficient technicians across the board in swimming, cycling, and running biomechanics, as well as in movement and stability.

Triathletes in Motion is about examining and developing functional movements specifically for triathlon. We provide all-encompassing principles of technique training as well as self-assessments, self-examinations, a system for coaches, and exercise remedies for the majority of movement limitations encountered

by triathletes. Technique training and those workouts are equally central to the book. These too are individually assessed using a unique training approach: *body lines* that establish standards for self-coaching and teaching by coaches for the assessment of technique and that provide a highly effective training progression plan. This approach to training technique in swimming, cycling, and running guides triathletes step by step in training the best postures and positions through specific segments and regions of the body.

In the technique chapters on swimming, cycling, and running, body lines are described for every benchmark of technique. Carefully teamed with lifestyle levels, baseline tests, and ACES (accurate, controlled, effortless, and smooth movements), the triathlete and coach can fully customize training. When coordinated with the functional movement assessments, test exercises, and improvements, body line training becomes the perfect match for the training of technique and better performance.

All triathletes and coaches must seriously consider changing their approach to training from more or less arbitrary techniques and drills to deliberate and purposeful postures that occur during every motion in swimming, cycling, and running. What we mean by *postures* is explained later in the book but involves breaking the process of training down into phases in which high-quality movements (which we call ACES—explained shortly) can be assessed, corrected, and mastered before progressing to the next phase. Through evidence-based training, the triathlete's functional movements via a complex mixture of skeletal, muscular, and soft-tissue coupling become the point of departure for training— earlier than any other aspect of coaching.

The human body is incredibly malleable, with an extraordinary capacity to adapt. This is primarily a benefit for triathletes but can also create problems when an adaptation to a postural abnormality produces an increase of strain on the body's supporting structures. This leads to less efficiency and balance over the base of support, resulting in increased energy use and greater risk of overuse injury. Such abnormalities, and the body's adaptations to them, must be assessed through testing and corrected through targeted exercises.

Think for a moment about your body and how technique mechanics increase or decrease your balance, posture, and the curves that compete against moving more efficiently. These elements are entrenched in how your body moves functionally, independent of swimming, cycling, and running. Uneven pressures at the joints and poor or inefficient body mechanics increase ligament strain and muscular work and thus pain, discomfort, and sometimes chronic injury.

Every triathlete has his or her own neurological capacities, muscular strengths and weaknesses, level of joint mobility, level of muscle flexibility (including hypermobility), and bone characteristics. No matter your set of attributes, through assessment and exercises to achieve closer to optimal function and by working on technique postures and positions, your functional motion will certainly improve. By improving your functional motion, you save energy by decreasing the amount of energy you need to sustain a given speed, which of course leads to better performance. By improving body postures and positions separately from swim, bike, and run workouts it is possible to boost performance even more.

Movements and Postures

As you know, most movements become more adept through training. But for optimal improvement in performance to occur, you need functional balance and stability throughout your body, with your pelvis acting as a nucleus (core) to transfer forces to your limbs. Any instability in the pelvis guarantees performance will be affected. We will talk repeatedly in this book about training your deeper core muscles—the pelvic area—to optimize your technique. Enhancing performance through improved technique requires a coordinated development of mobility, flexibility, and stability. Technique training (and any other type of training) and bike fitting should begin with assessing functional motion—that is, your body's movement apart from swimming, cycling, and running.

Once functional movement is determined, only then should technique corrections be applied. In each of the chapters on swimming, cycling, and running, the foundations and principles of movement are described within the unique body lines system of training that we mentioned earlier in the chapter. This system progressively trains specific body segments for technique development and for ACES. ACES stands for movements that are accurate, controlled, effortless, and smooth; achieving ACES is key to optimal training and will be referenced throughout the book.

If you think of every motion you make when you swim, bike, and run as an opportunity to improve your movement and posture, having a method for training makes sense. The body lines system of technique training does not include drills per se but rather postures and positions that you achieve and then repeat over and over with accuracy and control. This system takes highly complex motions and breaks them down for clear-cut training and evaluation of specific body segments for repeated rehearsal of effective postures. Each chapter on technique is where everything is clarified. But, quickly, by way of example, let's say you are swimming. During the swim, your head is considered a body line (see chapter 6, Head Line), and there are certain postures and positions during the stroke that you should attain for each body segment through progressive practices. When you achieve ACES in a particular posture, you are prepared to progress to training the next posture.

Triathletes in Motion proposes a 180-degree paradigm shift, a change in the way triathletes and coaches think about coaching and developing technique. This begins with the principle of individualization and the assessment of functional movement before and during training. Most coaches and triathletes work at high volumes and intensity, and some with considerable success. But as the sport of triathlon matures, that training method will become obsolete. More and more triathletes and their coaches believe that the intensity and volume–based system of training has reached a plateau. They are, however, also recognizing the value of assessing functional movement, stability, and training of more efficient technique so that each phase of training and each athlete can be specifically trained as needed. Such assessment allows for the development of better swimming motions, improved cycling power and bike-fitting solutions, and greater running efficiency.

Arguments against the oncoming trend toward assessment of functional movement do not hold merit. In fact, most sports have a long history of athletic trainers, physical therapists, and physicians performing evidenced-based movement and musculoskeletal screenings to assess and develop exercises that improve athletic capacity. Why should triathlon be different? Through assessing and correcting movement limitations, the triathlete learns how to move the body from the deep-layered core to transfer energy and force to the limbs. This leads to very basic advantages over triathletes who do not train the core in the proper ways.

Motor learning—the training of neurons to send finely tuned signals to the muscles—is at the heart of this book. Through proper training, improvements in motor learning can occur at any age. The acceptance of current movement status as static and untrainable is outdated. From the center of the body (core) to the limbs, there is an unlimited capacity for change, development, and improvement. Training hard and long is simple, and you have likely trained this way for years, possibly with a hard-nosed coach to push you to train even harder. But training to reshape your movements through a combination of corrective and stabilization exercises and techniques will take you further than any training program you have tried thus far.

Your goal as a triathlete (or coach) is to develop posture that is functionally suited for triathlon and results in balanced, symmetrical movements that increase efficiency. As you read on, you will see that posture is an element of *Triathletes in Motion*. You will stop thinking of posture only in terms of standing erect without slumping. Rather, your postures in triathlon are the movements your body makes in each segment during each phase. Depending on the individual, some postures are much more effective than others. If you think in terms of achieving an optimal posture in each segment and during each phase, and then practicing this posture over and over again, you will be on track for both improved performance and reduced risk of overuse injury caused by less than optimal technique.

As a triathlete, how you move your body during daily living, such as when sitting, walking, or standing, influences your skill when swimming, cycling, and running. For this reason alone, it is important to assess functional movements at the outset, before training begins. We might call this your functional movement factor, a baseline of your capacity to move functionally, apart from every other individual. In this book, we provide several levels of tests to help you assess your own factors of functional movement. This becomes the launching point in transferring your improvements in functional movement into better technique and movements in daily life.

At some point, every triathlete reaches an upper limit of aerobic ability in which further improvement relates primarily to economy of movement—that is, efficient technique. Less than optimal posture is frequently related to inherited traits, but it also often relates to technique that has been affected by postural faults, instability, lack of mobility, and habits caused by continued patterns of inefficient movements. Very often those imperfections or weaknesses are revealed in competition as the deeper stabilizing muscles can no longer hold; therefore technique diminishes and pace slows.

All facets of training are interconnected: the physical preparation of endurance, speed, strength, technique, flexibility, mobility, and stability; mental strategies; nutrition; tactical strategies; equipment; adaptation; absorption; progression; periodization; functional movement; and recovery—all of these are related. If any one of these areas is out of sync, performance will be affected. That said, perhaps the most meaningful facet of training for the triathlete—because it affects both technique and efficiency, which are so key to effective performance, and because they are often neglected—is functional movement.

A functional body has normal ranges of flexibility and stability in the muscles as well as mobility in the joints. During activity, muscles that move well and remain stable will perform better and be injured less often. Building triathlon performance on efficient movement and stability allows technique to be more skilled, leading to improved performance. There is little, if any, ability to increase maximum oxygen uptake once a high level of fitness is reached, but you can train to use a larger portion of oxygen as a result of increased efficiency (or economy).

Improved technique positively affects energy efficiency and performance. In swimming, excessive kicking increases oxygen consumption, so reducing the kick rate and force and generating movements in the right way will improve efficiency. Similarly, by maintaining a horizontal position and minimizing sideways body motion, drag is reduced, as is the energy needed to sustain a given speed. In cycling, a lower cadence and overloaded gears increase energy use and reduce efficiency, whereas a higher cadence and proper gear adjustments can make the most of the energy you burn. Finally, during the run, overstriding increases oxygen use by activating larger leg muscles, whereas foot strikes underneath the hips activate the more dominant and efficient running muscles. These are just a few examples of ways in which movement efficiency can be influenced through minor modifications.

As we exercise, our skeletal muscles react to neural signals that result in movement. These signals communicate with muscle-moving proteins (actin and myosin) and ATP (adenosine triphosphate), which provide the energy we need to move. As we increase the efficiency of our movements, the energy we use is reduced, and a corresponding shift occurs toward fat use rather than carbohydrate. This improves our ability to sustain performance intensity and duration.

A more efficient body is capable of higher outputs of work while using the same fuel or energy as a less efficient body. For triathletes, greater efficiency results from better technology and improvements in athletic skill, functional movement, and technique. By continually improving technique and the foundations of movement, triathletes make gains in performance, even with little or no increase in maximal oxygen uptake.

Performance: The Triathlete Foundations

To become a better triathlete, you must understand the interrelated variables associated with movement. These are balance and proprioception, cardiovascular fitness, flexibility, mobility, stability, technique, nutrition, and psychology. Each of these variables contributes to how you move and perform. They are the foundations of performance and serve to develop individualized training that meets your unique needs in functional movement and technique. Through assessment and exercises to enhance movement and stability, and by training your motor learning pathways with clear body segments of technique, you become more efficient and less prone to injury.

Nearly every triathlete has functional movement limitations in flexibility, mobility, or stability, and often in all three. These restrictions affect technique and efficiency and contribute to periodic or chronic injuries. The perfection of technique is a never-ending process that the best triathletes work on constantly. Nevertheless, some techniques cannot be fully realized because of the underlying functional proficiency of movement. The training model we put forward here joins functional movement analysis, progressive testing, and exercises with principal techniques in swimming, cycling, and running that you can use to revamp your training plan.

In the following section we provide a series of self-assessments to help you understand how your body moves and transfers loads and to recognize individual differences in functional movement. Ideally, in each of these assessments, all forces will come together to converge at the pelvis. These are preliminary tests that precede the more thorough assessments and exercises found in later chapters.

Balance and Proprioception

As you move, information comes to you via the senses, allowing you to assess the environment and make split-second decisions on pace, position, safety, tactics, and so on to aid you in making movements as purposeful as possible. For triathletes, balance control is important, but so too is a sharpened awareness of the positions of the limbs (arms and legs) when swimming, cycling, and running. Sensory receptors in the muscles, joints, and joint capsules provide signals of position in the limbs, including changes in muscle length, amount of force, and levels of pressure, temperature, and touch.

Balance for the triathlete is a continuum of adjustments, but fortunately the nature of each sport (swimming, cycling, and running) is more or less linear in motion and made up of repeated similar movements. Swimming stroke after stroke, repeated pedaling, and running one stride after the next at more or less the same intensity provide the basis for training the body's position to maximize the base of support for each sport.

The nervous system provides the sensory, motor, adaptive, and anticipatory processing mechanisms chiefly through the visual, vestibular, and somatosensory systems and the receptors for touch, temperature, proprioception, and pain. Through these systems, you perceive the position of your body and the movements you make. Assessing flexibility, mobility, and stability along with corrections, as needed, to enhance these systems will improve performance by bringing about better control of balance.

Developing better movements involves accepting, adjusting, processing, and learning how to collect and apply a seemingly unlimited amount of sensory stimuli. Skilled athletes can do this very well. This is what we see in the best triathletes as they perform with accurate, controlled, effortless, and smooth movements (ACES).

In swimming, the base of support is the water; the hand and arm anchors on to the water to hold and move the body over the hand and arm. In cycling, the pelvis sits stable atop the saddle, arms rest on elbow pads, and feet rotate like clockwork along the circumference of the pedal stroke. In running, the strides float airborne from one foot strike to the next. Each requires stability, mobility, flexibility, and balance control. The more functional the placement of the body during motion, and the greater the balance control, the more likely effective performance will develop.

Top-level triathletes demonstrate finely tuned balance. They have magnificent posture and stability and an ability to maintain the body's center of gravity over a base of support in near-perfect states of symmetry. There are variations in movement, but elite triathletes maintain a conscious awareness of their positions as they move (proprioception). Balance for the triathlete is the stability of posture and the ability to maintain movements uniformly from one swimming stroke, pedaling motion, and running stride to the next. Proprioception involves the sensory awareness of the positions of the hip, knee, ankle, and foot, such as when running. Balance is best when your body's center of mass positions your base of support in a stable, functional posture as you move. Proper technique, strong, mobile joints, and flexible muscles will help you maintain the most stable postures, making for greater efficiency.

When injured, your body's responsiveness to movement is impaired by unsettled and cautiously guarded movements. You might lose the ability to effectively control your movements, which can lead to less than optimal compensations. This is why it's important to learn how to move functionally and activate more muscle groups across multiple joints. You must be able to maintain alignment and control the central part of your body (pelvis) throughout the swim, bike, and run.

Think of balance as the control of motor functions; combined with sensory feedback, balance determines the position of your body in space. Constant feedback alerts your body's response to control the next movement to meet the current situation or conditions. Training is largely a process of programming your body's balance functions to better control the complex interaction of the nervous and musculoskeletal systems.

Cardiovascular Fitness

Triathlon places unique demands on the cardiovascular system. For cardiovascular endurance, active muscle fibers and skeletal muscles must be supplied sufficient amounts of oxygen and nutrients and be able to effectively remove heat and other waste products. Endurance training builds your capacity to use energy stores in the body and transport large blood flows to the working muscles. Think of training your cardiovascular endurance as the preparation of building a smooth highway of fatigue resistance by increasing oxygen delivery for extended periods; balancing waste removal, heat tolerance, and heat removal; and improving fuel efficiency. Endurance athletes train the cardiovascular system to supply active muscle fibers with sufficient oxygen and nutrients that help moderate metabolic heat and waste products, such as carbon dioxide (a by-product of cell metabolism and respiration in which energy from nutrients is converted for energy transport within the cells for metabolism).

There are many ways to train cardiovascular endurance, but you do this chiefly through extended workouts at moderate intensities. Yet to improve maximal capacity to consume oxygen, you must also work at higher levels of intensity. Long-duration training at lower intensities will definitely boost the cardiovascular system, but you must also stimulate and teach your nervous system how to best activate the muscles. This requires a combination of long aerobic workouts and periodic increased intensities of shorter durations with longer recoveries.

Of course, long and slow distance training does not prepare your body for high-intensity training. This is why, even during your base preparation training, you should combine your aerobic workouts with progressive amounts of duration intervals at higher intensities, rest of moderate to full recoveries, and strong focus on form. Even high-intensity training can improve the cardiovascular and aerobic systems by improving the tolerance of high intensity and increasing your ability to maintain higher speed with endurance.

Flexibility

Flexibility refers to the ability of muscle and soft tissue to flex and yield to forces during a stretch. There are single- and multiple-joint interactions that you should be able to move through without restriction. Muscles lengthen when stretched, and there is a stretch force transmitted to the muscle fibers in the connective tissues.

With restrictions (tightness) in muscle length, the body cannot move freely, affecting functional control of movement. Technique will be flawed, and recurring injury might result, as well as below-optimal performances. Such tightness leads to less muscular control and affects the health of tissues, and might begin a chain of compensations in other parts of the body. For this reason, triathletes must be assessed individually and provided customized exercise and movement remedies in balance and technique. General stretching exercises are not recommended because they lack individual assessment and might do little good or even worsen some conditions. For instance, you might be stretching muscles that are hypermobile (overly flexible and causing joint instability) and understretching the muscles that need stretching the most.

Through assessing flexibility individually, problems can be determined and condition-specific corrections implemented. Unnecessary, or even unfavorable, flexibility exercises can be avoided. Some triathletes will have tight, restricted, inflexible muscles that call for a combination of exercises to remedy flexibility loss.

The examination of flexibility helps assess stability (strength) as well. The hypermobile triathlete is often lacking strength in the muscles supporting a joint. This triathlete might think she is really flexible, but hypermobile joints have limitations in stability and strength where they are most needed, so it's important not to overstretch them.

Sensing Better Movements

Some individuals cannot feel the position of their joints and postures. They might also lack a clear perception of the forces being generated from the muscles and the timing of their firing during movements. Such individuals provide an illustration of how different capacities can be to feel or sense the body in space and time.

Skilled triathletes detect and apply sensory input effectively and efficiently in a continuum that enhances performance through constant refinement of technique and effort. To produce these skilled movements, the triathlete must *feel* the movements, train the right motions, and go about the process of improving skill through assessing and correcting both the actual movements and the intended movement.

Body lines, as described, train technique through emphasis upon certain body regions and applying postures and positions of technique with unrushed lower intensity. You train with full attention to the body region and postures to be achieved. When coupled with the assessment of functional movements and exercises to correct deficiencies, the triathlete will improve performance.

If no corrections in movement and stability are made, the body will often adapt to less efficient means of movement, resulting in the following movement matrix compensations:

- A decrease in mobility equals a constant misalignment in the body's ability to move in a symmetrical way.

- A decrease in flexibility equals a decrease in normal arc of motion as a result of restrictions in motion by tight muscles and the inability of weak muscles to move a body part properly.

- An increase in muscle tightness will maintain a faulty alignment regardless of body position, so lack of flexibility can result in less efficient movement and chronic injury.

- A weak muscle often causes corrective changes in body alignment and thus abnormal movements.

- A normal movement pattern sustains normal wear and tear on joint surfaces and normal distributions of weight and movement.

Mobility

The ability of the body to move or be moved and to initiate, control, and sustain movements defines functional mobility. In effect, mobility is related to flexibility and the integrity of joints that work together to provide unrestricted and pain-free movements. The body's motions are shaped by movements away from normal ranges, and these misalignments cause weight-bearing joints to become out of position. Such movement tendencies can result in increased forces in contrast with a normally aligned joint. For example, during running, when the hip medially (inwardly) rotates and the knee hyperextends (straightens), an outward (bow-legged) movement of the knee occurs. This position might cause load bearing during the stance phase of running to be away from the middle of the leg, hip, knee, and ankle.

This compensation is associated with a number of knee issues but is also related to tightness in the gastrocnemius and soleus (calf), piriformis (lateral rotator of the hip in the posterior pelvis), and biceps femoris (lateral hamstring muscle and external rotator of the tibia and femur). There might also be muscular weakness in the adductors (inside thigh muscles) and medial hamstring (semitendinosus), which, when stable, help to maintain alignment. The goal is not to necessarily make imperfect alignment issues perfect but

Where many triathletes (and some coaches) misjudge the learning and reshaping process of technique is in the practice, process, and stages of learning. Effectively reconstructing technique until accurate and controlled postures are achieved takes time. Only through constant and progressive training in which you achieve ACES can movements eventually become optimally efficient, less conscious, and more automatic. Trying to rush the process will result in movements that are not accurate, controlled, effortless, and smooth. To practice such movements ultimately sets you back in your training because your body must unlearn them and be retrained in the proper movements. For best results in your training, follow these guidelines in sensing your movements:

- Learn to describe and demonstrate your movements and express how they feel. This will help you progressively develop better movement feedback and train movement in smaller, learnable segments and body lines. As you move, ask yourself . . .
  - o What muscles were involved?
  - o Was there more or less tension (force), pain, or discomfort?
  - o Did the movement feel accurate, controlled, effortless, and smooth?
  - o What was the relative perceived exertion?
  - o Did the movement feel efficient and effective?
- Strive to develop the awareness to recognize purposeful movements and to detect and correct errors when movements do not achieve ACES.
  - o Self-assess and correct movements during individual training sessions.
  - o Do lower-intensity, progressive, and body segment-focused workouts, such as swimming 50 reps of 25 meters (or yards), emphasizing the entry and extension body line; cycling 12 reps of two minutes each with evenly placed bilateral foot-pad pressure during the downstroke; or running 30 reps of 100 meters, focusing on the elongation of the neck without deviations in stride.

to decrease the not-so-balanced movements that often cause other weakness or tightness, reduce performance, and increase injury risk.

A common problem in swimming, for example, is crossover during entry. This occurs when the swimmer's hand enters the water and extends inward as well as forward. This inward motion sometimes crosses over the centerline of the body, resulting in increased time before propulsion and lateral shifting of the hips caused by poor posture and entry position. Thus a swimmer's flexibility and joint mobility are at issue (restricted chest and back muscles), which means working on technique alone will not make for better stroke movements. Too often, coaches will simply instruct swimmers not to cross over at the entry, but what's really needed are mobilization and flexibility exercises to achieve more normal ranges of motion. Such training will allow the hand to enter the water in front of the shoulder and extend straight ahead instead of crossing over the body midline.

Stability

There are three subsystems of stability—bones and ligaments, active muscles, and the nervous system. When any of these is not providing normal support, overall stability is affected.

Think of your body's stability as your core, the deep muscles in which energy is

Yoga Movement and Stability

Yoga, group mobility, stability, high-intensity core training, and flexibility classes are popular, but unfortunately some participants, especially men, might be doing more harm than good. Poses in many of these disciplines are considered unisex, but because of significant differences in the female and male anatomies, they should not be done in the same way by males and females.

Some yoga poses and postures simply aren't for everyone. The idea that more flexible muscles are always better is a common misconception. Unnecessarily increasing flexibility isn't a good thing. Good muscles have tension in order to contract, lengthen, and shorten (and even remain the same), and problems can occur when there is too much flexibility in muscles and laxity in joints. The local stabilizers (discussed later in the book) are central to performance, and in many programs they simply aren't trained correctly. Being able to contort one's body into abnormally varying degrees of flexion, extension, and rotation is contraindicated for most triathletes.

That said, because of its emphasis on joining physical, mental, meditative, and spiritual components, yoga can be beneficial for triathletes. When yoga approaches are combined with an evaluation of movement and stability and implemented via an individually developed plan, they can likely be effective.

Just as each individual has unique characteristics in his or her capacity for movement, stability, and joint mobility, there are also gender differences to consider, such as the following:

- Men weigh 20 kilograms (42 pounds) more than women.
- Men are taller than women (the average male is 5 feet, 9 inches [~176 cm]; the average female is 5 feet, 4 inches [~162 cm].
- Women have about 30 more degrees in their pelvic arch (120 vs. 90 degrees).
- Men have shoulders that are about 10 percent wider.
- Women's backs are 15 percent shorter (from hips to top of shoulders).
- Men have longer hands by 5 percent.
- Women have shorter upper arms by 8.5 percent.
- Men have longer forearms by 10 percent.
- Women have wider hips by 10 percent.
- Men have longer feet by 9 percent.

transferred to your limbs. This is your base of support, and any increase in stability (along with joint mobility and the right amount of flexibility) will improve economy and technique. When running stride to stride, as your foot strikes the ground, the more stable your postures and positioning are, the more efficient you will be. Combining this stability with functional movement in the muscles and joints and proper technique is the very foundation of improved performance. Movements that sway the body into less efficient postures or fall outside of the center of mass because of muscle imbalances (tightness or weakness) or faulty technique can cause distal (away from the core) and less efficient muscles to overactivate in order to maintain stability. At some point, these global muscles will fatigue, resulting in compensations and slower speeds.

Though the stability of the body is affected by many elements, one of the key elements is the pelvis. Key forces are transferred from the pelvis, and any instability in this body region will affect posture. We will return to this point in a later chapter.

Because of the dynamic nature of our sport, stability and balance are importantly linked. How effectively the deep-layered muscles are stabilizing joint function is of utmost importance. The ability to maintain a constant state of functional posture—support of the body over the center of mass—is absolutely essential for the triathlete. Later chapters on posture, movement, and the core address this issue by focusing on the deep-layered muscles of the body and whole-body functional movements and tests.

Muscles play a particularly important role in stability. The muscles of the neck and trunk, for example, are primary stabilizers of the spine. Weakness in these muscles can alter posture and cause an adverse effect on functional movement and performance. Thus assessing movement for normal ranges of motion and stability is central to optimal performance.

A goal in this book is to provide assessment and exercise remedies to improve functional movement and stability. Although a triathlete's functional strength is specific to swimming, cycling, and running, strength is often trained generally to all regions of the body. This general approach can be beneficial for some triathletes, but improving strength via a targeted and individual approach is far better, as we will see in subsequent chapters.

Functional Strength

Strength in a muscle is the ability of the tissue to produce tension against the demands that are placed on the muscle. For triathletes, having more muscular strength than is required for optimal performance might be counterproductive. Certainly, building muscle mass to the level of a bodybuilder does not benefit endurance performance—the resistance that triathletes need to overcome simply does not require that degree of muscular strength.

However, a professional grand tour cyclist without a swimming background will likely lack the upper-body strength to become a proficient swimmer. He or she will probably not have the necessary chest, back, arm, and core strength. Strength assessment should always relate to the specific functional work that triathlon requires.

Functional strength is a key factor relating to the ability of the nerves and muscular systems (neuromuscular) to produce and control the forces of movement while swimming, cycling, and running. Through assessing functional strength and prescribing corrective exercises, these movements will become more efficient, smooth, and coordinated.

Muscular Power

Motor skills for movement in everyday living include both strength and speed. For the triathlete, the muscular power needed during performance is quite different from that required in daily tasks at work, home, or play. Power can be improved in two ways: by increasing the work a muscle can perform over time and by reducing the amount of time to produce a given force.

Training muscular power is related to the strength (force) and speed (rate) of muscular movement. Simply put, greater power provides the capacity to perform at higher intensities, which allows you to work for longer periods at higher outputs.

Endurance

Endurance exercise involves supplying active muscles with enough oxygen and nutrients to perform over time. Waste products such as metabolic heat and carbon dioxide need to be eliminated to maintain performance on a steady level. Triathletes understand endurance better than many athletes because the ability to work for prolonged periods of time is measured by the successful resistance to fatigue against time. Muscular and cardiovascular endurance are different in that the latter is based on the ability to perform dynamic movements (e.g., swimming, cycling, running) with large muscles for prolonged periods of time, whereas muscular endurance is the ability of isolated muscle groups to perform contractions over time.

For the triathlete, cardiovascular endurance training has many benefits and advantages and is particularly important for overall training adaptation, which further prepares the body for more intense training. These benefits include the following:

- Connective tissue (ligaments and tendons) is strengthened. Supporting muscles gain endurance, and there is increased resistance to muscle cell damage during heavy exercise.
- Slow-twitch muscle fibers gain size and strength. Training effectively stimulates slow-twitch motor neurons, which contributes to improving exercise economy.
- Increases in blood volume carry more hemoglobin (oxygen-carrying molecules) to the working muscles.
- The capacity for storage of muscle glycogen reserves increases.
- Capillary development and density improve (capillaries, the smallest blood vessels, are where oxygen is passed from the blood to the working muscles). Training increases the number of capillaries surrounding each muscle fiber, thus expanding aerobic capacity.
- There are increases in mitochondria (structures within the muscle cells that produce ATP, the cell's energy).
- Resting heart rate decreases.
- Stroke volume (amount of blood pumped by one contraction of the heart) increases.
- Temperature regulation (heat tolerance) improves via circulatory adaptations.
- Respiratory endurance (lung ventilation ability) increases.
- Oxidation of free fatty acids improves, which spares muscle glycogen.
- Muscle glycogen storage capacity increases.
- Body fat decreases.

Technique

The foundation of technique starts with the elements of motion—strength, flexibility, mobility, stability, and balance. Focusing on and optimizing these elements allow you to move more functionally during training and performance. When you move more function-

ally in your normal daily life, for example, you begin to progressively invest in efficient technique and reduce the risk of repetitive-motion injuries that are so common in triathlon. You begin to adapt and use more efficient movements instead of adapting to being good at less efficient motions.

Combining movement assessment, corrective exercises, and technique helps you learn to use your muscles more efficiently. Every triathlete has unique movements, and there is no single perfect form (though certain elements and principles are accepted as the foundations for better technique), but when movements are overly excessive or exaggerated, a loss of efficiency results, as well as a greater risk of injury. When the body moves ideally and functionally, there are fewer corrections necessary to maintain form; the result is better performance with much less chance of injury to joints and supporting muscles.

Through assessment, your unique movement and stability limitations can be identified. This begins the process of enhancing technique through improved functional movements—a process we'll discuss in far greater detail in chapters to come.

Nutrition for Training and Race Day

Proper nutrition is crucial for optimal performance and battling fatigue. Nutrition significantly affects metabolism (conversion of food into energy), which is needed for muscle contraction and to curtail dehydration. As muscles uptake fuels into the blood, the fuels are processed to provide energy used by the cells in the muscles for movement (contraction).

Carbohydrate

Carbohydrate provides energy to fuel the body and is essential for the proper functioning of the central nervous system. Because carbohydrate has limited stores in the body, it must be replaced during rest, training, and competition. Generally, the amount of carbohydrate to ingest is 30 to 60 grams when exercising 2 hours or less and 40 to 90 grams per hour when exercising more than 2 hours. If you ingest too little, your blood glucose levels will struggle to keep pace; if you ingest too much, absorption might slow down and cause gastrointestinal issues.

Here are some key points about carbohydrate ingestion:

- Intake of .5 gram per pound (1 to 1.2 grams per kilogram) of body weight each hour can improve performance, whereas more than this amount can slow absorption.
- Because muscle absorption increases over time, during the first hour or two of exercise it might be best to ingest water or a drink or food light in carbohydrate. After 90 minutes to 2 hours, the full carbohydrate recommendations are best for reducing fatigue.
- The body's major source of energy, carbohydrate spares the breakdown of protein and primes the metabolism of fat for use as a fuel for endurance. Maintaining carbohydrate levels permits you to sustain intensity.
- A steady ingestion of carbohydrate spares the use of liver glycogen and helps maintain blood sugar levels. Pre-exercise ingestion of carbohydrate is important to enhance liver stores.
- Movements and motor skills are more coordinated with adequate carbohydrate ingestion. The central nervous system can also be affected adversely by low levels of carbohydrate.
- Maintaining carbohydrate levels improves and sustains a feeling of well-being.

Fluid Intake

Sweat rates vary among individuals. An important point is that there's a limit to how much fluid can be emptied from the stomach and reabsorbed each hour. Thus there is a difference in how much fluid is lost and how much should be consumed. The triathlete's body is in a constant process of controlling body temperature and releasing excess heat. When the ability to maintain the body's core temperature is challenged, performance imbalances occur.

At either end of the spectrum—in hypothermia (low body core temperature) or hyperthermia (elevated body core temperature)—temperature imbalances can markedly slow you down and even become life threatening. One of the advantages we have as humans is the ability to remove heat from the body through evaporation. Through this process we are capable of extraordinarily long durations of exercise. However, because of this capacity to sweat and remove heat through evaporation, we must also replace fluids at regular intervals and in the proper amounts.

It is not sufficient to merely replace lost fluids based on sweat rate. As mentioned, there are limits to the amount of fluids that can be absorbed and emptied, and if we ingest more than these limits, the fluids are lost through the bladder. There are body mass losses from fluids lost from the lungs, skin, respiratory tract, and feces. These body mass changes also affect the amount of body weight lost. Weighing the body alone might not be a reliable means to determine postexercise water loss. Some triathletes actually gain total body water, and research suggests that this water comes from muscle glycogen and fluids in the gastrointestinal tract. Thus it isn't as simple as working out and weighing yourself to determine your sweat rates and fluid replenishment amounts and timetables.

The key is to establish individual differences for replacing nutrients and fluids within a range of guidelines and depending on duration and ambient temperature. There is not a single rule for everyone, but rather a range of how much or little fluid and carbohydrate should be ingested each hour. The general recommendation is no less than 400 milliliters (14 oz.) and no more than 800 milliliters (28 oz.) for each hour. For all triathletes, fluid replenishment should be a primary concern both during and after exercise. This is especially important for intense or long-duration workouts and in extreme environments.

Ingest too much fluid or sugars, and you will notice a delay of absorption and discomfort caused by too much water in the stomach and gastrointestinal tract. In contrast, not ingesting enough can result in dehydration, increased body temperature, and slowed performance.

Drink at regular intervals of 10 to 15 minutes with the goal of determining the right amount of water (or other fluids) to ingest each hour. Once you determine the right amount for you, practice repeatedly in training so that fluid replenishment becomes automatic.

Here are some key points for fluid intake:

- Drinking smaller, frequent quantities of water throughout the day provides better digestion and absorption than drinking larger quantities but less frequently. Drinking with meals or large quantities at once causes a lot of water to go speedily into the bladder because the body doesn't store extra water.

- Drink water first thing in the morning (triathletes are more dehydrated overnight) and monitor urine color pre- and postexercise (you want urine to be light yellow).

- Avoid beverages high in calories with limited nutritional value.

- Drinking cold fluids (41 degrees Fahrenheit; 5 degrees Celsius) improves absorption.

- Ingest 14 to 28 ounces (~400-800 ml) an hour depending on intensity, duration, and temperatures. Do not exceed 28 ounces (800 ml) in an hour because there's a limit in the rate of gastric emptying.

- Vary fluid ingestion depending on environmental conditions (hot, humid, cold).

- Do not ingest too much fluid during the later stages of an event, especially when fatigue and not dehydration is causing a slowing of pace.

- Do not rely on sweat rates to determine fluid replacement because other factors also contribute to body mass (weight loss).

- Some triathletes tolerate higher levels of dehydration and use fluids from glycogen stores more effectively than others.

- Develop a hydration plan that has been tested in training. Training and following good nutrient and fluid practices within ranges lead to better race performances.

Psychology

Imagine participating in a race in which you have no mental reaction to the sensations of physical effort. That is, you pace along mechanically and unemotionally with no mental interference whatsoever. There are no tactics or managing of pace, only a monotonous process of waiting for the best aerobic engine to cross the line.

Thankfully, athletic performances don't happen this way. Fatigue, anxiety, and negative thoughts affect performance adversely, just as positive attitude, mindful focus, and the desire to achieve good outcomes generally make for improved performance. In fact, mental training might be a triathlete's biggest asset. Once you have achieved a certain level of physical aptitude, training your brain's core (or default state of mind) to be positive, uncongested, and free of negative thinking might be the most productive training you can do. What if you view stress and anxiety differently? As a benefit that is a normal reaction of the process in preparation and anticipation. Instead of a negative physiological and psychological feature, stress and anxiety can be thought of as a much-needed part of living and competing. The anxiety is good for you—it's just your mind and body being enthusiastic and energized.

Very often overthinking, overprocessing, and speeding up the mind compromise execution. In fact, learning how to slow down unnecessary thoughts can allow you to speed up performance. The process begins with better understanding of your thoughts and feelings and of the processing and retraining of your mind. Just like your body, your brain can be trained to be more efficient. By recognizing and understanding unreasonable negative thoughts and rehearsing (training) reasonable, positive, and realistic thoughts, you have a far better chance of achieving your desired outcomes.

In the best circumstances and most productive relationships there is a clear line of separation of dependency between triathlete and coach. Great coaches (those who stand the tests of time) do not encourage dependence or heartlessly dictate but instead provide intelligent pathways to greater outcomes and best performances. So much in performance begins with a vision of attaining something special and believing in the course of action—a clear vision of how to establish goals and reach for desired outcomes. These goals provide the foundation for every workout. When you know your desired outcome, and recognize a realistic path to reach it, the entire process of training becomes charged with enthusiasm.

Just as positive thinking can yield positive results, the opposite also tends to occur. Whenever you have a difficult event in your life, you might see that difficulty reflected in your training and performance levels. At such times, consider using the cognitive training worksheet shown in figure 1.1. If you are a triathlete, this worksheet can be generally helpful in alleviating tough situations, but in a broader sense can also help you establish more rational thinking across the spectrum of life, training, and competitions. If you are a coach, the worksheet can pave the way for discussion. Ask your athletes to describe the situation, thoughts, emotions, and possible outcomes. Then ask them how they can change the circumstances to get the outcome they desire.

There is no question that anxiety, nervousness, and outright fear affect every triathlete at some level. Anxiety can hinder performance when levels are too high, but moderate amounts can in fact improve performance. Probably the best way to learn how to manage anxiety at your desired levels is through experience.

Elite athletes in explosive events, such as sprints, can tolerate very high levels of anxiety. Triathlon is obviously not an explosive event. In its nature, the sport requires calm, cool, and collected management of emotions and energy, both before and during competition. Different triathletes process anxiety differently, but a common element is always present: the desire to achieve a particular outcome. No matter how your anxiety is processed, the cognitive worksheet can help you achieve a state of mind that results in better outcomes through understanding when thoughts are misplaced and counterproductive.

Anxiety is real and is caused by thinking misplaced, unreasonable, and sometimes distorted thoughts. Some levels of anxiety are good for performance, and others are not. Everyone has issues, and they deal with them in many different ways, but one good way to deal with negative issues is to train yourself to focus on desired outcomes.

Developing Training Programs

No one perfect training program works for every triathlete every time. Yet somehow, time and again, the elite perform at the highest levels. Coaching and training programs are very important, but two factors—the way training is managed and psychological fortitude—might be what distinguish the elite from their closest competitors at the macro-level (not in specific workouts).

Training and training programs must be malleable. Good coaches are finding workouts scripted more than a few days in advance often do not work. Generic training plans have their place, but they are frequently ineffective, or insufficient, for triathletes who desire a thoroughly targeted program of workouts. Perhaps most important is the big picture of the program plan—that is, the phases of training, or the periodization of the program.

As any experienced triathlete knows, training programs can follow many forms of blocks, phases, and periods of emphasis. In the following sections we'll look at some general rules for base preparation, race preparation, peak preparation, and restoration periods. In each phase are targets or projected outcomes for training, based primarily on events planned for the upcoming season. Again, the overall planning of each phase, including a periodization plan, is perhaps most important because this provides a basis for the types of workouts for each phase.

Base Preparation Period

The base preparation period lasts from 4 to 24 weeks and includes a gradual increase in training volume, intensity, density, frequency of workouts, and transition training (bike-to-run workouts) with periodic fitness standard tests (performance field or laboratory tests) and a restoration period of 3 to 7 days in every 2-, 3-, or 4-week cycle. The general physiological

FIGURE 1.1   Cognitive Training Worksheet

Situation

Describe the circumstances of an actual event or stream of thoughts leading to an unpleasant emotion or situation resulting in an undesired outcome.

Automatic thoughts

Write down the automatic thoughts that correspond with or precede the event. What immediate thoughts did you have during or before the event?

Emotions

Indicate the grade of the following emotions, using this scale: 0 = none; 1 = very low; 2 = mild; 3 = midrange; 4 = high; and 5 = very high.

Fear ____	Envy ____
Anger ____	Frustration ____
Guilt ____	Shame ____
Depression ____	Denial ____
Jealousy ____	Offense ____
Self-pity ____	Negative thoughts ____
Anxiety ____	Regret ____
Resentment ____	Resentment ____

Outcome achieved?

Answer the following question yes or no. Did you get the outcome you desired? That is, is what happened, or your thoughts about it, what you truly wanted? If no, complete the next section.

Yes ____ No ____

Getting desired outcome

Specify how you would change the event, automatic thoughts, or reactions to achieve the desired outcome.

From M. Evans and J. Cappaert, *Triathletes in motion.* (Champaign, IL: Human Kinetics).

SARAH GROFF   Strength of Belief

The power of the limitations we place on ourselves can be staggering. This lesson was reinforced for me at the 2012 Olympic Games.

As seen through the view of Hollywood and most media outlets, Olympic athletes are exemplary specimens of humanity. Highly disciplined, focused, and with physiques chiseled by years of athletic practice, these athletes appear to be exceptional in both body and mind. According to pundits, such champions have been gifted—they left the womb with exceptional abilities that the rest of us can only dream of having.

Well, most of this could not be further from the truth.

The concept of innate ability is not only erroneous but is also highly damaging to aspiring athletes. I know this personally because I had to overcome this pervasive idea as a professional athlete. Over the years, I chipped away at this impossible image, realizing that even an unexceptionally talented and insecure athlete could become one of the best in the world in her sport.

Like many, I had long assumed that great athletes are born, not made. I lumped myself into a category of athletes with moderate talent who struggled in competition and assumed that I could reach only a low level of achievement. Though it took years for me to recognize the Sarah that others saw in me, my eyes eventually opened to my true potential. I learned I was not fated to be mediocre. Not at all. In fact, I had the possibility to make myself great.

It took me a while, but I learned that hard work and dedication, combined with a mindset of growth, can overcome many of our perceived shortcomings. It wasn't that I didn't have the potential to be an Olympic medal contender—my problem was that my perception of what it took to be good was flawed. I learned to place emphasis on consistent work and to stop berating myself for being too physically and psychologically imperfect. This lesson fundamentally shifted my mental approach to training and racing.

I began the 10K in the 2012 Olympics with the goal of being in the medal mix with one kilometer to go. Some people did not expect me to be in that position. However, because I believed it was possible, that's exactly where I found myself—in the mix with one kilometer remaining.

This result was a massive victory for me, indicating the growth I had achieved. I've grown more since and will be setting my sights a bit higher in 2016. No, I did not leave the womb a superhuman Olympic champion, but I've learned that nothing can keep me from shaping myself into one.

---

benefits and phase objectives of the base preparation period include the following:

- Endurance and connective tissue development occurs specific to triathlon.

- Stroke volume, blood volume, and enhancement of glycogen storage and capacity all increase.

- General aerobic endurance develops (extended workouts are of low to moderate intensity with high-level training intensity to stimulate neuromuscular development).

- Progressive development occurs in strength, flexibility, mobility, posture, and technique through deep-layered core training and constant practice of technical (biomechanical) improvements with training and exercise corrections.

- Improvement and ongoing practice of mental outcome strategies are promoted.

- Managing nutrition and rest and creating an effective program for restoration are emphasized.

Race Preparation Period

The race preparation period lasts from 3 to 8 weeks with a restoration period every 2 to 4 weeks for 2, 3, 5, or 7 days and daily mental training time (cognitive competitive outcome strategies and practice). The general physiological benefits and phase objectives of the race preparation period include the following:

- Specificity is increased (race specificity at or near event distance intensity, distance, and number of workouts).
- Periodic transitions (bike to run) at race-specific intensity and distances are strategically organized.
- Overall training volume reductions occur with expanding suprathreshold (above race-pace) training to elevate maximal oxygen uptake and anaerobic capacity.
- Posture and form positions are at highest levels under increased intensities.

Peak Transition Period

The peak transition period lasts from 1 to 3 weeks. The general physiological benefits and phase objectives of the peak transition period include the following:

- Training volumes are reduced.
- Peak conditioning is reached through further increases in suprathreshold and anaerobic threshold workouts.
- Potential and feel of speed and fluidity are increased.
- Psychological strategies are fine-tuned to achieve desired outcomes.

Restoration Period

The restoration period lasts from 1 to 4 weeks. The general physiological benefits and phase objectives of the restoration period include the following:

- Physiological and psychological restoration occurs.
- Occurrences of bacterial and viral infections might decrease.
- Training decreases in volume, intensity, and frequency can reduce chronic injury rates.
- Recovery and training balance performance (overload and recovery) and adaptation strategies (response to fatigue and progressions of training, workouts, and competitions) are reviewed and finely tuned.
- Performance evaluations assess training volume, intensity, frequency, recovery days, and number of competitions.
- Management occurs in four areas of potential fatigue: metabolic (energy stores and replenishment), neural (high or extensive muscular contractions that reduce the firing rate of muscles), psychological (training, racing, social stress factors), and environmental (travel, geography, heat, cold, climate).
- Active rest with varied cross-training activities reduces monotony of training.
- Adjustments are made in volume, intensity, duration, frequency, and type of workouts to enhance physiological, neural, and psychological states.
- A routine of restoration therapies is established (e.g., sleep, nutrition, deep tissue release, pool water immersion, gentle downhill running, spinning exercises on the bike, and light-intensity swimming).

The recommendations for these four training periods are general guidelines for you to adapt to your best needs as you gradually determine these precise needs via testing and training. The longer you train, the better tuned you will become with your body and the better you'll be able to recognize exactly what organization and periodization cycle work best for you. In the next section we turn to the adaptations that occur in the body during periods of training.

Adaptation

The changes that occur in your body systems during training are called adaptations to the training stimulus. As time passes, both your cardiovascular and muscular systems begin to process energy much more efficiently. Neurological and biochemical changes to both systems result in better performances in workload and intensity at a lower physiological cost because you are in better shape.

Improvements via adaptations to training are rooted in a solid understanding of energy system and intensity training, training volume management, recovery, and a knowledge of mixing the frequency (how often), intensity (how hard), density (workouts per week), and durations (training volume) of training. These factors are at the core of physiological training and workout design.

Triathletes and coaches tend to place predictable borderlines on the models they use for workouts, periodization, tapering, and recovery. How a particular triathlete adapts to the training loads (volume, intensity, duration of intervals, density and dosage of workouts, and recovery) depends on how these elements are organized. Training plans and workouts should be regarded as flexible, elastic processes built on how well you adapt to your training sessions. Of course, training will always place stress (fatigue) on the body, and rest will always bring a period of adaptation and growth of fitness via the reestablishment of energy stores and production of new proteins for restoration. But within these basic truths of training is a lot of room for improvisation.

As we have said before, training is not black and white, and no one training model is best for everyone. There are ranges in intensity and recovery that are well accepted and governed chiefly by common sense, but individuals can vary enormously in how they adapt to training volumes and intensity. Generic training plans often do not address these kinds of individual differences and should be viewed as only guidelines meant to be adapted.

During training, breakdowns in protein occur that require rest, proper fueling, and adaptation. Because our sport involves three far different activities, triathletes particularly need to pay close attention to getting just the right mix of training volume, intensity, frequency, and density (how workouts are organized and how far apart).

Whether you are coached or self-trained, the monitoring of adaptation is one of the most important aspects of training, in terms of the response to training frequency, intensity, and duration. The primary goal of training adaptation is to reduce training errors and unfavorable responses such as overreaching, overtraining, and overuse injuries and to increase overall progress in fitness and health. We discuss adaptation further in later chapters as it relates to particular body systems.

Ratings of Perceived Exertion

Certainly the best and latest technology, equipment, and external training devices (heart rate, power, watches, GPS) are useful and even necessary at times. But perhaps the most practical—and some would argue the most accurate—way of determining effort in the moment is using ratings of perceived exertion (RPE). These are the fundamental perceptions of intensity and feelings of effort before, during, and after activity and managing recovery through deeper levels of cognitive understanding.

The RPE scale was originally developed to monitor the efforts of training with cardiac patients during rehabilitation. The patients learned how to measure work intensity using the scale. It proved to be highly accurate and over the years has become part of most sport and exercise models to monitor effort. Monitoring and determining effort in the triathlete, especially when cycling, can be integrated with heart rate or power measuring devices.

In RPE monitoring, the cognitive perceptions of intensity are based on respiratory and nutritional (food and fluids) sensations as well as feeling in the arms, shoulders, and legs during training and racing. RPE is sensed effort determined by the training response desired and the distance of the competition.

As with every method of monitoring intensity, there are limitations in RPE measurement. Individuals have different capacities (physiological and psychological) that affect any method of determining exertion level. Perhaps the best approach is to combine several technologies with RPE at the nucleus.

MEREDITH KESSLER   11:30 Ironman to Ironman Champion

When I met Meredith Kessler, she was a keen amateur Ironman athlete. In fact, she had already completed 20 Ironman races; her best performance was 11 hours 28 minutes. Though she hadn't yet lit the world on fire, she did have consistency—her last 15 Ironmans were within a 10-minute spread. Meredith came to me with a simple request—she wanted me to make her good. How good she could get was certainly an unanswerable question on day 1, but taking her for an initial bike ride I noticed a few things about her, including her great grit and determination (we use the word gumption, which has become our mantra with Meredith for more than five years years), a big engine, and a startling lack of skills. Big enthusiasm . . . big engine . . . incorrect application of her assets. This all added up to an unpolished diamond.

Over the next 12 months, Meredith progressed from 11.5 hours to 9 hours 48 minutes. Within two years, she won Ironman Canada. She has gone on to become one of the leading Ironman athletes in the world, with five championships to her name thus far.

So what was the recipe? You might think it was a big increase in training load to build her fitness, but no, it was quite the opposite. General fitness was not a limiter for Meredith. In fact, on reviewing her training program, I was struck with how much training she was accumulating in the week. What also came out of the review was that most of this training was completed at a very similar intensity, and there was little regard for rest and recovery in her week. She trained, and trained a lot, but was consistently fatigued throughout the process.

The process with Meredith was to take a longer-term lens on her progression. I set up a four- to five-year road map that we embarked upon. For the initial two years, the plan included a pretty dramatic drop in volume of weekly training. The goal was to teach her the value of lighter sessions, recovery, and blocks of recuperation. I also wanted to evolve the range of intensities at which she could operate, because fitness was there—she simply couldn't go *fast*. Ironman power was the same as half-Ironman, which was the same as Olympic distance. I decided to integrate two or three lighter days each week, thus forcing reduced volume, so she would do *barely* enough extended duration training to prepare her for Ironman distance, focusing on increasing intensity and overall power potential. Our thought was to live off the foundational endurance she had created over the previous seasons. The results were immediate and dramatic, and she has since gone on to develop a full range of gears, even showing potential to be a very good Olympic-distance and half-Ironman athlete.

Of course, the approach must evolve, and as speed and power have been developed, we now refocus on more classic Ironman training. The key here, though, is that we'll approach that extended-duration training without forgetting our guiding principles. Recovery is built into the program, and the training is built around it. We *lead* with recovery and aim to execute highly specific and high-quality work.

Meredith's journey is not done; her improvements will be ongoing. By embracing specificity and recovery, as well as establishing a smart long-term road map, she has primed herself to make massive gains that will continue over the coming years.

—Matt Dixon, MSc

RPE is a proven and highly accurate method of regulating output and, as we'll see in later chapters, indispensable for the technique and movement testing in our training system.

With training and competitive experience, triathletes become increasingly attuned to their perceived (internal) effort of intensity. Ironman world champion Chrissie Wellington, in answering questions about using pace and power for determining effort, wrote, "I have never used power. I use pace on the run and a time clock in the pool, but on the bike I just prefer to go on feel. On perceived effort! But I know a lot of athletes use power, and do so effectively. But we always have to remember it is power over 8 to 9 hours that we need to be concerned about. Not just biking power!"

How proficient a triathlete becomes at being aware of the breathing, sweating, and feelings in the muscles is central to achieving best outcomes. This conscious awareness is at the center of successful triathlon performance; the principle behind RPE fuses physiological and psychological responses to effort through perceptions of the body's signals in the respiratory and metabolic sources and from the exercising muscles.

We do not mean to question the reliability of quantitative training measures, but we do want to insist that these external methods should include RPE for further feedback—because heart rate and power can be affected by many variables from day to day. Sometimes a fatigued triathlete cannot hold prescribed power or heart rate levels. In such cases he or she must be aware of shifts in physiological and psychological capacities that a number on a heart monitor watch or power meter alone cannot determine. Also, these technologies require experience to use because variations indicate upswings and downswings in fitness from day to day. Thus zones of effort must be established to use these systems effectively.

Heart-rate training is subject to slow responses to changes in effort, just as power training by measuring work rate for cycling is much different indoors versus outdoors. Temperature, body position, humidity, dehydration, training status, mood, nutrition status, time of day, and cardiac drift (increased heart rate caused by decrease in stroke volume) all affect how the triathlete feels, and both heart rate and power are affected.

Triathlon racing efforts are comparatively steady state, with workloads just under, at, or slightly above aerobic threshold. No matter the competition distance (sprint, Olympic, full triathlons), these efforts are for the most part completed with intensity moderately constant, though of course higher for shorter events. Triathletes should have an ideal pacing strategy in mind that matches intended effort, based mainly on racing experience and training preparation. This kind of self-governing of effort is learned through training at mixed levels of effort and durations, with RPE as the primary manager of training intensity, though other measures might be used as well.

If RPE is used as the primary measure of intensity, triathletes can more naturally adjust output to meet demands (duration, pace, environment, fatigue). Consider the far-different feelings of physical intensity you get from sleeping soundly, working at your desk, walking in a forest with a friend in conversation for hours, and performing light exercise with a group. Compare these feelings to what you feel when performing moderate exercise with a comfortably beating heart and comfortable breathing. Now compare these feelings to performing harder training with fuller breaths and body heat rising and mind focused on movements and nutrients, distance to be covered, terrain, and pace. Finally, compare all of these feelings to what you feel when performing very hard exercise that can last just minutes or seconds before you hit overdrive and your hands are on your knees. These feelings are the ranges of exertion the mind and body can feel, and no matter the environment, duration, or intensity, you have an innate ability to regulate and fine-tune your effort in accordance to your perceived exertion. You simply can't do that as precisely with any other system of measure.

Exertion, time to fatigue, and training characteristics (table 1.1) can help set the framework for working RPE into your program and training. You can use many types of technologies to evaluate velocity (mostly in

TABLE 1.1   Level of Exertion, Intensity, and Fatigue

Exertion level	Training zone	Time to fatigue	Training characteristics
No exertion at all		N/A	At rest
Extremely light to very light	1	Many hours	After intervals or event as cool-down
Light		Many hours	Aerobic conditioning or casual distance training
	1	Many hours	Aerobic conditioning—moderate-intensity distance training
Somewhat hard to hard	2	3.5-15+ hours	Subthreshold—half-Ironman to Ironman pace
Hard to very hard	3	2-3 hours	Functional threshold intervals—Olympic triathlon pace
Very hard to very, very hard	3 to 4	1-2 hours	Functional threshold intervals—sprint and Olympic triathlon pace
	4	20 min.-1 hour	Functional threshold intervals—sprint and Olympic triathlon pace
Very, very hard to extremely hard	5	2-8 min.	$\dot{V}O_{2max}$ and very high-intensity interval training
Extremely hard to maximal	6	30 sec.-2 min.	Suprathreshold lactate tolerance training—sprinting
Maximal	6+	10 sec.	Suprathreshold intervals lactate tolerance training—sprinting

cycling), but RPE during the swim, bike, and run is your best training pulse.

Training Technique Testing

The ability to improve performance through alterations in form and technique will benefit economy (i.e., efficiency) in triathlon. Said another way, the amount of oxygen you need in order to work at a given pace is reduced as you improve your technique. Today, there are thousands of articles from scientific and trade magazines, websites, and printed materials that relate to technique and training. It is very easy to find inexpensive training plans, workout suggestions, and technique recommendations of all kinds—the problem is there's not much standardization and a basis to build from.

One clear factor in technique and its effects on economy are the relationships among flexibility, joint mobility, and stability. Any triathlete can improve technique by improving any of the body regions in these areas. A cornerstone of this work is the assessment of movements and combining body lines training with ACES (accurate, controlled, effortless, smooth movements) to establish new neural pathways.

Body Lines and ACES Testing

The body lines system of training involves practicing triathlon skills and movements body segment by body segment with a goal of achieving ACES in each segment. The system takes complex movements and skills and breaks them down into parts to enhance the motor-learning process through progressive training workouts that are accurate, controlled, effortless, and smooth. This system has been designed expressly for this book and provides a functional and organized process to optimize technique through practical and individualized progressions of tests and exercises. The system develops gradually because motor learning and reeducating swimming, cycling, and running technique and movements take time. Muscular and nerve pathways must develop, as well as flexibility, mobility of joints, and muscle stability.

The body lines system promotes a built-in method for individual progression by delivering a process for enhancing technique and efficiency that is nongeneric. Each of the later technique chapters (chapters 6, 7, and 8) provides technique guidelines and training progressions to help you move better. A system for coaches to teach these guidelines or to incorporate their own system into the ACES method is also presented.

Generic methods of exercise training are outdated. To be most effective, training must be individualized to the specific needs of each triathlete. Movement and stability must be assessed, followed by exercise remedies that are individually targeted. Next, body line technique evaluations are made and specific regions of the body trained to best enhance form and movements. ACES training and com-

petency workouts are applied and completed with the practice of postures and positions followed by testing and progression (figure 1.2).

ACES were chosen as the main pass–fail criteria because ACES emphasizes the neuromuscular change in coordination that must take place in order to pass each segment test. A body line that has been mastered will reflect an accurate movement, will be performed in a controlled manner, will be perceived as effortless, and will be smooth and easy. This system is self-progressing, with the triathlete assessing movement, control, and sense of effort during training and testing.

As mentioned, motor learning and reeducating movements take time, particularly for triathletes, who must master three sports. For each sport there is a requirement of adaptation and a goal of increasing conditioning and training technique. Technique training should overload progressively in volume and intensity over time. In swimming, once competency is shown in technique (the swimmer has passed the test of each body line), technique-based training should include longer-distance workout sets so that physiological as well as biomechanical training occur. For example, a segment of a swim technique and fitness workout would focus on balance, extension, and arc. During the workout each movement is centered on maintaining balance and executing

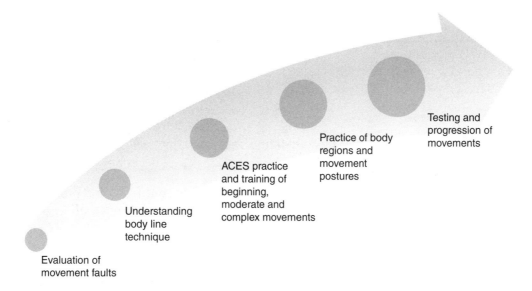

Testing and progression of movements

Practice of body regions and movement postures

ACES practice and training of beginning, moderate and complex movements

Understanding body line technique

Evaluation of movement faults

FIGURE 1.2 Movement, body lines, and ACES.

the accurate, controlled, effortless, and smooth positions of the extension and arc of the hand and arm. The workout set is long with short rest to simulate moderate levels of threshold training.

These workouts should not be so complex that the stimulus is lost—after all, the triathlete is an endurance athlete. The goal is to continuously and progressively stimulate a training response that builds threshold endurance and technique together. An intensity that is too high reduces the capacity to maintain body lines by pushing the anaerobic systems. If intensity is too low, there is not enough stimulus, and adaptation won't be sufficient. The swimmer should complete each test swim with ACES in three graded swimming test levels (this will become clear in chapter 6). With training, adaptations occur physically and biomechanically as the body becomes more efficient through absorption of increasing fitness and better training technique. Conditioning and technique training should overload progressing in specificity, volume, and intensity over time.

Before you begin testing, a baseline must be determined. Baseline tests should be taken before other assessments and training begin and should be taken in three training and testing zones:

- *Subthreshold (Sub-T)*—Sub-T tests are below race pace, aerobic, and evenly and comfortably paced. Form is easily maintained throughout the test. RPE is light.
- *Functional threshold (FT)*—FT tests are at race-pace threshold levels. RPE is hard. This test is *not* used for body line

assessment and progression but as a separate measurement of economy and aerobic threshold.

- *Suprathreshold (Supra-T)*—Supra-T tests are well above race pace and anaerobic (sprinting and high-speed tests). RPE is extremely hard to maximal. This test is *not* used for body line assessment and progression but as a separate measurement of economy and anaerobic capacity.

Table 1.2 shows the intensity for each of the three testing levels. Again, the Sub-T, FT, and Supra-T levels are used for baseline testing, but only the Sub-T level is used for body lines testing.

Once baseline tests have been completed, a lifestyle level test should be completed to determine the amount of body line technique work that should be done. A lifestyle level test allows you to adjust the amount of body lines training you do based on your yearly workout plan and time available for workouts (table 1.3). Note that body lines training and testing should only be done in the Sub-T training and testing zone to allow you to focus on the correct body line rather than a high-intensity workout. Also, after the body lines and ACES have been achieved and technique has improved, the baseline tests should be taken again to record improvement.

Because not all triathletes train continually year-round or have different lifestyle classifications and event goals, there are three classifications of baseline tests and weekly workout recommendations based on lifestyle levels and event goals and are indicated by different test lengths (table 1.4). In these tables, the lifestyle

TABLE 1.2   Baseline Test Intensity Levels

Baseline test level	Description
Sub-T testing	• Aerobic endurance; even effort that is controlled and maintains form • RPE: zone 2—somewhat hard; moderate, controlled effort
FT testing	• Lactate threshold—race-pace effort • RPE: zone 3 to 4—hard to harder; strong, race-pace effort
Supra-T testing	• Anaerobic—speed and sprinting effort • RPE: zone 6—very, very hard; sprinting effort with a 1:6 work-to-rest ratio and no less than 4 minutes or more than 5 minutes of interval time

TABLE 1.3 Triathlete Lifestyle Classification Based on Annual, Weekly, and Daily Training Hours

LIFESTYLE LEVELS	ANNUAL HOURS	WEEKLY HOURS (AVERAGE)		DAILY HOURS (AVERAGE)	
		Low	High	Low	High
1	250-500	5.25	10.5	.75	1.5
2	500-700	10.5	15.75	1.5	2.25
3	700-1,500+/–	15.75	31.5	2.25	4.25

TABLE 1.4 Recommended Baseline Training Adaptations Based on Lifestyle Level

SWIMMING			
	Lifestyle level 1 (250-500 hours)	Lifestyle level 2 (500-700 hours)	Lifestyle level 3 (700-1,500+ hours)
Number of training adaptation weeks	8	4-6	2-4
Workouts per week	3-5	2-4	2-3
Workout distance (main body line set)	800	1,500	2,000
ACES baseline test for swimming	4 sets of 8 × 25 m with 15 sec. rest after each 25 and 1 min. between rest sets	5 sets of 6 × 50 m with 20 sec. rest after each 50 and 1 min. rest between sets	4 sets of 10 × 50 m with 20 sec. rest after each 50 and 1 min. rest between sets
CYCLING			
Number of training adaptation weeks*	4-6	3-4	2-3
Workouts per week	3-4	2-3	2-3
Workout time (main body line set)	40 min.	30 min.	30 min.
ACES baseline test for cycling	4 sets of 5 reps of 2 min. with 1 min. soft pedaling recovery between sets	3 sets of 5 reps of 2 min. with 1 min. soft pedaling recovery between sets	3 sets of 5 reps of 2 min. with 1 min. soft pedaling recovery between sets
RUNNING			
Number of training adaptation weeks*	8	4-6	2-4
Workouts per Week	2-3	2-3	1-2
Workout distance (main body line set)	1-2 miles	2 miles	2-3 miles
ACES baseline test for running	16-32 reps of 50 m body line technique plus 50 m of relaxed tall-posture running	32 reps of 50 m body line technique plus 50 m of relaxed tall-posture running	32-48 reps of 50 m body line technique plus 50 m of relaxed tall-posture running

*You may retest baseline after two weeks if you achieve ACES.

level that corresponds to your annual hours of training can be found for swimming, cycling, and running. Next, the number of weeks you should train the body lines, how many workouts each week, and the total distance (main portion of the workout that focuses on the body region) are recommended. For example, if you train a total (all sports) of 500 to 700 hours a year, for swimming, table 1.4 indicates four to six weeks of adaptation to the body lines (specific regions of technique), two to four workouts each week that include 1,500 meters with focus on selected body lines. Those regions of the body are found in the tests in the swimming, cycling, and running chapters (chapters 6, 7, and 8).

Baseline testing is simply a data marker of performance. Testing is necessary to establish where you begin before training and then during and after achieving and improving technique. It is important to distinguish between these tests because body line tests are the training of body regions and focus on improving postures and technique, whereas baseline tests are the periodic testing of various distances and intensities in swimming, cycling, and running.

You might have baseline test protocols, distances, periods of and types of tests, intensities, and volumes different from the recommendations in the baseline test distance standards (table 1.5). If in doubt, go to the lesser lifestyle volume. We use three testing levels of varying distances and intensities to encompass the wide spectrum of cardiovascular output, force, and muscle activation. In addition, for each lifestyle level and primary event focus, there are test days columns with numbers 1 to 5, which indicate the following:

- 1 indicates testing should be performed on the same day (all three levels).
- 2 indicates testing should be performed on two consecutive days.
- 3 indicates testing should be performed on three consecutive days.
- 4 indicates testing should be performed over the course of four days.
- 5 indicates testing should be performed over the course of five days.

Testing should be separated by periods of training and technique adaptations following body lines training, or phases of training. The recommendation is four to eight weeks during the base preparation phase of the early season. During race preparation, there can be one or two tests. When uncertain about the test volume, go to a lower level and test with the same pretest rest and training conditions when possible. Also follow the intensity zones as closely as possible.

You can record your ongoing test results by using the baseline test and data record form (figure 1.3). This provides a journal for recording your results for each test, intensity, dates, distances, times, RPE, and other data markers. Take and record a baseline test, perform body lines training and retest the recommended baseline distances over time. Note that sub-T1, T2, T3, T4, FT1, 2, 3, 4, supra-T1, T2, T3, and T4 are columns provided for recording and tracking different tests over the training season. You may also choose to include other optional data markers, such as fatigue, fuel used, fluid intake, respiration rate, average or peak power, heart rate, altitude, average gradient, or peak speed.

Movement and Stability Testing

Baseline or technique testing without functional movement and stability evaluations and corrective exercises neglects a crucial area of performance. Triathlon is a technology-propelled sport, and it's with good reason that triathletes are captivated by every facet to produce free speed and monitor output. That said, the development of technique and the contributions to economical movements through muscle flexibility, mobility in the joints, and stability should never be underestimated.

If range of motion becomes limited or, for example, hip or foot and ankle stability is reduced because of injury, there is a corresponding reduction of economy in movement. In running, this can influence stride rate by diminishing hip extension. In cycling, the outcome of poor ankle mobility or stability can affect the connection and linkage of power

TABLE 1.5   Baseline Test Distance Standards

LIFESTYLE LEVEL 1 (250-500 HOURS)	SWIMMING BASELINE TEST DISTANCE			CYCLING BASELINE TEST DISTANCE			RUNNING BASELINE TEST DISTANCE		
	*Sub-T	FT	Test days	*Sub-T	FT	Test days	*Sub-T	FT	Test days
Sprint	400 m	200 m	1	10 m	5	2	4 m	2	1
Olympic	800 m	600 m	1	16 m	8	2	6 m	3	2
Long distance	1200 m	800 m	2	32 m	16	3	10 m	6	3
Full distance	2000 m	1000 m	3	56 m	28	3	12 m	8	3
LIFESTYLE LEVEL 2 (500-700 HOURS)	SWIMMING BASELINE TEST DISTANCE			CYCLING BASELINE TEST DISTANCE			RUNNING BASELINE TEST DISTANCE		
	*Sub-T	FT	Test days	*Sub-T	FT	Test days	*Sub-T	FT	Test days
Sprint	600 m	400 m	1	14	7	1	6	4	2
Olympic	1200 m	800 m	1	20	10	2	8	4	3
Long distance	1600 m	1200 m	2	42	21	3	12	8	3
Full distance	3000 m	2100 m	3	80	40	4	14	10	4
LIFESTYLE LEVEL 3 (700-1,500 +/– HOURS)	SWIMMING BASELINE TEST DISTANCE			CYCLING BASELINE TEST DISTANCE			RUNNING BASELINE TEST DISTANCE		
	*Sub-T	FT	Test days	*Sub-T	FT	Test days	*Sub-T	FT	Test days
Sprint	800	600	1	20	10	1	8	6	1
Olympic	1600	1400	2	30	16	3	10	6	3
Long distance	1800	1600	3	56	28	4	14	10	4
Full distance	3400	2600	4	90	56	5	16	12	5

Sprint course: swim 750 m (.47 mi.), bike 20 km (12.4 mi.), run 5 km (3.1 mi.); Olympic (standard) course: 1,500 m (.93 mi.), bike 40 km (24.8 mi.), run 10 km (6.2 mi.); long course: swim 1.9 km (1.2 mi.), bike 90 km (56 mi.), run 21.1 km (13.1 mi.); full course: swim 3.9 km (2.4 mi.), bike 180 km (112 mi.), run 42.2 km (26.2. mi.).

through the hip, knee, ankle, foot, and ultimately the pedal. The strokes of a swimmer with poor hip flexibility, mobility, or stability might be asymmetrical, resulting in less controlled motions that require greater effort.

When there are unbalanced, oblique, or lopsided movements in the body, these result in compensations of normal patterns of motions. Triathletes and coaches often address imbalances and unevenness in the off-season in order to program better motions in swimming, cycling, or running mechanics, which can make for long-term adaptations and enhanced technique. However, during high-load periods of training, preparation, and racing, the demands on the musculoskeletal system increase significantly, which can result in even greater compensations, caused by underlying weaknesses and instability at the local levels. With this in mind, the systems we have designed for assessing movement (chapters 3 and 4) provide simple movement

FIGURE 1.3 Baseline Test and Data Record Form

SWIM	SUB-T				FT				SUPRA-T			
	1 Date:	2 Date:	3 Date:	4 Date:	1 Date:	2 Date:	3 Date:	4 Date:	1 Date:	2 Date:	3 Date:	4 Date:
Distance												
Total time												
Average pace per 100 m												
Stroke rate average*												
RPE												

CYCLING	SUB-T				FT				SUPRA-T			
	1 Date:	2 Date:	3 Date:	4 Date:	1 Date:	2 Date:	3 Date:	4 Date:	1 Date:	2 Date:	3 Date:	4 Date:
Distance												
Total time												
Average miles (km) per hour												
RPM**												
RPE												
Temperature												
Wind conditions												
Terrain type												

RUN	SUB-T				FT				SUPRA-T			
	1 Date:	2 Date:	3 Date:	4 Date:	1 Date:	2 Date:	3 Date:	4 Date:	1 Date:	2 Date:	3 Date:	4 Date:
Distance												
Total time												
Average mile (km) pace												
Stride rate***												
RPE												
Temperature												
Wind conditions												
Terrain type												

*Count stroke rate for 50 at 1/4, 1/5, and 3/4 of the distance.

**Count RPM at halfway of the test time for two minutes and for the final two minutes.

***Count your stride rate at 1/4, 1/2, and 3/4 of the distance and during the final minute.

From M. Evans and J. Cappaert, *Triathletes in motion.* (Champaign, IL: Human Kinetics).

tests, progressions, and maintenance exercises to help you maintain functional form and movements.

Triathletes don't always have the assistance of gravity in activating and determining if local stabilizers are not functioning properly. Thus it's important to use baseline tests to determine the presence of an underlining dysfunction. In swimming, we use all four extremities to generate power or scull (holding water) our way through the water, which increases the demand for controlling rotational forces and transferring loads through the pelvis. The starting point for cycling is to be able to provide a stable base for the legs to generate power symmetrically throughout the pedaling motion and to optimally transfer forces through the pelvis. The more power that needs to be generated, the more stabilization we need through the deep core for maximum efficiency. During the run, we need our deep-layered core stabilizers to function well in order to generate efficient power and maintain posture and load transfer to dissipate the ground reaction and other forces acting on the body.

Stability in the pelvis and spine boosts load transfer when swimming, cycling, and running. Core training allows us to develop better movement and motion patterns that in turn increase the potential for higher and more efficient economy and use of oxygen. The most proficient triathletes possess excellent pelvic and spine stability, which we can witness in the efficiency of their movements. As they move, their stability meets the changing postures and demands of fatigue—such triathletes have the base of support and athletic, powerful rigidity in posture to move gracefully and quickly over long periods of time.

The next series of self-tests will help you quickly assess overall load transfer. These tests help confirm the need for in-depth movement screening, tests, and exercise remedies (chapters 3 and 4). Because the pelvis links to the limbs through complex movements and carries the burden of providing perpetual steadiness when swimming, cycling, and running, we can assess control and normal function through the single-leg stork test, forward-bend test, Trendelenburg test, multifidus test, sacral motion test, and ASLR (active straight-leg raise) test. In the description of the tests, don't let references to anatomical body landmarks (e.g., the posterior superior iliac spine) obscure what are relatively simple tests of your basic movements. Instead, focus on the photos and use the text to help you step by step.

Single-Leg Stork Test

The single-leg stork test assesses the ability of the low back, pelvis, and hips to transfer load (energy) on the weight-bearing leg and to determine if those regions of the body function efficiently and allow the pelvis to rotate optimally during swimming, cycling, and running. For example, when running or cycling, do the low back, pelvis, and hips transfer energy efficiently? The stork test assesses two phases—hip flexion and stability—during a single-leg stance. Table 1.6 tells you if you have passed this test or what has caused you to fail.

Hip-Flexion Phase

Standing with equal weight on both legs with feet together, place one hand on iliac crest with thumb palpating the inferior aspect of the posterior superior iliac spine (PSIS) on the side of the hip to be flexed (figure 1.4a). The opposite thumb palpates the midline of the sacrum level to the inferior aspect of the PSIS. Flex hip in a marching motion on the side of the hand palpating the PSIS (figure 1.4b). Note the quality of the posterior motion of the ilium relative to the sacrum. Compare this motion to the other side.

a   b

FIGURE 1.4   Single-leg stork test: hip-flexion phase.

Stance phase

With one hand palpate the iliac crest, with the thumb palpating the inferior aspect of the PSIS on the side of the weight-bearing leg. The opposite thumb palpates the midline of the sacrum level to the inferior aspect of the PSIS. Flex the opposite hip in a marching motion on the side of the hand palpating the midline of the sacrum (figure 1.5). Note the motion of the ilium relative to the sacrum.

FIGURE 1.5 Single-leg stork test: stance phase.

TABLE 1.6 Assessment of Single-Leg Stork Test Results

	PASS	FAIL
Hip-flexion phase	The PSIS rotates posteriorly relative to the sacrum (i.e., the thumb on the PSIS moves below the thumb on the sacrum).	The ilium rotates symmetrically relative to the sacrum (i.e., your thumbs stay level).
Stance phase	The ilium should either posteriorly rotate relative to the sacrum or remain still or level with the sacrum.	The ilium rotates forward or superior relative to the sacrum. The thumb on the PSIS moves above the thumb on the sacrum.

Forward-Bend Test

The forward-bend test assesses the ability of the low back, pelvis, and hips to maintain form closure (how the pelvis transfers load between the trunk and the lower extremities) and force closure (how and what extra forces are necessary to control two joint surfaces when load is applied to the pelvis during flexion of the hips and spine). During running and cycling, the hips flex, and this test evaluates how well the pelvis exchanges load from the torso and lower body. The forward-bend test assesses two body regions. Table 1.7 tells you if you have passed this test or what has caused you to fail.

Part I

Stand with equal weight on legs with feet and ankles touching. Palpate the inferior aspect of PSIS with thumbs. Bend forward as if to reach for toes (figure 1.6a).

FIGURE 1.6 *(a)* Forward-bend test: part I. **a**

Part II

One hand palpates the iliac crest and the thumb on the inferior aspect of the PSIS on the same side of one leg while the other thumb palpates the midline of the sacrum level to it. Bend forward as if to reach for toes through a full motion (figure 1.6b). Note the motion of the ilium relative to the sacrum; repeat on other side.

FIGURE 1.6 *(b)* Forward-bend test: part II. **b**

TABLE 1.7 Assessment of Forward-Bend Test Results

	PASS	FAIL
Part I	There should be no difference in relative motion between the two PSIS. Your thumbs should move symmetrically as a couple.	Asymmetrical motion occurs during palpation. One thumb moves above or below the other.
Part II	There is symmetrical movement of the ilium relative to the sacrum (i.e., the thumbs of the two fingers move together symmetrically or the thumb on the PSIS moves slightly below the thumb on the sacrum).	The thumb on the sacrum moves below the thumb on the PSIS.

Form and Force Closure

The triathlete's optimal pelvic stability (which provides overall body stability) is a function of joint anatomy—the shape of the surface and how the pelvis connects and fits together (form closure) and the compressive forces that act across joints and motor control (force closure) that are, in effect, the forces necessary to maintain the posture of the pelvis.

With limitations, instability, or pain in the pelvis, losses in muscle strength can result, making functional movement difficult. Technique and economy will be much less effective. Because the pelvis is the central distributor of force, it must be stable. When the pelvis is working effectively, the spine, legs, arms, and head are more efficient in posture control and movements. You'll be better at transferring loads from the pelvis to produce forward movement during swimming, cycling, and running.

Form Closure

Form closure is the shape, structure, or form of a joint that provides stability. That is, the shape of the pelvis, for example, and the ligaments attached help to optimize the form and stability and load-bearing ability. Any weaknesses or irregularities can reduce stability and increase movement in the pelvis. Form closure is achieved passively at the end range or by the shape of the supporting surface. The center of mass of one bone is passively supported over the horizontal aspect of the body of the adjacent bone (e.g., vertebral body on disc and body below or the femur on the tibial plateau while standing).

Force Closure

Compressive forces and congruency between two surfaces of a joint provide the friction to enhance stability. Force closure is achieved by the influence of an external force. There are four primary mechanisms of force closure: segmental stiffness, compression force closure (low-threshold and high-threshold systems), positional force closure, and torsion control (low-threshold and high-threshold systems).

Optimizing form or force closure enhances the stability and load-bearing ability of a joint complex. Minimizing form or force closure reduces stability and destabilizes the load-bearing ability, allowing for increased movement potential.

Trendelenburg Test

The Trendelenburg test assesses gluteal muscle dysfunction or a possible inability to transfer load through the pelvis. This is a common area of weakness for triathletes and results in inadequate stability and less effective load transfer—you'll note changes in running and cycling mechanics and power. Table 1.8 tells you if you have passed this test or what has caused you to fail.

Stand with equal weight on legs with feet and ankles touching. Palpate the left iliac crest and inferior aspect of the PSIS with the left hand and the right iliac crest and inferior aspect of the PSIS with the right hand (figure 1.7a). Lift one foot up, with bottom of foot pointing back (figure 1.7b). Note any motion between the two bony crests; repeat with other foot.

FIGURE 1.7 Trendelenburg test.

TABLE 1.8 Assessment of Trendelenburg Test Results

	PASS	FAIL
Trendelenburg test	Minimal motion occurs when one foot is lifted. PSIS and iliac crests remain relatively level.	There is notable superior or inferior movement of one PSIS and iliac crest relative to the other.

Multifidus Test

The multifidus is a muscle central in stabilizing the spine. The multifidus test assesses the ability of the myofascial system (soft tissue that supports and protects body structures) to assist with load transfer in the unloading leg. Table 1.9 tells you if you have passed this test or what has caused you to fail.

Stand with equal weight on legs with feet and ankles touching. Palpate the left and right sacral sulcus (a depressed area in the sacrum; figure 1.8*a*). This can be found by first palpating the left and right PSIS. Move your fingers slightly toward the midline of the spine off the two bony crests and onto soft tissue. Keep your fingers there. Take a half-step forward, shifting weight onto the forward leg and off the back heel (figure 1.8*b*). Note how the multifidus muscle swells up into your finger.

a   b

FIGURE 1.8 Multifidus test.

TABLE 1.9 Assessment of Multifidus Test Results

	PASS	FAIL
Multifidus test	The multifidus muscle boldly swells into your finger just as the back heel is lifting off the ground.	There is an asymmetrical, delayed, or faint swelling of the multifidus muscle as the back heel lifts.

Sacral Motion Test

The sacrum is the large triangular bone at the base of your spine. The sacral motion test assesses how the low back and sacrum maintain form and force closure of the pelvis and assist in load transfer through the pelvis. Table 1.10 tells you if you have passed this test or what has caused you to fail.

Part I

Stand with equal weight on legs with feet and ankles touching. Palpate the left and right sacral sulcus. This can be found by first palpating the left and right PSIS. Move fingers slightly toward the midline of the spine off the two bony crests and onto soft tissue. Keep fingers there. Bend backward, keeping knees straight (figure 1.9a). Note the movement of your thumbs inward or sinking in.

FIGURE 1.9 *(a)* Sacral motion test: part I. **a**

Part II

Stand with equal weight on legs with feet and ankles touching. Palpate the left and right sacral sulcus. This can be found by first palpating the left and right PSIS. Move fingers slightly toward the midline of the spine off the two bony crests and onto soft tissue. Keep fingers there. Moving slowly, slightly bend to one side, keeping knees straight (figure 1.9b). Note the ability of the thumb on that side to sink in or move inward. Repeat on other side and compare side to side.

FIGURE 1.9 *(b)* Sacral motion test: part II. **b**

TABLE 1.10 Assessment of Sacral Motion Test Results

	PASS	FAIL
Part I	Both thumbs sink in symmetrically.	Asymmetrical sinking occurs in the thumbs, or one thumb does not sink in at all.
Part II	There is symmetrical sinking in both thumbs on each side.	There is asymmetrical sinking in one thumb compared to the other.

Active Straight-Leg Raise (ASLR) Test

The ASLR test assesses the ability of the low back, pelvis, and hips to maintain form and force closure and effectively transfer load in a non-weight-bearing position. Here you are testing lumbar and spine stability as well as your ability to brace the abdomen with deep-layered stabilizers. Table 1.11 tells you if you have passed this test or what has caused you to fail.

Lie on back with legs straight (figure 1.10a). Lift one extended leg about 30 degrees (figure 1.10b). Note any movement in the thorax, pelvis, or opposite leg. Lower the leg and repeat with the other leg. Determine if one leg feels heavier or more difficult to lift than the other. Then gently compress your pelvis at the anterior superior iliac spine (ASIS) and repeat, lifting the first leg and then the second. After each leg is lifted, ask yourself if the leg feels lighter or easier with the compression. Repeat the sequence, compressing the PSIS together in the back.

FIGURE 1.10   ASLR test.

TABLE 1.11   Assessment of ASLR Test Results

	PASS	FAIL
ASLR test	The effort to lift each leg is symmetrical. There is no change in effort with compression of the pelvis in the front or back.	One leg feels heavier or more difficult to lift than the other without any compression. One or both legs feel easier to lift with compression either in the front or back.

In this section we have provided six pre-screening tests as ways to evaluate general overall movement and stability. These can be repeated as check-ups or field tests at any time. The all-inclusive tests in chapters 3 and 4 along with core tests in chapter 5 go much deeper and provide extensive remedies and progressions for assessing and improving movement and stability in all regions of the body.

You should now have a firm grasp of the principles of movement, RPE, body lines, ACES, and prescreening for mobility, flexibility, and stability. In the next chapter we will cover principles of triathlon training, including information on the energy systems, periodization, individualization, and adaptation. Note that this next chapter intends to be encyclopedic in nature and to serve as a resource for reference on the broader but principal themes of training. Feel free to skip or skim this chapter for now and move to the practical themes of assessing posture (chapter 3) and movement (chapter 4).

2 Principles of Triathlon Training

Triathlon performance is controlled by three physiological characteristics: maximal oxygen consumption capacity, lactate threshold, and economy. In this chapter we address the broader implications of these performance characteristics and discuss principles that are crucial to the development of elite triathletes.

In addition to understanding the principles of physiology, you must take into account race tactics, skill and technique, equipment use, psychology, the environment, fatigue, rest and recovery planning, nutrition, general health issues, injury management, and travel considerations. Triathlon training is complex, but with a foundation of knowledge and an understanding of training standards, you can build a successful training plan and effective workouts. Regardless of your training or coaching method, system, or style, sport science and training principles can give you a broader view of training. Don't abandon your unique style, however; individual ingenuity is perhaps the most stimulating aspect of training and coaching. The extensive information in this chapter is both accessible and appropriately researched so that you can confidently apply it to your particular method of training.

Physiological Aspects of Triathlon

Triathlon training principles are important because they can clarify many issues. However, as with any branch of learning or sport, triathlon training is marked by an endless evolution of theories and models, engineering, human adaptations, innovations, and hypotheses—and yes, opposing opinions. These divergent ideas create the ever-fluctuating continuum of performance improvement. Be that as it may, athletes, coaches, and scientists alike can benefit from today's principles and develop better training programs and athletes through transformations in coaching.

In the following sections we cover physiology principles that are a backdrop for any training program, workout, or coaching method. How you apply these principles will depend on your training or coaching emphasis and philosophy, level of experience, and other factors.

Maximal Oxygen Capacity ($\dot{V}O_2$max)

The body's ability to efficiently transport oxygen to exercising muscles is central to triathlon performance. One of the factors affecting this ability is the body's maximal aerobic power, or *capacity*. The body's capacity to use oxygen (maximal oxygen capacity, or $\dot{V}O_2$max) is measured while performing large muscle group activities such as swimming, cycling, and running. This straightforward but strenuous test comprises a series of incremental progressions of intensity. At a certain point the athlete reaches a plateau of oxygen intake and cannot develop any further cardiac output. It can be hard to pinpoint exactly why this happens because competing elements can limit further increases in speed.

The lungs, heart, blood, brain, and muscles all play important roles in how much force can be exerted and in the economy of movement. A key factor is how many motor units (i.e., muscle cells of the active muscles) are recruited. Elite athletes recruit more motor units and for longer periods—and this can be trained with higher-intensity intervals and improvements in form. Thus technique and movement function (flexibility, joint mobility, stability, and strength) also play crucial roles in maximal oxygen consumption and directly affect performance.

The oxygen you consume is delivered to muscle cells via a complex process that provides ATP (the energy compound) to the muscles to generate force. Endurance and your performance depend upon the blood to carry oxygen to active skeletal muscles to produce and sustain velocity when swimming, cycling and running. From inhaled air, oxygen flows into the lungs and from there into the blood and is delivered to the muscles via the arteries. Therefore, when you improve your functional movement, stability, and technique, you expand your body's ability to use energy and to recruit motor neurons (signals from spinal cord to produce movement) efficiently.

$\dot{V}O_2$ max tests, although not necessary, do provide a window into aerobic capacity. In fact, no test is more accurate at predicting performance potential. High oxygen capacity is associated with elite endurance performances in both long-distance running and cross-country skiing in both men and women.

However, it turns out that training improvements are not related to increased maximal oxygen capacity. Rather, they make the athlete more efficient at exploiting a larger fraction of that maximal capacity. Elite triathletes learn the optimal intensities of effort for certain distances or intervals. This allows these athletes to avoid creating too great a supply of blood lactate and thereby maintain a steady state.

Given that training does not increase maximal oxygen capacity, one of the goals of training should be to increase the percentage of maximal oxygen capacity at which steady state occurs. In doing so, the body can balance aerobic and anaerobic metabolism at a higher intensity. Following are benefits of working at a higher percentage of your maximal oxygen capacity:

- Increases the total amount of blood volume; reduces blood thickness so that it flows faster from the heart to the muscles.
- Increases the amount of air intake into the body.
- Increases the strength of specific muscle groups and their response to specific training.
- Increases cardiac output (the amount of blood ejected from the heart each minute).
- Increases the number of red blood cells for transporting more oxygen to the muscles.
- Increases the capillaries around muscle fibers, thereby increasing the oxygen available to working muscles.
- Improves how blood is shunted to the working muscles (i.e., more efficient delivery of blood to the muscles used during exercise).

Lactic Acid

During exercise, your body's first fuel source is mainly carbohydrate. Carbohydrate metabolism creates the by-product lactic acid within the working muscles. However, blood lactate levels (the levels of lactic acid in the blood) don't really change all that much until you reach a threshold of about 60 percent of maximal oxygen capacity. Thus learning how to train at appropriate intensities and increasing the percentage of maximal oxygen capacity at which the lactate threshold occurs are extremely important for triathletes.

Triathletes often refer to lactate in describing the burning sensation in the muscles following high-intensity exercise, but this is inaccurate. In fact, the muscles shift toward what is called *acidosis,* but the resulting lactate production is not what is causing the muscle burn. The burn has more to do with the coinciding accumulation of hydrogen ions, which is what slows muscle contractions and elicits the burning sensation.

Triathletes shouldn't experience muscle burn very often, but it's important to learn how to train the lactate threshold specifically for triathlon, which is a relatively steady-state activity. Triathletes should maintain intensity as high as possible without reaching the point at which muscles tighten and burning occurs. When performing in a steady state, a functional balance exists in the creation and removal of lactate in the exercising muscles. The goal is to perform at a high but steady level of physical exertion and without any abrupt or lengthy periods in which a decrease in lactate removal occurs. Training, then, becomes a practice of improving ability to raise the percentage of lactate threshold without redlining. For triathletes, the ability to sustain a high proportion of aerobic capacity is crucial for strong performance.

Functional threshold power (FTP) is determined simply as average power for a 30- to 60-minute time trial, which serves as an excellent practical alternative to a ramped lab test because it correlates very closely to oxygen uptake at lactate threshold. This gives a bottom-line measure of functional endurance performance. How triathletes evaluate, train to tolerate, and improve lactate threshold (or FTP) is a process of combining optimal effort with optimal duration with optimal technique.

Economy

The *economy* of exercise relates to the oxygen consumption necessary for a particular effort in exercise. There are of course differences from one triathlete to the next in the amount of oxygen consumed.

Equally trained triathletes with the same or comparable maximal oxygen capacity can have different performance results for a number of reasons, one being economy of movement (also called technique). As we discuss in later chapters, improvements in performance can be made as a result of constructive changes in flexibility, mobility, stability, or biomechanics. Thus maximizing triathlon and endurance performance becomes a process of reinforcing a group of principles. Achieving an optimal combination of volume, intensity, and density along with functional movement and

technique improvement during training paves the way for optimal performances.

Even the best training plan can't make up for limitations in functional movement. Economy of movement makes optimal use of aerobic capacity and lactate threshold possible. A solid, pragmatic approach to the systems of energy and how to apply them makes optimal training much more likely to occur. Coaches and advanced triathletes require a solid understanding of these systems and how they apply to training time, recovery from intervals, physiological benefits, and progression.

Cardiac Output and Stroke Volume

Cardiac output refers to the amount of blood pumped out by the heart. Total output is the multiplication of stroke volume (the amount of blood pushed out from the heart with every heartbeat) by heart rate (in beats per minute). Improvements in training fitness increase the heart's ability to supply oxygen to muscle fibers.

Training properly, triathletes can attain increases in cardiac output through increases in stroke volume. Training at long, slow intensities appears to be one of the best means of improving cardiac output. The lower training heart rate increases stroke volume because the heart can fill more completely with each beat. At higher intensities there's less time for the heart to fill with blood between heartbeats. Through low-intensity training, stroke volume will improve, allowing for higher-intensity workloads. The heart adapts and is able to fill with blood at a much faster rate, allowing a higher output of intensity.

Energy

The energy in the body exists in combinations of chemical molecules within five compounds that the body burns as fuel: adenosine triphosphate (ATP), creatine phosphate (CP), carbohydrate, fat, and protein. Which fuel, or combination of fuels, being burned during a workout depends on the intensity of the work. For optimal training benefits, and optimal performance, it helps to know which fuel is being burned, how much is being burned, and when a particular fuel supply is exhausted.

Energy Systems

Food contains carbohydrate, fat, and protein, all of which can be released as energy for muscle contraction. The calories in the foods are converted via biochemical reactions (the metabolism process) and released as energy, enabling your body to function and move. The intensity and duration of activity determine when and to what extent each metabolic system contributes. These systems are described in sections that follow.

ATP-CP System

The ATP-CP system is an anaerobic source of energy for high-intensity activities that last up to 10 seconds. This system has a very large power capacity for short, quick bursts of activity. Oxygen is not needed at this intensity because contractions can occur using only the ATP within the muscles. Only a small amount of ATP is present in the muscles, so sprints or heavy exertions deplete the stores rapidly.

Anaerobic Glycolysis (Lactic Acid) System

The lactic acid system provides major sources of energy for generally moderate-intensity activity lasting from 30 to 90 seconds. This activity might include high-intensity exercise that burns ATP-CP energy for the first 10 seconds and relies on anaerobic glycolysis thereafter.

Aerobic System

Any activity that lasts longer than a few minutes uses the aerobic system of energy. This system provides energy for many hours of exercise. Unlike the other energy systems, the aerobic system can be replenished during lower-intensity activity and is limited only by your aerobic resources, which are developed through incremental aerobic training. Once the aerobic system of energy has been activated, a reduction of lactate in the muscles occurs, along with a more efficient use of carbohydrate; combined, these conditions allow for extended and improved triathlon performance.

Adaptations occurring within the energy systems can allow you to exercise at a higher percentage of your maximal oxygen capacity. Combined with optimal technique, flexibility, and joint mobility, finely developed energy systems can vastly improve your performance.

Obviously, as a triathlete, you should maintain training intensities most beneficial for triathlon performance. Adhering to triathlon-specific guidelines for training intensities paves the way for optimal performance, no matter which coaching system you use. Thus how to use these guidelines within your training plan is a matter of individual choice and philosophy.

The energy you store allows you to move, permitting contractions of muscles to occur against resistance—the resistance of water as you swim, pedals as you cycle, and the ground as you run. Many scientific explanations exist regarding how energy is stored, replenished, and used by muscles, but of primary importance to triathletes is how energy is supplied to the body for continual muscular contraction. Optimal performance demands a high rate of oxygen consumption. Your body requires a high cardiac output and an ability to circulate blood most efficiently to the muscles most activated.

Triathlon Performance Principles

Desired conditioning, or cardiovascular, response can be produced only through proper training. The most effective training for our sport demands adhering to principles concerning intensity, duration, frequency, and volume; you should keep these principles forefront in mind when constructing your training plans and workouts.

When considering intensity, duration, volume, and frequency, perhaps the most challenging to manage well is frequency—that is, the way in which your workouts and rest are spaced. If the frequency of your training is not optimal, your training stimulus might be either lacking or beyond your capacity to develop in the way that you desire.

There is no single best approach for applying the principles behind intensity, duration, and frequency. Each triathlete has his or her own strengths and weaknesses and must learn to apply the principles accordingly. Some triathletes are exceptionally skilled at adjusting the principles intuitively. As they adjust the intensity, duration, and frequency of their workouts and develop their fitness levels, the focus on one aspect (swimming, cycling, or running) might move more toward skill training, whereas another is on physiological fitness and aerobic conditioning. Many triathletes and their coaches strive for a holistic approach to training in which a continuous interaction of training components occurs, one feeding off and fueling another as all progress as much as possible toward optimal development.

Of course, above all, training must be individualized. What works best for one triathlete might not work best for another. Also, it is not in the best interest of any triathlete to fashion an unyielding training plan or environment. Structure is important, but so is flexibility. Innovations of workout design, program planning, and management of stress and recovery should depend on the individual athlete and be somewhat a matter of individual choice. Training can be a wonderful journey, a never-ending challenge that cannot be completed because its ultimate end—perfection—cannot be reached. But there are elements of physical, technical, movement function, tactical, and emotional preparations that can always result in better outcomes as a consequence of better training.

The principles that govern the intensity, duration, and frequency of training are listed here:

Fitness principle

Individualization

Movement

Technique

Optimization

Overload

Specificity

Stimulus

Interval

Recovery

Periodization

Taper

Warm-up

Adherence to these principles allows you to train in an optimal yet individualized manner that ensures the best possible outcomes in training and performance. We'll look briefly at each of these principles in the sections that follow and expand our discussions in chapters to come.

Fitness Principle

Fitness involves more than the ability to train or compete for extended periods. Endurance is certainly important, but so too are many other elements of fitness. There are dozens of subcategories to fitness that can differ for each triathlete, including energy systems and cardiorespiratory system improvements; the composition of the body in terms of fat mass; flexibility and range of motion; joint structure function; muscular stability; and the neuromuscular system changes in movement for a more effective technique.

We'll look at these subcategories in detail later in the book. For now, the main thing to emphasize is that, when it comes to the subcategories of fitness, each triathlete has unique demands, training status, and goals. Triathletes are individuals, and no one single training component or technique of movement is best for everyone. This leads us to the principle of individualization.

DARREN SMITH   A Coach's Reflections on the 2012 Olympic Triathlon

I coach to help athletes express their absolute sporting capabilities on the one day it really matters. For some, the Olympics are that one day. The challenge is to develop physical, mental, and strategic abilities in your athletes.

The Olympics are a crazy environment. Much has been written about the need to prepare well, have structure, and develop competence well before arriving. There are so many more distractions at the Olympics than in any other world championship, as athletes go from competing for themselves to competing for nations. Many stakeholders come into the equation, not to mention the allure of an Olympic medal, which can be life changing. Outcome becomes the prime target, but this is largely a poisoned dart.

When it comes to training, my mantra is *routine, routine, routine*—and also management of expectations. In London in 2012 I had triathletes from six countries—five competitive females, all of whom had placed top five in rounds of the world series competitions, and one male. But since these were the Olympics, I had to hand over my athletes to their countries' head coaches. This happened four days ahead of the competition. Some of these coaches were entering their first Olympics and had less than a year's experience in coaching Olympians. Those four days were the longest of my life! But as one of my athletes, Kate Roberts of South Africa, reminded me: "Coach, don't stress. We are all fine—you taught us well!" Some of the athletes had been world class for years; others were new to this rarified level in 2012.

I guessed the running demands to reach the podium to within a second or so based on an average pace we would need to run for 9 kilometers, the last 1 kilometer, and the last 200 meters. We also guessed the numbers of athletes and their names still in contention with 1 kilometer to race, and we trained each of the athletes in our squad to maximize skills against these demands. Of course we also had race strategies.

Unexpected swim outcomes made some nations change plans. A major bike crash, including two of our team taken down, was a real kick. But as the race played out, the cream rose to the top. Those affected by the crash rose to the occasion, battled back into the race, and gave it everything they could.

With just 1 kilometer of the run to go, four talented ladies, including two from our squad, still had the chance of winning a medal. I sat in the stands next to the finish line, surprisingly calm, having faith my athletes would get the most out of themselves. Sarah Groff dropped off with a few hundred meters to go—a little sad, but this was the woman who clawed back into contention after being dropped by the lead athletes much earlier in the run! Three entered the sprint zone. Finally, I was standing, the crowd was going nuts, and a photo was needed to determine the winner. What a triumph for all three athletes! Our silver medalist, Lisa Norden, was delighted with her performance. If only everyone knew of the rocky times she'd been through to get there. I was extremely proud of the entire support team because we delivered the athletes to their special day in their best-ever shape. They were all ready, relaxed, and excited to express their talents.

Individualization Principle

We all recognize that we don't all respond to the same training in the same way. Every triathlete has his or her own set of talents, skills, and abilities that accompany differences in gender, age, fitness, training state, flexibility, mobility, stability, strength, mental and emotional levels, and general health. All of these factors must be considered when developing your training program.

Training in Groups or Teams

When preparing several triathletes for competition, a combination of individual and group training alternatives might come into play. In many situations, group training does not easily allow for individual differences among athletes—at least not without great demands on the coach. That said, coached group training for the professional or elite triathlete in cohesive groups with well-thought-out workouts can be a useful and even ideal method of training. Swim training does favor group workouts, mainly because of pool use constraints, and an experienced on-deck coach can organize and run extremely productive workouts in a group environment. Cycling training tends to combine group and individual training with coached and noncoached outdoor and indoor workouts. Finally, because of convenience, running favors an emphasis on individual training (particularly for amateurs) combined with coached and noncoached track workouts and group meetings for trail and long-distance runs.

Group training challenges the triathlete and coach to manage individual programs and progressions of intensity, frequency, and duration. Because it includes three modes of activity, triathlon training might demand even closer attention to training principles. There is a tendency in group training to push the pace, try to keep up, go longer distances, and train at a higher level of effort. It's important to decide on group training within the scope of the intended purpose of training and to self-regulate the intensity, volume or distance, and terrain. With noncoached groups, however, there is an unpredictability of pace that can be difficult to govern if a triathlete is not content to follow his or her own plan.

Today, triathlon coaches and clubs organize and administer a full range of services—from masters swim programs and group swimming, to track and trail running group workouts, to indoor and outdoor group cycling, to specialized individual coaching services for every group. Not-for-profit triathlon clubs and groups largely have volunteer coaching and perhaps a select number of coaches or companies who are paid for individual services. There are workouts for every level of athlete, including workouts for men and women, women-only workouts, youth workouts, and group-, club-, and team-training camps, with a host of combinations. These distinctions are important because triathletes working with coaches delivering customized workouts should factor in the increased intensity variations of group training.

Group training is an important part of the triathlon for both physiological and social reasons, but the built-in competitive nature of group training must be accounted for. If the varied duration, frequency, terrain, and intensities are not factored in, inconsistency in training and progression will result. Establishing a workout and training strategy before training (group or alone) will lead to better outcomes.

Genetic potential determines quite a bit in triathletes, but no matter where you currently stand, or whether you have been genetically blessed or cursed, *every* aspect of your training can create possibilities for greater improvement. The principle of individualization might be the most obvious of all the training principles, but it might also be the most important to remember—especially if you're a coach faced with the task of training many triathletes at once.

Movement Principle

Movement assessment particular to the triathlon continues to evolve. As happens in other specialties and technical fields, there are growing pains along with incremental improvements in approaches to providing proof that assessment is a valid science. But one need look only to the field of physical therapy to acquire the wealth of science and research available to bear out the basis for coupling movement analysis with technique training. Poor posture and weak or tight muscles can produce not only poor technique but also discomfort, pain, and even disability.

By making subtle adjustments, a physical therapist can help you produce better movements and improved body alignment and balance. On the other side, if you continue to repeat patterns of movement that are less than ideal, those can result in less than optimal performances and injury caused by compensations of movement.

In this book, the tests for movement, stability, and flexibility are based on the most current methods for improving flexibility, mobility, stability, strength, and functional movement patterns. The goal of every triathlete is to move forward with as much force and as little resistance as possible. An increase in resistance is often caused by imperfect technique, resulting from problems in stability, flexibility, or mobility. Over time, such problems can lead to inflammation of soft tissue and impaired joints that cause pain and hinder functional motion.

Movement is the central (core) starting point for triathlon performance. Motion (triathlon performance) is a collection of balance, stability, muscular performance, mobility, flexibility, cardiovascular endurance, and technique that every triathlete and coach should attend to as part of every training plan. With proper technique, functional alignment becomes visible—the body exhibits stability and muscular balance in both dynamic and static positions. We see this clearly in many elite triathletes.

Your purpose as a triathlete is to maximize the forces that move your body forward and to reduce the forces of resistance in swimming, cycling, and running. In swimming, producing more power is not effective, but enhancing technique and learning to slip through the water *are* effective. In cycling, you must have stability and a functional stance on the pedals in order to align limb movements seamlessly on the pedals, the points at which force and power are prevailing. In running, you must have sufficient stability to maintain balance from foot strike to foot strike and hold the torso in alignment, even when fatigued.

Within the principle of movement is the understanding that every triathlete has characteristic movements that affect performance beneficially or unfavorably (or both). Movement is never perfect, but the closer you can come to perfect in terms of flexibility, mobility, and stability, the better you will perform and the less likely you will be to suffer tissue damage or overuse injuries caused by problems in technique. The movement principle is discussed in greater detail later in the book.

Technique Principle

The smallest of changes in technique affect efficiency of movement, but this can be difficult to measure. However, illustrations of exceptional technique in such sports as swimming and Nordic skiing indicate that even the slightest deviation from the ideal will cause inefficiency and impaired performance. A good example is the difference in energy cost when comparing the classic diagonal ski stride to the V1 skate style. The classic technique uses 16 percent more energy than the V1 skate technique, vastly diminishing performance.

Olympic swimmers have been shown to use less power (propulsive force) to move through the water when compared to other swimmers. Instead of focusing primarily on power, elite swimmers focus on efficiency of technique. If their technique is optimally efficient, their strokes need not be as powerful; in fact, if their stokes are too powerful, efficiency will be compromised. The more efficient technique also contributes to improved body position in the water.

For triathletes, the reduction of energy cost and anything that arrests, limits, or reduces forward movement must be attended to. Today's triathletes spend tens of thousands of dollars on the most aerodynamic and slip-streaming bikes, bike fitting, aero-bars, tires, wheel sets, helmets, clothes, skin suits, wetsuits, and other equipment built to even slightly enhance performance. Businesses have blossomed and millions of dollars have been spent in the quest to help us swim, ride, and run faster. With a single-mindedness of improving performance through mechanics and cutting-edge equipment, technicians have changed the way we look at performance. More so than any other sport, triathlon has triggered innovation in mechanics, nutrition, equipment design, and even online coaching.

All that said, nothing is more vital to triathlon than proper technique. No bike, wetsuit, wheel set, nutrition strategy, or workout regimen can make up for poor alignment of the muscular or skeletal system. So, until you have reached the level of the most elite, focus on perfecting your technique rather than on saving for the best bike money can buy.

Optimization Principle

The optimization principle values working as close to your lactate threshold as possible. Most of the energy for competition and training in triathlon is derived from the aerobic system. Thus, from a physiological perspective, much of your training uses a system of steady-state energy output. To optimize performance, efficiency of movement (technique) and economy (i.e., how high a percentage of your maximal aerobic capacity you can use) should be emphasized during training.

The physiological demands of competition are necessary to practice and training plans, and workouts should develop individual fitness to reach maximal capabilities. Those goals and the process vary enormously from athlete to athlete; there are no exact blueprints of the right amount of intensity, volume, and frequency. How the triathlete and coach decide to test, prescribe the plan, and measure the threshold in swimming, cycling and running is a matter of choice (e.g. time, heart rate, power, RPE), but optimal performances are not simple to identify by numbers alone. Yet, understanding the specifics of competition and the backgrounds and capabilities of each triathlete will help identify the most effective and the optimal training intensities.

Overload Principle

The overload principle refers to how the body interacts with and reacts to physical training. Training can result in better, worse, or same performance, and which result you get often depends on how training loads (intensity, volume, and rest) have been applied. Very simply, your cells, tissues, organs, and energy systems respond to the physical demands of training, and with the right physical demands and appropriate recovery, you'll likely see improved performance. If after training you remain more or less unchanged in performance (not necessarily a bad thing), this might mean that training loads have not been sufficiently progressed to challenge your body to improve.

If you are an experienced triathlete, you know that you cannot continually increase the training intensity, volume, and frequency of your workouts. To achieve the desired training effect, you must allow time for adaptation to occur during a recovery period. Achieving an optimal ratio of training to recovery is as much art as science, but once you find the proper balance, results are likely to be positive, with fewer overtraining periods and fewer recurring injuries.

The benefits acquired through applying the overload principle can be alluring, but keep in mind that no one principle stands alone. By taking a holistic approach and considering all of the principles together, you will see better results than if you focus on a single principle and neglect the others. Each principle has its own attractive elements that might resonate more for one triathlete than another, but even as we achieve the results we're looking for we must strive not to neglect the other principles. For instance, if you emphasize the overload principle and ignore the stimulus principle (discussed soon), you probably won't get the results you're after.

Specificity Principle

The specificity principle provides the foundation for physical training for triathletes. This principle holds that our training adaptations should be specific to the energy systems, body structures, and movement functions we use during performance. Simply put, we should train how we race. Our energy stimulus, muscle groups, joint movements, and contraction speed all respond to the way in which we train. For instance, as triathletes, we know to emphasize aerobic training over anaerobic because of the endurance demands of our sport. Likewise, we steer away from training for muscular strength because bulky muscles don't serve us well in triathlons.

The specificity principle helps us focus on the best means of achieving our performance goals. Our training methods for swimming, cycling, and running are each brought to focus through specificity. Our training requires physiological adaptations (e.g., transition workouts from bike to run or swim to bike), volume, and intensity that are specific to triathlon.

When training under the specificity principle we must also remember the individualization principle—in fact, we could say the specificity principle in a sense *contains* the individualization principle. Under the specificity principle, we train while keeping the demands of our sport in mind; under the individualization principle, we train while keeping our own strengths and weaknesses in mind. As we discussed earlier, some triathletes might require extensive training to improve stability or mobility; others might require large cardiovascular improvements. Specificity, then, is the process of identifying the specific demands of our event along with the specific demands of our own individual situation, and then training in a way that best meets these demands.

Stimulus Principle

The stimulus principle can be more or less understood by an inversion of training intensity, frequency, and volume. That is to say, the greater the intensity and frequency (i.e., how much time separates one workout from the next within the same training session), the lower the total volume and longer recovery between training sessions should be. Similarly, when training volume and frequency increase, intensity should decrease. How the stimulus is spread depends largely on the demands of competition and individualization. Shorter competition time or distance, such as a 1.5-kilometer swim, 40-kilomter ride, and 10-kilometer run, call for greater demands on high-intensity training and lower volume, whereas long-distance triathlons, such as a

half-Ironman, require higher volume and lower intensity in training.

As we have discussed, training overloads your cells, tissues, organs, and systems. To be effective, training must have a stimulus *and* an overload—workouts must provide a progressive challenge over time, but for the greatest training benefit, recovery is required. Keeping an eye on how you respond to workouts and taking periodic recovery days (or weeks) of lighter activities can be one of the most important contributors to fitness and improved performance.

The stimulus designed into phases of training is known as *periodization*, which is an important principle in its own right and discussed at length later in the chapter. In short, periodization involves interspersing training periods with a goal of peaking at just the right time, such as on the day of your event.

Interval Principle

Intervals are an important part of training for triathletes. Intervals are prescribed periods of time or distances the triathlete repeats with targeted levels of intensity followed by periods of recovery. Recovery periods might be from a few seconds to a few hours, depending on the focus, phase, individual, and event target. Recovery periods are determined by an interval's intensity and duration. Short-duration intervals at high intensity have longer recovery periods between bouts of intervals compared to lower-intensity (race pace) intervals, which incorporate shorter recovery periods.

There are millions of ways to construct interval workouts, but to be most effective they should always adhere to a logical intensity, duration, and recovery ratio (see table 2.1). A period of work (intensity or force and distance) is followed by a period of recovery, and volume is progressed through phases of training.

How triathletes can benefit most from interval training is hotly debated, with many coaches and triathletes clinging to their own theories, but there are clear norms as well as scientific guidelines and principles that provide a basis for training the energy systems appropriately. Refer to table 2.1 for guidance

TABLE 2.1   Intensity and Interval Recovery

% of maximal heart rate	55-60%	61-75%	76-85%	86-92%	93-95%	96-98%	99%+
Training zone	1	2	3	3 to 4	4	5	6
Rating of perceived exertion (RPE)	Very, very light	Fairly light to somewhat hard	Somewhat hard+	Hard	Harder	Very hard+	Very, very hard
Attributes	Recovery from training and racing; interval recovery	Aerobic conditioning— foundation training	Sub-threshold development and endurance training	Race pace threshold training	Suprathreshold above race pace training	High-intensity $\dot{V}O_2max$ training	Speed, lactate tolerance, neurological development training
Interval durations	N/A	N/A	N/A	Intervals 1-120 min. with short rest (e.g., 5-30 sec.)	2-10 min.	2-8 min.	15 sec.-2 min.
Work–rest ratios	N/A	N/A	N/A	Short rest (5-30 sec.)	1:5	1:1	1:6

in applying the right mix of intensity and recovery to interval training; the table includes corresponding heart rate ranges, RPE, workout attributes and durations, and work–rest ratio recommendations.

Recovery Principle

Recovery for each triathlete will differ in accordance with the individualization principle. Triathletes with higher levels of fitness recover more quickly between training sessions. That said, there are recommended ranges for how much recovery is needed between various types of workouts, with fitness level, training status, volume (distance), and intensity being key factors. Stories abound of triathletes training in a constantly fatigued state. As a result, their training level and performance decline or plateau. Sufficient recovery must always occur between training sessions—how long the recovery should be depends on load, intensity, and volume but must always be long enough for muscle glycogen to be replenished.

Recovery should be monitored, such as through uncomplicated day-to-day record keeping (figure 2.1 is a sample). Sleep is often undervalued, and some triathletes might fail to appreciate the physiological importance of quality sleep, which requires a quiet and comfortable environment. Tiredness, low motivation for training and competition, changes in appetite, and resting heart rate are factors that influence recovery and are easy to assess and chart. Over time, you can trend your recoveries and make daily adjustments to your training.

The daily living score is helpful for managing day-to-day training. Strive for ratings in the top two zones for each factor, and adjust training accordingly with volume and intensity being the key points to manage. Monitor these results in order to maximize the work being done with recovery on a daily basis. Also effective are online record-keeping systems, which can shift training plans (workouts) within days or sometimes weeks or longer in advance up to the day and minute.

There is no one best practice with the exception that triathletes and coaches should consider moving away from generic workout planning toward more daily and weekly prescribed workouts (matching the phase of training and the results of workouts). There

FIGURE 2.1 Daily Living and Recovery Template

INFLUENCING FACTOR	DAY 1-31
Quality of sleep	1 2 3 4 5 6 7 8 9 10 11 12 13 14 15 16 17 18 19 20 21 22 23 24 25 26 27 28 29 30 31
Length of sleep (hours)	
Very deep = -1	
Normal = 0	
Restless = 1	
Bad with breaks = 2	
Not at all = 3	
Tiredness	1 2 3 4 5 6 7 8 9 10 11 12 13 14 15 16 17 18 19 20 21 22 23 24 25 26 27 28 29 30 31
Very rested = -1	
Normal = 0	
Tired = 1	
Very tired = 2	
Painful tiredness = 3	
Training willingness	1 2 3 4 5 6 7 8 9 10 11 12 13 14 15 16 17 18 19 20 21 22 23 24 25 26 27 28 29 30 31
Very good = -1	
Good = 0	
Poor = 1	
Unwilling = 2	
Did not train = 3	
Appetite	1 2 3 4 5 6 7 8 9 10 11 12 13 14 15 16 17 18 19 20 21 22 23 24 25 26 27 28 29 30 31
Very good -1	
Good = 0	
Poor = 1	
Eat because I should = 2	
Did not eat = 3	
Competitive willingness	1 2 3 4 5 6 7 8 9 10 11 12 13 14 15 16 17 18 19 20 21 22 23 24 25 26 27 28 29 30 31
High = -1	
Average = 0	
Low = 1	
None at all = 2	
Resting heart rate	1 2 3 4 5 6 7 8 9 10 11 12 13 14 15 16 17 18 19
Enter morning resting heart rate	

From M. Evans and J. Cappaert, *Triathletes in motion*. (Champaign, IL: Human Kinetics).

are many ways to best establish a balance between the stress (stimulus) of training and (rest), but this too is individually applied. Note that rest is not always a complete time of inactivity, and that what works for one triathlete might not be effective for another. In fact, for many highly trained triathletes, a rest day often includes light training in swimming, cycling, or running, or all three.

How much recovery time is needed—and how much is too much—differs among triathletes, but generally speaking, it's very important to have regular, planned periods of rest and recovery. Planning rest from workout to workout, day to day, week to week, month to month, and phase to phase helps keep you fresh and allows for important adaptation to and regeneration from training.

The aim of the recovery principle is to restore the mind and body to preexercise or precompetition levels and to strategically progress through a coursework of training and rest cycles. The principle is complex, with rest, nutrition, exercise, and treatment such as stretching, massage, and deep-tissue therapies implemented to improve and speed up restoration.

How to determine the right amount of recovery time between training and racing is as much feel as science. If you feel fatigued, you probably are, even if your training records and history say you shouldn't be. One way to assess if you are overtraining and need more rest is to use central nervous system (CNS) repetitive tests. These tests look at your increasing or decreasing ground contact time. A simple series of three to six single-leg hops on both legs can test if contact time is increasing, and distance covered decreasing. If contact time increases, you are likely fatigued. Used prior to training, CNS tests can help you decide how to design your workout.

After racing and training, you should exercise lightly with an active recovery that boosts the removal of the processes of metabolic waste from the muscles, establishes fluid balance, begins to restore energy reserves, and elicits relaxation in the active muscles. Light and short-duration exercise speeds recovery and the rebuilding of muscles and tissues. A light-intensity and short recovery (less than 5

minutes; any more can delay replacing muscle glycogen) keeps blood flowing and places more glucose in reach of the muscles to begin the process of recovery even sooner. Combining a few minutes of light postevent or workout exercise with fluids and carbohydrate will go a long way toward restoring your body.

Every race or training session causes a breakdown of protein. Protein supplies the basic tissues of the body, but it is constantly broken down and replaced. Training and racing increase the rate of protein turnover, so part of your recovery is eating nourishing foods, including protein.

In a well-designed schedule, recovery is of equal value to training. Recovery allows for adaptations from periods of training to occur. In theory, recovery functions as the process of adaptation that, little by little, produces a higher level of fitness. As we've said, every triathlete recovers differently. Older athletes recover more slowly than younger athletes. Males tend to recover faster than females because of higher levels of testosterone. There are many factors that come into play, including nutrition; environment; travel; and intensity, duration, and frequency of exercise.

Periodization Principle

Triathletes seek well-organized and comprehensive training plans. The resources for training plans are numerous, including the Internet; generic plans offered by coaches, teams, and clubs that can be customized; and written media such as books and magazines.

Triathletes in quest of elevating performance know training variations are important for modifications and alterations in the training stimulus. Through periodization, the volume, intensity, frequency, density, and recovery are manipulated to produce (stimulate) specific adaptations. Responses obtained vary, but as a principle, training must be fluctuated—and for some triathletes this is the most difficult part of training because it involves both time-management skills and constant and regular assessment.

In a periodization plan, a season is framed into periods of training. The best periodization plans cover dozens of factors in the training process and provide a framework for developing the workouts phase by phase, week by week, and day by day. A key point of any periodization plan is progression; unfortunately, improvement is always a process—there's no way to instantly achieve high performance.

The category, classifications, events, phases of training, dryland training, allotment of phase, weekly and daily volume, intensity of training, tests, distance and intensity of transition (bike to run sessions), and the periodization of the energy systems (closely managed dose of training intensity for up to six levels of energy system training) are just some of the manageable aspects of training. Which components to train, how training is fluctuated, how many weeks to allot, and which activities to perform (and at what volume and how much intensity) will all determine what we call your training block, or training phase. Because of the many differences among triathletes (including wide ranges in strengths and weaknesses, not to mention genetic and training histories), a generic one-size-fits-all training plan is not practical. That said, there is a place for a good plan even if it's not written directly for the triathlete.

Triathletes can and do respond positively to almost any organized approach that progresses and provides sufficient time for adaptation. In fact, most triathletes do some form of group training, and even elite athletes training among an expertly coached squad often do very similar workouts. The key is that these workouts are targeted, with periodization always forefront in mind, and never random.

We'll look at the most popular periodization models in the sections that follow. A helpful way to think about periodization is from the viewpoint of weight training because weight training—with its structured phases and blocks of sets, repetitions, rest intervals, exercise type, and varying levels of resistance (weight) is the most obviously conducive for periodization. Of course with its three modes of activity, triathlon training is more complex than weight training, but we can learn a lot from the weight training model. After all, every triathlete would agree that changes in

volume, intensity, and frequency of training must occur in the training process.

Traditional Cycle (Block) Periodization

Block periodization includes preparatory, precompetition, competitive, tapering, and transition phases managed by macro-, meso-, and microcycles. The macrocycle is the overall view of the training plan (that is, you can see the training focus for each block). A mesocycle is a specific block lasting weeks with technical and physiological goals to achieve. The microcycle is a week of training—actual workouts are developed based on macro- and mesocycle specifications.

Accepted variations of block periodization popular among triathletes intelligently reinvent, but simplify, the traditional format, with periods that we call prep, base 1, base 2, base 3, build 1, build 2, peak, race, and transition. This format gives us the macro overview of the season in which our sub-blocks and daily workouts can be developed according to the purpose of the phase of training.

Step-Up Periodization

Step-up periodization is similar to the traditional model but with a different approach as the training intensity and volume rises and lowers (steplike) over the course of each phase. Very often the steps are organized into blocks of weeks that fluctuate upward in terms of volume, intensity, and frequency over three weeks; this is followed by a step down for the fourth week to training of less volume and reduced intensity.

There are many variations to the step-up approach and unlimited ways to change the number of weeks (steps) upward or downward or evenly spaced (back-to-back weeks of the same dose) all for the purpose of applying stimulus and recovery in a progressive way.

Other Models of Periodization

Linear, nonlinear, random, undulating (wave), and overreaching periodization models are applied with as many variations as there are coaches, but the success of these is based on the individual response to the training stimulus. Your overall plan, or training blueprint, remains most important. Working from a well-designed blueprint, your day-to-day workouts can be targeted precisely and progression managed more effectively.

Not everyone needs a customized program of training, and many group and generic approaches provide sound principles of training and planning. Though not individually designed, these approaches do provide some structure, manage workloads over time, and might be sufficient for neophyte, recreational, or even competitive triathletes who compete only from time to time. If you are serious about triathlon, however, periodization must be a key piece of your training program, especially from the standpoint of the training phases. Only via the consistent training that periodization helps manage can you achieve the highest level of fitness. Of course to accomplish this level, there must be few interruptions caused by illness or injury.

Through periodization you organize and manage, based on your individual goals, your sequenced workouts, intensity workloads, technique focus, strength and functional training, planned recovery (weekly, monthly, and by phase), physiological assessment and skills practice, and competitive events. Each phase has its own goals, objectives, and tasks and is managed in training volume and training intensity. Traditionally, periodization involves a continuously organized flow of preparation, competition, and transition phases of training. Each phase has specific goals such as building general stamina, stability, movement function and technique, and fitness during the preparation phase and transitioning into the competition phase during which workouts are targeted to help you peak at just the right time. The transition phase is a recovery period between events.

In the real world, periodization does not follow a perfectly straight line, except perhaps in group or club programs where there is a general plan in place. The best periodization and training programs are dynamic and flexible and serve primarily as a guide and not an unequivocal plan. However, the objectives and the process for the achievement of your intended goals and peaking at the best time for optimal performance are well defined.

Many periodization programs involve three weeks of progressive volume and intensity building (might be more or less than three weeks, depending on the block or phase of the training season) followed by a week of reduced loads. Such programs, however, are likely more generic or group-oriented rather than individualized because of all the circumstances—seen and unforeseen—that can affect the flow of training.

When necessary, adjusting workouts to accommodate life's events—travel, wedding, family matters—can be built into a periodization plan, as long as you have some notice before the event occurs. Of course, there is always a chance for unforeseen complications such as unexpected personal matters, injuries, illness, problems at work, and family issues that can disturb the flow of training.

Base, build, general preparation, and off-season phases should follow guidelines established by the goals of your program. For the precompetition, competition, tapering, and transition (recovery) phase, the same is true—each phase should target specific training and related goals. Program objectives will guide your training for each phase, including physical, technical, tactical, equipment, movement function, technique development, mental strategies and cognitive training, and tests and standards.

Within a periodization program, the principles of loading and unloading of intensity apply as they relate to volume and frequency. For the body to adapt most successfully to training there must be reduced stimulus (load) and sufficient recovery time to allow for restoration. If sufficient time isn't built into your program, you run the risk of overtraining.

The principle of loading and unloading chiefly involves the management of the volume of intensity. In 1997, in my book *Endurance Athlete's Edge*, I described a table of periodization that I developed to manage progressive loading and unloading of intensity for every phase of training. I still use that system today, but as more of a guide to manage the amount of each intensity training zone included in workouts by day, week, and phase. Views differ on how much load (intensity and volume) and when to rest, but there can be little disagreement that intensity and training volume must be incorporated into every training plan.

Taper Principle

Training breaks down tissue and fatigues triathletes for the purpose of producing the training effect and to boost performance. Generally, training produces short-term fatigue as a result of dehydration, a depletion of energy stores, and other metabolic changes. When training intensity or duration is reduced, then the training effect might decrease as well.

To maintain training effects and remove the fatigue that training causes during a taper, the volume and frequency of training must be reduced. Successful tapering and peaking seem to be best achieved with a decrease in volume and maintenance or an increase in training intensity, or both. The principle of tapering is important to consider because much research supports the connection between tapering and improved performance.

There are many types and lengths of tapering methods, but they all decrease volume and increase intensity—only the rates will vary. For example, there is a linear taper (a straight line but a slower reduction in volume and frequency), an exponential fast decline or slow decline (curved shaped reductions in training load), or a step taper, which involves sudden drops in training load. Scientific studies on tapering show that physiological, psychological, and technical performance improvements occur fairly quickly during the period before competition. Improvements in performance with effective tapers range from 1 to 6 percent (significant improvements for competitive triathletes). By progressively reducing training volume and either maintaining or increasing training intensity over 7 to 21 days prior to events, there are observable improvements in performances. The important point to keep in mind is that the total training volume must be reduced and the intensity of training increased. How much of a reduction and how

great an increase will depend on your training status, athletic history, and goals and the nature of the event.

For priority events, there is agreement that 7 to 21 days of tapering are effective when using progressive volume reduction and intensity increase. The decrease in training volume places you in a position to benefit from increased rest. On the other hand, there is ample evidence that the most effective tapering models include either maintained or increased intensity that is equal to or slightly faster than anticipated race pace.

An effective taper will minimize the build-up of fatigue from previous training workloads and maintain the physiological adaptations achieved during that training. But too much rest without stimulus might waste the training effects achieved during training. A good taper moves you into your fitness peak, achieving this through reductions in training volume and frequency and increases in intensity (intensities at race pace and above).

Warm-Up Principle

At rest, the blood flow to the muscles is quite low—about 15 to 20 percent. In addition, many of the capillaries (blood vessels) are still closed. After about 12 minutes of exercise, the blood flow directed to the skeletal muscles rises to about 70 to 75 percent. In order for the muscles to work at their maximal aerobic capacity, all of the blood vessels need to be opened (dilated). Similarly, the elasticity of muscles increases their metabolic processing as their tissues warm. A warmed muscle can achieve greater length and apply more force while reducing injury risk caused by cold tissue. For these and other reasons, a warm-up under all conditions is important.

Warm-up routines will vary depending on air temperature. You must know your body well enough to know how much warm-up you need under various conditions. This will help you avoid physiological and psychological surprises before competition. Triathletes are challenged by both the natural environment and the sequence of swimming, cycling, and running. Each of these activities has distinct challenges in terms of body temperature regulation.

In nearly every circumstance, a warm-up will improve performance. There are both physiological and psychological reasons for this. The minutes before a race can be stressful, with many unknowns, but with a prescribed rehearsal both the physiological and psychological pieces can be managed and practiced in training. Obviously, anxiety can prevent you from performing optimally. Practicing a well-prepared preevent routine can give you the mental calmness and perspective you need for optimal performance. Training is the time to practice your warm-up rehearsals. In the following sections we give some tips for warming up. The key is making the warm-up familiar enough to be automatic as you prepare your mind and body for competition.

Swim Warm-Up

Because the swim comes first, you warm up for it last, following your warm-up for the bike and run. The swim sets the stage for the race, and whether you are competing with or without a wetsuit, a warm-up is necessary. The intensity of the competition determines the type and length of the warm-up, with shorter events requiring longer and more intense warm-ups and longer events needing less intensity and time. Some triathletes choose to use the swim portion of the race as their warm-up, but to perform well and feel ready for the start of the swim, a warm-up of 8 to 12 minutes is recommended (depending on fitness and experience level).

Several minutes of light-intensity strokes will raise your body temperature slowly. The warm-up should help prepare you physiologically, psychologically, and tactically for the start of the race. After the easier strokes, three to five race-pace (or even slightly faster) accelerations of 20 to 30 seconds are beneficial. Follow this with 30 seconds of light swimming.

Also, to open your lungs up even more and rehearse the start, several 10-second strokes at well above race-pace intensity, with very full and deep lower abdomen breathing, can increase ventilation, which will reduce carbon dioxide levels during exhalation.

When there is no possibility for a preevent warm-up for the swim (timing mix-up, weather, event logistics), there are dryland methods for warming up that include shoulder and active warm-up exercises as well as using stretch bands with light resistance to simulate water movements (see chapter 6).

The last part of your warm-up should be light, effortless, and controlled swimming. Your mind should be clearing and body temperature elevated; oxygen delivery has prepared your muscles for supple and smooth motions. Your cardiovascular system is ready for competition.

To maintain beneficial effects of the warm-up, try to finish your swim warm-up 5 to 10 minutes before the race starts. If there is a postponement, a few more minutes of light, relaxed, and smooth swimming are recommended.

Bike and Run Warm-Up

The bike and run warm-up should precede the swim warm-up and will vary depending on distance and expected intensity of the race. You should plan and practice various warm-up scenarios. For events under two hours, warming up for each discipline (swim, bike, and run) is more important than doing so for competitions of longer duration. Each warm-up should take between 8 and 12 minutes and include light effort and relaxed movements at the outset, followed by several race-pace intervals of 20 to 30 seconds each, as well as several intervals at greater than race pace. This warm-up will warm your muscles and get your heart and lungs prepared so that you are ready, body and mind, for the upcoming race. See chapters 7 and 8 for further details on warming up for the bike and run.

The principles discussed in this chapter provide the nucleus for your training and should be the building blocks for your training program. The principles of individualization, movement, technique, optimization, overload, specificity, stimulus, interval, recovery, periodization, taper, and warm-up all work individually as well as in combination to get you optimally prepared for performance.

Your training program should be developed progressively. There should be periods of high volume and low intensity, high volume and moderate intensity, moderate volume and high intensity, and lower volume and even higher intensity. Interspersed between these are periods of rest and recovery for further training adaptation.

$\underline{3}$ Assessing Posture

When swimming, cycling, and running, efficiency in so many ways is directly connected to posture. *Posture* is more than how we stand—it is also how we move and how stabilized we are when sitting, bending, lifting, standing, and performing all the motions that training and competing require. In this chapter we explain how posture shapes performance. We discuss faulty postures common among triathletes, tight and weak muscles and how these influence movement, and how to recognize the symptoms of poor posture, what causes them, and how to remedy them. We present training exercises and techniques to correct posture deficiencies and describe how to reposition movement for better posture in sport and daily life. Finally, we provide assessment tools and a quick way for coaches to evaluate triathletes in the field.

Technique, a key term in the chapter, can be described as the preservation of fundamental postures—no matter the motions. Developing technique is coupled with functional movement and posture. *Biomechanics*, another key term, is the practice of how the body is affected by internal and external forces. Being able to make the smallest of adjustments to the body's motions through improved muscle awareness, better technique, and physical training is a huge factor in performance.

Triathletes continue to break fresh ground in so many areas of performance by using external means to enhance performance, such as aerodynamics in cycling and wearing speed suits for the swim. The end of these means is often reduced costs of energy to overcome resistance. In triathlon, any forces that impede, oppose, or sway forward movement and increase or decrease the energy needed for swimming, cycling, and running have been keenly studied by elite triathletes, coaches, and, yes, companies that make products. Yet with all the cutting-edge equipment used in our sport, it is the movement variations affected by posture and the mechanics of technique that can have a significantly more powerful influence on performance, energy cost, and power output. Despite the common use of revolutionary equipment, triathletes must still execute mechanically correct motions, train the physiology, and apply rest and regeneration from workouts to improve.

Posture and Stability

Think of posture as a composite of the positions of all the joints of your body at any given moment, coupled with muscle balance. Performance is affected by posture because technique is enhanced or diminished by unevenness in movements. For the endurance athlete, posture and stability need to be not only statically (i.e., fixed, not moving positions) trained but also exercised in ways specific to swimming, cycling, and running with dynamic (moving) techniques. These techniques are best performed while maintaining fundamentally sound posture in the head, neck, truck, and hips through the feet.

The effect on alignment by immobile joints, for example, results in compression on moving surfaces and puts sizeable tension and stress on bones, ligaments, and muscles. For triathletes, this limit in mobility causes stiffness in joints and the body's alignments. Fundamentally, technique and economy are now affected by the body's posture and result in counterbalances with uneven and, very often, uncoordinated movements.

In upright posture there's not a significant amount of muscle activity necessary to maintain posture of the spine. However, small changes in support cause overstressed motions and can cause injury from overuse elicited by continual corrections as well as reduce the efficiency of movement and performance. When corrections or compensations go unaltered over time, muscle strength and flexibility become imbalanced as muscles become weaker, tighter, and less able to move efficiently. Triathletes must have sufficient muscular endurance to maintain proper posture through the countless motions of swimming, cycling, and running. If the support system—proper posture—is absent, there will likely be

Classic Postures of Elite Athletes

The triathlete's posture is a collection of running, swimming, and cycling positions built on a fundamental blend of every joint in the body. Few individuals have textbook posture, but there are ways of improving carriages in daily life that will benefit the triathlete in training and competition.

It is worth noting that every triathlete has distinctive techniques, and many achieve high levels of performance. The aerobic engines of world-class triathletes are extraordinary and provide the gateway toward peak levels of performance. That said, at the elite level, movement, stability, and technique limitations are very often the difference in taking home the silver or bronze instead of the gold.

Posture is technique connected to your training, joint mobility, stability, and strength. Evaluate your posture as you plan your phases of training and perform your workouts. The smallest improvement in your posture can have a significant impact on performance. Functional motions (flexibility, mobility, and stability) and posture play key roles in performance outcomes. At the Olympics, great athletes fall short because their posture weakens at the wrong time. Such outcomes could have been avoided through small, gradual corrections and training rehearsals that mimic the demands of competition.

Here are a few examples of some athletes who exemplify good posture:

- World-record holder and highly regarded technique coach Karlyn Pipes has water posture that is stroke by stroke a picture perfect demonstration of symmetry. Karlyn works from her inside (core) to outside (extremities) along an extremely stable head-to-toe center line.

- As a top three Ironman Hawaii finisher, Torbjorn Sindballe has bike positioning and power output that are extraordinarily efficient, flowing, and balanced. His bike posture made him a compelling force on the Queen K of Kona. Even since his retirement in 2009, many regard his posture and bike positioning as the best in the sport.

- Few triathlete runners deliver such an ideal demonstration of posture as multiple Ironman and world champion Craig Alexander, whose head, torso, hips, knee, and foot strike lines never stray at any time. His posture is nearly perfect, and the energy savings and propulsion he achieves are remarkably efficient.

increased stress with increased risk of injury and less ability to maintain proper technique, which of course will hinder performance.

Nearly every muscular pain you encounter as a triathlete is mechanical in nature and is usually caused by faulty postures or biomechanics. Trying to correct technique without taking into account the principles of posture and movement is ill advised. To be sure, there are fundamental key techniques in swimming, cycling, and running that can and should be maintained, but these are generally basic and not a source of problems for the experienced triathlete. When an experienced triathlete has difficulties, they are often caused by problems in motor learning or movement boundaries. Thus training should be individualized to allow for unique adaptations for correcting any flexibility, mobility, or stability issues that are present. Training should focus on accurate, controlled, effortless, and smooth (ACES) skills training. Any motions and techniques you use should be varied enough to promote better mechanics in combination with movement and stability (dryland) exercises that work to correct your movement limitations.

Whenever you experience an unexpected drop in performance or suspect the onset of an injury, the first thing to do is have your posture assessed. There are hereditary and often habitual postural faults that are caused by errors in how we sit, stand, squat, work, reach, lie, stoop, and bend. In this chapter you'll learn to identify these faults and to change your posture patterns by improving alignment and correcting muscular imbalances caused by weakness and tightness.

Teaching and Relearning Postural Alignment

A normal stationary posture functions as the basis for evaluating the alignments in the triathlete. Comparing triathletes side by side with models of optimal posture and working to make corrections via daily living remedies, along with strengthening, stretching, and mobility exercises, we can help them improve posture and develop better move-

ments, more efficient motions, and improved performances.

Whether pushing, standing, pulling, squatting, rotating, extending, or flexing, maintaining proper posture is fundamental for developing better body mechanics. Teaching technique—no matter the sport—is much easier when all movements are made with a foundation of good core posture. This method teaches the triathlete to move from within, from deep inside the center of the body, and to rely less on less coordinated hand, head, and feet movements.

When practicing technique, triathletes must maintain core posture (a tall, functional standing posture). Difficulties achieving proper technique are associated with neuromuscular pathways (brain to muscle) and possible flexibility restrictions, limitations in joint mobility, and instability caused by muscular weakness. One or more body regions might need alignment and stability remedies, but the practice of feeling the proper movements, and how muscles generate those movements, is very useful in postural correction. To do this, the triathlete should be mindful of (pay extra close attention to) a particular body region and how it moves and feels during movement. What is this region's most natural posture and position? When learning new techniques or performing new drills or exercises, the triathlete might have difficulties in properly executing the unfamiliar movements. Maintaining core posture in every exercise or skill you perform makes it more likely you will execute and repeat the movement more efficiently over time.

Reinforcement of movement that comes only with attentive practice should be part of the regimen. Whether you are trying to correct a fault in the posture of a particular body region and technique or practicing to reinforce proper posture, try these exercises that help you absorb the feel of your movements:

- *Verbal reinforcement*—a coach or partner uses verbal commands and cues to help the triathlete reinforce movement corrections of posture; the triathlete begins with slow, controlled movements to learn how the muscles move and the postures feel. (This exercise can also be done alone with the triathlete simply speaking the verbal cues.)

- *Visual reinforcement*—videos, mirrors, or photos can help the triathlete see and feel his or her proper postures and alignments and couple them with verbal prompts to promote better body mechanics.
- *Tactile reinforcement*—by having someone touch the muscles that need to contract (generate force), the triathlete can absorb, feel, and learn proper positions and alignments.

Pelvis and Low Back

In the neutral standing position there is a normal curve to the front of the low back, and the plumb line passes through the middle of the trunk and greater trochanter (bone on side of hip at top of femur). The pelvis is predominant for maintaining good posture and alignment, and when imbalances occur in the muscles that maintain a neutral posture of the pelvis the result can be adverse effects on parts of the body above and below. Instability on one side of the pelvis can result in a forward or backward shift or tilt. This slanting of one side causes a kinetic (movement) unevenness in motions, especially in the lower body when running.

Hip and Knee Joints

With good posture viewed from the side, the plumb line passes just behind the hip joint and slightly in from of the center axis of the knee. With a forward and backward alignment there can be increased muscular effort to maintain balance, increasing expenditure of energy.

Ankle

The plumb line in good posture passes slightly in front of the lateral malleolus (bony prominence on the sides of the ankle) and through the middle of the foot arch. Triathletes with ankle instability and lateral ankle sprains can have difficulty with postural control.

Feet

In normal barefoot standing, heels are about three inches (7.6 cm) apart with a slight toeing-out of approximately 8 degrees on both feet. The joints of the foot allow pronation (an inward rotation with sole facing somewhat laterally), supination (an outward rotation with sole facing medially inward), abduction (movement away from the center of the body), and adduction (movement toward the center of the body) at the ankle and in the forefoot.

Head and Neck

The head and neck postures are balanced and require only a small degree of muscular effort to maintain ideal alignment. The head is not tilted up or down, sideways, or downward; the chin is not drawn in. The plumb line passes through the lobe of the ear toward the shoulder joint.

Thoracic Spine

The thoracic spine is the middle segment of spine between the head and abdomen. In ideal posture, the upper back curves slightly back and arms hang in a normal alignment relative to the thorax.

The body is interconnected from the head, thorax, lumbar spine, and—perhaps most important for triathletes—the pelvis. Good characteristics or faults in posture in any of these regions affect the other regions and performance. The triathlete's swimming, cycling, and running motions are influenced by these relationships to a large extent, and posture plays a key role. Coaching and learning technique begin with posture—the triathlete must maintain posture (head to toe) in swimming, cycling, and running. Maintaining posture results in evenness is right- and left-side movements and is the basis of all good technique.

- Movements away from the normal alignment of good posture, especially under the long-term stress of triathlon, might increase energy demands and strain the joints, ligaments. and muscles.
- Initiate movement from the center of the body (proximal generation), from the pelvis, core, and finally from the arms and legs. When movements are away from the center (distal) there are more likely uncoordinated motions and less efficiency. By holding posture and,

for example, the head in alignment, the body and limbs will more likely move symmetrically.

- Identifying which muscles are inflexible or weakened can help improve postural alignment with corrective exercises and changing habitual postures (see chapters 2, 4, and 5).
- The pelvis is the link between the spine and lower extremities of the body. How the pelvis moves causes action, including motions in the hips and spine. The pelvis *must* be stabilized to prevent excessive motions through the upper and lower body.
- The triathlete techniques in swimming, cycling, and running are in principle a reflection of posture, and improving technique should begin with assessing posture and applying exercises to adjust, adapt, and enhance movements before making wide-ranging changes to technique.

Exercises to help improve posture include strengthening, stretching, core stability, mobility, and improvements in daily living postures when walking, sitting, standing, bending, pushing, and pulling. See chapters 4 and 5 for tests and exercises. Here, in the sections that follow, we give recommendations for changes in daily posture and positions. The tests in chapters 1, 4, and 5 assess posture in numerous ways; completing the test exercises correctly means you have the posture necessary to perform these motions. When the test exercises cannot be completed, performing

ANGELA NAETH   Playing to Your Strengths

You often hear that you need to work on your weaknesses, and while that's definitely true, you can also pick races that play to your strengths. For instance, if you're a strong cyclist but struggle on the run, look for races with tough, hilly bike courses but flatter runs. If you're not a strong swimmer, avoid the ocean swims and pick races in lakes or rivers, which are usually a little calmer on race day. Personally, I love the heat, so I tend to excel when racing in hot weather and gravitate to warmer races. Physiologically, am I any better at racing in the heat than any of my competitors? Maybe not—but mentally I think I have an edge, and that can really help on race day.

Which brings me to an important point: Don't underestimate what the right mental attitude can do for you, and don't forget to cultivate that attitude in both training and racing. Often, things that happen to you are colored either good or bad depending on how you react to them. For instance, I was able to set a bike course record in St. Croix in 2012 despite having to ride the last six miles with a flat tire. Racing is tough, and especially in longer races, you'll have rough patches or encounter problems or difficulties. If you let these things rattle you, they'll throw you off your game and can wreak havoc on your race plan. If you focus too much on your problem, you'll forget other important things, such as staying on top of your nutrition, which could ultimately have a greater impact on your race. If, however, you can quickly decide how you're going to deal with the issue, you can get back in your zone, put your head down, and get on with it. This doesn't just magically happen, though. You can't just decide you're going have the right mental attitude—it's something that needs to be trained, just like your swimming, cycling, and running. Practice it any time you're having a rough patch on a long run or your stomach is giving you trouble on the bike.

Get good at not losing your head (or your positive attitude) when you have to deal with rough patches or flats in training and you'll be way better prepared to handle issues when they arise on race day.

the exercise will help correct the posture over time.

In the following sections we review several common postures. The point is to learn how to begin to correct your posture throughout your daily living at home or at work. Each section provides several key postural points to keep in mind once you've determined the type of posture you have. Improving posture with daily living activities will go a long way toward establishing even better function once the more comprehensive exercises are started (in chapters 4 and 5). For now, you want to learn to correct faulty postures in the most basic way: while performing daily-life activities such as sitting, standing, bending, turning, and reaching.

Hypererect and Forward Chest Posture

This upright posture's signature is a flat upper back and resembles an upright military-style posture. It is not common in most people, but triathletes can take on all or parts of this posture before events because of stress, eagerness, and readying the mind for the race. This posture tends to be very upright with knees hyperextended and balance on the balls or toes of the feet. The posture looks like this:

- Head in neutral position
- Upper-cervical spine curved normally with small forward lean
- Midthoracic spine normal but slightly backward
- Lower lumbar spine hyperextended
- Pelvis at a forward (anterior) slant
- Knee at joints somewhat hyperextended
- Ankle joints slightly plantar flexed

You can make corrections to this faulty posture with attention to how you sit, stand, bend, and reach during daily living activities.

- Be mindful of standing with proper posture.
- Breathe into your back.

- Increase upper-back curve lean when standing.
- Avoid using the spine extensors to stand straight. Use hips and legs instead.
- Use abdominals and diaphragm to support rib cage.

Forward Head and Rounded Upper-Back Posture

This posture is distinctive with the head forward, neck extended, shoulders rounded, abdomen extended, and pelvis tipping forward (increasing the curve in the lower back). Each of these areas can affect performance because of compensations in movements to overcome weak, tight, or otherwise poor habits. The posture looks like this:

- Head forward
- Increased curve in neck
- Cervical spine hyperextended
- Scapula abducted (turned outward)
- Increased hunching (kyphosis) in thoracic spine (upper back)
- Collapsed chest and ribs
- Increased curve (lordosis) in lumbar spine
- Pelvis rotated forward (anterior tilt)
- Hip joints flexed
- Knee joints slightly hyperextended
- Ankle joints slightly plantar flexed

Make corrections to this posture with attention to how you sit, stand, bend, and reach during daily living activities.

- Maintain a neutral tilt position of pelvis.
- Avoid slouching of thoracic spine.
- Keep chin in a head-up posture.
- Avoid stiff-legged actions, especially when running.
- Breathe into rib cage for chest expansion.

This posture is accompanied by muscle shortness in the quadriceps, abdominals (deep-layered transversus abdominis and multifidus), lower back, and back of neck. The exercises in chapters 4 and 5 can help you achieve flexibility and core stability. This posture is also accompanied by muscle weakness in the external obliques, hip flexors, front of quadriceps, upper back, and front of neck.

Swayback Posture

Swayback is gravity-less type of posture in which stability yields to muscle weakness and fatigue; in many instances, the triathlete favors a relaxed or slouching body position. The swayback posture causes the pelvis to tilt back and the spine and knees to extend; when standing, you might put most of your weight on one side of the pelvis. Any of these issues can significantly affect triathlon performance. The posture looks like this:

- Head forward
- Cervical spine (neck) slightly extended forward and curved
- Collapsed upper chest (flattens chest wall)
- Long thoracic spine (upper back rounded)
- Lumbar (lower back) spine more flattened
- Hip joints hyperextended and forward of vertical plumb lines
- Knee joints hyperextended
- Ankle joints neutral

Correct the swayback posture with attention to how you sit, stand, bend, and reach during daily living activities.

- Activate the hip flexors to actively bring leg forward.
- Maintain a neutral position of pelvis by drawing in the abdomen.
- Use the gluteal muscles to extend hip when walking.
- Hold chin in and level.
- Avoid slouching of the upper spine.

This posture is accompanied by muscle shortness in the hamstrings, abdominals, and lower back. Muscle weakness in the abdominals, hip flexors, front of quadriceps, upper back, and neck flexors is also common.

Flat-Back Posture

The flat-back posture is characterized by a forward head and a straight back, with little or no curving of the spine. The lack of curve in the spine can reduce the shock-absorbing ability of the lumbar spine. The cause of this posture can be slouching, flexing when sitting or standing, or an overemphasis on exercises that flex the spine. The posture looks like this:

- Head forward
- Cervical spine slightly extended
- Increased curve in upper thoracic spine; lower part straight
- Lumbar spine flattened and straight
- Hip joints extended
- Knee joints extended and sometimes flexed
- Ankle joints slightly plantar flexed

Make corrections to the flat-back posture with attention to how you sit, stand, bend, and reach during daily living activities.

- Engage the hip flexors slightly, generating force to actively bring leg forward.
- Maintain pelvis in a neutral position.
- Use the glutes to extend hip.
- Maintain an upright head position with chin in.
- Avoid slouching of the thoracic spine.
- Maintain a lumbar curve.
- Maintain a neutral scapula position.

This posture is accompanied by muscle shortness in the hamstrings and abdominals and muscle weakness in the front of the quadriceps and lumbar erector spinae (muscles of the spine at the lower back).

The scapula, or shoulder blade, is a flat, triangular-shaped bone that connects the humerus (upper arm bone) with the clavicle (collar bone). A normal position of the scapula is flat against the upper back with no angles or noticeable bulging edges. Many movements of the scapula are associated with movement at the upper extremities in triathletes. Muscle imbalances (length and strength) will alter mechanics and increase energy use. In running, the scapulae stabilize and synchronize movements of the upper body; when sufficiently stable, they can have a significant impact on posture and performance.

With upper-extremity motion, the muscles of the scapula work together to stabilize and control the position. With weakness, the ability to control and move the humerus (the long upper-arm bone from the shoulder to the elbow) is reduced. In swimming, the stabilizing muscles of the scapula (trapezius, rhomboids, and serratus anterior) move the scapula but do so by stabilizing this large flat bone from each angle. If not stable, the humerus cannot be positioned to provide leverage and can alter mechanics of the underwater swim stroke.

A triathlete's shoulders should be equally even with no unusual elevation, depression, or postural misalignments. The shoulders flex, abduct (away from the body), adduct (inward), medially and externally rotate, horizontally abduct and adduct, and extend using a wide array of muscles from the deltoids, pectorals, latissimus dorsi, and teres minor and major. Any weakness or tightness in any one area affects others and will have a definite negative impact on performance.

Asymmetries of the shoulder and scapula commonly seen in triathletes include the following:

Abducted and Elevated Scapula With Humeral (Upper Arm) Inward Rotation

An abducted and elevated scapula during inward humeral (upper arm) rotation is when the scapula is moved further away from the center of the spine, inwardly rotates, and the inside of the scapula becomes more vertical. The posture looks like this:

- Round shoulders and upper back
- Depressed chest
- Tight pectoralis minor
- Longer thoracic curve
- Increased upper thoracic curve
- Forward head posture

Depressed and Abducted Scapula

A depressed and abducted scapula is when the scapula is moved further away from the center of the spine and shoulders slope downward sharply, accentuating broadness with internal rotations of the arms. The posture looks like this:

- Rounded and depressed shoulders sloping downward
- Full broad back
- Long well-developed erector spinae
- Internally rotated arms
- Depressed rib cage and protruding abdominals

Elevated Shoulders and Adducted Scapula

Elevated shoulders and adducted scapula are when shoulders are shrugged upward, the angle of shoulders is square, and the scapula is adducted, with the medial border of scapula closer to the spine. The posture appears like this:

- Decreased curve in thoracic spine
- Forward head posture
- Externally rotated shoulders
- Arms behind body (from side view)

Assessing Posture and Functional Movements

One of the quickest and most effective ways to assess a triathlete's posture, flexibility, joint mobility, and stability is with the deep-squat self-test. This test is often used as an initial method for evaluating movement and prescribing exercise remedies. We'll delve much deeper into assessments in chapters 4 and 5, but the deep-squat self-test presented in this chapter is one of the best screening tools for triathletes.

At its center, the deep-squat self-test provides an evidence-based approach for the assessment of movement as it relates to a triathlete's ability to execute technique. Inability to move freely, functionally, and with stability during this test very often shows up in less than efficient swimming, cycling, and running technique. If a triathlete tests well in the screening, the training focus shifts to technique and periodization.

There are other common testing models, such as musculoskeletal assessments performed by physical therapists, but the deep-squat self-test gives you a quick and effective initial screening and can also be used for ongoing field test evaluations. The remedies are not especially complicated, and retesting is simple, as are the steps for progressing the sets and reps to help determine the necessary corrective exercises to improve posture, movement, and stability.

Part of learning how to move more functionally is learning where muscular forces originate. Efficient swimmers work from deep inside the core and pelvis and transmit force from inside to outside. Beginning and recreational swimmers tend to attempt to apply forces from the outside (with arms and legs often flailing about). The deep-squat self-test can inform you how to generate forces from deep within toward the limbs outward in swimming, cycling, and running. The deep-squat self-test can also help assess the behavior of overactive and underactive muscles and identify common symptoms and causes of musculoskeletal injury caused by imbalances.

Before you begin the deep-squat self-test, you will need

- a dowel 4 to 5 feet (1.2-1.5 m) in length,
- a slick surface such as a slide board or linoleum,
- socks (so feet slide on the slick surface),
- a grid to evaluate movement (optional), and
- a video-recording device

To perform the deep-squat self-test, stand with feet hip-width apart and aligned straight forward from heel to toe (figure 3.1a). Arms are straight overhead with wrists straight (you may hold a dowel overhead, if you choose). Squat as if sitting in a chair (moving buttocks backward) and descend as far as possible or until hips are level with knees (figure 3.1b). Complete three squats while being filmed from the front (anterior) and three more while being filmed from the side (lateral).

When viewing the video, look for these key points:

- Heels flat—both heels are flat with no visible anterior weight shifting onto the balls of the feet.
- Feet parallel—feet point straight ahead and remain parallel from heel to toe with no visible sliding; the longitudinal arch is maintained.
- Arms overhead—at the deepest point in the squat, arms and hands are overhead and aligned from hands through ear, shoulder, and hip.
- Torso—at the deepest point in the squat, the torso remains parallel to tibia (lower legs).
- Torso migration—torso does not lean forward or tilt back more than 10 degrees.
- Hips horizontal—hips are horizontally aligned with the knee (within 10 to 15 degrees)
- Knees aligned—the center of both knees are aligned over the second toe with no adduction or abduction during the squat.

a   b

FIGURE 3.1   Overhead deep squat.

Figure 3.2 is a deep-squat self-test form that helps you easily assess functional movement. To use the form, enter a numeric value to evaluate your movement and stability benchmarks. The values are determined during the downward squatting. Repeating three consecutive squats (with video) is normally enough to complete the form. These are the numeric values:

- 0 = There is pain in one or more areas regardless how the squat is performed.
- 1 = The squat cannot be executed (too many restrictions).
- 2 = The body region movement is less than perfect.
- 3 = The squat body region is perfect.

Once you have completed the test form, review your video and use figure 3.3 to help identify corrections, as needed. Place a checkmark alongside the appropriate body region listed under Asymmetry (e.g., if feet rotate externally during the self-test, check that box). Then use the form to locate the likely cause of the problem and the correction for it. The correction exercises appear later in the chapter (see Stretching, Functional Movement, and Strengthening Corrective Exercises).

Figure 3.3 provides a way to quickly identify asymmetries in movement. However, one of the problems with corrective exercise training is the process for the progression of sets and repetitions. That is, how many repetitions should you do, and for how long? Refer to table 3.1 for guidance in progressing through the exercises, based on your proficiency in executing accurate, controlled, effortless, and smooth (ACES) movements through three respective stages. In stages 1 and 2, you are perfecting form, improving flexibility, joint mobility, and stability of the body regions selected and trained. Once you have completed those exercises, you progress to the stage 3 maintenance phase, which begins with higher repetitions and hold times but is done only once or twice per week. Following is a detailed description of the three stages.

Stage 1

- Sets with reps and hold-time exercises: one or two sets for 10 reps, but hold the posture in the exercise for 30 seconds.
- Sets with reps only: three sets of 30 reps with one-minute rest.
- Sessions per week: four or five sessions of flexibility, joint mobility, and stability exercises.

FIGURE 3.2   Deep-squat self-test form.

Body region and standard	Left side of body	Right side of body
Heels Both heels flat on the floor	☐0 ☐1 ☐2 ☐3	☐0 ☐1 ☐2 ☐3
Feet Feet remain straight ahead and parallel (no sliding inward or outward).	☐0 ☐1 ☐2 ☐3	☐0 ☐1 ☐2 ☐3
Arms Arms are overhead and aligned with lower leg and ankle.	☐0 ☐1 ☐2 ☐3	☐0 ☐1 ☐2 ☐3
Hips Hips remain level, with top of each thigh and hips evenly aligned (above or below scores a 2).	☐0 ☐1 ☐2 ☐3 ☐0 ☐1 ☐2 ☐3	☐0 ☐1 ☐2 ☐3 ☐0 ☐1 ☐2 ☐3
Knees The middle of the knees align with the second toe.	☐0 ☐1 ☐2 ☐3	☐0 ☐1 ☐2 ☐3
Torso Torso and dowel are aligned and don't fall forward more than 10 degrees in front of torso; torso is parallel to tibia.	☐0 ☐1 ☐2 ☐3 ☐0 ☐1 ☐2 ☐3	☐0 ☐1 ☐2 ☐3 ☐0 ☐1 ☐2 ☐3

From M. Evans and J. Cappaert, *Triathletes in motion.* (Champaign, IL: Human Kinetics).

FIGURE 3.3   Identification form for deep-squat self-test corrective exercises.

Asymmetry: what the body region does during the squat	Common tight (inflexible) muscles	Stretching and functional movement exercises	Common weak muscles	Strengthening and stability exercises
Feet flatten (the arch collapses down and inward)	Gastrocnemius: ankle plantar flexion (pointing), knee flexion, and foot eversion Peroneals: Foot eversion, ankle plantar flexion (pointing), support longitudinal arch and depression of first metatarsal (bone of the big toe) Tibialis anterior and posterior: ankle dorsiflexion (flexing), foot inversion (supination), support longitudinal arch of the foot	Ankle dorsiflexion: incline board stretch Gastrocnemius: standing upper calf stretch Soleus: standing lower-calf stretch Peroneals: foot eversion and inversion	Muscles that control posture during single-limb stance (gluteus medius) Gluteus medius: pelvic control posture during single-limb stance Tibialis anterior and posterior: ankle dorsiflexion (flexing), foot inversion (supination), support longitudinal arch of the foot	Gluteus medius: side-lying hip abduction with resistance Gastrocnemius and soleus and Achilles: eccentric calf raise Peroneals: foot eversion and inversion

> *continued*

> *continued*

Asymmetry: what the body region does during the squat	Common tight (inflexible) muscles	Stretching and functional movement exercises	Common weak muscles	Strengthening and stability exercises
Heels rise	Gastrocnemius and soleus (the bulging shape of the calf): foot plantar flexion, inversion, and knee flexion	Gastrocnemius and soleus, Achilles, foot, and ankle function and knee flexion: overhead deep squat with elevated heels	N/A	N/A
Feet externally rotate	Gastrocnemius and soleus (the bulging shape of the calf): foot plantar flexion, inversion, and knee flexion Piriformis: hip external rotation and some hip abduction Hamstrings: flexion of the knee and external rotation and hip extension and external rotation	Gastrocnemius: standing upper calf stretch Soleus: standing lower calf stretch Piriformis: Supine piriformis stretch Hamstrings: three-way hamstring stretch	Gluteus medius: pelvic control posture during single-limb stance Adductors (longus, brevis, magnus): hip adduction, flexion, and external rotation	Gluteus medius: prone external leg slides Adductors: supine flexed knee medicine ball squeeze
Knees adduct (move inward)	Adductors (longus, brevis, magnus): hip adduction, flexion, and external rotation Iliotibial tubing: flex, abduct, and medial rotation of the hip via association with other muscles Tibialis anterior: ankle dorsiflexion	Adductors: supine hip 90-degree wall-leg slide Iliotibial band: ITB side-lying with strap Tibialis anterior: foam roller slide from side bridge	Gluteus medius: pelvic control posture during single-limb stance Gluteus maximus: hip extension, external rotation, abduction, adduction and stabilization of the knee	Gluteus medius: Supine with lateral elevation Gluteus maximus: unilateral squat on horizontal or vertical half foam roller
Knees abduct (move outward)	Hamstrings (biceps femoris): knee flexion, external rotation; hip extension, external rotation Iliopsoas: hip flexion, trunk flexion, hip external rotation, lateral bending Piriformis: hip external rotation and small amount of abduction of flexed hip	Hamstrings: hamstrings with strap plus foot eversion Iliopsoas, rectus femoris: stability ball overhead lunge Piriformis: seated 90-degree stretch	Gluteus medius: pelvic control posture during single-limb stance Gluteus maximus: hip extension, external rotation, abduction, adduction and stabilization of the knee	Gluteus medius: 90/90 gluteus medius with internal rotation Gluteus maximus: bilateral squatting on horizontal half foam rollers

Asymmetry: what the body region does during the squat	Common tight (inflexible) muscles	Stretching and functional movement exercises	Common weak muscles	Strengthening and stability exercises
Increased lumbar extension and hip flexion (pelvis tilts forward)	Iliopsoas: hip flexion, trunk flexion, hip external rotation, lateral bending Rectus femoris: knee extension and hip flexion Hamstrings: knee flexion and internal rotation, hip extension and internal rotation Erector spinae (iliocostalis, longissimus, spinalis): extension, lateral flexion, rotation of spine Latissimus dorsi: extends, adducts, and internally rotates the shoulder, hyperextension of the spine and adducts raised overhead arm against resistance (swimming), elevation of the pelvis	Hip flexors: stability ball overhead lunge Rectus femoris (quadriceps): elevated extension with squat Hamstrings: 3-way hamstring stretch Erector spinae: kneeling slump to arch-back stretch Latissimus dorsi: kneeling stability ball 45-degree stretch	Gluteus medius: pelvic control posture during single-limb stance Gluteus maximus: hip extension, external rotation, abduction, adduction and stabilization of the knee Deep-layered abdominal muscles: transversus abdominis, multifidus, quadratus lumborum Rectus abdominis: flexion of the spine and posterior tilt of pelvis Erector spinae (iliocostalis, longissimus, spinalis): extend, lateral flexion, rotation of spine	Gluteus medius: elevated unilateral hip dip and hike Gluteus maximus: supine hip extension to bridge with alternate march Deep-layered core: supine bridge contralateral stability ball
Increased lumbar flexion (pelvis tilts backward with increased forward trunk lean)	External oblique: flexion of the trunk tilts pelvis back, elevates pelvis; trunk rotation and lateral bending Rectus abdominis: flexion of the spine tilts pelvis back and compresses abdomen Hamstrings (biceps femoris, semitendinosus, semimembranosus): knee flexion and internal rotation; hip extension and internal rotation Hip flexors (illiopsoas): hip flexion, trunk flexion, hip external rotation, lateral bending	External oblique: lateral hand over head on stability ball Rectus abdominis: supine extension on stability ball Hamstrings: three-way hamstring stretch Hip flexors: stability ball overhead lunge	Erector spinae (iliocostalis, longissimus, spinalis): extend, lateral flexion, rotation of spine Gluteus medius: pelvic control posture during single-limb stance Gluteus maximus: hip extension, external rotation, abduction, adduction and stabilization of the knee Deep-layered abdominal muscles: transversus abdominis, multifidus, quadratus lumborum	Erector spinae: prone extensions on stability ball Erector spinae and deep-layered abdominals: prone sweeping contralateral arm and leg extensions Gluteus medius: elevated unilateral hip dip and hike Gluteus maximus: supine hip extension to bridge with alternate march Deep-layered abdominals: circuit lateral bridging and prone to lateral bridging

> continued

> continued

Asymmetry: what the body region does during the squat	Common tight (inflexible) muscles	Stretching and functional movement exercises	Common weak muscles	Strengthening and stability exercises
Abdomen protrudes	Hip flexors (illiopsoas): hip flexion, trunk flexion, hip external rotation, lateral bending	Hip flexors (iliopsoas): hip extension with lateral torso stretch	Deep-layered abdominal muscles: transversus abdominis, multifidus, quadratus lumborum	Deep-layered abdominals: transversus and multifidi standing draw-in
Arms fall forward	Latissimus dorsi: extends, adducts, and internally rotates the shoulder, hyperextension of the spin and adducts raised overhead arm against resistance (swimming), elevation of the pelvis Pectoralis major: adducts, flexes, and internally rotates the shoulder	Latissimus dorsi: kneeling 45-degree stability ball stretch Pectoralis: standing corner wall L stretch	Trapezius (middle and lower), posterior deltoid, rhomboids: stabilizes scapula with arm movement Rhomboids: adducts and elevates scapula Serratus anterior: abducts and upward rotation of scapula Pectoralis minor: elevation of ribs and scapula abduction	Trapezius, posterior deltoid, and rhomboids: YTWL postures on stability ball Rhomboids: corner press-outs Serratus anterior: scapular stabilization circuit Pectoralis minor and serratus anterior: scapular Protraction with resistance
Elbows flex	Pectoralis major: adducts, flexes, and internally rotates the shoulder	Pectoralis: standing corner wall L stretch	Trapezius (middle and lower), posterior deltoid, rhomboids: stabilizes scapula with arm movement	Trapezius, posterior deltoid, rhomboids: YTWL postures on stability ball
Hips are above horizontal	Hip flexors (illiopsoas): hip flexion, trunk flexion, hip external rotation, lateral bending	Gastrocnemius and soleus, Achilles, foot, and ankle function, and knee flexion: overhead deep squat with elevated heels	Gluteus maximus: hip extension, external rotation, abduction, adduction, and stabilization of the knee Quadriceps (rectus femoris, vastus lateralis, intermedius longus and vastus oblique): extension of the knee and hip flexion Hamstrings (biceps femoris): knee flexion, external rotation and hip extension and external rotation Gastrocnemius and soleus: plantar flexes ankle, knee flexion, foot eversion and inversion	Gluteus maximus, quadriceps, hamstrings, gastrocnemius, shoulder, back extension, hips, ankles: Olympic hang and clean to squat Gluteus maximus and quadriceps: unilateral squat on horizontal or vertical half foam roller Hamstrings: supine leg curls on stability ball Gastrocnemius and soleus and Achilles: eccentric calf raise

TABLE 3.1   ACES—Evans' Self-Progression Exercise Training System for Posture

ACES progression stage	Sets with reps and number of breaths			Sets with reps only			Sessions per week
Stage 1	1-2 sets	10 reps	2-4 breaths	3	20- 30	1 min. rest	4-5
Stage 2	2-3 sets	5 reps	4-6 breaths	2	35-45	30 to 45 sec. rest	3
Stage 3	1 set	1 rep	6-10 breaths	1	60-90	N/A	1-2

Stage 2

- Sets with reps and hold-time exercises: two or three for five reps, but hold the posture in the exercise for 60 seconds.
- Sets with reps only: two sets of 45 reps with 45-second rest.
- Sessions per week: three sessions of flexibility, joint mobility, and stability exercises.

Stage 3

- Sets with reps and hold-time exercises: one set for one rep, but hold the posture in the exercise for 90 seconds.
- Sets with reps only: one set of 90 reps.
- Sessions per week: one or two sessions of flexibility, joint mobility, and stability exercises.

Stretching, Functional Movement, and Strengthening Corrective Exercises

The general assessments have been completed, exercises established, and the ACES system has told you how much and how often to train. In the following sections we describe the corrective exercises. The key to proper execution of the exercises is to maintain posture and work through each exercise with accurate, controlled, effortless, and smooth movements before moving onto the next stage. Later, in chapters 4 and 5, you will progress into much deeper levels of assessment and exercises.

The exercises that follow are listed in sequence by asymmetry and body region for tight, inflexible muscles and then weak muscles.

Incline Board Stretch

This exercise stretches and addresses the functional movement of ankle dorsiflexion. Step onto an incline board with feet up and heels down (figure 3.4). Lean forward to increase the stretch and draw the abdominals in gently to maintain a neutral pelvis. Inhale through the nose and exhale through the mouth for the number of breaths according to your stage (table 3.1). Repeat on the other side.

FIGURE 3.4 Incline board stretch.

Standing Upper-Calf Stretch

This exercise improves the flexibility and functional movement of the gastrocnemius. Place both hands against a wall, straighten the left leg, and push left heel into the floor (figure 3.5). Draw in the abdominals gently to maintain a neutral pelvis. Inhale through the nose and exhale through the mouth for the number of breaths according to your stage (table 3.1). Repeat on the other side.

FIGURE 3.5   Standing upper-calf stretch.

Standing Lower-Calf Stretch

This exercise improves the flexibility and functional movement of the soleus. Place both hands against a wall, flex knees by squatting down (squatting removes tension on the gastrocnemius), and press your weight into your feet (figure 3.6). Draw in the abdominals gently to maintain a neutral pelvis. Inhale through the nose and exhale through the mouth for the number of breaths according to your stage (table 3.1).

FIGURE 3.6   Standing lower-calf stretch.

Foot Eversion and Inversion

This exercise improves the flexibility, functional movement, stability, and strength of the peroneals. Sit on floor and wrap a resistance band around the outside and inside of one foot. Attach the ends to something sturdy. Evert (turn outward) the foot slowly against the resistance (figure 3.7*a*). When everting, the sole of the foot turns outward, but the thigh does not rotate. Then invert (turn inward) your foot slowly against the resistance (figure 3.7*b*). When inverting, the sole of the foot turns inward, and the thigh does not rotate. Draw in the abdominals gently to maintain a neutral pelvis. Inhale through the nose and exhale through the mouth for the number of breaths according to your stage (table 3.1). Repeat on the other side.

a   b

FIGURE 3.7 Foot *(a)* eversion and *(b)* inversion.

Side-Lying Hip Abduction With Resistance

This exercise improves the stability and strength of the gluteus medius. Lie on side with knees flexed 90 degrees, heels not touching, and feet resting on a 3- to 5-inch (8-12 cm) bolster against a wall (figure 3.8*a*). Gently draw abdomen in toward spine to stabilize pelvis, and hold throughout. Raise upper knee by generating movement from upper buttocks (figure 3.8*b*). Refer to table 3.1 for the number of sets and reps appropriate for you. Repeat on the other side. (Optional: Place a band above the knees for additional resistance.)

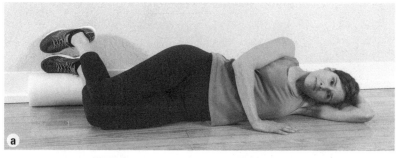

FIGURE 3.8 Slide-lying hip abduction with resistance.

Eccentric Calf Raise

This exercise improves the stability and strength of the gastrocnemius and soleus muscles and Achilles tendon. Stand on a step or platform and raise heels of both feet (figure 3.9*a*). Shift weight to right foot and lower while maintaining a neutral foot so that the arch does not collapse (figure 3.9*b*). Gently draw in abdominals to maintain a neutral pelvis. Inhale through the nose and exhale through the mouth for the number of breaths according to your stage (table 3.1). Repeat on the other side.

FIGURE 3.9 Eccectric calf raise.

Overhead Deep Squat With Elevated Heels

This exercise improves the flexibility and functional movement of the gastrocnemius and soleus muscles and Achilles tendon and develops foot and ankle function and knee flexion. Stand with both heels elevated atop a platform that is three quarters of an inch to two inches (2-5 cm) high (figure 3.10*a*). Squat until hips are aligned with knees (figure 3.10*b*). Gently draw in abdominals to maintain a neutral pelvis. Refer to table 3.1 for the number of sets and reps appropriate for you.

FIGURE 3.10   Overhead deep squat with elevated heels.

Supine Piriformis Stretch

This exercise improves the flexibility and functional movement of the piriformis. Lie on your back with left leg flexed and right leg crossed over the knee. With both hands under the left thigh, pull knee toward the chest (figure 3.11). Inhale through the nose and exhale through the mouth for the number of breaths according to your stage (table 3.1). Repeat on the other side.

FIGURE 3.11 Supine piriformis stretch.

Three-Way Hamstring Stretch

This exercise develops stretching and functional movement of the hamstrings and isolates the three hamstring muscles. Face an elevated object and place right heel on top, with supporting foot (foot on floor) in one of the three following positions:

1. Position 1: supporting foot faces forward (figure 3.12a).
2. Position 2: supporting foot is angled 45 degrees (figure 3.12b).
3. Position 3: supporting foot is placed at 90 degrees (figure 3.12c).

For all positions, flex forward from the hips and keep the knee steady. Gently draw in abdominals to maintain a neutral pelvis. Inhale through the nose and exhale through the mouth for the number of breaths according to your stage (table 3.1). Repeat on the other side.

a

b

c

FIGURE 3.12 Three-way hamstring stretch with supporting foot *(a)* forward, *(b)* angled 45 degrees, and *(c)* placed at 90 degrees.

Prone External Leg Slide

This exercise improves the stability and strength of the gluteus medius. Lie face down with a pillow under the abdomen and fingers placed on the bones under your pelvis to monitor movement (figure 3.13a). Contract the abdominal muscles by drawing navel toward a firm spine throughout the movement. Contract the buttocks. Slide right leg out to side as far as possible without any pelvis or spine movement (figure 3.13b). Return slowly to starting position. Refer to table 3.1 for the number of sets and reps appropriate for you. Repeat on the other side.

a

b

FIGURE 3.13 Prone external leg slide.

Supine Flexed-Knee Medicine Ball Squeeze

This exercise improves the stability and strength of the adductors. Lie on the floor with knees flexed holding a moderate-weight medicine ball between knees (figure 3.14a). Squeeze knees together while drawing in the core and contracting gluteals as the knees flex and the feet lift off the floor (figure 3.14b). Gently draw in abdominals to maintain a neutral pelvis. Refer to table 3.1 for the number of sets and reps appropriate for you.

FIGURE 3.14 Supine flexed-knee medicine ball squeeze.

Supine Hip 90-Degree Wall-Leg Slide

This exercise focuses on stretching and functional movement of the adductors. Lie on your back with hips flexed 90 degrees and heels against a wall (figure 3.15a). Draw in your core and slowly allow legs to slide outward (figure 3.15b). Inhale through the nose and exhale through the mouth for the number of breaths according to your stage (table 3.1).

FIGURE 3.15 Supine hip 90-degree wall-leg slide.

ITB Side-Lying Stretch With Strap

This exercise improves the flexibility and functional movement of the iliotibial band. Lie on one side with knees flexed and with a strap around the ankle of the upper leg and the other end over your upper shoulder. Note that an optional two- to five-pound weight on the lateral thigh can be used to increase the stretch. The femur (thigh) of the upper leg is flexed and adducted with slight lateral rotation until tension is felt along the lateral knee of the iliotibial band (figure 3.16). Gently draw in abdominals to maintain a neutral pelvis. Inhale through the nose and exhale through the mouth for the number of breaths according to your stage (table 3.1). Repeat on the other side.

FIGURE 3.16 ITB side-lying stretch with strap.

Foam Roller Slide From Side Bridge

This exercise improves the flexibility and functional movement of the tibialis anterior. Assume a quadruped position with right ankle across a foam roller and knee slightly bent with foot turned inward. Extend right leg, sweeping backward (figure 3.17), and return rolling on the outside of the shin. Work along the path with both long and short repetitive strokes in areas of increased tightness and pain. Control the pressure by controlling the amount of weight on the roller. Gently draw in abdominals to maintain a neutral pelvis. Inhale through the nose and exhale through the mouth for the number of breaths according to your stage (table 3.1). Repeat on the other side.

FIGURE 3.17   Foam roller slide from side bridge.

Supine With Lateral Elevation

This exercise improves the stability and strength of the gluteus medius. Lie on your back with knees bent, tubing around knees, feet on top of a two-inch (5 cm) block, back flat on the floor, and tailbone slightly raised. Raise left foot, turn knee, and move this leg laterally (away) from the right leg against and into the resistance of the tubing (figure 3.18). Generate force from the outside hip and slightly lift the heel off the floor slightly while squeezing the buttocks and pressing through the forefoot. Gently draw in abdominals to maintain a neutral pelvis. Inhale through the nose and exhale through the mouth for the number of breaths according to your stage (table 3.1). Repeat on the other side.

FIGURE 3.18   Supine with lateral elevation.

Unilateral Squat on Half Foam Roller

This exercise improves the stability and strength of the gluteus maximus and quadriceps. Stand barefoot on one leg on a horizontal foam roller and draw in your core (figure 3.19a). Squat three to five inches (8-12 cm) controlling the alignment of the knee with the second toe and generating forces from the buttocks (figure 3.19b). Continue the contraction during the squat and extension to the starting position. Gently draw in abdominals to maintain a neutral pelvis. Refer to table 3.1 for the number of sets and reps appropriate for you.

a   b

FIGURE 3.19   Unilateral squat on half foam roller.

Hamstring Stretch With Strap and Foot Eversion

This exercise improves the flexibility and functional movement of the hamstrings. Lie on your back with a strap over one foot and leg elevated until a moderate stretch is felt; then evert the foot and allow the leg to fall slightly to the side (figure 3.20a). Gently draw in abdominals to maintain a neutral pelvis. With foot everted, pull leg toward shoulder and hold (figure 3.20b). Inhale through the nose and exhale through the mouth for the number of breaths according to your stage (table 3.1). Repeat on the other side.

a

b

FIGURE 3.20 Hamstring stretch with strap and foot eversion.

Seated 90-Degree Stretch

This exercise improves the flexibility and functional movement of the piriformis. Sit on a chair or bench with left foot on floor and right knee crossed over left knee (figure 3.21a). Grasp the front of the right knee with both hands and pull your body down (figure 3.21b). Inhale through the nose and exhale through the mouth for the number of breaths according to your stage (table 3.1). Repeat on the other side.

a   b

FIGURE 3.21 Seated 90-degree stretch.

90-90 Gluteus Medius With Internal Rotation

This exercise improves the stability and strength of the gluteus medius. Lie on your back with feet flat against a wall and knee and hips bent 90 degrees with a ball between knees and tubing over ankles. Gently squeeze the ball and shift right hip up so right knee is slightly above left knee. Hold briefly; then slowly remove left foot from the wall and turn left ankle to the side (figure 3.22). Inhale through the nose and exhale through the mouth for the number of breaths according to your stage (table 3.1). Repeat on the other side.

FIGURE 3.22 90-90 gluteus medius with internal rotation.

Bilateral Squat on Horizontal Half Foam Roller

This exercise improves the stability and strength of the gluteus maximus. Stand barefoot on a horizontal foam roller and draw in your core (figure 3.23a). Squat three to five inches (8-12 cm), controlling the alignment of the knee over the second toe by generating forces from the buttocks (figure 3.23b). Continue the contraction during the squat and extension to the starting position. Gently draw in the abdominals to maintain a neutral pelvis. For a less challenging option, place foam rollers in a vertical position (figure 3.23c). Refer to table 3.1 for the number of sets and reps appropriate for you.

a   b   c

FIGURE 3.23 Bilateral squat on *(a-b)* horizontal half foam roller and on *(c)* vertical half foam roller.

Stability Ball Overhead Lunge

This exercise improves the flexibility and functional movement of the hip flexors. Sit astride a stability ball with right foot forward. Roll forward until a moderate stretch is felt on the left hip. Squeeze left buttocks and slowly roll an inch (2.5 cm) or so forward as you raise left hand overhead (figure 3.24). Inhale through the nose and exhale through the mouth for the number of breaths according to your stage (table 3.1). Repeat on the other side.

FIGURE 3.24   Stability ball overhead lunge.

Elevated Extension With Squat

This exercise improves the flexibility and functional movement of the rectus femoris. Elevate right foot about 30 to 36 inches (.7-.9 m) (figure 3.25a) and squat about 3 to 6 inches (8-15 cm) (figure 3.25b). Inhale through the nose and exhale through the mouth for the number of breaths according to your stage (table 3.1). Repeat on the other side.

a   b

FIGURE 3.25 Elevated extension with squat.

Kneeling Slump to Arch-Back Stretch

This exercise improves the flexibility and functional movement of the erector spinae. Assume a position on hands and knees, allowing your back to slump down (figure 3.26*a*). Arch your back as high as possible (figure 3.26*b*). Inhale through the nose and exhale through the mouth for the number of breaths according to your stage (table 3.1).

FIGURE 3.26   Kneeling *(a)* slump to *(b)* arch-back stretch.

Kneeling Stability Ball 45-Degree Stretch

This exercise improves the flexibility of the latissimus dorsi muscle (extension, adduction, and internal rotation of the shoulder, lifting, and a powerful swimming muscle—it works against the resistance of the water during the catch). Kneeling on floor with hands and forearms on a stability ball, flex forward from hips, lowering torso and head (figure 3.27a). Extend arms at a 45-degree angle to the left (figure 3.27b) and to the right. Another option is to perform the stretch on the floor without the ball. Inhale through the nose and exhale through the mouth for the number of breaths according to your stage (table 3.1).

FIGURE 3.27 Kneeling stability ball 45-degree stretch.

Elevated Unilateral Hip Dip and Hike

This exercise increases the stability and strength of the gluteus medius, a muscle that helps in lateral stability of the pelvis and is especially important in running and cycling during the loading (stance and downstroke) phases. With hands on the hips (iliac crest), place left foot on a 4- to 12-inch (10-30 cm) step with the right foot dorsiflexed and hanging to the side of the step. The toes of the left foot are spread and the arch is maintained. Let the right hip drop by unloading the left gluteus medius; keep the right ankle flexed. Return the right hip up so that it's level with the left by engaging the left gluteus medius muscle (figure 3.28 *a* and *b*). Refer to table 3.1 for the number of sets and reps appropriate for you. Repeat on the other side.

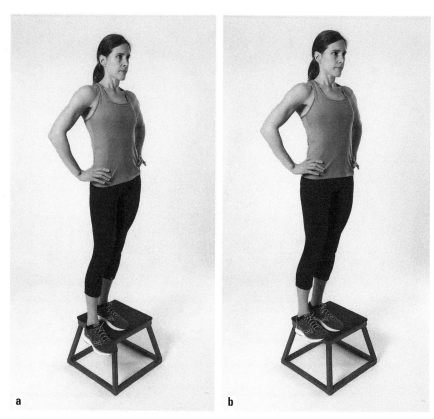

a   b

FIGURE 3.28 Elevated unilateral hip *(a)* dip and *(b)* hike.

Supine Hip Extension to Bridge With Alternate March

This exercise improves the stability and strength of the gluteus maximus. Assume a bridge position on a stability ball with hips level (figure 3.29a). March the left and then the right knee (figure 3.29b). Lower hips toward the floor (figure 3.29c). Squeeze gluteals, press heels into the floor, and bring hips level. Gently draw in the abdominals to maintain a neutral pelvis. Refer to table 3.1 for the number of sets and reps appropriate for you.

FIGURE 3.29 Supine hip extension to bridge with alternate march.

Contralateral Supine Bridge on Stability Ball

This exercise improves the stability and strength of the deep-layered core. Assume a bridge position on a stability ball with hips level and abdomen fully drawn in to stabilize the pelvis. Simultaneously raise right arm and left leg to be level with hips (figure 3.30). Inhale through the nose and exhale through the mouth for the number of breaths according to your stage (table 3.1). Repeat on the other side.

FIGURE 3.30   Contralateral supine bridge on stability ball.

Prone Extension on Stability Ball

This exercise improves the stability and strength of the erector spinae. Place both feet against a wall and lie on belly with chest over stability ball and hands behind neck (figure 3.31a). Squeeze gluteals and raise chest up and off the ball slowly (figure 3.31b). Keep gluteals engaged and lower to the starting posture. Refer to table 3.1 for the number of sets and reps appropriate for you.

FIGURE 3.31 Prone extension on stability ball.

Prone Sweeping Contralateral Arm and Leg Extension

This exercise improves the stability and strength of the erector spinae and deep-layered abdominals. Assume a position on hands and knees (figure 3.32a). Extend right arm and left leg together to full extension (figure 3.32b). Return to starting position and sweep the left arm and right leg to the extended posture. Refer to table 3.1 for the number of sets and reps appropriate for you.

FIGURE 3.32   Prone sweeping contralateral arm and leg extension.

Bridging Circuit

This exercise improves the stability and strength of the deep-layered abdominals. Bridge on the left elbow with a straight torso aligned with the pelvis (right hand on hip to monitor movement) with the feet stacked (figure 3.33a). Inhale through the nose and exhale through the mouth, holding the position for the number of breaths indicated in table 3.1. Then rotate by rolling into prone position onto the right side while maintaining the longitudinal posture (figure 3.33b). Inhale through the nose and exhale through the mouth for the number of breaths according to your stagte (table 3.1). Repeat on the other side.

FIGURE 3.33 Bridging circuit on (a) elbow and in (b) prone position.

Lateral Hand Overhead on Stability Ball

This exercise improves the flexibility and functional movement of the external obliques. Lie on your right side on a stability ball with left foot forward and left hand over head (figure 3.34). Inhale through the nose and exhale through the mouth for the number of breaths according to your stage (table 3.1). Repeat on the other side.

FIGURE 3.34 Lateral hand overhead on stability ball.

Supine Extension on Stability Ball

This exercise improves flexibility and functional movement of the rectus abdominis. Lie supine on a stability ball positioned at the lower curve of the spine with both hands over head (figure 3.35). Inhale through the nose and exhale through the mouth for the number of breaths according to your stage (table 3.1).

FIGURE 3.35   Supine extension on stability ball.

Extended Hip With Lateral Torso Stretch

This exercise improves the flexibility and functional movement of the iliopsoas. Stand with hands on hips and step forward with left leg until right heel lifts from the floor. Reach right hand overhead and bend hip away from extended right leg (figure 3.36). Inhale through the nose and exhale through the mouth for the number of breaths according to your stage (table 3.1). Repeat on the other side.

FIGURE 3.36   Extended hip with lateral torso stretch.

Transversus and Multifidi Standing Draw-In

This exercise improves the stability and strength of the deep-layered abdominals. Stand tall (draw the clavicle back and align it with the back of the neck and draw the scapulae toward the hips) and place right palm on abdomen and back of left hand on low back (figure 3.37). Draw belly in toward left hand; there should be little to no pressure against the hand. Inhale through the nose and exhale through the mouth for the number of breaths according to your stage (table 3.1 ACES).

FIGURE 3.37 Transversus and multifidi standing draw-in.

Standing Corner Wall L Stretch

This exercise improves the flexibility and functional movement of the pectoralis. Stand about 12 inches (30 cm) from and facing a corner of a wall, holding arms in an L position with elbow, forearm, and palm against the wall (figure 3.38a). Lean body forward from ankles with knees slightly flexed (figure 3.38b).

Inhale through the nose and exhale through the mouth for the number of breaths according to your stage (table 3.1).

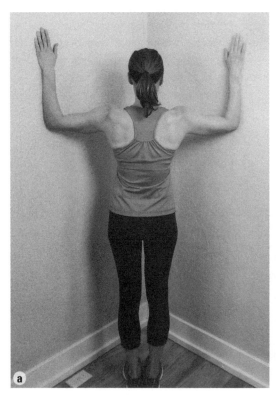 

FIGURE 3.38 Standing corner wall L stretch.

YTWL Postures on Stability Ball

This exercise improves the stability and strength of the trapezius, posterior deltoid, and rhomboids. Lie face down with chest on a stability ball; raise both arms and shoulders to form the following letters:

- Y (figure 3.39a)
- T (figure 3.39b)
- W (figure 3.39c)
- L (figure 3.39d)

Inhale through the nose and exhale through the mouth for the number of breaths according to your stage (table 3.1).

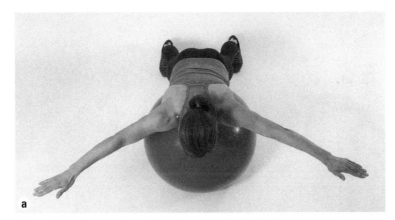

FIGURE 3.39 Postures on stability ball: *(a)* Y, *(b)* T, *(c)* W, and *(d)* L.

Corner Press-Out

This exercise improves the stability and strength of the rhomboids. Stand with back facing a corner of a wall and shoulders abducted to 90 degrees with elbows, forearms, and upper arms against the wall (figure 3.40*a*). Press elbows into walls and push body away from corner (figure 3.40*b*). Inhale through the nose and exhale through the mouth for the number of breaths according to your stage (table 3.1).

a   b

FIGURE 3.40 Corner press-out.

Scapular Stabilization Circuit

This exercise circuit develops stability and strength of the serratus anterior. To complete the circuit, do the following exercises one after another.

90/45 Scapula

Sit on a stool with back against a wall and flex arms up to 90 degrees horizontal so that you set the shoulder blades flat (clavicle back, scapulae down the hips) against the wall, not winging (figure 3.41a). Draw in the lower back toward the wall and fully raise both arms to approximately 45 degrees above horizontal while maintaining the set and low back position (figure 3.41b). Return to the start position. Inhale through the nose and exhale through the mouth for the number of breaths according to your stage (table 3.1). Refer to table 3.1 for the number of sets and reps appropriate for you.

FIGURE 3.41 Scapular stabilization circuit: 90/45 scapula.

Push-up plus

Begin in the up position of the push-up against a wall (or in a standard push-up position on the floor for more resistance) with the hands slightly to the sides of the shoulders (figure 3.42a). Then, push up a little extra to protract the scapulae (figure 3.42b). Inhale through the nose and exhale through the mouth. Refer to table 3.1 for the number of sets and reps appropriate for you.

FIGURE 3.42 Scapular stabilization circuit: push-up plus.

Scapular Protraction With Resistance

This exercise improves the stability and strength of the pectoralis minor and serratus anterior. Stand (or sit) with elbows at sides flexed to 90 degrees with tubing in the hands (figure 3.43*a*). Push forward against the resistance to round the upper back without rotating the body or moving the pelvis (figure 3.43*b*). Inhale through the nose and exhale through the mouth. Refer to table 3.1 for the number of sets and reps appropriate for you.

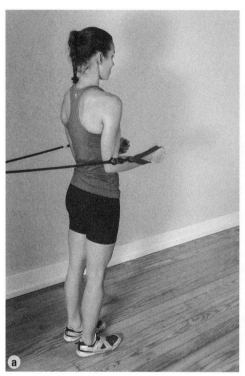 

FIGURE 3.43 Scapular protraction with resistance.

Supine Leg Curl on Stability Ball

This exercise improves the stability and strength of the hamstrings. Lie on your back with both feet on a stability ball. Pressing your heels into the ball, come up to a bridge (figure 3.44a) and pull in toward buttocks without arching low back (figure 3.44b). Slowly release, but stay up in a bridge. Inhale through the nose and exhale through the mouth. Refer to table 3.1 for the number of sets and reps appropriate for you.

FIGURE 3.44 Supine leg curl on stability ball.

Olympic Hang and Clean to Squat

This exercise improves the stability and strength of the gluteus maximus, quadriceps, hamstrings, gastrocnemius, shoulder, back extension, hips, and ankles. Stand with feet hip-width apart and facing forward. Hold a barbell in an overhand grip with elbows rotated outward so the barbell is hanging about midcalf. Squat with bar (figure 3.45*a*) and jump upward by extending body, beginning with a shrug of the shoulders to pull bar upward with arms and allowing elbows to flex out to sides, keeping bar close to body (figure 3.45*b*). Slide body under bar by lifting elbows up (figure 3.45*c*) and catch the bar on shoulders and upper chest while moving simultaneously into a squat (figure 3.45*d*). Squat until hips are horizontal and then immediately stand up. Return to start position by bending knees slightly and lowering the bar to midthigh position. Inhale through the nose and exhale through the mouth. Refer to table 3.1 for the number of sets and reps appropriate for you.

a   b   c   d

FIGURE 3.45   Olympic hang and clean to squat.

Posture is one of the most important elements for effective performance. To obtain better posture, your functional movements (flexibility, joint mobility, and stability) must be operating in good form. One of the keys (especially in running and even daily living) is keeping the clavicle back and the shoulder blades down and rotated. Practicing technique without assessing and understanding how to maintain posture through every movement, position, and posture of each sport neglects one of the most important principles of triathlon training—that every triathlete is an individual. This principle is one of the foundations of training.

4 Assessing Movement

As a triathlete, the reason you need to assess your functional movement (flexibility, joint mobility, and stability) is to improve performance as a result of achieving better technique, because you can move better and reduce recurring injuries caused by misaligned or compensating movements. Unique to this book are assessments along with progressive and self-correcting exercises that help you come closer to perfecting your technique. Once you can repeatedly execute a movement with accuracy, you simply move on to the next assessment and subsequent exercise.

Progressing from the basic assessments and exercise recommendations presented in chapters 1 and 3, we move in this chapter to deeper, more innovative levels of movement assessment. These pass-or-fail tests are like exercises that progress through stages with ACES and are exceptional training for triathletes at any level, from beginner to Olympian.

Training Better Movement Patterns

In this chapter we provide steps for you to assess compensatory movement patterns. From earlier chapters, you'll recall that you should precede any change in technique with movement assessment to identify any weaknesses or limitations.

Triathletes often attempt to apply technique that gets in the way of best possible perfor-

mance, and if they persist with such training, chronic injuries from overuse can result from overloading muscles and damaging soft tissue structure. A body in motion outside of its primary and most efficient pattern of stability and mobility can continue to be functional, but it will be diminished in its ability to achieve optimal performance and will be more susceptible to injury.

The human body has an amazing ability to adapt and compensate for limitations in motion by developing alternative patterns of movement. Unfortunately, these alternate patterns can establish themselves as the *primary* patterns after only two weeks of constant recruitment. This can ultimately place limits on the triathlete's development and optimal performance. Although the ability to perform at a high level might remain, optimal neuromuscular capabilities are hindered, resulting in a greater risk of getting caught in a cycle of constant injuries when trying to advance training.

When limitations of motion appear at any joint in the body, to achieve the total movement desired, the body will require more motion from other joints or segments of the body to perform that motion. As long as those joints or segments are able to control the additional amounts of motion being demanded of it, then no big deal. A lack of control of motion by the local (deeply placed muscles closer or directly attached to joints, where they remain neutral and work most optimally) and global (larger, fast-working superficial muscles for transferring loads and movements) stabilizing muscles often presents itself as an uncoordinated and lopsided motion when those movements are performed slowly, or as an increased perceived exertion in isometric or static low-load holding-type exercises, such as planks, prone, and lateral bridging exercises for the core.

Ideally, stability should always accompany mobility because each one can have a profound effect on the other. A lack of stability can restrict motion by demanding more from the global mobilizing muscles. Joints that lack stability show an increase in activation of the global mobilizing muscles surrounding them. (See table 4.1.) This increase in activation is a reactive protective mechanism to not only produce compression at a joint as an alternative and compensating way of creating stability at that joint, but also as a way to limit motion at that joint. When the global mobilizing muscles of the body remain active, and not completely at rest, their ability to shorten and lengthen completely is diminished, along with other key functions. These limitations restrict the amount of motion and force that are capable of being produced at any joint it crosses over. Stability, however, can be sacrificed to maintain mobility. This is done at the expense of the joint itself as well as its surrounding soft tissue structures (such as ligaments and the joint capsule). When a joint is left unprotected and unable to control excessive motion, overloading, or sudden forces, it creates an environment that can accelerate degeneration and lead to recurring injuries.

Power and force generation are created from the more central parts of the body, such as our trunk, pelvis, hips, and shoulders. The more distal segments of the body are designed for more fine-motor adaptation and sensory output. This sensory output provides vital real-time data to the central nervous system (spinal cord and brain; CNS), allowing it to respond instantly with muscular activation. For example, the CNS permits the feet to make quick adjustments to maintain balance when walking over uneven surfaces and the ability to manipulate buttons and zippers with the hands. When the more proximal segments of the body are not capable of providing the stability needed to generate the amount of force or motion needed, greater demand is placed on the more distal segments to make up for that loss. Thus a myriad of compensatory movement patterns can develop, and it's crucial to have a means or formula to help in identifying the sources of these patterns.

To maximize performance, you must have appropriate load-transfer ability through the pelvis, accompanied by an ability to control stability through the core and proximal joints. You must learn to identify faulty patterns of movement and address them if you want to progress to higher levels of individually based training. By identifying and retraining the functional control of body segments, you can begin to correct movement instability and apply much more precise movements in technique. The local and deep postural stabilizers (closest to the joints) along with secondary (midlevel stabilizers) are the most important to train because they fatigue slowly (slow twitch) and provide stability because of their location and the control of joint postures. The more superficial muscles are fast twitch and build tension rapidly and only provide stability when conditions are extreme, resulting in lack of body control and more uncoordinated movements (often seen in competition when the local stabilizers have fatigued).

TABLE 4.1   Local and Global Stabilizers, Global Mobilizers

	Local stabilizers	Global stabilizers	Global mobilizers
Function and characteristics	Deep, single-joint muscles are closest to joints (crossing over one joint). Deep postural stabilizers are always holding against gravity and are not direction dependent. Slow twitch (more fatigue resistant triathlete). First to activate due to a built-in mechanism to become more active before the global muscles fire to produce movement. Many muscle spindles, much more than global muscles, meaning they provide much more input to the central nervous system and brain about what is occurring at that joint, allowing the brain to make appropriate responses to changes of force that act on that joint at any time. Provide proprioceptive feedback for the brain to make decisions on. Work eccentrically (during lengthening, unloading) to stabilize movement through static holding of joints. Increase muscle stiffness to promote mechanical stability. The most important core muscles to train.	Intermediate-depth single-joint superficial muscles maintain posture and transfer loads between upper and lower extremities between the pelvis and spine, working across multiple segments to maintain center of mass. Biomechanically suited to generate forces that control (keep the motions produced by global mobilizers in check). Generate forces to control range of motion of trunk and limbs	Largely superficially layered multijoint muscles produce the speed, torque, and force for power and acceleration (larger movements). Work concentrically (during shortening, loading) with acceleration to produce power. Concentric production of movement by means of longer levers (legs and arms). Assist in shock absorption of load. Build tension very rapidly (fast twitch) under higher levels of resistance; they fatigue quickly. Become overactive in dysfunction and are more dominant, less functional. Contract and relax and work concentrically.
Examples	Transversus abdominis, deep lumbar multifidus, psoas major, pelvic floor	Erector spinae, internal oblique, gluteus medius, gastrocnemius	Rectus abdominis, gluteus maximus, hamstrings, external obliques, psoas, pectoralis, latissimus dorsi

DAVE SCOTT Maximizing Core Potential

The most common functional compensation in triathletes I coach is the absence of joint and movement symmetry. In fact, I've never seen an athlete with complete bilateral symmetry. Generally, one side of the body is dominant, resulting in asymmetry (lopsidedness), less power, and instability. Any one of these issues can alter movements in swimming, cycling, and running. What is lacking is a beneficial way to train, use, and command under stress the inner core muscles. If you can do this, you will reduce pressure on the vertebral spine and improve stability during movements.

Inherent in triathletes I've coached are weaknesses in the upper hamstring and gluteus maximus, and the low back and hip flexors on the same side are restricted (tight). The effect is global compensations in technique and a loss of power and stability. The triathlete cannot conceal these limiters under the stress of racing.

The primary stabilizer for the core is the transversus abdominis (TrA). If this muscle is not used, or taught how to be used, the triathlete might rely on the rectus abdominis (RA), a secondary stabilizer muscle, to generate power. The core is identified from the front of the body beginning with the mid-ribcage and passing along the abdominals, pelvis, and quadriceps. From here the posterior core muscles pass the length of the hamstrings, pelvis, gluteals, low back, and midback.

The deepest abdominal muscle, TrA, is located under the internal oblique and runs anterior to lateral around the low back. This muscle is corsetlike in providing stability in the lower front and back abdominal area. The TrA, in comparison to the RA (the six-pack muscle), is slow acting, but the TrA can be activated to maximize the potential of this important vital stabilizer.

Exercises and techniques that force TrA output and teach the triathlete how to command stability under stress are important. By training and activating the TrA in the right way, you can reduce pressure (compressive forces) on vertebral discs and reduce the use of secondary movers. Training and learning to fire the TrA help brace the spine and help the triathlete work more efficiently. A simple way to engage the TrA is when exhaling—you can force the TrA to contract (stabilize) by drawing your navel in toward your spine during the exhale.

A good exercise to activate and train the TrA is performed on your back. Arms are out to sides and knees bent. Lift both knees toward chest and bring heels back down (feet on the floor) three times. This establishes the back into its natural curved posture (there is a slight and normal curve in the low back—the back is not flattened to the floor). Place the first and middle fingers of both hands on the belly opposite the navel. Drawing in the belly, press the navel toward the spine while simultaneously flexing the right knee just beyond 90 degrees. The fingertips should feel the TrA activate while the knee is flexing. Slowly lower the flexed leg (foot) to the floor for a count of six. The rectus abdominis won't be contracting now (that's a spinal flexor, like doing a crunch), but with practice the TrA will contract and develop more capability for stability. Do six to eight repetitions on each side. As your proficiency improves, try bringing both knees at the same time toward your chest. This can be more challenging because the RA can contract more—so concentrating on keeping the TrA fully engaged during the flexing and extending the knees back to the floor are necessary.

The single-leg soar is another great exercise for the TrA. Stand tall with ribs high (just ribs, not the chest) to activate the TrA. Hands are at sides, palms facing forward (figure 4.1a). Relax shoulders (low) and contract shoulder blades as if placing something in your back pockets. At the same time, draw in the TrA (arms will lift slightly away from body). Shift weight to the left foot with toes spread and weight on heel (figure 4.1b). Tighten the left gluteus and quadriceps (maximal contraction). Hold the TrA, right gluteus, and quadriceps tightly and lift right leg straight off the ground (figure 4.1c). The right foot is dorsiflexed in alignment (not pointed inward or outward to prevent load transfer). The navel points down as the right leg is lifted 30 to 45 degrees (for beginners, and up to 90 degrees when proficiency builds). At 90 degrees, both the swing leg and torso are aligned and level with the ground. Do three or four sets of 20- to 60-second holds for each leg.

You'll notice all the muscles of the foot, lower leg, quadriceps, pelvis, and gluteals are firing fairly high and, most important, that the TrA is fully activated. By purposely relaxing the TrA, the low back muscles contract (increasing compression) and the RA fires (making it difficult to talk freely). Resetting the TrA reduces the pressures on the vertebral spine. The single-leg soar is similar to the positions in triathlon, and the TrA is fully maximized when done properly.

a   b   c

FIGURE 4.1 Single-leg soar.

Movement Assessment and Exercises

The process of adapting and renovating technique begins with assessing which body regions have more or less control of functional movements. As we've discussed, limitations in performance or technique are often caused by overactivation of the mobility muscles generated by underactive inhibited stability muscles that provide control and protect the joints. Think of these underactive areas as potential weak links in the chain of kinetic movements. We want to identify and repair these weak links. Our goal is to correct any uncontrolled or compensatory motions and retrain them to be conducive to optimal technique.

Every test and exercise we'll present in this chapter focuses on the following:

- The assessment of seven body segments that affect movement and stability: cervical, scapulohumeral, thoracic, trunk, pelvis, femoral, and feet

- Assessing muscle imbalances and the effects of contributing weaknesses to alignment and technique in swimming, cycling, and running

- Improving the alignment of torso, pelvis, knees, and head

- Control and awareness of muscle recruitment (during flexion and extension) and effort

As in earlier chapters, we'll use ACES (accurate, controlled, effortless, and smooth) exercise progressions for both assessment and training. ACES assesses movements at three stages of proficiency and is a simple system of gauging correct test exercise technique. As you might recall, the ACES progressions are based on your ability to perform the tests' movements correctly. Body lines (techniques, postures, positions of body, and regions of training in chapters 6, 7, and 8) are measured with ACES through unhurried movements at lower intensities that progress to longer distances or time intervals that focus on one specific movement.

Endurance athletes require ideal functional movement and stability for long periods, and often at high levels of aerobic output. To meet these demands, you must be able to perform increasing numbers of repetitions, well beyond those in traditional exercise programs. Thus many of the test exercises in this chapter have high numbers of repetitions (or long durations). That said, the tests and progressions are not intended to cause you undue exertion. Rather, the demands of the tests will assess the level of your functional muscular control, stability, and mobility under triathlon-like conditions. The tests use a pass–fail system in which you continue to do an exercise until accurate, controlled, effortless, and smooth results are attained. Then you progress to the next stage (see table 4.2). Once you have met the demands of the highest stage of testing, continue the exercise in a maintenance phase.

Before we get to the tests, let's clarify what low- and high-load testing means. Low-load testing assesses the recruitment of muscles

TABLE 4.2 Self-Progression Exercise Training for Movement

ACES progression stage	Sets with reps and number of breaths			Sets with reps only			Sessions per week
Stage 1	1-2 sets	10 reps	2-4 breaths	3	20-30	1 min. rest	4-5
Stage 2	2-3 sets	5 reps	4-6 breaths	2	35-45	30 to 45 sec. rest	3
Stage 3	1 set	1 rep	6-10 breaths	1	60-90	N/A	1-2

through normal ranges of joint motion and the stability of proximal segments throughout that motion with little weight or challenge. High-load testing assesses the ability of the musculature to stabilize proximal segments (pelvis, trunk, shoulder blades) under higher loads or challenges. The differences between the two tests are important to note.

Low-load testing assesses segmental function of the local stabilizing muscles (deep inner core muscles such as the transversus abdominis and multifidus) and the global stabilizing muscles (outer core muscles such as the rectus abdominis and external and internal obliques) with minimal activation of the global mobilizing muscles (the larger, powerful muscles) in the absence of any impact on load transfer through the pelvis. Thus low-load tests assess if there is a pure recruitment dysfunction in the local or global stabilizing muscles in absence of (or in the facilitation from) the global mobilizing muscles.

High-load testing assesses the function of the stability muscles under more strenuous challenges. This not only tests their ability to meet the stability demands being placed on it by the mobility muscles, but also tests the body's ability to transfer loads effectively.

For many low-load motion tests, the stabilizing muscles are evaluated and then trained correctly. For the high-load tests, the focus becomes more specific to the required movements and demands of swimming, cycling, and running during training and racing. This is when the local and global stabilizers must be able to control the amount of forces being placed through the joint by the global mobilizers that are producing movement, power, and acceleration during training and competition.

Multisegmental Low-Load Tests

Multisegmental low-load tests using the overhead deep squat help identify certain segments of the body that might lack proper stability and control during functional movements. If stability is not present during lower loads, it will not be sufficient during the higher loads of training and competition, resulting in compensations.

Overhead Deep-Squat Test

This overhead deep squat helps to identify zones of symmetry and asymmetry in the joints, flexibility in the muscles, and lumbopelvic and overall body stability. You'll need a slick surface such as a slideboard or linoleum, socks, and a video recorder at the front, back, and sides.

To perform the overhead deep-squat test, stand with feet hip-width apart and aligned straight forward from heel to toe, with arms straight overhead (figure 4.2a). Squat down as if sitting in a chair (moving buttocks backward) and lower as far as possible while keeping arms as vertical overhead as you can (figure 4.2b).

Complete three squats filming from the front (anterior), three squats filming from the side (lateral), and three squats filming from the back (posterior). Observe the squat from the side and back. A perfect overhead squat will have these qualities:

- Heels are flat with no anterior (front) weight shifting onto the balls of the feet.
- Feet remain straight ahead and parallel from heel to toe with no noticeable sliding; the longitudinal arch is maintained.
- At the deepest point in the squat, arms and hands are overhead and aligned through the ear, shoulder, torso, and hip joint.
- Your torso at the deepest point remains parallel with lower legs (tibia) and does not lean forward more or less than 10 degrees.
- Hips are horizontally aligned with knee (within 10 to 15 degrees above).
- The centers of both knees are aligned over the second toe with no adduction (inward) or abduction (outward) movement during the squat.

The segmental assessment (low load) tests identify the stability to control specific regions of the body (segments). The tests focus on isolated body regions (segments). Any compensation in one segment will affect others. If you fail a test, continue the exercises (remedies) until you achieve ACES. Then move to the next stage.

FIGURE 4.2 Overhead deep-squat test.

Corrective Exercises for Overhead Deep Squat, Cervical Segment

To pass the overhead deep-squat test in the cervical segment, head and ears must stay in line with arms and shoulders. You fail this test if head or chin extends (juts) forward.

To correct faults in the cervical segment, lie on back with knees bent and a small towel under neck to fill space between neck and floor. Place one hand around front of neck. Very slowly slide back of head on towel, lengthening back of neck and nodding chin down (figure 4.3). Maintain this position and lift head one to two inches (2.5-5 cm) off towel. Focus on holding the lengthening of back of neck; do not let chin poke forward. Refer to table 4.2 for number of sets and reps.

FIGURE 4.3   Corrective exercise 1 for overhead deep squat, cervical segment.

The second test exercise to correct faults in the cervical segment is to lie on your belly, propped up on elbows and forearms. Upper back is rounded into a hunched position, keeping belly on floor (figure 4.4a). Nod head by lifting base of skull up and lengthening back of neck (figure 4.4b). Slowly extend at the bottom of neck, trying to get ears in line with shoulders, and maintain the lengthening of back of neck while keeping ears in line with shoulders (figure 4.4c). Refer to table 4.2 for number of sets and reps.

FIGURE 4.4   Corrective exercise 2 for overhead deep squat, cervical segment.

Corrective Exercises for Overhead Deep Squat, Scapulohumeral Segment

You pass the overhead deep-squat test in the scapulohumeral segment if arms stay in line with body and elbows stay straight and do not bend or flex. You fail this test if arms bend or lower or if shoulder blades elevate or rotate downward.

To correct faults in the scapulohumeral segment, stand facing a wall with elbows level with shoulders and bent 90 degrees. Hands are open with pinkies and forearms against the wall and body line is vertical (figure 4.5a). Slide arms up wall, extending elbows off wall without rotating elbows outward or wider than shoulders (figure 4.5b). Go as high as you can without forcing or muscling arms up and without arching lower back, leaning toward wall, or elevating shoulders. Refer to table 4.2 for number of sets and reps.

FIGURE 4.5 Corrective exercise 1 for overhead deep squat, scapulohumeral segment.

The next exercise to correct faults in the scapulohumeral segment is to stand facing a wall with feet four to six inches (10-15 cm) from wall and arms placed overhead in a Y. Your pinkies are on wall and elbows are straight (figure 4.6*a*). Gently rotate clavicle back and squeeze shoulder blades down toward buttocks without arching low back (a key position of running and activities of daily living). Lift pinkies off wall for one or two breaths and keep elbows straight while maintaining shoulder blade position (figure 4.6*b*). Refer to table 4.2 for number of sets and reps.

FIGURE 4.6   Corrective exercise 2 for overhead deep squat, scapulohumeral segment.

Corrective Exercises for Overhead Deep Squat, Thoracic Segment

You pass the overhead deep-squat test for the thoracic segment if your upper and mid-back stay in neutral position. You fail this test if your upper or midback flexes or extends.

To correct faults in the thoracic segment, stand with back against wall, feet hip-width apart and 12 inches (30 cm) from wall with knees bent. Your head faces forward slightly off the wall (figure 4.7*a*). Gently roll clavicle backward, flattening shoulder blades against wall; hold this position for one or two breaths (figure 4.7*b*). Very slowly flatten lower back against wall and hold. Do not let head jut forward or shoulders come off wall. Refer to table 4.2 for number of sets and reps.

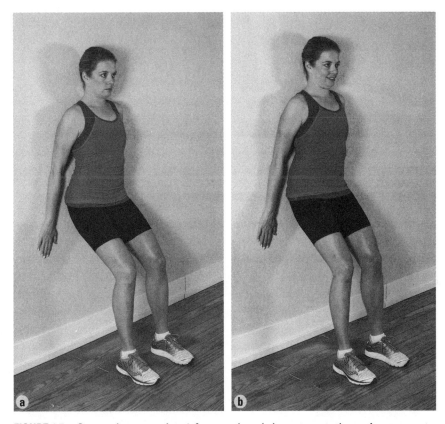

FIGURE 4.7   Corrective exercise 1 for overhead deep squat, thoracic segment.

The next progressive test exercise to correct faults in the thoracic segment is to sit with feet unsupported. Tip the small of your back inward to sit up tall with your rib cage (not your chest) high (figure 4.8*a*); then slowly lower down. Bend your chin to chest, exhale, and slump forward into a slouched position, squeezing the bottom of your sternum toward your navel (figure 4.8*c*). Staying in this slumped position, tip the small of your back forward, as before, and hold this position for one or two breaths. Do not let your head, shoulder, or sternum lift up. Refer to table 4.2 for number of sets and reps.

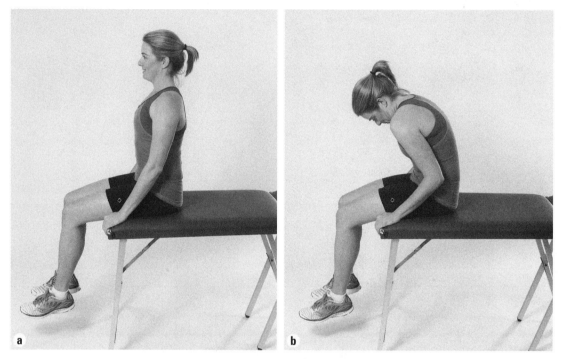

FIGURE 4.8   Corrective exercise 2 for overhead deep squat, thoracic segment.

Corrective Exercises for Overhead Deep Squat, Trunk Segment

You pass the overhead deep-squat test for the trunk if your lower back stays in neutral position. You fail this test if your lower back flexes or extends (arches or flattens).

To correct faults in the trunk segment, stand with lower back in neutral position and bend forward at hips, keeping lower back neutral and knees straight (figure 4.9*a*); hold for one or two breaths. Rise back to starting position (figure 4.9*b*). Refer to table 4.2 for number of sets and reps.

FIGURE 4.9 Corrective exercise 1 for overhead deep squat, trunk segment.

The next exercise to correct faults in the trunk segment is to sit on an edge of a table with only half your thigh supported. Lie on your back and bring your feet up onto the edge of the table (figure 4.10*a*). Lift both feet off the table, flexing in hips to 90 degrees; place hands palms down under both sides of your pelvis (figure 4.10*b*). Gently flatten your back into your hands, and hold this position during the test. Now lower one foot over the edge of the table and down until the back of your thigh touches the table (figure 4.10*c*); then rise to the starting position. Do not allow your pelvis (changing the pressure on the hands) to rotate down with your leg or your back to arch. Refer to table 4.2 for number of sets and reps.

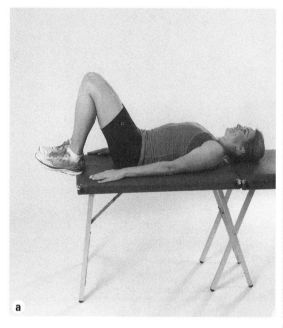

FIGURE 4.10 Corrective exercise 2 for overhead deep squat, trunk segment.

Corrective Exercises for Overhead Deep Squat, Pelvic Segment

You pass the overhead deep-squat test for the pelvis if your pelvis stays neutral and level. You fail this test if your pelvis rotates, tilts, or hikes to either side.

To correct faults in the pelvic segment, lie on side with body straight and one hip directly over the other. Place upper hand on upper pelvis to monitor any unwanted movement (rolling forward or backward or hitching; figure 4.11*a*). Keeping upper knee straight, turn leg upward to externally rotate it (figure 4.11*b*). Very slowly raise that leg up, keeping it externally rotated and your pelvis steady for one or two breaths (figure 4.11*c*). Slowly lower to starting position and then immediately rise again without relaxing your leg. Refer to table 4.2 for number of sets and reps.

FIGURE 4.11 Corrective exercise 1 for overhead deep squat, pelvic segment.

The next progressive test exercise to correct faults in the pelvic segment is to stand with back against a wall with feet together four to six inches (10-15 cm) from wall. Keeping upper back and shoulder blades against wall, gently flatten your lower back (figure 4.12a). Slowly lift one leg up, flexing at the hip (figure 4.12b), and rise as far as you can without rotating on your stance leg or allowing your body to slide on the wall. Your goal is to reach 90 degrees of hip flexion, but you might have to start with 30 degrees. Refer to table 4.2 for number of sets and reps.

FIGURE 4.12   Corrective exercise 2 for overhead deep squat, pelvic segment.

Corrective Exercises for Overhead Deep Squat, Femoral Segment

You pass the overhead deep squat test for the femoral (thigh bone) if patella (kneecap) stays directly over first two toes. You fail this test if the varus (outward direction) or valgus (inward direction) of knee is lateral or medial of toes or if unable to squat to 90 degrees.

To correct faults in the femoral segment, lie on side with legs together and hips and knees bent to 90 degrees. Keep big toes together and heels apart throughout the exercise (figure 4.13a). Slowly rotate upper leg upward until knee is slightly above hip level (figure 4.13b); then slowly lower, touch lower leg, and immediately raise leg again. Do not let upper leg relax when you lower it; there should be no motion in pelvis or trunk during the motion. Refer to table 4.2 for number of sets and reps.

FIGURE 4.13 Corrective exercise 1 for overhead deep squat, femoral segment.

The next exercise to correct faults in the femoral segment is to lie on back with one knee bent and foot at opposite knee (figure 4.14a). Place hand palm down under pelvis of straight leg and gently flatten lower back into hand. Starting with bent knee in line with navel, slowly lower the bent leg outward to 45 degrees (figure 4.14b); then slowly return. Do not allow your pelvis to rotate or rise off your hand. Refer to table 4.2 for number of sets and reps.

FIGURE 4.14 Corrective exercise 2 for overhead deep squat, femoral segment.

A final exercise to correct faults in the femoral segment is to lie on your belly with a pillow folded under your navel and pelvis and hands placed on pelvis with one knee bent to 90 degrees (figure 4.15*a*). Slowly raise bent leg 20 to 30 degrees off floor, moving at hip only, and take one or two breaths (figure 4.15*b*). Do not allow pelvis to rotate or back to arch. Slowly lower leg, touch floor without relaxing it, and raise it again. Focus on lifting and lowering with gluteal muscles and not hamstrings. Refer to table 4.2 for number of sets and reps.

FIGURE 4.15   Corrective exercise 3 for overhead deep squat, femoral segment.

Corrective Exercises for Overhead Deep-Squat Test, Feet Segment

You pass the overhead deep-squat test for the feet segment if your toes stay pointed straight forward and your arches don't collapse. You fail this test if your feet turn outward or your arches collapse.

To correct faults in the feet segment, sit in a chair with feet and ankles together on the floor and knees directly over your ankles (figure 4.16*a*). Keeping your ankles together, lift your heels off the floor, rising onto your toes (figure 4.16*b*); take one or two breaths. The weight through your feet should be between your first two toes. Slowly lower your heels to touch the floor, then immediately rise again without relaxing. Keep ankles together throughout the motion. Refer to table 4.2 for number of sets and reps.

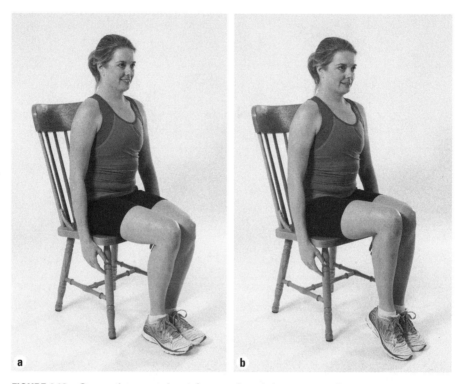

FIGURE 4.16   Corrective exercise 1 for overhead deep squat, feet segment.

The next progressive test exercise to correct faults in the feet segment is to stand with heels and big toes together (figure 4.17a). Slowly bend knees to about 30 degrees (figure 4.17b) and rise back to starting position, keeping toes and heels together. Refer to table 4.2 for number of sets and reps.

a   b

FIGURE 4.17 Corrective exercise 2 for overhead deep squat, feet segment.

Standing Rotation Test

This standing rotation test is another valuable tool in identifying your zones of symmetry and asymmetry in the joints, flexibility in the muscles and lumbopelvic region, and overall body stability. You'll need to video-record from the front, back, and sides.

To perform the standing rotation test, stand with feet together and aligned straight forward from heel to toe, with arms relaxed by your side. Rotate your body as far as possible, keeping arms relaxed (figure 4.18). Don't pull with your shoulders.

Complete one rotation on each side while being filmed from the front (anterior), one rotation on each side while being filmed from the side (lateral), and one rotation on each side while being filmed from the back (posterior). Observe from the back and sides. A perfect standing rotation will have these qualities:

- Big toes and heels stay on the floor.
- Knees remain straight and do not bend.
- Hips and pelvis rotate together without any anterior or posterior tilt.
- Thorax stays erect without any side bending or lateral tilt.
- No protraction (forward) or retraction (backward) occurs in the shoulders.
- Head faces forward in line with the sternum.

The segmental assessment (low load) tests identify the stability to control specific regions of the body. The tests examine regions of the body in an isolated way. Any compensation in one section (segment) will affect others. If you fail a test, continue the exercises (remedies) until you achieve ACES before moving to the next stage.

FIGURE 4.18 Standing rotation test.

Corrective Exercises for Standing Rotation Test, Thorax Segment

You pass the standing rotation test for the thorax if there is 45 degrees of hip rotation combined with 45 degrees of thoracic rotation. You fail this test if there is less than 45 degrees of hip rotation or less than an additional 45 degrees of thoracic rotation.

To correct faults in the thorax segment, stand with feet together six to eight inches (15-20 cm) from a wall with knees straight and back against the wall. Lock your fingers together behind your head, and place elbows back against the wall (see figure 4.19). Gently flatten your lower back, keeping your elbows against the wall. Very slowly slide your pelvis laterally on the wall from side to side, keeping your arms and back against the wall and knees straight. Refer to table 4.2 for number of sets and reps.

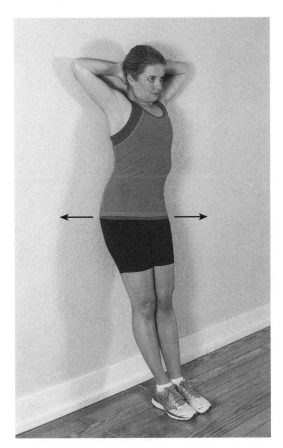

FIGURE 4.19 Corrective exercise 1 for standing rotation, thorax segment.

The next progressive test exercise to correct faults in the thorax segment is to stand with feet six to eight inches (15-20 cm) from a wall with your knees straight and your back against the wall (figure 4.20*a*). Place one arm shoulder level, elbow bent to 90 degrees; the other arm stays relaxed at your side. Gently flatten your lower back, keeping your elbow and arm against the wall. Very slowly slide your arm up the wall, reaching as high as you can while keeping the arm against the wall (figure 4.20*b*). Do not allow any part of your body to come off the wall or tilt. Refer to table 4.2 for number of sets and reps.

FIGURE 4.20   Corrective exercise 2 for standing rotation, thorax segment.

March Test

The march test is a simple test that assesses the body's ability to control motion at the core (hips, pelvis, and trunk). You are evaluating mobility in active hip flexion. You'll need video from the front and back.

To perform the march test, stand with feet together and aligned straight forward from heel to toe with arms relaxed at sides (figure 4.21a). March one knee up to 90 degrees of hip flexion and hold for five seconds (figure 4.21b).

Complete one march on each side while being filmed from the front (anterior) and one march on each side while being filmed from the back (posterior). Observe from the front and back. A perfect march will have these qualities:

- Big toes and heels stay together on the floor.
- Knees remain straight and do not bend, there's no femoral (thigh bone) internal rotation, and patella (center of knee joint) stays forward.
- Hips (femur and thigh bone) remain neutral; do not rotate while lifting knee to 90 degrees.
- Pelvis stays level.
- Thorax stays erect with no side bend or lateral tilt.
- No protraction (forward) or retraction (backward) occurs in the shoulders.
- Head faces forward in line with sternum.
- There's minimal weight shift and minimal lateral displacement of pelvis.

The segmental assessment (low load) tests identify sufficient stability to control specific regions of the body. The tests focus on body segments in an isolated way. Any compensation in one segment will affect others. If you fail a test, continue the exercises (remedies) until you achieve ACES before moving to the next stage.

FIGURE 4.21 March test.

Corrective Exercises for March Test, Trunk Segment

You pass the march test for the trunk if your trunk stays facing forward. You fail the test if the trunk rotates forward or backward on the standing leg.

To correct faults in the trunk segment, lie on one side with body in a straight line and one hip directly over the other (figure 4.22*a*). Place upper hand on your pelvis to monitor movement. Rotate your upper leg outward, pointing your toes upward and keeping your knee straight (figure 4.22*b*). Slowly lift your upper leg straight up about 12 inches (30 cm) from the lower foot without letting your pelvis roll forward or backward (figure 4.22*c*). Slowly lower down to the opposite leg without relaxing; repeat. Refer to table 4.2 for number of sets and reps.

FIGURE 4.22 Corrective exercise 1 for march test, trunk segment.

Corrective Exercises for the March Test, Pelvic Segment

You pass the march test for the pelvis if your pelvis stays level. You fail the test if your pelvis opposite to your standing leg hikes up or drops down below the level of the pelvis on the standing leg.

To correct faults in the pelvic segment, stand with back against a wall and feet together four to six inches (10-15 cm) from the wall. Keeping upper back and shoulder blades against wall, gently flatten your lower back. Slowly lift one leg up, flexing at the hip, and rise as far as you can without rotating in your stance leg or allowing your body to slide on the wall (figure 4.23). Your goal is to reach 90 degrees of hip flexion, but you might have to start with 30 degrees. Refer to table 4.2 for number of sets and reps.

FIGURE 4.23 Corrective exercise 1 for march test, pelvic segment.

Corrective Exercises for the March Test, Femoral Segment

You pass the march test for the femur if your foot, kneecap, and pelvis remain facing forward. You fail the test if there is any inward or outward rotation of the standing leg or pelvis.

To correct faults in the femoral segment, stand with feet together, keeping your pelvis level, and march one leg up to 30 degrees (figure 4.24*a*). With pelvis level, rotate together your upper body and pelvis on your standing leg. For example, standing on your left leg, rotate your left leg and hip together internally (figure 4.24*b*). Rotate as far as you can with your pelvis level and without moving your upper body. Slowly rotate back to facing forward. Refer to table 4.2 for number of sets and reps.

a   b

FIGURE 4.24   Corrective exercise 1 for march test, femoral segment.

Multisegmental High-Load Tests

The multisegmental (high-load) screening test is performed using the single-leg three-hop test. This test helps identify segments that control multiple regions of the body during challenging movements. The test evaluates more than one body region.

Single-Leg Three-Hop Test

The single-leg hop test evaluates athletic movement and assesses the body's ability to provide stability and control under higher loads. This test also provides a means to examine the body's ability to absorb impact from ground reaction forces during high-load activities such as running. This involves your movement symmetry from each side and your neuromuscular control. For this test you'll need cycling shorts and a video camera. You will need video from the front, back, and sides.

Stand with feet together and aligned straight forward from heel to toe with arms relaxed at sides (figure 4.25a). March one knee up to 90 degrees of hip flexion (figure 4.25b) and hop up and down in place three times. Your feet must leave the floor with every hop.

Complete one video of three hops from the front (anterior), one video of three hops from the side (lateral), and one video of three hops from the back (posterior). Observed from the back and sides, a perfect hop has these qualities:

- Feet leave the ground.
- Knee stays at 90 degrees of hip flexion on non-weight-bearing leg.
- No pelvic tilt or rotation; pelvis is level and facing forward.
- No movement in the trunk; lower back stays in neutral position.
- No varus (outward direction) or valgus (inward direction) at the knee; patella stays forward and over first two toes.
- Hip drops down vertically over the ankle and does not turn forward over the foot.

The multisegmental tests identify the stability needed to control isolated regions of the body (segments). If you do not pass a test, continue the exercises (remedies) until you achieve ACES. Then move to the next stage.

a   b

FIGURE 4.25 Single-leg three-hop test.

Corrective Exercises for Single-Leg Three-Hop Test, Trunk Segment

You pass the single-leg three-hop test for the trunk segment if trunk remains facing forward and lower back remains in neutral position. You fail this test if trunk turns inward toward standing leg or if lower back flattens.

To correct faults for the trunk segment, lie on back with knees bent. Place hands behind lower back with palms down. Lift knees up, flexing hips to 90 degrees; gently flatten your lower back into your hands (figure 4.26a). Slowly lower feet to one to two inches (2.5-5 cm) above floor with back flat against hands (figure 4.26b). Keeping lower back flat, extend knees out straight, keeping feet one to two inches (2.4-5 cm) off the floor. Return to starting position—knees bent, hips flexed to 90 degrees, and back flat. Refer to table 4.2 for number of sets and reps.

FIGURE 4.26 Corrective exercise 1 for single-leg three-hop test, trunk segment.

The next exercise to correct faults in the trunk segment is to stand with lower back in natural neutral position and arms lifted overhead (figure 4.27a). Bend forward at hips, keeping lower back in neutral position and knees straight (figure 4.27b). Rise back up to starting position. Refer to table 4.2 for the number of sets and reps.

a   b

FIGURE 4.27   Corrective exercise 2 for single-leg three-hop test, trunk segment.

Corrective Exercises for Single-Leg Three-Hop Test, Pelvic Segment

You pass the single-leg three-hop test for the pelvis if pelvis remains level. You fail this test if pelvis on unsupported leg drops down below level of pelvis on standing (hopping) leg.

To correct faults in the pelvic segment, stand in a door frame with feet hip-width apart and the outside of one foot against door frame (figure 4.28*a*). Lift foot against the frame up, bending (flexing) knee to 90 degrees (figure 4.28*b*). With light but constant pressure, press bent knee against door frame (figure 4.28*c*). Squat up and down on standing leg (to 30 degrees) while letting other knee slide up and down door frame (figure 4.28*d*). Keep lower back in neutral and patella in line with first two toes. Refer to table 4.2 for number of sets and reps.

FIGURE 4.28 Corrective exercise 1 for single-leg three-hop test, pelvic segment.

Corrective Exercises for Single-Leg Three-Hop Test, Femoral Segment

You pass the single-leg three-hop test for the femoral segment if patella (center of knee) stays directly over first two toes. You fail this test if the varus (outward direction) or valgus (inward direction) of knee moves either lateral or medial of first two toes.

To correct faults in the femoral segment, lie on back with hands behind head and knees bent, feet flat on floor (figure 4.29a). March one knee up to 90 degrees of hip flexion, and lift toes of down leg up so only heel is on floor (figure 4.29b). Keeping lower back in neutral posture, push down through heel of down leg and raise buttocks off floor high enough so body is in line with thigh (figure 4.29c). Slowly lower buttocks back to floor and raise again without relaxing. Refer to table 4.2 for number of sets and reps.

FIGURE 4.29 Corrective exercise 1 for single-leg three-hop test, femoral segment.

The next exercise to correct faults in the femoral segment is to stand with feet hip-width apart, toes straight forward, and hands on pelvis. March one leg up and hold (figure 4.30*a*). Bend standing knee to 30 degrees, keeping back in neutral and dropping buttocks over heels (figure 4.30*b*). Keeping weight on heel, slowly swing knee side to side (figure 4.30*c*). Keep pelvis still, with no rotation or tilt. Refer to table 4.2 for number of sets and reps.

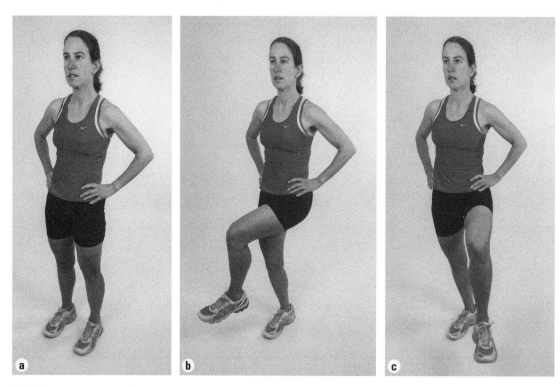

FIGURE 4.30 Corrective exercise 2 for single-leg three-hop test, femoral segment.

Corrective Exercises for Single-Leg Three-Hop Test, Feet Segment

You pass the single-leg three-hop test for the feet segment if toes stay pointed straight forward and arches do not collapse. You fail this test if feet turn outward or arches collapse.

To correct faults in the feet segment, stand with feet and ankles together and bend knees to 30 degrees (figure 4.31a). Lift heels off floor as high as you can (figure 4.31b). Slowly lower heels back down. Refer to table 4.2 for number of sets and reps.

a   b

FIGURE 4.31 Corrective exercise 1 for single-leg three-hop test, feet segment.

The next exercise to correct faults in the feet segment is to stand with feet and ankles together and lift one leg without letting the arch collapse on the standing leg (figure 4.32*a*). Without arch collapsing, slowly squat to 30 degrees on standing leg (figure 4.32*b*) and rise back up. Keep pelvis level and facing forward. Refer to table 4.2 for number of sets and reps.

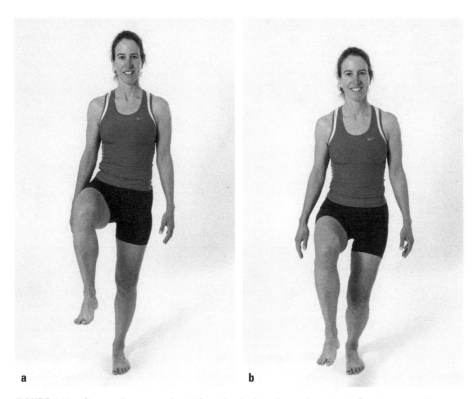

a   b

FIGURE 4.32 Corrective exercise 2 for single-leg three-hop test, feet segment.

Incline Push-Up Test

The incline push-up test is another simple test to evaluate movement and assess the body's ability to provide stability and control under higher loads through the upper quadrant. You'll need an edge of counter or back of chair, no shirt for men and a sports bra for women, and a camera to record from the front and side.

To perform the incline push-up test, stand with feet together and hands on edge of counter, keeping body straight and at a 45-degree angle (figure 4.33a). Lengthening back of neck so face is in line with sternum, tip shoulder blades up by gently rolling clavicle slightly backward and the inferior angle (lowest part) of shoulder blades forward under armpits (figure 4.33b). Maintain this alignment as you perform 10 push-ups.

Take one video of 10 push-ups from the back and one from the side. Observed from back and sides, a perfect incline push-up looks like this:

- Face and sternum stay in line.
- Chest does not cave in or shoulder blades pinch together.
- Body stays straight with no bend in waist.
- Elbows bend down toward sides, not out away from body.

The multisegmental (high-load) tests identify the stability to control isolated segments of the body. These tests are of higher force and test you under high-load exercises. If you fail a test, continue the exercises (remedies) until you achieve ACES. Then move to the next stage.

FIGURE 4.33   Incline push-up test.

Corrective Exercises for Incline Push-Up Test, Cervical Segment

You pass the incline push-up test in the cervical segment if face and sternum stay in line with one another and ears stay in line with shoulders. You fail this test if head falls forward of sternum or chin juts forward.

To correct faults in the cervical segment, lie on back with knees bent and gently arch the small of your back. Push down through heels, lifting buttocks off floor one to two inches (2.5-5 cm) while keeping lower back arched. Very slowly and gently slide back of head on floor, lengthening back of neck and nodding chin down. Maintain this position as you lift head one or two inches (2.5-5 cm) off floor (figure 4.34). Focus on holding the lengthening of back of neck; do not let chin poke forward. You can lower buttocks after your head between each set. Refer to table 4.2 for number of sets and reps.

FIGURE 4.34 Corrective exercise 1 for incline push-up, cervical segment.

In the next exercise to correct faults in cervical segment, get down on floor on hands and knees with knees directly under hips and hands directly under shoulders (figure 4.35a). Put one hand out on floor in front, followed by other hand (figure 4.35b and 4.35c). Shift weight forward onto hands so hands are directly under shoulders again (figure 4.35b). Tip shoulder blades upward by gently rolling clavicle slightly backward and the inferior angle (lower part) of shoulder blades forward under armpits (figure 4.35c); let head hang down (figure 4.35d). Nod head by lifting base of skull toward top of head and lengthening back of neck. Slowly extend bottom of neck, trying to get ears back up in line with shoulders (figure 4.35e). Maintain lengthening of back of neck while keeping ears in line with shoulders. Refer to table 4.2 for the number of sets and reps.

FIGURE 4.35 Corrective exercise 2 for incline push-up, cervical segment.

Corrective Exercises for Incline Push-Up, Scapulohumeral Segment

You pass the incline push-up test for the scapulohumeral segment if shoulder blades stay in neutral position. You fail this test if shoulder blades shrug up toward ears, rotate downward, or pinch together.

To correct faults in the scapulohumeral segment, stand with feet together and body straight in a vertical line at arm's length from wall (figure 4.36*a*). Keep hands against wall at shoulder height and step backward one foot length. Tip shoulder blades upward by gently rolling clavicle slightly backward and the inferior angle of shoulder blades forward under armpits. Lower one arm down by side, keeping other arm straight out in front of shoulder (figure 4.36*b*). Keeping hand on wall, lower elbow to wall below palm (figure 4.36*c*) and push back up. Body should remain straight with no rotation or bend at waist. Refer to table 4.2 for number of sets and reps.

FIGURE 4.36 Corrective exercise 1 for incline push-up, scapulohumeral segment.

Corrective Exercises for Incline Push-Up, Thorax Segment

You pass the incline push-up test for the thorax segment if thoracic spine stays in neutral position. You fail this test if chest collapses forward or shoulder blades pinch together.

To correct faults in the thorax segment, stand with back against wall and feet together six to eight inches (15-20 cm) from wall with knees bent so they are directly over ankles (figure 4.37a). Tip shoulder blades upward by gently rolling clavicle slightly backward and the inferior angle of shoulder blades forward under armpits (figure 4.37b). You should feel shoulder blades flatten against wall. Lift arms out front so elbows are directly in front of shoulders and bent at 90 degrees, palms facing you; gently flatten lower back against wall (figure 4.37c). Slowly raise arms upward, palms still facing you and elbows in (figure 4.37d). Make sure to keep lower back flat and shoulder blades against wall. Refer to table 4.2 for number of sets and reps.

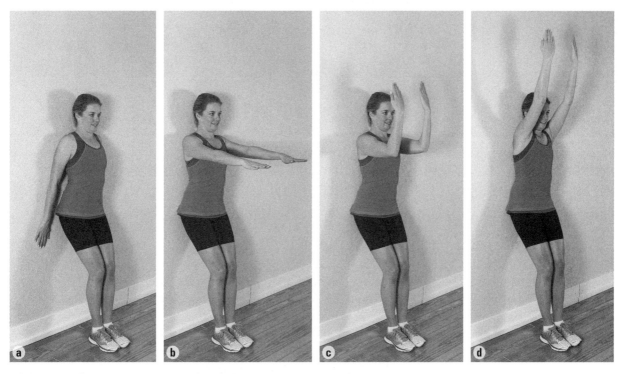

FIGURE 4.37   Corrective exercise 1 for incline push-up, thorax segment.

The next exercise to correct faults in the thorax segment is to lie on back with knees bent and feet flat on floor as you gently and slightly arch small of back and hold (figure 4.38*a*). Lift arms straight above shoulders and hold (figure 4.38*b*). Push down through heels and lift buttocks one to two inches (2.5-5 cm) off floor and hold. Curl head and neck up by squeezing bottom of sternum toward navel and reaching up with hands (figure 4.38*c*). Slowly lower. Make sure to keep lower back in a slightly arched position. Refer to table 4.2 for number of sets and reps.

FIGURE 4.38 Corrective exercise 2 for incline push-up, thorax segment.

Corrective Exercises for Incline Push-Up, Trunk Segment

You pass the incline push-up test for the trunk if lower back stays in neutral position. You fail this test if lower back arches forward or bends at waist.

To correct faults in the trunk segment, lie on back with knees bent and place hands behind lower back, palms down (figure 4.39a). Lift knees up, flexing hips to 90 degrees; gently flatten lower back into hands (figure 4.39b). Slowly lower feet to one to two inches (2.5-5 cm) above floor, keeping back flat against hands (figure 4.39c). Keeping lower back flat, extend knees out straight; feet remain one to two inches (2.5-5 cm) off floor. Return to starting position of knees bent, hips flexed to 90 degrees, and back flat. Refer to table 4.2 for number of sets and reps.

FIGURE 4.39 Corrective exercise 1 for incline push-up, trunk segment.

In this next exercise to correct faults in the trunk segment, stand with lower back in neutral position and lift arms overhead (figure 4.40a). Bending forward at hips maintain lower back in neutral position and knees straight (figure 4.40b). Rise back up to starting position. Refer to table 4.2 for number of sets and reps.

a   b

FIGURE 4.40 Corrective exercise 2 for incline push-up, trunk segment.

Group Training and the Triathlete

When you choose triathlon as your sport, you know you are choosing a lonely road. You will likely train many hours alone because your work, family, individual skills, and aspirations differ from those of most people you know. That said, many triathletes like to do some of their training with others. The social aspect makes training more pleasurable and tends to make you more accountable and demanding of yourself. Many elite athletes have told me that group training workouts were pivotal for them in preparing for competition. Professionally coached squads are the most sophisticated with much fewer differences in performance capacities. These are much more easily managed than teams, clubs, and groups of your friends. Group training can work well for swimming, cycling, and running when managed within an individual's training program and with the right mix of planning for volume, intensity, and flow. When training with others, a primary concern is not to let anyone influence your individual regimen. Your goals are your own, and you must train accordingly. But as long as you stick to your chosen path and retain your individual goals, group training can be beneficial.

- Yoga is a popular group activity among triathletes, but remember that some yoga positions place the body in high tension, with spinal compression at the joints. You can also develop excessive swelling of the face and neck caused by respiratory distress brought on by vigorous and complex yoga movements. Yoga has its benefits—relaxation, social connectedness, improved flexibility and stability, and movement enhancement—but if pain, particularly low-back pain, develops, be sure to seek medical care. If you have a history of low-back injury or pain, avoid the following positions:Static postures including prolonged positions of flexion, twisting, or lateral bends of the spine
- Intense torso and spine movements
- Movements that increase the compressive forces on the low back, such as repeated lumbar flexion

In all exercises, the key is to avoid inefficient movements or positions in posture and to improve or sustain normal movements that most effectively train, retrain, and enhance technique. The best way to do this is to begin by assessing functional movements in relation to normal ranges of flexibility and joint mobility and stability. If you cannot perform an exercise (or part of an exercise) that a coach or friend recommends (or that other triathletes are doing) without compromising your current functional capacity, then don't do the exercise. Train your areas of weakness as instructed in this book and then reassess function, before attempting the exercise again.

Whether training in a group or alone, make sure you have good knowledge and know your body's limits about which positions or exercises to include in your training and which to steer away from altogether.

For any body segment identified as failing during the testing, you must not only train that particular segment but also assess adjacent segments above and below that segment. For example, if your scapulohumeral segment fails a movement test, your cervical and thoracic segments must be assessed. In addition, if any end segment should fail (cervical or feet), you must test two segments above or below that segment. Because the global mobilizing muscles (producers of range of motion, power, and acceleration) responsible for movement cross over more than one joint and can affect stability at any joint that it overlaps, testing must be done at adjacent segments to any failed segment. For example, if the cervical segment fails a test, both the scapulohumeral and thoracic segments must be assessed. If your feet segment fails a test, both the femoral and pelvic segments must be assessed.

Individual movement and stability are at the nucleus of every part of this chapter in which functional movement, stability, and technique are indisputably connected to performance. All triathletes should be individually and comprehensively assessed so that their training is specific to their needs rather than generic. One of the central benefits of individual assessments is the discovery of individual differences in stability. At some point in competition, those weaknesses are exposed, resulting in less control and efficiency. Assessments can help you deliver the skill to make better movements.

5 Assessing and Strengthening the Core

Triathlon is a cadenced endurance sport requiring hundreds of thousands, if not millions, of movement repetitions in the extremities and torso. As you train, you experience ongoing stages of movement, adaptation, and skill learning as you progress toward advances in technique and fitness. Constant interplay occurs in the intricate and interrelated processing of movement, including cognitive skills (understanding what needs to be done), motor skills (executing the skills), functional movement (moving in full ranges of motion), and functional and stable performance (maintaining body posture through the core).

Stability of the core is crucial to optimal performance. Movements begin deep inside your core and are transferred to your extremities. Your core controls not only your spine to maintain alignment but also movements relative to your spine. A stable core enhances skill and efficiency and can limit recurring injury by reducing stress caused by movements working against each other.

Your core is your body's stabilization system. Every aspect of motor learning and skill development is enhanced by a stable core, including postural control, functional movement, limb coordination, muscle exertion to produce tension and force, and neuromuscular control.

Performance stability is your body's ability to maintain an even, balanced, and graceful posture during all movements. The best triathletes demonstrate precise and stable movement fully observable by the most untrained eyes. Your muscles must be stable and specifically trained to move efficiently. Functional movements connect to muscular stability and, when optimal, allow muscles to work in accordance with their structure and ability. Stability must be present on both sides of the body to provide a base for equal and balanced movements.

Stability increases your capacity for potential energy and the storage of elastic energy to further optimize movement. For example, while swimming, you load and unload with changing forces during the catch, insweep, and outsweep. In cycling, the pedaling and loading of muscles and corresponding structural stability are necessary when your hip extends during the downstroke. During the run, your muscles play a critical support role during the stance phase, without which stability would be impossible.

For many triathletes, the control and coordination of movements at some point become more accurate, more controlled, and even automatic. Others struggle with developing efficient movement patterns and have difficulty refining, adapting, and putting into practice the movements that are most efficient. In such cases, there's often an underlying instability in which muscles are weak or underactive, preventing normal motion and contributing to inflexibility in muscles and joints, which are very often exposed in competition as fatigue increases. The stronger your deeper-layered core, the more stable and effective technique can be. In this chapter we'll focus on assessing, strengthening, and training your core in ways that work the deepest stabilizers and postural muscles.

The Deeper Core: Triathlete's Performance Center

Think of your core as the epicenter of your body. It is a collection of muscles that support your spine, back, hips, and pelvis. Functional triathletes are especially stable from the deepest muscles of the core—the primary and secondary stabilizers. These deep core muscles are at the axis of motion, attach to the bony segments of the spine and joints, control

positioning of and provide stability and are made up of slow-twitch (type 1) muscle fibers for muscular endurance that fatigue slowly. They function at low loads and do not produce much, if any, force or torque for movement in swimming, cycling, or running, yet they play a vital role in controlling the positions of your joints. For the best transfer of load, your joints must be in optimal position for generating the highest amount of efficient energy for movement. Your deep core functions to hold your joints in neutral positions by responding with just the right amount of force during changes to posture caused by outside forces such as foot strikes while running, water pressure while swimming, and pedaling forces while cycling. See table 5.1 for a list of the core stabilizer and mobilizer muscles and table 5.2 for their characteristics.

Every level of triathlete can benefit from assessing functional capacity of the core and learning how to move from within the center

TABLE 5.1 Local and Global Stabilizer and Mobilizer Muscles of the Core

STABILIZERS		Mobilizers (global)
Primary (local)	Secondary (global)	
Multifidus	Gluteus maximus	Iliopsoas* Rectus femoris
Transversus abdominis	Quadriceps	Hamstrings
Internal oblique	Iliopsoas*	Tensor fasciae latae
Gluteus medius	Subscapularis	Hip adductors
Vastus medialis	Infraspinatus	Piriformis
Serratus anterior	Upper trapezius	Rectus abdominis External oblique Quadratus lumborum*
Lower trapezius	Quadratus lumborum*	Erector spinae
Deep neck flexors		Upper trapezius Levator scapulae
		Sternomastoid
		Scalenes
		Rhomboids
		Pectoralis minor
		Pectoralis major

*These muscles can work in multiple ways (secondary stabilizers or mobilizers).

TABLE 5.2   Characteristics of Core Stabilizers and Mobilizers

STABILIZERS		
Primary	• Deep, close to joint • Slow twitch • Usually monoarticular (one joint) • No significant torque • Short fibers	• Build tension slowly, more fatigue resistant • Better activated at low levels of resistance • More effective in closed-chain movement • In muscle imbalance tend to weaken and lengthen
Secondary	• Intermediate depth • Slow twitch • Usually monoarticular (one joint) • Primary source of torque • Attachments are multipennate (featherlike muscles)	
MOBILIZERS		
	• Superficial • Slow and fast twitch • Often biarticular (two joints) • Secondary source of torque	• Build tension rapidly, fatigue quickly • Better activated at high levels of resistance • More effective in open-chain movements • In muscle imbalance, tend to tighten and shorten

points of the body to the outside limbs most effectively. Talented triathletes of all ages tend to demonstrate balanced and symmetrical movements with sureness. These efficient motions are accomplished through years of training and further enhanced by training the deep-layered muscles of the core. But training these deep-core muscles—chiefly, the transversus abdominis, multifidi, and quadratus lumborum—is far different from common high-intensity core exercise training. These muscles are not trained through intense workouts but through controlled deep-layered techniques and body-region-specific exercises.

The most efficient athletic movements are those that originate from the center of the body. As a triathlete develops more efficient skills, energy expenditure is minimized as movements consolidate. Early on, however, if limitations in flexibility, mobility, and stability are ignored, movements can remain error prone, sometimes stiff and halting, and there can be an unnecessary and inefficient use of

the extremities. Asymmetrical motions can produce compensations not only in functional movements but within the stabilizing muscles of the core.

A fitting expression among physical therapists and movement practitioners is that proximal stability enhances distal mobility. The core (stability center) provides the most effective way to transmit energy to the limbs (from inside to outside). For example, instead of pulling, the capable swimmer will anchor the hand and arm (slowly) and engage and transfer power from the centerline (spine, pelvis, and hips) through the hand and arm holding (sculling) against dense water. An efficient cyclist similarly works from inside to out by maintaining a level pelvis, straight spine, and limited swinging or tilting in the upper body. The triathlete runner above all depends on core stability and posture and position of the upper back and scapulae to provide ample support of the body during the exchange of foot strikes.

Hollowing Maneuver

As a triathlete, when you swim, bike, and run, you anticipate movements of your arms and legs and respond by stabilizing your spine and pelvis in many directions of movement. Studies have shown the transversus abdominis precedes the movement of the arms and legs between 30 and 100 milliseconds for individuals with normal core function. For all of the exercises in this chapter, the transversus abdominis is activated by the hollowing maneuver to establish the pelvic floor muscle function and training this pivotal deep core muscle.

Research demonstrates that the hollowing technique is best for coactivating the deep-core stabilizers. Once you learn it, you can activate the technique in all of the exercise positions (lying, sitting, or standing) in this chapter and when swimming, cycling, and running. Keep in mind that the transversus abdominis encircles the trunk and, once activated, the waistline draws inward and tension is felt.

Here we describe the starting point for setting the transversus abdominis and training the multifidi. Progress and practice slowly, performing the motion in sequences. As with any technique or stability exercise, you will build the motor patterns progressively until you have the endurance to maintain the position or technique.

To perform the hollowing maneuver, lie on your back with knees somewhat flexed. Feet and heels are on the floor with toes relaxed and hands under pelvis (figure 5.1). Raise hips off floor momentarily and, with no changes in your low-back posture, lower the hips to the floor (this establishes your natural and neutral posture—do not flatten your back to the floor). Breathe in and breathe out several times and while holding the breath out, gently draw your navel in toward your spine (no movement in the spine), keeping your back neutral. There should be minimal or no movement of the pelvis, no flaring or lifting of the rib cage, and no bulging (distention) of the abdominal wall. You will feel tension in your central abdomen and a hollowing along each side of the navel, but you should be able to speak. There should be no increased pressure on your heels. Under control, continue drawing in your navel as far as you can, breathing all air out and pulling in toward the back, with no movement in the spine. Hold for 10 seconds; perform 10 repetitions. Note that this maneuver can be done while standing, with one palm across your lower abdomen and the back of the opposite hand across your lower back. Your palm on your belly will draw in alongside the hollow areas on both sides of your navel as you exhale. The hand on the back does not move or feel any pressure change. Draw in as you exhale, and hold this posture as you breathe out and continue to hollow out the lower abdomen with no lower-back or spine movements.

FIGURE 5.1 Hollowing maneuver.

Thus, training the underlying deeply placed core muscles is not accomplished through high-intensity core strength workouts and training systems. Rather, the stability and control of position in the joints are the initial and primary focus for building the foundation of better technique. During movements, experienced triathletes generate force from inside the body (the core) to the extremities (limbs). Beginning or less stable triathletes (at any level) might tend to move in the opposite manner (from outside in). When this occurs, movements are less forceful, appear uncoordinated, and require more energy over time to sustain. Elite and Olympic triathlon coach Darren Smith of Australia explains, "Triathletes with nonswimming backgrounds must learn how to stabilize the body through swiveling and a pivoting of the hips in connection with the placement of the hand in dense, still water. Our triathletes learn how to improve the activation of the core by swimming with bands holding the ankles together. If the athlete uses the arms only, they will sink. The athlete must learn to connect the hips and thus, the core." With enhanced stability at the deep core, you gain the ability to accomplish, maintain, and preserve posture and thus to apply better technique. Core stability at the local level can greatly enhance your capability to achieve maximal stability for longer periods of time and reduce injury caused by movement compensation as a result of an unstable core and postural muscles. Again, high-intensity core training works the superficial muscles and not the deep-layered stabilizers. Those are the most important for triathletes to concentrate on.

Dynamic Posture

The upper and lower extremities can contract, accelerate, and decelerate in a graceful display of motion. The more stable the proximal (center) core musculature, the more efficient the distal (away from the center) body movements of the extremities (arms, legs, and head). Triathletes and Ironman world champions Mirinda Carfrae and Chrissie Wellington are superb examples of core stability (neutral

spine and pelvic control) when running. A stable triathlete is balanced, and the displays of force are moving the body forward with extraordinary proficiency. Gravity gives the impression of abandonment as the runner floats horizontally forward with exceptional running motion. Propulsion is remarkably functional, powerful, and stable at each stride. For example, observe the pelvis and hips of a runner with an imagined box or rectangle providing an indication of core stability. With the upper parts of the box over the pelvis, a neutral (normal) pelvis and hips remain level and inside the box (figure 5.2). Excessive rotation of turning motions, forward tilting (accompanied by low-back arching), and elevation of the hip are movement compensations signaling lack of control in the pelvic, hip, and lumbar spine segments.

At the joint level, the body moves along several planes simultaneously—all functional movements are in three dimensions. The pelvis, for example, is the central nexus between the spine and the lower extremities. For the triathlete, stability is vital for posture, force, power generation, and the positions that make up efficient technique. The goal

FIGURE 5.2   Triathlete with a neutral pelvis.

CHRISSIE WELLINGTON Being a Champion

In my view, you don't actually become a champion. You act like one—adopting the behaviors and habits of a champion on a daily basis. Put another way, it's the manner in which you try to achieve your potential that makes you a champion, not the outcome. So what are the key strategies for success in triathlon?

Have a Clear and Realistic Yet Ambitious Goal

Success is a decision, not a gift. So decide what you want and, even more important, why you want it. You need to know where it is you are heading. Otherwise training becomes unfocused and unsatisfying. Ask yourself, "What *is* my dream?" Yes, you might be scared and worried about failing or not being able to remove your wetsuit, but face those fears. Champions try. So have an ambitious, yet realistic, vision that inspires and excites you. Focus on it. Don't spread yourself too thinly by trying to do too much. Then document and communicate it. Make the goal *real*—tape a note on your front door, type it in as your screensaver, go public with it on social media, whatever it takes to put the goal in front of you and make it your own.

You also need to know *why* you want to achieve the goal. For instance, your goal might be to complete your first half Ironman, and the reasons you want to do it might be to improve your health, meet new people, prove to yourself that you can meet the challenge, and raise money for charity. You must be passionate, excited, and energized about your goal and the reasons behind it rather than doing something because you feel you ought to or because your friends are. When my motivation wanes, I keep my goal and my reason for it forefront in mind, and I know that each session is a step closer to achieving it.

Set Smaller Tasks (Stepping-Stone Goals)

It was important for me to have smaller, transitional goals to make the long-term goal seem less overwhelming and to ensure I enjoyed the journey. These stepping stones might be difficult training sessions, or B races en route to my big A race. I also applied the same principle to individual sessions and races, dividing them into smaller, manageable segments. If I had a big swim workout (e.g., 40 × 100 m), I focused on the first 5 × 100s. I never thought about the next 35. Plus, at around the two-minute mark, your cells more easily use oxygen as a fuel, muscle temperature rises, and exercise becomes easier.

During Kona 2011 I got through the race by mentally breaking the race down into stages—the next swim buoy, the next aid station, or even the next step forward. I promised myself that once I reached a certain point I could either stop or keep going. Giving my brain the reward of having completed these smaller goals created positive momentum. (And the answer is *always* keep going!)

Aspire to Greatness

Mediocrity is a choice. Excellence is a choice. Seeking excellence in every part of your life is a conscious decision. My goal was always to be the best I could be. That goal—and that decision never to settle for mediocrity in effort—is what drove me every day.

Create a Strategy or Practical Plan

You need a detailed and focused plan to give you direction and structure and to help prevent procrastination. My plan had to be realistic and tailored to *me* and was focused as much on my weaknesses as on my strengths. Every action required a goal. Nothing was done without a reason. I also viewed training holistically. My schedule comprised swim-bike-run sessions, nutrition, strength and conditioning, massage, and relaxation. In this sense, I trained 24/7. That is, I focused each minute, hour, and day on training my body to be the best it could be.

Developing my plan also required knowledge and information about different training methods, nutrition, my competitors, race courses, and so forth. I took responsibility for learning about my sport and everything associated with optimizing performance.

Be Prepared to Be Flexible, Adapt, and Take Risks

If you risk nothing, you risk everything. It's easy when you're at the top to rest on your laurels. But where is the challenge? For me, it wasn't simply about winning—it was about being the best I could be. Striving for outperforming myself, not just for first place. This meant being prepared to assess, adapt, and evolve, and to take calculated risks. As a structured, regimented person, I had a hard time embracing change; but I had to refine my physical, technical, tactical, and mental skills to stay ahead of the game. This might mean trying a new coach, a new training location, or a new technique. If you always do what you've always done, you get what you've always got. This doesn't mean blindly adopting every new innovation—sometimes simple, time-honored techniques are best—but the key is be prepared to take small risks for large gains.

It was also important for me to inject different workouts and equipment into my schedule every once in a while. It might sound oxymoronic, but motivational malaise can strike when the regimen becomes too regimented. Slight changes and adaptations kept me physically and mentally fresh and stopped me from getting stuck in a routine rut.

Create a Supportive Environment

It's important that your training environments support your plan, such as a gym, track, and pool that are convenient and financially affordable in the long term. As an amateur, I kept my running clothes at the office so I could do a quick session on my lunch hour. I also biked to work to get bang for my commuting buck. As a pro, I needed to optimize the conditions for performance—being in the same town as my coach and with good training partners, being close to a main airport to limit travel time, living at altitude or in a place with varied and safe roads to cycle on. We can all make slight changes to our environment to help us be the best we can be.

Use Motivational Media

I used various tools to motivate myself. These included a playlist of songs that were guaranteed to get me jumping, moving and grooving during sessions and before races. I carried a dog-eared copy of Rudyard Kipling's *If* with me everywhere and even wrote the words on my race water bottles. I used to watch uplifting movies or YouTube clips of others overcoming huge hurdles to achieve their dreams—a quick peek at Kona DVDs the night before a race never failed to get my blood pumping!

Keep a Log

I always kept a training log. I made sure I highlighted any accomplishments and successes, noted my reaction and emotions, and celebrated getting up and over little

> continued

> *continued*

milestones. Whenever I found my motivation flagging, I looked at that book and recalled difficult times when I had struggled but overcame lethargy, tiredness, and discomfort. I knew that if I had jumped over those hurdles in the past I could do it again.

Learn to Lean on Others

Triathlon is an individual sport, but we never get to the start line alone. It was hard for me, as a fiercely independent person, to lean on others, but I couldn't have achieved what I did without technical, physical, financial, and emotional support from outside. For me, this support came from my coach, family, training partners, massage therapist, local tri club, sponsors, the media, and even my competitors. The word *competitor* is taken from a Latin root meaning "to seek together"—and with the help of my competitors I learned to dig deeper and discover reserves I never knew existed. As a champion, your path to success is paved with so many more hands than just your own.

See the Positives and Banish Negativity

The only thing certain in triathlon is that things rarely go exactly as planned. I have sunk in the swim, had bike mechanicals, catapulted over crash barriers, relieved my GI tract in bushes. I came in sixth in a race and was devastated. I've been injured. I didn't start the World Championships in 2010 because I got sick. I crashed two weeks before the World Championships in 2011 and didn't even think I could start the race. It's these kinds of mishaps and mistakes that help us learn, become slightly wiser, slightly

is to maintain a neutral alignment to reduce or eliminate excessive shifting, lateral tilt, or rotation in the pelvis. Many of these traits can be observed through assessment and to some extent can be seen as a triathlete swims, bikes, and runs.

To maintain optimal functionality in technique, the muscles of the core are constantly challenged. Functioning normally, the stability system of the core provides the support to meet the demands of training and competition and the various postures in swimming, cycling, and running. When operating optimally, the deeper core reduces the size of the neutral range of motion by an increase in the stiffness in the muscles. The purpose is to preserve equilibrium for each movement during swimming, cycling, and running. The beginning process of assessment is looking closely at posture alignment. A triathlete's muscular balance affects posture, alignment, and performance and can lead to recurring injuries caused by misalignment. Faults in alignments also cause excessive stress and strain to the bones, joints, ligaments, and

muscles. By assessing the position of joints, it can be determined which areas are in balance and which are imbalanced because of tight, restricted, inflexible muscles or weak, overactive muscles.

Core Assessment and Exercises

Assessing your core helps you confirm that the muscles that control the positions in your joints are working effectively. The stability of your spine and pelvis is most important for maintaining a functional body position as you swim, bike, and run. These movements are connected with every one of your body's segments; the lack of functional control or stability in one segment can produce compensations in technique that compromise movement and cause injury.

As we have learned in previous chapters, the ACES (accurate, controlled, effortless, smooth) system simplifies the self-progression of exercises. Some of the regions of your core will need more or less training than others to achieve normal function. Each of the exercises

stronger, slightly bolder, and much more determined. Champions are patient, resilient, and tenacious. They view obstacles as opportunities to scale new heights. They know that perfection is the ability to overcome imperfections perfectly.

Sometimes I had to recognize negative self-talk and consciously replace the thoughts with positive affirmations. "This is too hard" and "I am too tired" were replaced by "I am strong. I *can* be an Ironman!" I had a mantra to repeat ad infinitum: *Never ever give up.* I wrote these words on my race wristband and water bottles. I also spent time on visualization, picturing myself training and racing, imagining myself as strong, confident, and successful, seeing myself cross the line, hearing the roar of the crowds, falling into the arms of loved ones, overjoyed with the feeling of accomplishment. You are only as powerful as your mind, and I used my mind to give me the confidence to overcome hurdles and achieve more success than I ever dreamed of.

I'll finish with a few important Ps: The first P is perspective. Champions retain it. Win, lose, or sink, triathlon shouldn't define you. Never wed your emotions to a specific outcome. The journey is what matters. If you have given it your all, then you've already won. Last but not least are positivity and passion. Champions exude these. Not all the time, admittedly. On occasion, even the most cup-overflowing individuals get down in the dumps. But an ability to trade *I can't* for *I can,* to believe in yourself and all that you are, is what makes you a true champion.

that follow must be performed as accurately as possible while maintaining control throughout the range of motion. There might be a degree of muscular challenge, depending on your level of fitness in each region, but all movements should be accurate, controlled, effortless, and smooth.

Using ACES as a means of assessment, stage 1 assesses each exercise for stability and competency. At each of the subsequent stages, you must achieve ACES before progressing to the next stage (table 5.3). Once you have reached the fourth stage, continue to do the exercises once or twice a week for maintenance.

Transversus Abdominis (TrA)

The TrA is a flat abdominal muscle that gets its name from the way its fibers pass horizontally across the abdomen. The deepest of the abdominal muscles, the TrA works to create tension that makes for a girdle-like support around the abdomen and lumbar spinal column. This stabilizing muscle has a deep-layered and far-reaching mechanism for supporting the body. It is the only abdominal muscle active in the abdomen during both flexion and extension. The TrA is also an anticipatory muscle that coordinates with

TABLE 5.3 Self-Progression Exercise Training for the Core

ACES progression stage	Sets and reps	Sessions per week
Stage 1	1 set of 10	Testing level
Stage 2	3 sets of 10 reps	4-5 (adaptation phase)
Stage 3	2 sets of 15 reps	3 (absorption phase)
Stage 4	1 set of 30 reps	1-2 (maintenance phase)

respiration during exercise. This highly unique muscle is the first active muscle preceding the movement of the limbs. In effect, the central nervous system signals activation of the TrA to stabilize the spine in anticipation of forces and movement.

Signs of weakness in the transversus abdominis are

- an extension (distension) of the abdomen when standing and
- an increased lordosis curve (low back arches).

As described earlier in the chapter, the hollowing method is an effective way to produce and activate the TrA when training. Studies show that a weak TrA functions with delayed activation in individuals with back pain. This might indicate less stability during movement (less anticipation by the TrA). Studies document that training this muscle for posture control and stability can provide relief for patients with back pain. The key as a triathlete is how the TrA supports spine stability when swimming, cycling, or running. Arm and leg motion functioning about a stable and adequately strong spine and pelvis can improve performance. Training the TrA is a primary exercise and can lead to long-term enhancement in movement efficiency.

Testing TrA Stability

Test the stability of your transversus abdominis with this quick self-test. Lie on your back with knees bent and both feet on the floor. Place fingertips of both hands on the iliac crest (tip of pelvis on both sides) and relax spine so it's neither arched nor flattened against the floor (figure 5.3a). Breathe out slowly while at the same time drawing your navel inward and lifting one foot off the floor (figure 5.3b). Repeat on the opposite leg.

A strong, stable TrA has the following characteristics:

- The pelvis on either side does not move in any direction.
- The back does not flatten.
- The back does not arch.

FIGURE 5.3 Transversus abdominis self-test.

Transversus Abdominis Exercises

Exercises for the transversus abdominis result in these benefits:

- Improved stabilization of the spine and pelvis during movement of the arms and legs
- Improved ability to maintain a neutral spine and pelvis

- Improved rotation
- Improved isometric stability of the TrA, external obliques, and rectus abdominis
- Improved ability to move the lower extremity without moving the pelvis or spine

See table 5.3 for the progression of sets and reps. Once you have achieved ACES at one stage, move to the next stage.

Transversus Abdominis Leg Flexion and Extension With Supported Foot

Lying on your back, bend hips and knees with feet on floor; place left hand on the outside of the abdomen between pelvis and ribs. Contract abdominal muscles by pulling navel toward spine (hold this position throughout the exercise). Lift and hold right knee at chest using right hand (figure 5.4*a*). Lift left foot off floor by extending lower leg (figure 5.4*b*); hold for one or two breaths. Lower foot, maintaining abdominal contraction. Return right leg to starting position and repeat with other leg. Refer to table 5.3 for number of sets and reps.

a

b

FIGURE 5.4 Transversus abdominis leg flexion and extension with supported foot.

Transversus Abdominis Leg Flexion and Extension With Unsupported Foot

Lying on back, bend hips and knees with feet on floor. Place fingers of both hands on the outside of abdomen between pelvis and ribs. Contract abdominal muscles by pulling navel toward spine (hold this position throughout the exercise). Lift right foot 90 degrees off floor toward chest (figure 5.5*a*). Lift left foot off floor by extending lower leg without moving back or pelvis (figure 5.5*b*); hold for one or two breaths. Return left foot to floor. Return right leg to starting position and repeat with other leg. Refer to table 5.3 for number of sets and reps.

a

b

FIGURE 5.5 Transversus abdominis leg flexion and extension with unsupported foot.

Transversus Abdominis Bilateral Hip and Knee Flexion and Extension With Unsupported Foot

Lie on back with legs and hips straight. Place fingers of both hands on outside of abdomen between pelvis and ribs. Contract abdominal muscles by pulling navel toward spine (hold this position throughout the exercise). Lift both feet off floor so knees are flexed 90 degrees (figure 5.6a). Extend knees and lower legs (figure 5.6b); hold for one or two breaths. Lower legs to starting position. Refer to table 5.3 for number of sets and reps.

FIGURE 5.6 Transversus abdominis bilateral hip and knee flexion and extension with unsupported foot.

Gluteus Medius

The gluteus medius (GM) is a hip abductor that controls lateral pelvic tilt. With a loss of stability in the GM, the hip on the weak side shifts and loses steadiness. It is perhaps the most important muscle for pelvic stabilization and body control while swimming, cycling, and running. This muscle stabilizes the triathlete during weight bearing (e.g., running stance phase and the pedaling downstroke). Insufficient stability or strength affects alignment of the lower legs and joints and can cause recurring injury.

The primary role of the GM is to stabilize and control hip position and the transfer of forces from the lower extremity through the pelvis and to the upper extremities. This alone is ample motivation for triathletes to maintain stability of the GM and all muscles of the hip, including the gluteus maximus. An underactive and weak GM will cause an athlete to compensate for instability with irregular movements in technique. Signs of weakness in the gluteus medius are

- lateral pelvic tilting (on the side with tightness or weakness),
- limping or rocking to the weight-bearing side when walking or running, and
- trunk lean toward the side of weakness (shifting center of gravity for balance).

You need a neutral pelvis for efficient swimming, cycling, and running. In swimming, a neutral pelvis allows you to maintain the centerline (head, sternum, pelvis) of your body during each stroke. A stable core and GM help to deliver a narrow, streamlined, core-driven, and energy-efficient stroke as force transfers from the core to the limbs. In cycling, the GM will increase the stability of your pelvis on the saddle and assist in force transfer to the pedals. This steadiness transfers energy from your hip through the center of your knee onto the second toe of your foot and to the pedal. In running, you'll achieve best energy transfer with your GM stabilizing your pelvis, especially during single-limb foot strikes, midstance, and push-off.

Testing Gluteus Medius Stability

Test the stability of your gluteus medius with this quick self-test. Stand on one leg by lifting opposite foot (facing back) off floor (figure 5.7). If your GM (hip abductor) is strong, your pelvis will remain level. If your GM lacks strength, the iliac crest of your nonstanding leg will lower.

Gluteus Medius Exercises

Exercises for the gluteus medius will result in these benefits:

- Improved hip abductor and gluteus medius muscle performance and stability
- Improved hip extensor muscles (gluteus maximus and hamstring muscles)
- Improved hip adductor muscles (mid- and inner-thigh adductors magnus, brevis and longus, pectineus, gracilis)
- Improved stretch in the hip abductor muscles (tensor fascia latae, iliotibial band)
- Improved performance of the lateral abdominal muscles

See table 5.3 for progression of sets and reps. Once you have achieved ACES at one stage, move to the next stage.

FIGURE 5.7 Gluteus medius stability self-test.

Gluteus Medius Face-Lying Lateral Abduction

Lie face down with a pillow under your abdomen, legs straight and close together, and toes pointed. Place fingers on bones under pelvis to monitor movement (figure 5.8a). Contract abdominal muscles by pulling navel toward spine (hold this position throughout the exercise). Contract buttocks and slowly slide right leg out to side as far as possible without any pelvis or spine movement (figure 5.8b). Return leg slowly to starting position; repeat on other side. Refer to table 5.3 for number of sets and reps.

FIGURE 5.8   Gluteus medius face-lying lateral abduction.

Gluteus Medius Side-Lying Lateral Leg Abduction

Lie on side with legs and feet together; rotate pelvis slightly forward. Place hand on hip or on gluteus medius to make sure hip remains motionless during the entire exercise. Contract abdominal muscles by pulling navel toward spine (hold this position throughout the exercise). Lift top leg upward and slightly backward so leg and heel are slightly behind body (figure 5.9). Do not let pelvis move or back arch when lifting. Return leg to starting position; repeat on other side. Refer to table 5.3 for number of sets and reps.

FIGURE 5.9   Gluteus medius side-lying lateral leg abduction.

Gluteus Medius Side-Lying Hip Abduction

Lie on side with knees together and slightly flexed; place a pillow between ankles to separate heels (figure 5.10a). Slowly rotate top knee up from hip (figure 5.10b). Do not let pelvis move or back arch when lifting. Return leg to starting position; repeat on other side. Refer to table 5.3 for number of sets and reps.

FIGURE 5.10 Gluteus medius side-lying hip abduction.

Multifidus

One of the most important stabilizers of the spine, the multifidus is key in controlling position and stiffness of the spine. This very thin muscle is the deepest-layered muscle of the back. The multifidus plays an important role in preserving posture in swimming, cycling, and running.

The multifidus attaches at the sacrum, the triangular bone at the base of the spine that joins the hip bones forming the pelvis. The multifidus fills the grooves on the sides of the lower vertebrae and functions to extend, rotate, and laterally bend the spine. Signs of weakness in the multifidus include chronic low-back pain and lumbar or thoracic kyphosis (arched low back and rounded upper spine).

Testing Multifidus Stability

Test the stability of your multifidus with this quick self-test. Lie face down with a small pillow under your lower abdomen. Breathe normally and maintain maximum cervical flexion (flexed neck) and gluteal muscle contraction (for pelvic stabilization) while holding sternum off the floor (see figure 5.11). Termi-

nate the test if you cannot keep your sternum off the floor, if you have pain, or after two minutes (for females) or three minutes (for males). If you held the contracted position for two minutes (for females) or three minutes (for males), your multifidus is stable and strong. Holding the contracted position for under 90 seconds (for males) or under 60 seconds (for females) indicates a weak, unstable multifidus with likely accompanying low-back pain.

Multifidus Exercises

Exercises for the multifidus result in these benefits:

- Improved stability and activation in back extensors
- Improved bracing of the abdominals and a neutral spine
- Improved control of maintaining neutral joint positions
- Improved performance of the abdominal muscles
- Improved control of the spine by preventing rotation
- Improved balance control
- Improved ability to control the pelvis
- Improved lateral bending and extension

See table 5.3 for the progression of sets and reps. Once you have achieved ACES at one stage, move to the next stage.

FIGURE 5.11 Multifidus stability self-test.

Multifidus Quadruped Hip Extension With Knee Flexion

Get on hands and knees with spine straight and head aligned with spine. Shoulders are over hands; hips are centered over knees (figure 5.12a). Rotate the scapula down toward the hips and keep the clavicle back and level. Keep abdominals drawn in (navel pulled toward spine) throughout the exercise. The pelvis and spine do not move at any time. Keeping knee bent 90 degrees, lift one leg from hip up and backward (figure 5.12b). Hold flexed knee for 10 seconds; return to starting position. Repeat with other leg. Refer to table 5.3 for number of sets and reps.

a

b

FIGURE 5.12 Multifidus quadruped hip extension with knee flexion.

Multifidus Quadruped Hip and Knee Extension

Get on hands and knees with spine straight and head aligned with spine. Shoulders are over hands; hips are centered over knees (figure 5.13a). Rotate the scapula down toward the hips and keep the clavicle back and level. Keep abdominals drawn in (navel pulled toward spine) throughout the exercise. The pelvis and spine do not move at any time. Lift one leg back from the hip, keeping leg and hip straight (figure 5.13b). Hold flexed knee for 10 seconds; return to starting position. Repeat with other leg. Refer to table 5.3 for number of sets and reps.

a

b

FIGURE 5.13 Multifidus quadruped hip and knee extension.

Multifidus Quadruped Hip-Knee Extension With Shoulder Flexion

Get on hands and knees with spine straight and head aligned with spine. Shoulders are over hands; hips are centered over knees. Keep abdominals drawn in (navel pulled toward spine) throughout the exercise. Rotate the scapula down toward the hips and keep the clavicle back and level. The pelvis and spine do not move at any time. Lift one arm and opposite leg at the same time (figure 5.14). Lift from the hip (keep leg, hip, and arm straight). Hold flexed knee for 10 seconds; return to starting position. Repeat with other leg. Refer to table 5.3 for number of sets and reps.

FIGURE 5.14 Multifidus quadruped hip-knee extension with shoulder flexion.

Quadratus Lumborum

Another important muscle for spine stability is the quadratus lumborum (QL). From the rib of the thoracic spine (T12) to lumbar and iliac crest (L3) of the pelvis, this muscle attaches to each of the lumbar vertebrae and is particularly effective in managing load and stress on the pelvis and spine.

Think of this muscle as reinforcement for many movements in triathlon. Triathletes move in many planes of motion, and this muscle predominantly stabilizes movements of flexion, extension, and bending to the sides. The QL is not a particularly large muscle—much smaller than the back extensors—and its role in spine stabilization results from where it is attached to the spine. The QL muscle is often overtaxed by intense core exercises or yoga stretches, especially in the presence of instability, hypermobility, or joint immobility. Such training can be a formula for low-back pain, injury, and increased instability and overstretched muscles that reduce the forces the muscles can generate. Thus training the stability of the QL is crucial for all triathletes.

The QL is optimally positioned to provide control of lateral flexion and rotation. The key is the QL's ability to provide control during the return to neutral positioning. Being able to maintain control of the spine and pelvis and the interrelationships during movement prevents stress caused by instability and reduces compensating motions in technique.

Signs of weakness in the quadratus lumborum include the following:

- Low-back pain
- Sacroiliac joint instability caused by weakness in the QL or abnormal movement in the joint
- Irregular frontal gait in which feet flatten, toes turn in or out, knees move inward, and pelvic rotation is excessive at heel strikes

Testing Quadratus Lumborum Stability

Test the stability of your quadratus lumborum with this quick self-test. Lie on your side with legs extended and foot of the top leg in front of lower foot. Support body on one elbow and feet so that hips are off floor and body is straight along its entire length (figure 5.15). Hold opposite arm across chest, placed on support arm's shoulder. Hold this position until straight posture or hips return to the floor. Repeat on the other side. Try for 90 seconds on each side.

FIGURE 5.15   Quadratus lumborum self-test.

Quadratus Lumborum Exercises

Exercises for the quadratus lumborum result in these benefits:

- Improved control and balance in pelvis
- Improved stability in the abdominal muscles
- Improved control of the spine to lessen rotation
- Improved ability to elevate pelvis, extend spine, and control the stability of lateral bending of the lumbar spine

See table 5.3 for the progression of sets and reps. Once you have achieved ACES at one stage, move to the next stage.

Quadratus Lumborum Side-Lying Bridge With Flexed Knees

Lie on side with body propped on elbow for support; spine and torso are aligned with back of head. With feet stacked, flex knees 90 degrees. Place free hand on opposite shoulder to stabilize it or along the side of body to add more load to the bridge. Contract (draw in) the abdominals throughout the exercise. Raise hips off floor (figure 5.16). Hold for number of breaths according to your stage. Refer to table 5.3 for number of sets and reps.

FIGURE 5.16   Quadratus lumborum side-lying bridge with flexed knees.

Quadratus Lumborum Side-Lying Bridge With Rotation

Lie on side with body propped on elbow for support (or on the hand, for increased difficulty). Spine and torso align with back of head. Foot of upper leg is in front of the underneath support leg. Raise hips off floor and place free hand on opposite shoulder to stabilize it (figure 5.17a) or alongside of the body to add more load to the bridge. Contract (draw in) the abdominals throughout the exercise. Maintaining alignment, slowly rotate upper shoulder by rolling torso toward floor to strengthen front and back abdominals (figure 5.17b). Transfer weight on to both elbows (or hands) with body face down. Slowly rotate to opposite side, ending in starting position. Hold for number of breaths according to your stage. Refer to table 5.3 for number of sets and reps.

a

b

FIGURE 5.17   Quadratus lumborum side-lying bridge with rotation.

External and Internal Obliques

The external obliques (EO) are the largest abdominal muscle, curving around the lateral and front sides of the ribs. This muscles flex the trunk, control or prevent forward pelvic tilt, elevate the pelvis, and rotate the torso. They are also important accessory muscles during expiration and elevate the diaphragm muscle. The internal obliques (IO) are the upper-abdominal muscles; they are smaller and thinner than the EO and lie under the lateral wall of the abdomen. The IO primarily flex the spine but also assist in lateral bending, rotation, and elevation of the pelvis. They are also active during expiration and for the elevation of the diaphragm muscle. The IO are commonly exercised abdominal muscles (via trunk curls or sit-up crunches with legs extended), which can cause overtraining in the IO and rectus abdominis, leading to muscular imbalance (shortening) in the EO.

In both the EO and the IO, moderate weakness decreases the efficiency of respiration (forced exhalation). With weakness on both sides of the external obliques there can be forward tilting in the pelvis. And when tightness of EO and IO is present there can be a swayback posture with pelvis tilting forward and thorax (area between neck and abdomen) positioned back.

The obliques together with the transversus abdominis control and contain the entire abdomen and thus are important for spine stability for triathletes.

Signs of weakness in the external and internal obliques include swayback posture and posterior pelvic tilt.

Testing External and Internal Oblique Stability

Test the stability of the external and internal obliques with this quick self-test. Lie on back with knees and feet extended; place fingertips behind the ears, lightly touching. Perform a

FIGURE 5.18   External and internal oblique self-test.

sit-up with trunk, neck, and head aligned and elbows pointed away from body (figure 5.18). Common signs of weakness are a curled trunk, arched back, flexed head, and elbows pointed toward feet.

Exercises for External and Internal Obliques

Exercises for the external and internal obliques result in these benefits:

- Improved respiration and support of abdominal intestines
- Improved rotation stability of the vertebrae
- Improved elevation of the pelvis (neutral stabilization)
- Improved control of flexion of the trunk and spine
- Improved control of posterior pelvic tilt during movement of the lower extremity (reducing compensations in movement)

See table 5.3 for the progression of sets and reps. Once you have achieved ACES at one stage, move to the next stage.

Oblique Feet Slide to Extension With Single Flexion

Lie on back with feet on floor. Place fingertips of both hands on iliac crest (figure 5.19*a*). Contract (draw in) abdominals throughout the exercise. Slide both feet and heels along the smooth surface of the floor to full extension while contracting abdominal muscles (figure 5.19*b*). Return one knee to chest, holding knee lightly. Lift opposite foot off floor and hold for 10 to 15 seconds (figure 5.19*c*). Repeat 3 × 30 seconds or 1 × 90 seconds on each side. Refer to table 5.3 for number of sets and reps.

FIGURE 5.19 Oblique feet slide to extension with single flexion.

Oblique Feet Slide to Extension With 90-Degree Flexed Knees

Lie on back with legs extended. Place fingertips of both hands on iliac crest (figure 5.20*a*). Contract (draw in) abdominals throughout the exercise (maintain a fixed position of the lumbar spine). Slowly flex hips and knees and slide heels on floor while contracting abdominal muscles (figure 5.20*b*). Lift knees toward chest and pause (figure 5.20*c*). Lower feet to floor and slide feet to starting position. Refer to table 5.3 for number of sets and reps.

FIGURE 5.20 Oblique feet slide to extension with 90-degree flexed knees.

Oblique Bilateral 90-Degree Knee Flexion With Feet Slide

Lie on back with legs extended while contracting (drawing in) abdominals. Abdominals remain contracted throughout the exercise. Place fingertips of both hands on iliac crest (figure 5.21*a*). Slide heels on floor, flexing hips and knees until feet are flat (figure 5.21*b*). Slowly flex hips and knees and lift heels off floor (figure 5.21*c*). Lift knees to 90 degrees and pause (figure 5.21*d*). Lower feet to floor and slide feet to extension. Refer to table 5.3 for number of sets and reps.

FIGURE 5.21 Oblique bilateral 90-degree knee flexion with feet slide.

Serratus Anterior

When the arm is elevated overhead, as in the full extension of the swimming stroke, the serratus anterior (SA) works with the trapezius to rotate the scapula upward. The SA is one of the most important muscles for shoulder and upper-back stability. Constantly firing during the underwater stroke phase and from beginning to end of recovery, the SA sustains position of the scapula. This muscle's stability is of central importance for the triathlete not just in swimming but also in cycling and running because it assists in preserving a flat back and functional posture.

Signs of weakness in the serratus anterior include the following:

- Winging of the scapula
- Inward and downward rotation of the scapula
- Difficulty raising arm into flexion (overhead), resulting in increased winging of scapula
- Difficulty raising one arm overhead
- Scapula adducted (drawn inward) during the upward motion of a push-up

Testing Serratus Anterior Stability

Test the stability of your serratus anterior with this quick self-test. Stand with head, upper back, and buttocks against a wall. Place right hand under armpit, reaching fingers around back. Elevate left arm as high as possible (figure 5.22). With a normal serratus anterior, the scapula rotates slightly forward (away from wall). With an abnormal or weak SA, the scapula will wing into the wall during flexion of the arm overhead.

Serratus Anterior Exercises

Exercises for the serratus anterior result in these benefits:

FIGURE 5.22 Serratus anterior stability self-test.

- Improved stability of the scapular and shoulder motions
- Improved ability to raise the arm overhead while maintaining a neutral position (e.g., stretching forward during extension when swimming)
- Improved running posture by stabilizing the scapular and shoulder positions during forward and backward swinging of the arms
- Improved aerodynamic performance position when cycling by stabilizing the upper back for greater support, resulting in better leverage

See table 5.3 for the progression of sets and reps. Once you have achieved ACES at one stage, move to the next stage.

Serratus Anterior Press with Elastic Tubing

Secure elastic tubing behind at shoulder level through pulley. In a seated or standing position (figure 5.23a), flex shoulders 90 degrees and extend elbows with arms even with shoulders. Push outward against the resistance without rotating body (figure 5.23b). Movement comes from the scapula and SA. Refer to table 5.3 for number of sets and reps.

FIGURE 5.23 Serratus anterior press with elastic tubing.

Serratus Anterior Push-Up Plus

Stand in one of these three positions: hands against a wall so arms are straight at shoulder level (optional: stability ball between wall and hands), leaning on a table, or lying in push-up position on the floor (figure 5.24a). With hands slightly to the sides of shoulders, push trunk up and away from wall, table, or floor (figure 5.24b). At full range, push up, using upper-back muscles to achieve more extension. Refer to table 5.3 for number of sets and reps.

FIGURE 5.24 Serratus anterior push-up plus.

Serratus Anterior YTWL on Stability Ball

Lie face down on a stability ball with feet in one of three positions: shoulder width, hip width, or together. Hold a one- to five-pound dumbbell in hands on floor in front of shoulders. For the following positions, focus on maintaining a stable scapula during the entire movement:

1. Raise arms in a Y (figure 5.25a).
2. Raise arms to sides in a T (figure 5.25b).
3. Raise arms to sides in a W (figure 5.25c).
4. Raise arms to sides in an L (figure 5.25d).

Refer to table 5.3 for number of sets and reps.

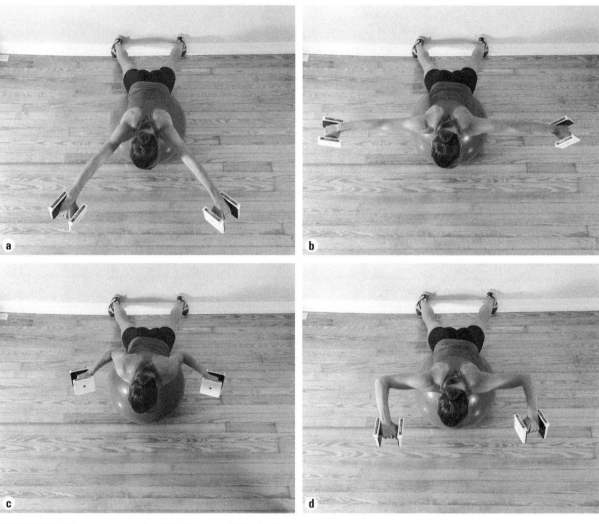

FIGURE 5.25 Serratus anterior YTWL on stability ball.

Upper, Middle, and Lower Trapezius

The trapezius (TrP) is a triangular muscle lying over the back of the neck (upper), shoulder (middle), and upper thorax (chest). The TrP assists in stabilizing, elevating (upper), and depressing (lower) the scapula during movements, such as during hand entry and forward extension and shoulder position with the high elbow catch when swimming. In cycling, these muscles assist shoulder and cervical postures important for balance and power transfer. For running, head, cervical, shoulder, and scapular postures are enhanced and help maintain the proper lines of the trunk and head. The lower TrP muscle brings the scapula in and down and lifts upward for rotation. Affecting the inward, upward, and elevation of the scapula, the TrP stabilizes the cervical spine and posture of the head. Triathletes benefit from a strong trapezius muscle group.

Signs of weakness in the trapezius include the following:

- Restricted ability to raise arm overhead
- Upward or outward scapula
- Shoulder in a forward position
- Increased tendency toward kyphosis (abnormal curve of the thoracic region of the spine)

- Decreased ability to extend or raise the head in a prone position (e.g., looking up from an aero pose on the bike)

Testing Trapezius Stability

Test the stability of your middle and lower trapezius with this self-test of bent-over rows. Stand alongside a bench with a dumbbell on the floor. The amount of weight should be 5 to 10 percent of body weight in kilograms.

Place one knee and one hand on the bench and lower torso to parallel to the floor while gripping the dumbbell (figure 5.26a). Extend dumbbell up until upper arm is parallel to floor (figure 5.26b). Lower arm to starting position. Do three sets of 15 reps on each side with 30 seconds between sets to test your competence.

Test the stability of your upper trapezius with this self-test of shoulder shrugs. Stand with feet shoulder-width apart and hold a dumbbell in each hand at sides, leaning forward slightly at hips (figure 5.27a). The amount of weight should be 20 to 30 percent of body weight in kilograms. Elevate shoulders as high as possible with a shrugging motion up and then down (figure 5.27b). Do three sets of 15 reps on each side with 30 seconds between sets.

FIGURE 5.26 Middle and lower trapezius self-test.

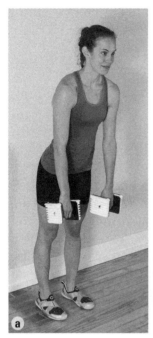
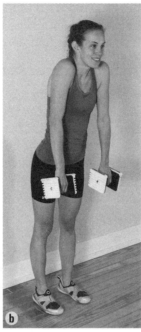

FIGURE 5.27   Upper trapezius self-test.

Trapezius Exercises

Exercises for the trapezius result in these benefits:

- Improved performance of the trapezius muscle group
- Improved stability of the scapula during arm movements
- Improved ability to balance the head in neutral position while swimming, cycling, or running

See table 5.3 for the progression of sets and reps. Once you have achieved ACES at one stage, move to the next stage.

Trapezius Stability Seated Arm Slide

Sit on a stool with back against a wall and hands and arms at sides. Draw in navel to contract abdominals throughout the exercise. Flex elbows by pulling arms back at a 90-degree angle; touch wall with back of hands at head height (figure 5.28a). Raise arms overhead (in line with shoulders) using the upper-back TrA muscles (figure 5.28b). Refer to table 5.3 for number of sets and reps.

FIGURE 5.28   Trapezius stability seated arm slide.

Prone Overhead Flexed Arms

Lie face down with pillow under chest, arms overhead and slightly outside shoulders, elbows flexed slightly, and thumbs pointed upward (figure 5.29a). Lift arms by pulling shoulder blades together and slightly down so that hands are higher than elbows (figure 5.29b). Refer to table 5.3 for number of sets and reps.

FIGURE 5.29   Prone overhead flexed arms.

We need to see a shift from the "harder is better" approach to training the muscles and stability of the core. Too many sport performance companies, training systems, personal trainers, coaches, and triathletes assume that hard, fatiguing exercise must be good. Yes, some discomfort is necessary for progress, and there are many exercises that do just that. But above all, the deeper-layered muscles that provide stability and allow for the transfer of load from the joints must be trained for optimal stability. Optimal posture must be maintained, or else movements will be compensated by distal (away from the core) body reactions that are uncoordinated and less effective. Those will show up in competition just when stability from the inner core is needed the most. The exercises in this chapter are the best way to achieve joint stability, especially in the pelvis, and to produce the best posture and potential for improved technique and efficiency, and injury-free training and performances.

TORBJORN SINDBALLE   Beating the Heat

In 2003 I competed for a Kona qualification slot in Ironman Wisconsin. The September day was uncharacteristically hot and humid—above 90 degrees. At the 9-mile mark my running suddenly went from smooth to ugly. My chance of qualifying was running away quickly in the horizon. However, I was not the only one suffering that day, so a deep surge secured the spot despite a run split 20 minutes slower than usual. That day the heat won.

Heat has a profound impact on performance, and I was not immune. From the onset, normal paces melt away as effort and fatigue increase. The days where I ran smoothly were infrequent in the heat, a battle I faced all too often. In Kona 2004 and 2005 as well as in Ironman Austria 2006, I faced the same issue. Ten miles into the run I faltered to a painful shuffle. We checked hydration levels and electrolyte balance, we tried a conservative strategy on the bike to save energy for the run, we tried cooling my head and neck with ice, but nothing helped. After Austria in 2006 I swore I would never again compete in another major race in the heat.

A few weeks later during the Danish Triathlon Championships (another hot summer day), I noticed a strange pattern. Going out, I had a tailwind; coming back, I had a headwind. While I should be faster in the tailwind, I felt terrible and ran slow. Into the wind, however, I felt great and ran strong. The effect was immediate as I turned back into the wind I felt better and my speed dropped nearly 15 seconds a mile. How could my performance and mood change so rapidly?

Afterward, I went back to my physiology textbooks and then collaborated with University of Copenhagen professor Lars Nybo Nielsen, a leading scientist in exercise temperature regulation. The resulting hypothesis was that my core temperature limited my performance rather than dehydration, overhydration, or electrolyte imbalance.

At 180 pounds I was 20 pounds heavier than most professionals. Calculations revealed those 20 pounds spiked heat accumulation while running because I was not able to get rid of it in hot and humid conditions. My brain would shut down the firing to my muscles and make it impossible to maintain pace.

The normal cooling mechanism during exercise is evaporation through sweating. In addition, humans achieve a cooling effect from convection (air around the skin is replaced with cooler air). In hot and humid conditions both of these mechanisms work less efficiently than when in dry heat or cooler temperatures. Instead we needed to look elsewhere for a solution to my 10-mile heat barrier.

Some years earlier I read a study form Stanford where scientists enhanced the performance of football players by cooling their palms. I adopted the same technique using a rubber glove filled with ice, which instantly made my heart rate drop by 8 to 10 beats. The hand is a much more effective place to cool the body than the head because of the higher density of capillaries close to the skin. In addition, I ran in a white long-sleeve shirt and wore arm coolers during the bike leg that minimized the heat obtained from sun radiation and made it possible to enhance the evaporation of water and sweat from the material and my skin.

The third and final part of the puzzle was to identify the speed that I could maintain without overheating. After extensive testing in the Kona lava fields, we determined that I could hold a 7-minute-per-mile pace without spiking my core temperature. In October 2007 I bettered my marathon split under the scorching Hawaiian sun to 2:57 and finished third overall in the race, beating the heat in the process.

6 Analyzing and Improving Swimming Technique

Swimming efficiently is rewarding, but it remains a challenge for a large population of triathletes to master. Swimming requires a deep commitment to practice in order to make essential changes in technique. After reading this chapter, you should have a firm grip on the principles of swimming and how to apply the right postures and positions of technique. You should also be able to implement a body lines training system that helps you make better movements via posture-based workouts. In earlier chapters we have highlighted functional movements and posture. In this chapter we continue to focus on functional movements, particularly flexibility, joint mobility, and stability as they pertain to swimming.

Improving the freestyle stroke for triathletes, particularly for those without a swimming background, is not easy. Learning how to swim better begins with assessing posture out of the water and then working on limitations and corrections through the test exercises in the earlier chapters. Improved stability and functional movements out of the water will help you attain postures that ease execution in swimming.

To make the most of your technique work, your body must be as balanced as possible in stability, joint mobility, and flexibility. Because swimming, biking, and running are rhythmic, symmetrical sports, it follows that the better your body can move functionally and main-

tain body lines, the better your balance and more efficient your technique and economy. In this chapter, we will reshape your swimming technique through the practice of postures and positions in all regions of the body. If you are a coach, the method of coaching we promote here will allow an effective approach to teaching and correcting mechanics individually and in groups.

Before starting this swimming chapter, prepare your body for technique work by reviewing chapters 1, 3, 4, and 5; implementing the exercises; making self-assessments of balance; stability, and flexibility; and monitoring progress using the ACES assessment tests. If you do this before practicing the principles in this chapter, improvements in technique will come more quickly and easily.

You first need to learn how to streamline and balance your body along a horizontally level plane. This begins out of the water, with posture as the foundation. Maintaining a position of good horizontal posture is central to all movements of the swimming stroke. Next begins the intricate task of learning to coordinate and synchronize the limbs' depth, width, length, height, and force around the balanced body. Breathing, arm strokes, kicking, and body roll all must come together, accompanied by the proper pathways and varying velocities of the hands and arms.

Through careful, deliberate practice of technique, you can become a much more efficient

Training Equipment in Swimming

You can better learn to swim if you rely less on swimming aids such as pull buoys, bands, tubes, fins, training paddles, and mittens. That said, some kinds of equipment are better than others. Here we provide a list of recommended swimming products that do not compromise the posture of the swimmer or impede the development of ACES in swimming.

Training Fins

The best training fin is made of soft foam that channels water in such a way that represents and improves flexibility, stability, and mechanics of the kick. Fins should be extremely comfortable and streamlined and not alter swimming mechanics. Avoid fins that are stiff and long and disrupt the natural kicking tempo.

Tempo Training Devices

This device is placed underneath the swim cap alongside the ear so that an audible beep can be heard. The adjustable rate of the beep helps to develop tempo, evenness, bilateral symmetry, and stroke rate. These aids can also be used for dryland training to develop tempo in the stride rate while running or in cycling cadence.

Contoured and Airfoil Paddles

Contoured and airfoil swim training paddles provide lift along the very slightly curved pathway the hand and forearm use when swimming. This pathway provides the optimal lift and water-holding capacity used by the most efficient swimmers. These paddles enhance this motion and teach the swimmers the most efficient motions and postures of the fingers, hands, wrist and forearms. Swimming is not a strength discipline, and improving technique is paramount to better performance.

The shape of the paddles should match the natural shape of the hands when holding water. The hand is not flat, and flat paddles incorrectly train the hand pathway, but a cup-shaped paddle more accurately trains the pathway and hold and develops a better feel.

Alignment Kickboard

An alignment kickboard is used for maintaining posture and alignment and does so without hyperextending the neck or lower back. Avoid conventional kickboards, which can cause hyperextension. An alignment kickboard can be used with one or both arms.

---

swimmer. Improving, understanding, and focusing on technique before intensity are a central theme of this chapter. You will learn the right movements and repeat patterns over and over, and gradually you will attain the right mix of training volume, frequency, and intensity. Stability and functional movements go hand in hand with efficiency and are central to improving swimming technique. For coaches, determining how flexible, mobile, and stable your triathletes are should be fundamental in both group and individual programs and should precede all training workouts. This is a shift in thinking that will make you better able to execute the techniques in this book.

In the same way as aerobic capacity training, technique training must be specific and provide progressive adaptations. For acclimatization to better technique to take hold, training of distance is especially important for triathletes. Progressively building endurance along with technique builds a foundation for optimally developed movements. For swimming success, technique is more important than strength. Good technical skills reduce energy costs at any speed. Such skills are best acquired through learning how to balance and streamline the body in and through the water. In addition, there are underwater hand paths (phases), or sweeps of diagonal motions, that when applied in normal ranges at varying accelerations can improve swimming.

For hundreds of years swimming technique has been of keen interest to humans. Coaches, scientists, and technique experts have studied the biomechanics and physiology of every conceivable aspect of swimming. A few areas of continual interest are increasing propulsion; reducing resistance, drag, and lift; hand-shaping patterns; buoyancy; vortex and laminar flows; leg forces; turbulence; and water characteristics. Plenty of information on all of these elements is available in many printed sources and online.

Our focus in this chapter is a bit different. We stick to swimming principles and the accepted mechanics of swimming, but we use a fresh approach. We discuss mechanics in terms of body segments, or phases, and we present a simple testing method using the body lines system presented in earlier chapters. This method has been proven to be an effective, measureable, and progressive learning system for freestyle technique.

Mechanics of Swimming

There are two main mechanical concepts that apply to achieving fast swimming speed: maximizing propulsion through the effective use of propulsive forces and minimizing resistance from the water (drag).

A study conducted during competition at the Olympic Games shows that elite swimmers do not power their way through the water. In fact, they use less propulsive forces than their slower counterparts. Elite swimmers use propulsive forces *more efficiently* and have significantly better body position in the water. Elite swimmers finesse the water and have been shown to use significantly less power to swim as many as three seconds faster

for 100 meters. They use technique to reduce the effects of drag.

Following are some principles related to drag, surface area, buoyancy, body roll, sculling, breathing and balance to help you with the deeper foundations of swimming. Later, the technical and step-by-step features of the freestyle stroke, body lines, exercises, and ways to improve and correct faults are reviewed.

Drag (Resistance) From the Water

Passive drag from the water has been studied for many decades by towing a swimmer in a prone (face down) position at different speeds. Passive drag is influenced mainly by body composition, height, posture, and limb lengths—essentially, your shape, postures, and positions. Because the density of the water can't be changed, the next point to consider is speed. This is important because it takes a lot of energy, effort, and power to make a small increase in swimming speed due to the water's resistance.

Frontal surface area is measured from a frontal view. A balanced and more horizontal body position has low frontal surface area. However, if hips or legs sink in the water, this adds to the frontal surface area, and drag is increased. This results in more turbulence. Every arm, body, and leg movement disturbs or moves water and creates turbulence. Minimizing unnecessary movements and maintaining a balanced and horizontal body posture helps to reduce turbulence and thus reduce drag.

Think of swimming as slipping through the water in a narrow horizontal position. Because drag forces are one of the determining factors to success in swimming, let's look at several ways you can reduce drag.

Frontal Surface Area

Frontal surface area is easy to understand in theory—a smaller frontal surface area is better because it creates less resistance. During swimming, the body has the smallest frontal surface area when in a horizontal position. However, buoyancy works against the body staying horizontal in the water.

Buoyancy and the Buoyancy Force

When a body floats face down in the water, the feet, arms, and hips tend to sink. This is caused by a mismatch in the line of action of the buoyancy force from the water and the center of gravity of the body. When a body is floating in water, the buoyancy force acts at the center of the displaced water, which is typically in the midtorso area (figure 6.1*a*). The center of gravity is typically just below the navel. This mismatch causes the body to rotate (legs downward) until the forces match (figure 6.1*b*).

Part of what influences how far your legs will sink is the density of your body, which depends on your body composition—fat has a low density and tends to float, bones are roughly neutral, and muscle has a high density and tends to sink. The body composition of triathletes tends to skew toward high levels of muscle and low levels of body fat. This higher body density is one factor that puts triathletes at a disadvantage during non-wetsuit and pool swimming. Without a doubt, the wetsuit changed triathlon. This piece of equipment allows swimmers of all levels to be safe, warm, and buoyant in open water. Triathlon would not have grown to such worldwide popularity without the wetsuit. Still, learning better tech-

nique and body positions and postures—even in a wetsuit—is necessary.

Another factor that influences how far legs will sink is the placement of the limbs of the body. Specifically, lengthening the arms in front of the head helps the body be more horizontal. A long-streamlined posture raises the center of gravity toward the center of buoyancy (note that the center of gravity is not a static point on the body; it is a point that represents the average of all the body's mass). When the center of mass (CM) and the center of buoyancy are closer together, the body does not need to rotate as much for forces to align. The body, in effect, floats more horizontally.

Elite swimmers apply this principle by using a modified version of a catch-up (front quadrant) stroke and an early exit midtorso. Using this technique, at least one arm stays above the head during most of the arm pattern (figure 6.2). This helps raise the CM toward the head (toward the buoyancy force) and reduce the body rotation that causes the lower body to sink.

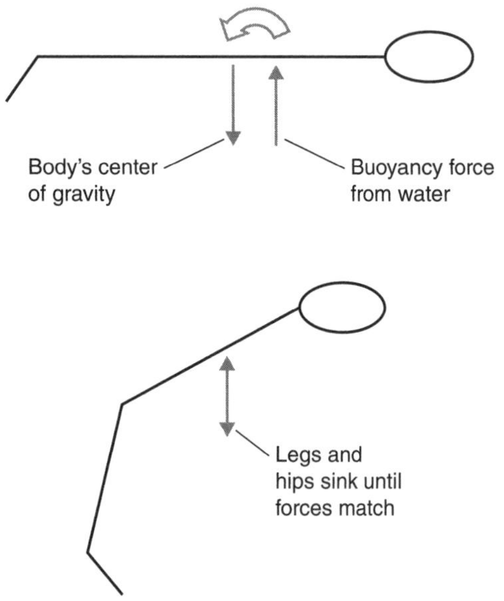

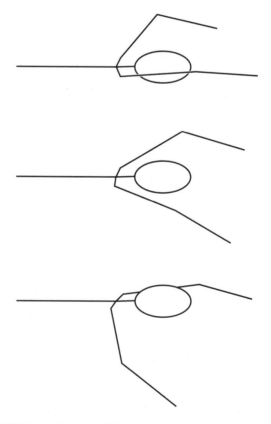

FIGURE 6.1 Buoyancy force.

Body's center of gravity

Buoyancy force from water

Legs and hips sink until forces match

FIGURE 6.2 Catch-up (front quadrant) stroke.

Body Roll

Proper body roll helps to streamline the body with every stroke. Body roll should be limited to a rotation about the longitudinal (head to toe) axis of the body and should not include any up-and-down or side-to-side motion. The centerline axis (center of the chest, or sternum through the middle of the pelvis) of the body should be constantly aligned to the direction of travel—straight down the pool. Any flexing, extending, lateral, or unnecessary motions can be influenced by functional movements and stability. So, you are not only learning how to apply better technique but also ensuring your movements are not restricting your ability to achieve better body lines.

By rolling the body around a centerline posture, the frontal surface area (as viewed from the front) can be reduced. Body roll allows you to mimic the V shape of the bottom of a boat (figure 6.3a) rather than the flat bottom of a barge pushing through the water (figure 6.3b).

Additionally, a more V shape helps to cut through the water. When traveling the same speed, the wake (or turbulence) of a barge is much higher than the wake of a boat. This turbulence affects the amount of drag the swimmer must overcome. Thus proper body roll has the double positive effect of reducing frontal surface area and reducing turbulence (the coefficient of drag).

Breathing

Breathing should be synchronized with body roll. The head should roll with the body and not lift to breathe. Lifting the head immediately causes the unwanted reaction of lowering the lower body. Also, during training, breathe to both sides of the body for a set portion of workouts and remain aware of the center posture of the body where the chin, sternum, and middle of the pelvis are aligned and connected on an axis. Breathing on only one side of the body develops strength imbalances in the upper body.

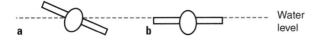

a   b   Water level

FIGURE 6.3 Body roll.

Learning to breathe on either side (bilateral breathing) also benefits open-water swimming. Waves, swells, and other competitors can hamper the tempo of your stroke, so the ability to bilateral breathe is an advantage. That said, during racing or high-intensity training, breathe on your dominant side, and do not alternate. You don't want to risk hypoxia (less oxygen reaching the body's tissues), especially when working at functional threshold. There are form and technique benefits in bilateral breathing, but these should be used only during lower-intensity technique training.

Propulsion

In freestyle swimming, 70 percent or more of propulsion is generated by the arms. The phrase *feel for the water* is used by coaches to describe a swimmer with good technique for propulsion. It can be difficult to teach feel for the water, but when a swimmer has it, it's easy to recognize. These are the swimmers who move gracefully and effortlessly through the water.

One of the best ways to develop feel for the water is through sculling drills. Sculling is the basis of each stroke. In teaching freestyle swimming, coaches typically demonstrate strokes as sweeping S-shaped patterns moving from above the head to the hips. But in the water, there is very little backward motion of the arm and hand relative to the water. The body is moving past the hand, and the hands and arm are working the same small volume of water. This is why tapered sweeping motions are so important—yet not with exaggerated motions but with very small deflections of the hand and forearms. The simplest way to describe the sweeping motion is that the hand sweeps downward, outward, inward, and outward again in a figure-8 motion. Although there are downward and upward motions as well, each is mainly a slight sculling motion—an oblique movement to capture and hold water.

These smaller, skillful sculling or sweeping motions allow the hand to find still water. If the hand and arm moved straight back toward the feet without sculling, the hand would get caught in a channel of moving water and could not forcefully push against the water. However, there is merit to a straight line of hold during the catch because the high elbow and holding of the hand and forearm more vertically allow the body to move over this fixed hand (holding water via small, oblique side-to-side, down, out-and-back motions).

A common question is if swimmers are sweeping side to side, how do they go forward? The answer is that the minute sculling motions allow swimmers to use both lift and drag forces for propulsion (modeling the hand like a hydrofoil). The use of lift force helps to direct propulsive forces forward instead of sideways. This is the key to creating propulsion in the water. For these reasons, sculling drills should be included in workouts and are a foundation to achieving propulsion. There is a trend to push straight back with a more vertical hand and forearm, with the pathway directed straight backward; this is correct, but there are very minute sculling elements at play, so learning to skillfully scull and use the foil-like motions is an important part of efficient swimming. Thus, rather than there being one best way to swim, swimming is best understood as a collection of methods, and each method has merit. That said, the ability to feel the water will always make for better swimming.

There is no better way to learn this feel than by practicing the fluctuating orientations and positions for the fingers, palm, undersides of the forearm, and upper arm. Sculling (table 6.1) and developing the ability to propel the body through changes of hand pitch with continuous and rhythmic pressure of the hand and arm should be a primary practice for every level of swimmer.

As mentioned, you can best learn to benefit from and develop lift propulsion through sculling. This technique spotlights the lateral motions of the hand and arm from the catch through the upsweep phases of the stroke. There are phases of different peaks of acceleration (how fast or slow the hand and arm moves) of the hand and forearm when swimming. It is not a constant speed but a continuum of varying sweeps of acceleration and deceleration. Sculling teaches the motions of the downsweep, insweep, and outsweep in a swimming-specific way.

In the following sections we describe the principles of sculling in the face-down, face-up, vertical, and lateral body positions.

Balance

The orientation of the body should be maintained in each plane. The head is aligned with the spine and hips are level in the water. The kick is minimal, but the body must be level or aligned.

Breathing

Breathe to the side or use a snorkel to maintain head alignment. There should be no hyperextending or lifting of the chin and head.

Hand and Arm Position

The hand should not scull near the surface. The elbow is slightly flexed above the hand, wrist, and forearm, pointing up. Beginning with hands outstretched in front of head and about 6 to 12 inches (15-30 cm) below the surface (elbow is above hand at all times), palms press outward to about shoulder width with little finger pointed toward the surface. Round off by rotating hands, pressing inward with thumb pointed up. There should be a slight finger spread (no more than 10 degrees) with hand held in a naturally cuplike manner (don't overextend or tense the fingers).

Feel the water pressure in both directions and do a figure-8 with hands at about the same depth throughout. A winglike or boomerang shape (discussed later in this chapter) of the hand, forearm, and upper arm is central to swimming. This shape sweeps against the water by rotating, pitching, and moving laterally like an airfoil against the water to create propulsion and lift. This is the central element of effective swimming in terms of hand and arm movement—the slight sweeping motions with a flexed and high elbow are ultimately necessary for improved swimming.

The motions are accomplished together as a whole, from the upper back, shoulder, arm, and hand (not with only the hand and forearm) and not too much, if any, exaggerated flexing of the elbow. There should be constant and rhythmic back-and-forth pressure on the hand and forearm (e.g., thumbs down, then thumbs up).

Kicking

The kick should be minimal but light and steady and maintaining rhythm.

The shaping of the hand and arm during the underwater stroke does change some in angles of attack, or pitch. It is neither an entirely straight-back nor an exaggerated S-type pull. Rather, it is the ability to hold water by making very small deflections, or sweeps, that change the angle and pitch and result in increased hold on the water. Good swimmers do not pull or push back but hold or maintain the hand in a near-fixed place in the water. As we have said, sculling should be part of the regimen of every swimmer wishing to improve efficiency and feel for the water.

Phases of the Freestyle Swimming Stroke

There are variations in mechanics unique to each individual, but the phases of the freestyle stroke can always be recognized. In this section we progress through these phases, presenting principles for you to build on. First we'll explain the phases and primary terms related to the freestyle swimming stroke. Then we'll describe how to develop better movement through lower-intensity training that enhances motor learning by breaking down complex movements into what we call body lines.

TABLE 6.1 Sculling Positions and Technique

Body position	Body direction and position	Description	Hand and arm position
Face down	Forward	On belly with body horizontal with light kicking. 1. Open-hand sculling. 2. Open to four, three, two, and one fingers sculling. 3. Closed fingers (fist) sculling.	Overhead in stretched position 6-12 in. (15-30 cm) below surface; scull no wider than shoulder-width apart.
Face up	Forward	On back with feet pointing in direction of travel.	Overhead in stretched position 6-12 in. (15-30 cm) below surface; scull no wider than shoulder-width apart.
	Backward	On back with head pointing in the direction of travel; knees flex, then extend.	Hands scull at the midtorso, close to sides of body.
Vertical (head up, feet down)	Stationary, forward, backward, and circular	Scull in a vertical position, moving the body forward or backward or in a circle.	Hands are below surface 6-12 in. (15-30 cm), palms down; scull outward and inward 6 to 12 in. (15-30 cm) back and forth.
Lateral (on sides)	Side lying; the body moves forward	Scull in small figure-8s with gentle kick to keep body horizontal.	Forward hand stretched forward; opposite hand is placed on same hip; scull with forward hand.

The way that triathletes train is increasingly separate from the traditional and individual sports of swimming, cycling, and running. To be sure, technique and training similarities remain, but these are fluctuating as the specificity of triathlon training develops. The key concept today is specificity. Training specific to the nature of triathlon competition includes the following protocols:

- An increase in frequency of open-water group swimming sessions at both aerobic and race pace as events approach, including practice in calm, choppy, and unsteady conditions and in colder water. There is training focus on change of pace, direction, shifts in body position, periodic alternate-side breathing, congestion, and drafting under racelike open-water conditions.

- An emphasis on sighting skills, including lifting head and torso in alignment above water line until eyes are clear of water. When possible, large, stationary points are used as sighting landmarks (observed beforehand and while swimming) instead of buoys until within 100 meters. Conditions can change because of weather, so multiple sighting options are important, along with learning to swim without goggles or with fogged-up goggles.

- Practice starts (beach, in water, with and without warm-up), entries, and rounding buoy techniques under varying circumstances.

Nonfreestyle swimming strokes (butterfly, backstroke, breaststroke) are very useful for improving freestyle mechanics and open-water swimming. These strokes have many crossover benefits, including balance, coordination, good body position and postures, scapular stability, flexibility, and, most important, sculling—the feel for the water.

Beyond this, the deep-core stabilizers of the trunk and back (transversus abdominis, rectus abdominis, internal oblique, external oblique, and erector spinae) are developed and improve freestyle technique (because you are swimming from the center of the body, using the deep core and pelvis to deliver and transfer energy to the outside arms and legs). Multistroke training crosses over by developing many of the muscles used for freestyle swimming.

Limits in stability (strength) can alter the movements of technique and reduce capacity to generate force; they also increase the risk of recurring injury. Your skeletal muscles transfer and generate force and change the angles of joints. In swimming, the muscles of the hand, wrist, arm, and shoulder are very active, such as during the underwater pull. Yet it's the muscles that are further away and well anchored nearly the spine that might be most important. It's not surprising that the smaller muscles of the shoulder, such as the deltoids, are active during the catch and hold, but when compared to the larger pectoralis (chest) and latissimus (back) muscles, they cannot generate near the force because of their size. Thus it's especially important for the base muscles to be functionally strong and stable in support of the smaller muscles. The base muscles in effect anchor the smaller muscles to enhance swimming efficiency and reduce injury risk.

When swimming, you position your arms in the water using your shoulder muscles, but these muscles are supported by your ribs and spine, which are the prime movers of the shoulder and apply the most forces. The muscles surrounding the front and lateral sides of the trunk (rectus abdominis, internal and external obliques, and transverse obliques), when strong and functional, provide stability and power for the smaller muscles. Your swimming power comes not so much from the joints about your arms and shoulders as from your core. The muscles at the center of the body transfer energy to muscles further from the center.

Efficient mobility (ability to move the body functionally) in the arms and legs correlates to stability in the center of the body. For your hands, arms, shoulders, legs, and feet to function optimally, core muscles must be strong and stable.

How we walk, sit, stand, and carry our posture during daily activities affects how we move in our sport. It is especially important to learn how to move from the inside to outside of the body. Primarily, this means presenting a posture that permits the most efficient use of the muscles of the hips, legs, and torso (the core). Learning to engage these muscles during flexion, extension, and rotation is central to performing better movements in all sports and begins with proper posture.

Standing with anatomically correct posture begins the process for establishing and enhancing all body lines in swimming. Learning to take this position into the water and maintaining the centerlines of movement will take you further toward improved swimming than just about any technique. In assessing flexibility, mobility, and stability, movement tendencies become evident—you can tell to what extent you use your core muscles in your basic movements. For coaches, assessment can provide teaching moments in which to educate your triathletes how to be more aware of using the core muscles. Practicing functional movements teaches the body to use core muscles deep inside the body to affect movement of the limbs and achieve more efficient technique.

The muscles in the hip region are frequently unstable in triathletes. Notably, the gluteus medius (a muscle that prevents tilting or sagging of the pelvis) is an important pelvic primary stabilizer. When the gluteus medius is weak, other muscles or movements must compensate for the weakness in everyday activities, such as standing up from a chair. This compensation results in less efficient, less functional movements. Over time, the muscular, nervous, and skeletal systems become affected by these repeated less functional movements and sustained faulty postures.

Swimmers who move functionally on land transfer their skills remarkably well into the water, improving in symmetry of swimming motions and performance and reducing the risk of overuse injury. Balanced and symmetrical swimming movement begins in the proximal muscles at the body's core (below the chest to above the knees), which support the outward, or distal, muscles near the head, arms, hands, legs, and feet. An excellent technique to engage the deep core muscles is to draw in when exhaling to activate these muscles and help stabilize the pelvis, which result in better streamlining and better movements.

Thus optimal posture on land transfers directly to swimming and eases motor learning in the water. By learning to control your body during flexion (sitting) and extension (standing) through the use of your core muscles, you begin the process of establishing more functional movements. Movements controlled by active engagement and stability from the proximal muscles affect the functionality of the distal muscles during swimming (figure 6.4).

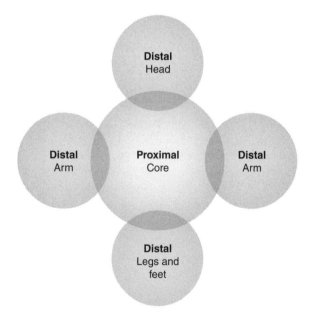

FIGURE 6.4 Proximal and distal—swimming from inside to out.

Front Quadrant

The front quadrant is defined as the front half of the freestyle stroke underwater (figure 6.5).

In front-quadrant swimming, at least one hand is in the front quadrant during the entire stroke cycle. This requires a shift in stroke timing. Traditional teaching dictates finishing hard with one arm past the hips and entering the water with the other arm. In front-quadrant swimming, the right arm's entry into the water occurs during the insweep phase of the left arm (along with an exit at midtorso). When done correctly, there should be no gliding—that is, no point at which propulsion is not being applied.

One advantage of front-quadrant swimming is that it keeps the body long, with one arm always out in front or above the head. Having one arm above the head raises the body's center of mass and helps reduce torque from the buoyancy force that causes the legs to sink. Also, as is well known in ship building, a longer hull is more streamlined than a shorter hull. In front-quadrant swimming, you lengthen the hull of your body. Another advantage of front-quadrant swimming is that it changes the timing of your breathing. In traditional stroke timing, as one hand enters the water and stretches out in front, the other arm is finishing the stroke. This has been taught as the best opportunity to breathe, using momentum of the finishing arm to help rotate hips out of the water. Unfortunately, this timing of the breath leaves the hips vulnerable to sinking as the head turns and lifts to breathe (figure 6.6).

Using front-quadrant swimming forces the breath to begin earlier in the stroke, when one arm is more underneath the body (figure 6.7; breathing occurs between the two images). The position of the arm in the water out in front serves as an anchor, creating forces that support the hips and keep them from sinking.

Entry Phase

Each entry into the water begins with the hand meeting the water about half an arm's length in front of and just outside the tip of the shoulder (figure 6.8). This must be as

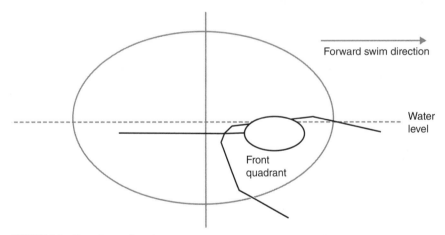

FIGURE 6.5 Front quadrant.

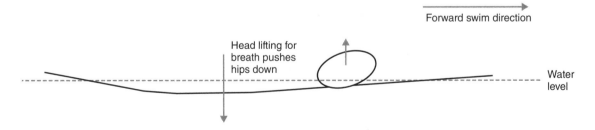

FIGURE 6.6 Posture is affected when the head is lifted or extended when breathing.

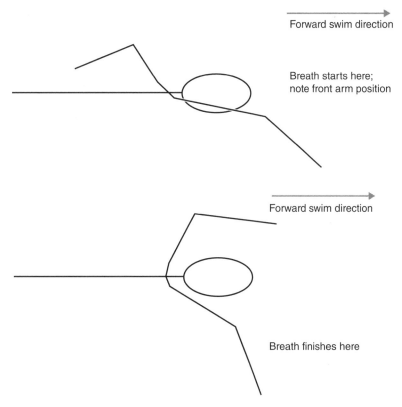

Forward swim direction

Breath starts here;
note front arm position

Forward swim direction

Breath finishes here

FIGURE 6.7 Breathe early when the front arm is beginning the catch posture.

streamlined as possible, with a minimum of splashing, slapping, or turbulence. Ideally, the fingertips are relaxed and lead the entry into the water, and the rest of the arm follows directly along the path of the fingertips. This motion disturbs the least amount of water and reduces resistance.

Extension Phase

Following the entry, the hand extends fully forward in a slightly downward arcing motion (figure 6.9). This acceleration forward against the water creates additional drag and must be as streamlined as possible. A common stroke

FIGURE 6.8 Entry phase.

FIGURE 6.9 Extension phase.

flaw is to drop the elbow during extension. The elbow must remain above the wrist and hand and pointed more upward. A dropped elbow adds to the frontal surface area and increases drag.

Small and Oblique Sweeping Phases

For years we have heard the terms *elliptical, S-shaped,* and *sweeping* to describe the limb motions of the freestyle stroke. These techniques can be difficult to describe and are often overused. People differ in their opinions on whether an elliptical, oblique (sideways or lateral) sculling motion is more or less advantageous than a straight-arm pull with a high elbow. Most likely, a hybrid of these methods is most effective. There are very different movement and stability factors at play as well. But some confusion exists on the meaning of pulling and sweeping. We use *sweep* to describe holding on to the water by using very slight shaping and sculling motions to purchase and anchor the hand and arm against the water, as opposed to the straight-arm pull (both with a high elbow and lower forearm and hand during catch). Sculling, described earlier, is a method for holding water by using the limbs to establish a more fixed point—a point of leverage.

The desired sweep is accomplished via minute lateral movements of the hand and forearm during the downsweep, catch, insweep, outsweep, and upsweep—the principal phases of the underwater motions. These lateral movements (sweeps) are subtle but can be easily learned once you know how to perform them and how they benefit the stroke. Note again that the sweeps are not performed with exaggeration, but they should always occur. Sculling practice goes a long way toward teaching and learning these motions. Coaches are correct in recommending a straighter pathway, but these lateral motions (sweeps) are needed to capture still water—because water pushing straight and directly backward results in a slipping of the hand. Thus a small degree of lateral motion is necessary for optimal performance.

Downsweep Phase

One of the most important parts of the freestyle stroke, the downsweep paves the way to the catch and the in-, out-, and upsweep phases. There is not a significant propulsive movement in the downsweep before the catch; it occurs in sequence as a continuation of the extension and has the feeling of a forward extension and downward arcing, or positioning the arm around a barrel (figure 6.10). You should use only gentle action, with soft pressure downward, forward, and out to the side until the hand, forearm, and upper arm are nearly facing backward. The elbow should be kept high as fingertips carve gently forward and downward to make the catch. Note that your limits in joint mobility and muscle flexibility will affect how high and vertical the elbow and forearm can be. Work in smaller ranges of 15, 30, 45, and up to nearly 90 degrees while improving movement and stability with dryland exercises.

The pathway for the downsweep is both a long extension and a downward, deep, and slow-arcing motion. Imagine a semicircular curving line that the hand and forearm follows. This places the hand, inner forearm, and upper arm in excellent position for the catch and engages the core musculature for the insweep and sweeps up and out.

FIGURE 6.10   Downsweep phase.

Catch Phase

The catch is the point where the extension and downsweep phase end and the body begins to accelerate forward as a result of catching, or holding on to, the water. The catch occurs somewhere about one third of the way into the underwater stroke in a frontward and downward motion. The high-elbow catch is favored, allowing the desired hand and arm position (figure 6.11). Some coaches refer to this pathway as the early vertical forearm. Proper training of this position and correcting errors help you to achieve and master the desired movement.

A common stroke flaw, and another cause for a dropped elbow, occurs when too much force is used before the forearm is pointing backward. A soft positioning of the vertically oriented forearm and hand is more effective. The fingertips, hand, wrist, and forearm should point in a downward position. But use

FIGURE 6.11 Catch phase.

only limited force in achieving this setting of the hand and forearm. Keep hand and wrist relaxed as you rotate hand, wrist, and forearm downward. At this point, the next and more propulsive phases of the stroke begin. Note that executing the high elbow and early position without progressing accurately through the entry, stretch, extension and downsweep can make you fall short of the optimal catch. Later in this chapter, and in the swim tests, we discuss the importance of the fingertips and how learning to use the tactile properties of *feel* and working the stroke along designated lines and pathways is most effective.

At that point, propulsive forces can increase while keeping the elbow in a high position above the forearm and hand (there should be no dropping, lifting, or moving out, in, or back of the elbow). Next, the insweep, outsweep, and upsweep phases begin and are performed with the elbow flexed like a wing (or boomerang shaped). As propulsive forces begin to increase during the catch, the hand rounds the bottom corner in preparation for the insweep.

An effective way to learn (or teach) the concept of a vertical high elbow and the position and posture of the hold line is via the fingertip wall slide exercise. To perform this exercise, stand a forearm's length from a wall with both hands overhead and palms on wall (figure 6.12*a*). Slide forearm and hand down until fingertips touch the wall; the elbows do not move (figure 6.12*b*). Next, slide fingertips, hands, and forearms down to shoulder height; this is the vertical posture of the high-elbow position (figure 6.12*c*). Do 5 to 10 sets of 10 reps on the wall, and then swim 100 meters using this same posture. (You can do this while standing in the water imagining the wall vertically before you.)

Insweep Phase

One of the most propulsive parts of the swimming stroke, the insweep begins as the catch is made with the arm sweeping in toward the body. The hand and arm move in a slightly curved pathway lateral and outward, backward, and finally in an inward pathway as they

FIGURE 6.12 Fingertip wall slide.

near the ribs (figure 6.13). There should not be an exaggerated sweeping or inward sculling motion of the hand and arm. Rather, the upper arm, forearms, and hands are positioned as a single unit while the insweep rotation comes from the shoulder and back.

FIGURE 6.13 Insweep.

The strong back and shoulder muscles drive this powerful phase in a boomerang-shaped motion. A key point is for the scapula to remain flat, not winging up, in, or out. You will learn to apply and spread forces at different velocities following the catch to the insweep, upsweep, and outsweep. Maintain the high elbow and flexed shape as you sweep from one phase to the next. The insweep phase is completed as it reaches peak propulsion, rounds off, and moves into the upsweep.

Upsweep and Outsweep Phase

This phase is the continuation of the last part of the insweep as the arm and hand sweep up, out, and backward and end between shoulder width and the midline of the body (figure 6.14). Pressure is now released as the hand and arm push back and outward, with additional peak propulsive forces generated. It is important to exit the water well before the hips because the energy used to push back is high and the resulting propulsive forces low. Rather, an early exit at midtorso is recommended.

FIGURE 6.14 Upsweep and outsweep phase.

Release Phase

The release occurs as the hand lets go of the water and slides outward and up at about midtorso (early exit), not at the hip. The elbow bends upward to begin the recovery of the arm. The greatest amount of propulsion has already taken place, and there's no need to push water past the hips. By releasing earlier (early exit), you can recover more smoothly, use less energy, and be in the front quadrant more easily.

Recovery Phase

The recovery begins as the shoulder elevates the upper arm horizontally forward. It's important to move the shoulder and arm in the direction of travel and not lift upward toward the sky or midline of the back; rather, use the shoulder, flat and stable scapula, and latissimus dorsi muscles in an upward and forward motion. The elbow is flexed and first to exit the water with the upper arm. The forearm, wrist, and hand are relaxed and remain lower than the elbow. The arm swings forward during the body rotation and should occur close to the body (or with any posture that does not shift the center of mass up, down, or sideways to disturb the direction of travel). In some conditions (e.g., waves, rounding buoys, or congestion from swimmers), recovering in open water with a straight arm is necessary to maintain balance. However, swinging out too wide otherwise can increase energy. If the arm recovers straight (high above the body) and wide, it can act as a weighted lever rotating the body against the natural body roll. This interferes with the opposite hand and arm sweeping (holding) positions under the water.

Technique Training and Testing for Swimming

In 1927, William Bachrach, legendary swimming *coach* of the Illinois Athletic Club and coach of Johnny Weissmuller (Olympic gold medalist and of *Tarzan* TV fame), stressed that races are won on form, not on fight. Bachrach had many philosophies that resonate today; perhaps the one that relates most to this book was his emphasis on learning the parts to best learn the whole. Before we move on to describing the essential parts of the freestyle stroke, let's look at a few more scientific concepts, standards of movement, and body positions that serve as foundational principles for coaches, triathletes, and swimmers.

Body line training—our version of Bachrach's training the parts—improves swimming form and efficiency through the application of a clear and straightforward standard of technique. This system evaluates postures and positions at regions of the body and trains them using the ACES system of learning and testing efficiency. However, before much progress can be made in particular postures or regions, attention must first be paid to functional movement and stability. Assessing how your body performs out of and in the water with purposeful and progressive technique training is a primary goal of this book. Methods for such assessment were provided in chapter 3, and for deeper evaluations, chapter 4 contains evaluations and test exercises for improving functional movement, stability, efficiency, and technique.

The following section begins with the most foundational and essential aspects of swimming technique, which will function as a standard for each of the following sections. Learn these motions and practice them well

ENEY JONES Combating the Elements With Open-Water Skills

There are many techniques that will work and are advisable in the pool, but in open water you must have access to combat whatever the open-water elements might throw at you.

Head Position in Open Water

Triathletes swimming in open water need to learn head position in the following situations:

- *Rage*—when the wind is going in one direction and the current the other direction
- *Washing machine sea*—when there are no clear wave patterns in open water
- *Cross current*—when swimming perpendicular to the current
- *With the current*—when swimming with the current (increase distance per stroke)
- *Against the current*—when swimming against the current (increase cadence)

Many swimmers and triathletes are taught to press their chest and to keep the head in line with the chest. Picture a burrowing animal—this is what the position looks like; it is confining and not very productive. Instead, lift your sternum and stretch out your diaphragm so that your head lifts and is in line with your lifted chest. Relax your neck. Lift from your sternum, and keep your neck in line. Use wider entry and catch. This alignment presents these benefits:

- A higher head, sternum, and neck position offers less resistance and is more functional.
- A breaking-the-tape body position allows breathing to be easier and less constricted.
- You will have better access to sighting without needing to break your stroke or strain your neck.

Breathing in Open Water

In open-water swimming, breathing strategies such as these are helpful in some situations:

- *Density breathing*—when water is rough, you might have to density breathe. Lifting your head out of water to breathe might not be possible, so you breathe in air with water in your mouth—which you can do because the two elements have different densities. Practice breathing air with water at the base of your mouth.
- *Relaxation breathing*—inhale through your mouth and exhale through your nose. This will make your exhale last longer, and you'll do more strokes before you think you need air. This can be helpful if you have anxiety during the swim.
- *Disciplined breathing*—breathe toward the front of your stroke. Be disciplined about it. When you have finished your inhale, put your head back down and start the exhale.

before advancing to the more specific body line training. The workouts are in meters, but yards can be used equally as well.

Developing swimmers from beginner to elite is a process that can take years. Attempts to correct stroke flaws do not always result in improvement because of individual differences in motor learning capabilities and underlying limitations in flexibility, mobility, and stability. Our focus in chapters 3 and

4 was to minimize the flexibility, mobility, and stability limitations just mentioned. The exercises and tests were developed to improve strength, flexibility, stability, balance, and mobility and also to provide tools to monitor individual progress. To achieve the most from efforts in technique, mobility, flexibility, and stability must be maximized and balanced.

Any swimmer can improve technique by coupling form training with the improvement of movement asymmetries related to weak or immobile muscles and joints. However, there is a process of taking in information, with signals received from sense organs that are then converted to movements. One of the more challenging parts of training technique is the difficulty for individuals to assess their own movement performances. It's not easy to detect your own errors in movement. The ACES training and workout protocol and body line test exercises have been developed to help you mature in both the cognitive and physical awareness of position (proprioception) regarding where your limbs are in time and space. This occurs over time via accurate repetitions and learning how to feel and pay attention to those postures and positions as you move.

In the following discussions of body lines we cover the postures, positions, and characteristics to strive for as you progress toward masterful swimming. Adapt your training protocols as necessary to accommodate these all-important movements and corrections. It is a good idea to video-record your swimming above and if possible below the water before, during, and after each body line. Seeing your postures and positions firsthand goes a long way in helping you and your coach develop more accurate, controlled, effortless, and smooth technique.

Each baseline body line test consists of evaluating your movements with a pass or fail on each ACES parameter. Are the postures accurate, controlled, effortless, and smooth? Again, a video is the best way to assess the movements as describe in the text. An underwater camera and small (4- to 6-inch legs) tripod can sit along the pool bottom and record and immediately play back your body lines.

In each table are additional entries for your Sub-T time and pace per 100 meters and the number of strokes per 50 m you've taken (each time the hand enters the water) at 25 percent, 50 percent, 75 percent, and the last 50 meters of your swim test distance.

Stroke rates (SR) are variable from swimmer to swimmer. Unlike with running and cycling, it's problematic to specify a narrow range of the best stroke rates per minute. Swimmers tend to reduce their SR as their competence and swim times come down. However, there is variability, and selection of SR appears to be freely chosen and adjusted by a feel of a continuation of movement—no gaps, deceleration, or loss of continuous propulsion with an efficient stroke.

This interindividual variability is important because many coaching methods suggest across-the-board lower SR for all swimmers. However, higher SR can be effective, and studies indicate decreased RPE in most strokes when combined with lower swim times. On the other hand, lower SR and faster swimming increase RPE. Again, the principle of individualization is important here. Each swimmer will find a preferred cadence (SR) over time. Generally speaking, once swimming technique is mastered, SR becomes fairly consistent and decreased swim times occur as the result of longer stroke length.

There are ranges of inefficiency in SR that are more obvious. These are stroke rates that are either too high or too low. A too-high SR has a characteristic of slippage, exaggerated sweeping of the hand and arms underwater, and uncoordinated motions in general. Too-low SR is observed with swimmers gliding where there is a loss of continuity or propulsion. The important point here is that with improvements in technique and movement function, there will be a lessening of RPE and swim time. There will also be improvements in ACES and a honing of preferred and most efficient SR (up and down).

Practice these body lines using the testing tables that follow the explanation. These tables outline repetitions and distances (in meters, but yards can be used).

Posture, Balance, and Streamlined Body Lines

Here we'll discuss how to assess movement errors and develop the right positions and posture for training the body lines. The body lines should be trained at lower intensities and at light speed with a focus on achieving perfect form—or as close to perfect as possible. Your goal is neural control and reshaping technique, which require shifts in positions, postures, and timing.

Posture and Balance Lines

As noted earlier in the chapter, posture is of central importance in swimming, which is why posture is the first body line we'll address. Swimmers must always be mindful of the body's vertical, lateral, and horizontal positions in the water. These positions should be uniform throughout the freestyle stroke. Uniformity is achieved by maintaining the posture line—that is, head, torso, hips, and feet are aligned along the center axis of the body. A principle of posture is keeping the sternum and the center or the pelvis connected and aligned. This will improve overall body positioning by streamlining from head to toe and increase the transfer of forces from the deep inner core and pelvis.

A typical position for the swimming triathlete is sinking of the hips and legs, often accompanied by out-of-sync positioning of the arms and shoulders. Some of this is caused by low levels of body fat, but anyone can improve balance and natural buoyancy lines through attentive training. Reducing drag can increase swimming speed, and less energy or muscular power is needed to maintain the same speed. As we have emphasized, it is not propulsive forces but minimizing resistance, in combination with good technique, that most improves swimming. Each technique (body line) and every stroke of your workouts should be performed in a smooth, streamlined, balanced, and level (horizontal) body position.

Common faults of the posture and body symmetry lines include the following:

- Poor horizontal and lateral proprioceptive awareness of alignment of the body in the water
- Differences in the timing and positions of the left and right sides
- Lateral shifting of the hips due to misalignment of the sternum and pelvis
- Overrotation of the head
- Late breathing (beginning breath with the catch)
- Overreaching to the midline during the entry
- Contralateral stroke with one hand at the hip and the other extending overhead, placing the swimmer out of the front quadrant

In proper technique for the posture and body symmetry, the head, torso, hips, and feet are aligned at all times (center of axis). A posture with one hand overhead in a V or Y position is what you want to achieve when in the water (figure 6.15). Initially, concentrate on maintaining a long, fully lengthened body with the chest downward slightly. Lengthen-

FIGURE 6.15 V or Y position.

ing and keeping the chest down will naturally raise your hips and legs through a shift in the center of mass and use the buoyancy in the lungs. Another effective technique is to alter your stroke by catching up (front quadrant)—that is, keeping both arms in front of the head and shoulders for most of the stroke or at least until the stroking arm begins the insweep (figure 6.16).

Streamline Line

A swimmer who is streamlined is in the most hydrodynamic position and moves through the water with less resistance. By streamlining the full line of the body, you encounter much less resistance to forward movement. The energy of the stroking arms can then be used more efficiently, which results in further distance for each stroke, thus fewer strokes.

Common faults in the streamline line include the following:

- Taking up too much space (sideways, height, depth) or moving with unnecessary motions with the body and limbs causes increased resistance, or drag.

- Holding the head too high (extending chin away from chest) pushes hips and legs down. Raising the head can double the drag from the water because the frontal surface area increases dramatically.

- Kicking too deep increases the amount of space occupied by the body in the water. This increases the frontal surface area, causing greater drag.

Proper technique for streamlining is to begin every turn, push from the wall, and entry into the water with as narrow, horizontal, and elongated a body as possible (with the sternum and middle of the pelvis aligned). Each phase of the stroke should effortlessly preserve this body position along the length of the pool. From the wall push-off, hands are placed one atop the other, head is between biceps, and eyes are looking down. At the entry and extension of one arm, the small, narrow frontal surface is maintained by continuing the narrowest and highest (horizontal) body positions (figure 6.17).

Posture, Balance, and Streamlines ACES Test

Practice and test posture, balance, and streamlines together. When you have mastered these, retest by matching your lifestyle level in table 1.3 and your baseline test distance in table 1.4 for a Sub-T, as described in the note for figure 6.18.

FIGURE 6.16 Front quadrant.

FIGURE 6.17 Narrow and small frontal surface.

FIGURE 6.18   ACES body lines test: posture, balance symmetry, and streamline.

*BASELINE TEST DISTANCE: _____	ASSESSMENT				COMMENTS
ACES	Pass	Fail			
Accurate (pass–fail)					
Controlled (pass–fail)					
Effortless (pass–fail)					
Smooth (pass–fail)					
Meter time for sub-T	_____				
Pace per 100 meters	_____				
**Number of strokes per 50 m: _____	25%	50%	75%	Last 50	
Rating of perceived exertion					

*Sub-T baseline test distance (see table 1.4).

**Number of strokes per 50 m—count the number of strokes taken per 50 meters at 25 percent, 50 percent, and 75 percent of distance and the last 50 meters.

From M. Evans and J. Cappaert, *Triathletes in motion.* (Champaign, IL: Human Kinetics).

Breath, Head, and Eye Lines

The breath, head, and eye lines are among the most important body lines in swimming. Excessive flexion, extension, or rotation of the head transfers to every other part of the body and affects efficiency. The postures and positions of each of these body lines are fundamentally important to master and make every other technique position better.

Breath Line

As swimmers inhale oxygen, they do so through the nose and mouth and deep into the lower diaphragm. Through the windpipe (pharynx), the air makes its way through the bronchi, bronchioles, and alveoli. From this point, some oxygen makes its way into the bloodstream. The rate and the depth of breathing are in response to the body's metabolic needs—the intensity of effort. Over time, you learn to breathe in and exhale naturally within the tempo and rhythm of your strokes. There is a different tempo and pattern of breathing for each sport (swimming, cycling, and running), and these differences are learned through training. Thus some novices might struggle for a time in developing tempo and skill for breathing while swimming.

Because the body does an incredible job of making physiological adjustments to the work rate and moving air in and out of the lungs, there should not be an overly deliberate or forced effort to modify your breathing. Still, some athletes do not use the diaphragm (major muscle for inspiration) effectively, particularly under stress, and this is the primary muscle for normal inspiration of air.

When working correctly, ventilation (exchange of air to and from the body via breathing) is low during relaxed breathing and is much more efficient. Physical and emotional stress can affect normal breathing patterns, altering the normal muscle work to accessory muscles, which causes a decrease in ventilation. Learning to use the diaphragm in a natural way can improve ventilation and relaxation, decrease the work rate of breathing, and improve the exchange of gas and oxygenation (air into body that travels through the blood).

Common faults of the breath line include the following:

- Labored, short, rapid, and shallow breath
- Breath held underwater
- Breath forcefully exhaled through the mouth

- Breaths taken too early or too late in the stroke, disrupting the natural rhythm of the breathing pattern
- Use of accessory muscles to breathe that increase chest expansion and lower the use of the primary diaphragmatic muscles

In proper technique for the breath line, the head and torso begin to rotate slowly to the side as the catch and insweep begin the breath. The movements are symmetrical (i.e., together, not separate), and there should be no tension about the face, jaw, or muscles of the neck. The head turns slightly, and breath (inhalation) is back and to the side to maintain the eye-goggle line with a broad but relaxed outward expansion of the ribs (bilateral costal expansion). Inhalation is increased once at the full turn. Think of expanding the lower ribs and the back fully outward to take in a full and complete breath. The shoulders and chest should be relaxed, allowing the abdomen to rise lightly and fully for inhalation.

When the face returns underwater, let the air flow naturally, slowly, and fully out of the nose, keeping muscles relaxed. The mouth should be only slightly open as air slightly bubbles and seeps through the lips. This maintains the natural tempo of breathing while holding the air in the lungs for a longer time to maintain balance in the body. Note that if you expel air too rapidly you might feel breathlessness caused by hyperventilation.

Head Line

Your head's position in swimming should be in a neutral line with your spine. As you rotate to get air, your torso and head should pivot, preserving this alignment. There will be a slight break in alignment at the moment of taking in air, but in general it's best to maintain neutral alignment throughout your stroke.

Common faults of the head line include the following:

- Too much separation (chin not aligned with spine), resulting in poor shoulder, hip, and leg lateral alignment and expanded drag

- Turning head directly to the side (into the wake of the water line)
- Holding head too high, too low, and out of alignment with spine
- Rotating head too far up and back when breathing

In proper technique for the head line, the chin is kept in line with the center of the chest (sternum) and to some extent with a slight tilt downward when turning to breathe (figure 6.19). The head is turned to the side and slightly back into the trough (channel created by the head, producing a wake and air pocket) when breathing. With position of the head in a neutral posture (as when standing), the eyes are looking straight down to very slightly forward.

Backstroke swimming is outstanding for head-line training. The head is best held motionless with no lateral (side-to-side), flexion, or extended motion. Connecting and aligning the sternum with the middle of the pelvis will improve this posture as well. The arms, torso, and legs move about the center axis of the body, and the head remains positioned along this line.

Eye Line

From a neutral head and spine position, rotate both at the same time and in alignment to take air. The aim is to minimize movement,

FIGURE 6.19 Head line.

maintain a narrow frontal body, and be as streamlined as possible in the water.

Common faults for the eye line include the following:

- Nose and both eyes are out of the water. This excessive rotation and separation of the head and spine shift body alignment and cause preventable limb motions that increase effort to overcome drag.
- Head rotation, flexion, and extension, are too active when breathing, resulting in counteractions in the hips, legs, and feet, which create drag.

In proper technique for the eye line you turn your body and head and maintain an aligned, neutral orientation until one eye's goggle has broken the plane of the water line. Your mouth opens and curls somewhat upward to take a breath. You should see the water line during technique training.

Breath, Head, and Eye Line ACES Test

Practice and test the breath, head, and eye positions together. When you have mastered these, retest by matching your lifestyle level in table 1.3 and your baseline test distance in table 1.4 for a Sub-T, as described in the note for figure 6.20.

Fingertip, Entry, Extension, Wrist, and Downsweep Lines

In this stroke sequence, the body lines move into the sensitivity in the fingers and each line through the downsweep. Practicing each line with ACES over time will improve efficiency; some swimmers need to train all lines, whereas others can focus on fewer.

Fingertip Line

Research indicates exquisite capacity of the human brain to detect, localize, delineate, classify, and quantify specific sensations from the input of certain types of single sensory units, particularly in the fingertips.

Common faults in the fingertip line include the following:

- The fingers and hand are held too tightly.
- The fingers and hand are extended (flat).

In proper technique for the fingertip line, you can imagine an arcing, rounded line being followed by the fingertips (figure 6.21). By reaching forward, over, downward, and outward with the tip of the elbow pointed up, the catch is made sooner and increases the volume of water held.

FIGURE 6.20 ACES body lines test: breath, head, and eye lines.

*BASELINE TEST DISTANCE: _____	ASSESSMENT		COMMENTS		
ACES	Pass	Fail			
Accurate (pass–fail)					
Controlled (pass–fail)					
Effortless (pass–fail)					
Smooth (pass–fail)					
Meter time for Sub-T	_____				
Pace per 100 m	_____				
** Number of strokes per 50 m: _____	25%	50%	75%	Last 50	
Rating of perceived exertion					

*Sub-T baseline test distance (see table 1.4).

**Number of strokes per 50 m—count the number of strokes taken per 50 meters at 25 percent, 50 percent, and 75 percent of distance and the last 50 meters.

From M. Evans and J. Cappaert, *Triathletes in motion*. (Champaign, IL: Human Kinetics).

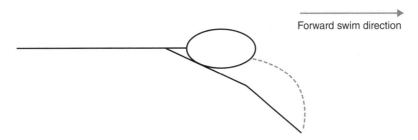

Forward swim direction

FIGURE 6.21 Arcing of the fingertip line.

Entry Line

The entry is particularly important and perhaps the most significant for setting up the correct positions and limb postures throughout the phases. There is a "feel" component here as the water flows from and along the fingertips, hand, and forearm. The elbow should be pointing up and never be under the wrist or hand as the hand feels the pressure of the water. There is momentum (forward movement) from the body moving forward when the fingertips enter the water—this can be described as oncoming flow. It is at this point that you should make an effort to sensitize and be fully aware of the water's feel against your fingers, hand, and forearm. There should be minimal interference and turbulence as the fingers, hand, wrist, elbow, upper arm, and finally shoulder enter the water.

The feel for the water that we have referred to is particularly evident during this phase. Good swimmers feel the flow, pressures, and the lift like that of a wing as it provides upward and underside forces during lift-off. This is the early stages of the wing line that will be discussed later. Sculling drills greatly improve this sensitivity to the angles, speed, and optimal positions of the hand and arm. If the entry is not accurate, controlled, effortless, and smooth, there is a strong likelihood other phases will be similarly affected. This phase is when the body begins the most balanced and elongated position as the hand and arm lengthen forward and slightly downward to begin the next phase.

Common faults in the entry include the following:

- Tension is felt in the hands (fingers closed tightly), shoulders, and neck.

- The hand slaps the water.
- The entry is too far in front of the shoulder (entry should be about half an arm's length in front of or just outside the shoulder line).

In proper technique for the entry line, the fingertips, hand, wrist, and then elbow follow the same line, all passing through the entry into the water created by the fingertips. They should enter the water in front of the head and even with or slightly outside of the shoulder. There are variations of hand pitch or angle, such as a thumb angled downward (diagonally pitched outward) or entering with the middle finger first, but in all cases the fingertips should make smooth entry first. The palm and underside of the forearm should be aligned in the same direction to keep the elbow slightly flexed and above the hand before making the extension.

Extension Line

The extension, or stretch, is a continuation of the entry line as you lengthen and stretch your leading hand and arm in a long and somewhat downward and arcing path. Your hips release as your body pivots along its axis to provide more forward extension of the hand and arm. Maintain your elbow above your wrist and hand with a slight flex. You will feel an increasing pressure on the underside of your aligned palm and forearm (facing the same direction). The movement is a shallow arc in a forward and slightly downward motion.

Common faults of the extension line include the following:

- Straightening the arm places the elbow underneath the hand and wrist, resulting in a less effective propulsive position.

- You begin a downward press onto the water ahead of the opposite hand beginning the exit line.
- The body has too much lateral rotation.
- You glide, which is counterproductive to maintaining a continuous motion of the body. You should have constant motion with no periods of deceleration.

In correct technique for the extension line, the elbow remains above the hand with the elbow slightly flexed and following the entry line of the fingers and hand. You move forward, arcing slightly downward. When your opposite hand has finished near midtorso (early exit), it is time for the next phase—the wrist line.

Wrist Line

The wrist is not excessively bent but only slightly cupping down. This motion traps the water under the hand (reduces air so fewer bubbles are present), which deflects still water away to provide leverage, a posture for the upcoming catch phase.

Common faults in the wrist line include the following:

- Too much force is applied (should be a soft positioning and feeling of the water on the hand and forearm).
- There is no excessive wrist flexion.
- Increased extension occurs in the wrist (fingers point up).
- The wrist is not aligned with the forearm (they should face the same direction).

In proper technique for the wrist line, you make a slight flexion of the wrist (to slightly cup the hand) as fingers near the fullest stretch and hips have rotated along their axis. This motion happens together with the release of the stroking arm at the hip line.

Downsweep Line

The downsweep is one of the most important elements in swimming but is often incorrectly applied. The downsweep should follow the entry and extension (stretch) and is especially important for creating the most favorable underwater hand path for the catch, insweep, upsweep, and outsweep. The motion of the hand and arm is smooth and effortless as it passes gradually downward, forward, and slightly outward, with the elbow remaining high and flexed as the body is moving forward. Because of its connection to and from important phases (entry, extension, catch, and insweep), this movement sets the tempo and effectiveness of the pathways for each phase. However, the fingertips are the sensory leaders to achieving more efficient pathways and movements and should lead the hand and arm into and from each of the phases of the stroke.

The early posture of the downsweep begins once the fingers enter the water and stretch forward with a slight arcing downward motion during the extension. The elbow remains directed upward (this flexes the elbow and forearm into a winglike lever) and remains above the hand through the stroke. As the stroking arm nears its completion of the release of pressure at the hips, the leading hand and arm are sweeping downward (fingertips leading) in a drawn-out and curved flow.

Use the very ends of the fingertips to lead and sense the water and to determine the gentle sloping forward and downward motion of the downsweep. Doing so elongates the stroke and lets the positioning of the hand and forearm for the catch to be made more naturally. Swimmers often rush this part of the stroke and apply downward pressure that disturbs forward propulsion.

This positioning, a soft and easy movement, can be imagined by picturing the fingertips guiding the hand, wrist, forearm, and elbow along a sloping pathway in an elegant and effortless maneuver that not only sets the high elbow catch and allows for the opposing hand and forearm to complete the most propulsive phases (insweep, upsweep, and outsweep) but also works to narrow the body in the water for better streamlining. A very old but completely accurate description is that the fingertips lead over a barrel that is sideways. The fingers reach over, out, down, and around until the pressure against the hand and underside of the forearm make the catch. There should be very little downward pressure against the water during this maneuver. Done accurately, the downsweep is a positioning movement, and any downward pressure against the water disrupts forward momentum by changing the direction of resulting forces.

Common faults in the downsweep include the following:

- Gliding the hand and arm at the surface and failing to arc over and downward
- Too much downward pressure
- Beginning the catch before the hand and arm have arced over the barrel
- Sweeping and pulling down at the extension, causing a missed catch and counter forces that do not move the body forward

In proper technique for the downsweep line, the downsweep begins at the same time that the opposite hand finishes the upsweep. The downsweep is for position and not propulsion, so take care in arcing forward and downward without any propulsive pressure, which is an essential part of learning to position the hand and arm in a leverage and winglike position. The elbow from entry, extension, and downsweep must be above the hand—this ensures better leverage against the water for the following sweeps of the stroke. Align the palm, inner forearm, and upper arm as the elbow is flexed for the catch. At the end of the extension, the wrist flexes slightly (downward and outward) as the hand and arm sweep forward in a gently downward and forward pathway. The movement is smooth and accurately controlled over a rounded arc downward, such as over an imaginary barrel.

Fingertip, Entry, Extension, Wrist, and Downsweep Lines ACES Test

Practice and test the fingertip, entry, extension, wrist, and downsweep lines together. When you have mastered these, retest by matching your lifestyle level in table 1.3 and your baseline test distance in table 1.4 for a Sub-T, as described in the note for figure 6.22.

Catch and Wing Lines

The catch and wing lines are an indispensible part of efficient swimming. As with each body line, achieving the correct posture is central to reshaping and improving swimming. Of course, this is dependent on functional posture, neurological (the brain's signals to muscles) transfer, athletic history, flexibility, joint

FIGURE 6.22 ACES body lines test: fingertip, entry, extension, wrist, and downsweep lines.

*BASELINE TEST DISTANCE: _____	ASSESSMENT				COMMENTS
ACES	Pass	Fail			
Accurate (pass–fail)					
Controlled (pass–fail)					
Effortless (pass–fail)					
Smooth (pass–fail)					
Meter time for Sub-T	_____				
Pace per 100 m	_____				
**Number of strokes per 50 m: _____	25%	50%	75%	Last 50	
Rating of perceived exertion					

*Sub-T baseline test distance (see table 1.4).

**Number of strokes per 50 m—count the number of strokes taken per 50 meters at 25 percent, 50 percent, and 75 percent of distance and the last 50 meters.

From M. Evans and J. Cappaert, *Triathletes in motion*. (Champaign, IL: Human Kinetics).

mobility, and stability both out of and in the water, and how the triathlete trains.

The fingertip wall slide described earlier (see figure 6.12) is an exceptional out-of-the-water way to train the posture and position of the catch and wing lines. This drill is so effective because it's done while holding an erect body posture and maintaining clear positions of the fingertips, forearm, and elbow.

Catch Line

The limb position for the catch line is important for generating propulsion. The catch occurs at the end of the downsweep at the deepest part, where the hand and arm catch the water. At this moment the body is accelerating forward, but the catch does not occur until the hand and arm are about 14 to 20 inches (35-50 cm) deep into the water. This is a soft position with little muscular forces applied at this time. The hand and underside of the forearm must be directed back before applying too much, if any, force. Doing so earlier increases downward, inward, and outward forces, which do not provide forward momentum at this moment of the stroke. The best swimmers hold back on exerting force and work to position the hand and arm in the highest leverage location, about a third of the way into the stroke.

Common faults of the catch line include the following:

- Putting too much force into the early phase of the downsweep to catch with a high elbow can cause shoulder tendinitis. Wait until the hand and forearm align more vertically (they are pointing downward with undersides facing backward; they need not be completely vertical to be effective).

- Raising the elbows while pushing the arms back. It's better to fix elbow position by stabilizing the shoulder and then using leverage to hold water as the body moves over a more or less fixed hand placement (better swimmers hold or anchor the hand and arm in the water).

In proper technique for the catch line, the forearm and hand are in a more or less vertical position (elbow flexed and high); the underside of the palm, underside of the forearm, and upper arm are aligned and facing backward (refer to the catch phase of figure 6.11). Think of the catch as a limb-positioning maneuver. This position places the hand and forearm in a leverage-like position, extending capacity to hold the water. Much is said about the high elbow and early vertical forearm, but you don't hear a lot about the best way to arrive at this position and what forces are necessary to attain it.

Little, if any, muscular effort is applied downward, inward, backward, or upward until the undersides of the palm and forearm are aligned and facing backward. For triathletes, particularly those without extensive swimming experience, the catch is perhaps best achieved by visualizing and applying an arcing forward and downward motion. A technique going back at least into the 1960s and perhaps aptly attributed to James Councilman (legendary swimming coach of Olympic gold medalist Mark Spitz) is the practice of extending and arcing the hand and arm over a barrel to make the catch. At this instant, an increasing pressure is felt by the hand and forearm as the catch is made fully and deeply, with a complete purchase of the water, which sets you up for the next phase of the stroke—the insweep.

Wing Line

Lateral and vertical (diagonal) sculling motions are perhaps of most importance for improving, increasing, and generating propulsion during the stroke. These are sweeping motions that do not involve pulling the hand and arm back, as the term pull certainly implies. Perhaps a change in language is needed to describe this phase of the stroke. Efficient swimmers do not pull but hold the water via effective lateral and vertical—and to some degree horizontal—patterns of movement. Biomechanists have proposed for over 30 years that there is a three-dimensional aspect in optimal swimming, with hand and arm motions moving laterally, vertically, and horizontally in sweeps and sculls. Thus the word *pull* does not really describe what happens during an efficient swimming stroke. The hands do not press backward by pulling but instead hold the water by shaping, deflecting, and moving the hand and arm laterally and vertically (sculling), and very slightly backward. Thus an efficient swimmer moves the body forward relative to the position of the hand. In effect, the body moves over the anchored or stable point of the sculling hand and arm.

Hand and arm sculling drills are recommended for learning the feel for how the body can move economically through the water via lateral and vertical motions. There is a winglike shape of the upper arm, elbow, lower arm, and hand when doing these drills and swimming naturally. This shape positions the forearm and hand in an optimal position to scull, shape, and hold on to the water in much the same way a bird wing is shaped during flight.

Common faults in the wing line include the following:

- Winging (not flat) scapula
- Pushing water forcefully backward (horizontally)
- Pushing the hand past the hips
- Hands slipping though the water following the extension and beginning of the catch
- Elbow underneath the wrist and hand (a dropped elbow)
- Armpit closing down during the insweep and outsweep

In proper technique for the wing line the elbow remains fixed from the entry, extension, catch, insweep, and outsweep phases. This is the high-elbow position that is most effective for leveraging and sculling water diagonally. The armpit is kept open, especially during the insweep and outsweep diagonal portions of the stroke; the hand, forearm, and upper arm catch the water as if reaching over and around a large barrel (figure 6.23). An open armpit causes the elbow to remain flexed so palm and forearm can be directed backward to secure a better hold against the water. The key point is to reach over the barrel for position and optimal leverage. A deeper catch in

FIGURE 6.23 Wing line.

open water has less turbulence and can be held more effectively.

Catch and Wing Lines ACES Test

Practice and test the catch and wing lines together. When you have mastered these, retest by matching your lifestyle level in table 1.3 and your baseline test distance in table 1.4 for a Sub-T, as described in the note for figure 6.24.

Insweep, Upsweep, and Outsweep Lines

The subtle sweeps (in, up, and out) occur diagonally and deflect water, resulting in increased water-holding potential, which is what you want. Practicing these regions and techniques along with sculling will improve efficiency.

Insweep Line

The body moves forward at its fastest during the insweep, which is a very slight diagonal and inward rounding off as the body rotates over the arm following the catch. The term *sweep* is perhaps confusing because the hand and arm are actually held in still water (water

FIGURE 6.24 ACES body lines test: catch and wing lines.

*BASELINE TEST DISTANCE: _____	ASSESSMENT		COMMENTS
ACES	Pass	Fail	
Accurate (pass–fail)			
Controlled (pass–fail)			
Effortless (pass–fail)			
Smooth (pass–fail)			
Meter time for Sub-T	_____		
Pace per 100 m	_____		
**Number of strokes per 50 m: _____	25%	50%	75%	Last 50	
Rating of perceived exertion					

*Sub-T baseline test distance (see table 1.4).

**Number of strokes per 50 m—count the number of strokes taken per 50 meters at 25 percent, 50 percent, and 75 percent of distance and the last 50 meters.

From M. Evans and J. Cappaert, *Triathletes in motion.* (Champaign, IL: Human Kinetics).

not moving straight backward). With the elbow flexed (above the hand) as the body rotates and moves over the forward point of the hand, you hold water with a downward and inward sculpting motion without pulling or pushing water backward.

There is pressure on the palm of the hand, forearms, and underside of the upper arms, which form a winglike position. You trap and hold water with the fullness of the hand, forearm, and upper underside of the arm with the elbow flexed. No sweep of the hand or arm is necessary; rather, the powerful shoulder and back muscles hold the wing position (elbow flexed and high).

Common faults in the insweep include the following:

- Sweeping past or well under the midline of the body reduces propulsive forces.
- Not sweeping laterally enough—there should be some inward rounding-off with the palm and underside of the forearm
- Moving the arm (flexing the elbow too much) and hand instead of holding the water
- Making an exaggerated S-like stroke with the arms and hand

In proper technique for the insweep, the hand and underarm of the forearm sweep inward slightly and round off for the next propulsive phase—the outsweep and upsweep. A noticeable increase in limb acceleration occurs at this phase until another rounding-off for the out- and upsweep. The elbow should remain bent like a wing for maximal generation of propulsive force; the hand and forearm should remain aligned in the direction of the sweep.

After the catch (over the barrel), the hand sweeps downward, backward, and rapidly accelerates inward. The palm and underside of the forearm move slightly and quickly inward, holding water as the body moves over the diagonal positioned hand and forearm.

Upsweep and Outsweep Line

The upsweep and outsweep is a pronounced outward and upward movement of the hand and forearm following the insweep. The speed of this movement increases to the same or higher velocity of the insweep.

There is continual acceleration of the hand and forearm, but the elbow remains flexed and does not extend. Rather, this sweeping motion deflects water in such a way that there is a sensation of an ever-increasing hold on the water, creating leverage and pressure against the hand and arm from which to propel forward. At this point the body moves over a fixed hand (held against still water) with greater propulsive force. As the hand and forearm collect and hold still water, the transition from the insweep to the up- and outsweep begins with the highest sweeping and an active rounding-off angling of the hand and forearm in an upward, outward, and backward pathway.

Common faults in the upsweep and outsweep include the following:

- Pushing backward past the hip (hand should exit at midtorso)
- Pushing back and upward
- Extending the elbow at the finish and release of the hand before recovery

In proper technique for the upsweep and outsweep, the hand and forearm remain aligned and round off from the insweep. The hand and forearm sweep backward, upward, and outward; the elbow remains flexed and high.

Insweep, Upsweep, and Outsweep Lines ACES Test

Practice and test the insweep, upsweep, and outsweep together. When you have mastered these, retest by matching your lifestyle level in table 1.3 and your baseline test distance in

table 1.4 for a Sub-T, as described in the note for figure 6.25.

Exit, Recovery, and Scapular Lines

The exit, recovery, and scapular body lines are the later phases of the stroke cycle, but their positions, timing, and performance connect to each other phase. For each of these phases, focus on proper posture and achieving ACES in each movement.

Exit Line

The exit of the hand (release) is timed with the entry, extension, and downsweep and coordinates with the moment of the catch of the opposite hand. Though gliding might be an accurate description of the nonstroking arm (entry, stretch, and downsweep), such a description might also be misleading.

At the moment of release (exit), the stroking arm has just completed the highest propulsive phases (insweep and outsweep). At the same time, the opposite arm and forearm are now arcing forward and downward (with low force) to position for the catch. It is at this instant that the catch and the exit are equally timed to sustain momentum.

The exit (release) and the catch occur at exact same time. This prolongs momentum

FIGURE 6.25   ACES body lines test: insweep, upsweep, and outsweep lines.

*BASELINE TEST DISTANCE: _____ ACES	ASSESSMENT		COMMENTS		
	Pass	Fail			
Accurate (pass–fail)					
Controlled (pass–fail)					
Effortless (pass–fail)					
Smooth (pass–fail)					
Meter time for Sub-T	_____				
Pace per 100 m	_____				
**Number of strokes per 50 m: _____	25%	50%	75%	Last 50	
Rating of perceived exertion					

*Sub-T baseline test distance (see table 1.4).

**Number of strokes per 50 m—count the number of strokes taken per 50 meters at 25 percent, 50 percent, and 75 percent of distance and the last 50 meters.

From M. Evans and J. Cappaert, *Triathletes in motion*. (Champaign, IL: Human Kinetics).

and maintains velocity. Gliding, on the other hand, indicates instant nonpropulsion. If the opposite arm is gliding at the exit, an immediate loss of forward speed begins.

Momentum is maintained by keeping strokes constant and the tempo from left to right side uniform. The position of the limbs, time taken from one stroke to the next, and the body's rotation should be equal and balanced.

Common faults in the exit include the following:

- Pushing backward toward thigh with palm facing upward (which pushes hips down)
- Pushing upward on the water with palm pointed upward as it nears and passes hips
- Fully extending hand and arm toward midthigh, increasing glide by lengthening recovery time because exiting arm must now travel a greater distance before entry
- Flexing or extending the wrist, putting hand, wrist, and forearm out of alignment
- Pressing too deep, causing an upward motion of the palm, a downward alignment of the hips, and increased drag and deceleration

In proper technique for the exit line, hand pressure is released midtorso and before the hips for an early exit following the upsweep and outsweep. You stop pushing up, out, and backward at the top of the hip and exit with little finger first and palm turned inward.

Recovery Line

The upsweep thrust provides the momentum to begin the recovery. The recovery includes the breath and the beginning of the downsweep on the opposite hand and arm. It begins with the elbow exiting the water first. There are differences in recovery techniques, but most successful swimmers use the following pattern:

1. Exit the water with shoulder and elbow leading.

2. Elbow is flexed as soon as it exits the water.
3. Elbow leads the hand and forearm until at the shoulder.
4. Recovery is unhurried and relaxed and does not alter the rhythm of the stroke.

The recovery should not be forced or hurried and is characteristically made with the elbow higher than the hand (high elbow and low hand). The shoulder leads the elbow; the hand and forearm follow. The middle deltoid is active to abduct and lift the arm during recovery as the supraspinatus couples with the deltoids for stability and the anterior deltoid abducts and begins the flexing of the humerus.

Common faults in the recovery include the following:

- Too wide or swinging arm—a high hand and arm result in lateral alignment problems, increasing drag and causing unnecessary waggling motions of the hips, head, shoulder, hands, arms, and legs.
- The elbow is brought up and inward toward the spine (overrotation).

In proper technique for the recovery, recovery begins before the hand has exited the water, with the elbow exiting first by lifting the shoulder. The arm is flexed at the elbow with the hand completely relaxed underneath as the shoulder brings the hand and arm forward to make the entry in front of the shoulder. The recovery should be relaxed, smooth, and unhurried, matching the opposite arm and hand progressing into the downsweep (a nonpropulsive but important positioning movement).

Scapular Line

The scapula (shoulder blade) connects the upper-arm bone (humerus) with the collar bone (clavicle). Upper-arm motions are accompanied by scapular motions using the upper trapezius, rhomboids, levator scapulae, serratus anterior, and pectoralis minor muscles to elevate, depress, abduct (move away from the body), adduct (bring inward), upwardly rotate, and downwardly rotate the scapula.

Each of these motions is part of the swimming stroke, and shoulder girdle and scapular stability are particularly important. Because the shoulder has just one bony attachment there is significant mobility in the joint. Stability is provided between the scapular and glenohumeral joint (shoulder joint) muscles. The muscles of the scapula help stabilize and control the position and maintain the most effective length and tension of the upper arm. If these muscles are not stable, control is reduced, and faults in technique and posture can cause imbalances.

Stroke mechanics adapt as a result of weakness in the scapula because muscles cannot stabilize the shoulder blade. For example, a forward tilt in the scapula (forward-leaning head) decreases the flexibility of the pectorals (chest), levator scapulae (posterior neck muscles that elevate and adduct the scapula), and scalenius (posterior neck muscles) and weakens the serratus anterior (muscles of the thorax that rotate the scapula) and trapezius (large triangular muscle that stabilizes the scapula in most movements of the arm).

Common faults in the scapular line include the following:

- Winging of the scapula
- Elevated or rounded shoulders
- Downward rotation of the scapula
- Inability to maintain a stable and flat shoulder blade during downsweep, insweep, outsweep, and upsweep

In proper technique for the scapular line, each of the sweeping phases works to maintain a stable and flat shoulder blade. Separately, you should work on each phase of the stroke and isolate the position of the scapula for the most functional and stable position possible.

Exit, Recovery, and Scapular Lines ACES Test

Practice and test the exit, recovery, and scapular lines together. When you have mastered these, retest by matching your lifestyle level in table 1.3 and your baseline test distance in table 1.4 for a Sub-T, as described in the note for figure 6.26.

Kick Line

For the distance pool and open-water swimmer, the kick is a stabilizer of the body, and overkicking uses a lopsided amount of energy in relation to the amount of propulsion achieved. Most common are the two-beat and the two-beat crossover kicks for most distance swimmers. Some will use a four- or a six-beat kick. Even this is changing: Distance

FIGURE 6.26 ACES body lines test: exit, recovery, and scapular lines.

*BASELINE TEST DISTANCE: _____	ASSESSMENT		COMMENTS		
ACES	Pass	Fail			
Accurate (pass–fail)					
Controlled (pass–fail)					
Effortless (pass–fail)					
Smooth (pass–fail)					
Meter time for Sub-T	_____				
Pace per 100 m	_____				
**Number of strokes per 50 m: _____	25%	50%	75%	Last 50	
Rating of perceived exertion					

*Sub-T baseline test distance (see table 1.4).

**Number of strokes per 50 m—count the number of strokes taken per 50 meters at 25 percent, 50 percent, and 75 percent of distance and the last 50 meters.

From M. Evans and J. Cappaert, *Triathletes in motion.* (Champaign, IL: Human Kinetics).

swimmers now use a constant six-beat or a rhythm of six kicks during each stroke cycle of the arms. Whichever kick you prefer, your goal is to develop an energy-protecting rhythm that matches your stroke rate and fitness. Learning to swim is complex and challenging; so much trial and error can take years of practice, but this time can be shortened by using body line training techniques and a model for motor learning that provides a framework for developing and teaching better motions and how to move in the water.

For triathletes, the kick is reduced substantially when wearing a wetsuit. The technology is continually developing a more streamlined, functionally mobile, and hydrodynamically perfected speedsuit for open-water swimming. The kick with a wetsuit is minimal, if any, because buoyancy gives hips and legs (the areas of the body that sink) substantial horizontal lift. The result is that your legs float more or less behind you, especially if you are wearing a high-density wetsuit. For the beginning to intermediate swimmer, this can be an advantage because kicking symmetry has likely not been developed. However, for the advanced to elite swimmer there can be some changes to stroke mechanics with a wetsuit that is too buoyant in the wrong places. For example, an excessive arching or extension of the neck and lower body can occur caused by extra buoyancy in the legs and arms.

Regardless of pool or wetsuit, the rhythm, movements, and motions of the kick from hips to feet is important to train to unify the stroke. You must learn how to coordinate and control the various muscle groups to achieve the best proficiency in swimming whether or not a wetsuit is worn.

The freestyle kick has a small production of propulsive force, but its impact is meaningful because an efficient kick helps reduce resistance to forward motion by maintaining a horizontal body position. If you cannot make forward progress with hands in a streamlined position along the length of the pool because your feet are sinking or splashing (or even staying in place or moving backward), you need motor learning and practice.

Common faults in the kick include the following:

- Rapid, fluttering kicking that is untimed with the stroke
- Deep and forceful kicking
- Dorsiflexed feet (toes pointing down)
- Everted feet (toes pointing out and down)
- Shallow and splashing at surface
- Bending at the knee because of dorsiflexed feet (toes not pointed—also known as a runner's or biker's kick); an excessive knee bend disrupts streamline by taking up more space in the water
- Legs too low in the water (sinking)

In proper technique for the kick, the knee bends only slightly, with feet providing flipperlike action; lift comes from the top of the foot surface. Toes are pointed inward and are relaxed and supple. Feet should be slightly angled inward; sometimes toes are touching. Keeping the sternum and middle of the pelvis in alignment narrows the body and enhances kick symmetry.

Kicking Methods

The kick is not significantly propulsive in distance freestyle, but poor or inefficient kicking disrupts the flow of water and streamline and can affect stroke tempo. A good kick begins from the pelvis and core, where load transfer is generated.

If you feel tightness when sitting on your feet, when using foam rollers, during deep-tissue therapies, or when kicking with ergonomic and flexible foam swimming fins, you should stretch the plantar flexion in your ankles.

The following in-water kicking exercises are superb for learning how to generate forces from the core parts of the body, streamline postures, and time your kick. They also improve ankle and foot mechanics.

Vertical Kicking

For freestyle vertical kicking, descend with feet first and hands streamlined overhead in 9 to 13 feet (about 3-4 m) of water. Fully exhale through the nose. Flutter kick to surface with toes pointed and initiating the kick from hips for three to five minutes (resting at the surface by sculling until you've recovered). For dolphin vertical kicking, descend with feet first and hands streamlined overhead in 9 to 13 feet (about 3-4 m) of water. Dolphin kick (undulating and wiggling entire body with the feet and legs together) to surface with toes pointed, initiating the kick from hips for three to five minutes.

Horizontal Kicking

For horizontal kicking, use a snorkel rather than a kickboard, which puts the body into extension—a poor posture. A snorkel allows the head to remain neutral and hands in a streamlined position with body horizontal. Push off wall into a narrow and rapid flutter kick (generate forces from hips) to a full, narrow streamlined position for a full length (may use soft foam fins).

Kick Line ACES Test

Practice and test the kick line. When you have mastered the kick line, retest by matching your lifestyle level in table 1.3 and your baseline test distance in table 1.4 for a Sub-T, as described in the note for figure 6.27.

Technique Exercises and Workouts for Swimming

Including technique and body line training in workouts is smart—it's not always about how far and how fast. Technique can be part of any training session or workout that focuses on developing form through thoughtful and purposeful training.

Technique Exercises for Swimming

Training form follows function, and in the following section we'll key on one body line, body region, or technique with added instruction on applying these in training workouts. Keep in mind triathlon is not pool swimming so in-season open-water training is important to include; the techniques in this section are good ones to put into those workouts. Fifty-meter (long course) training should be added to the program whenever possible. In short-course pools, swimming these workouts with lane mates using a pace clock to keep the rhythm of intervals and continuing neural adaptations might be incorporated from time to time.

Here you are working on modifying technique and improving economy through better

FIGURE 6.27   ACES body lines test: kick line.

*BASELINE TEST DISTANCE: ____	ASSESSMENT		COMMENTS
ACES	Pass	Fail	
Accurate (pass–fail)			
Controlled (pass–fail)			
Effortless (pass–fail)			
Smooth (pass–fail)			
Meter time for Sub-T	____		
Pace per 100 m	____		
Rating of perceived exertion			

*Sub-T baseline test distance (see table 1.4).

From M. Evans and J. Cappaert, *Triathletes in motion*. (Champaign, IL: Human Kinetics).

movements. High-intensity and longer-distance intervals should not be a part of this approach, but there are benefits in including shorter distances (25 to 50 meters) at very high outputs, always with a focus on the trained body lines and ACES.

Good posture in swimming is essential. Every good swimmer has good posture; the best swimmers have great posture. Every stroke of the arms should be executed while holding the lines of the body as stable as possible. Drawing in the lower abdominals (with a light activation of the hollow areas to each side of the navel) during exhalation helps stabilize the pelvis and spine. As you swim each stroke from left to right, strive for symmetry by working about an axis (line dividing the body from head to pelvis) with little downward, upward, or sideways movement in the shoulder, torso, pelvis, hip, or foot.

The following are the central points and principles of swimming that are the foundations of every movement and stroke. A warm-up might include swimming 50 to 100 meters focusing on each of these standards to help set and train these fundamentals.

- The entry is slightly outside the shoulder into a V or Y body posture.
- The head turns with the center of the body only as far as needed to get air, generally no further than the center of the head; in calm water only one eye is out of the water during breathing.
- Elongate the back of the neck and reach forward until shoulders rotate from 20 to 30 degrees.
- Alter the tempo and timing of the stroke to be in the front quadrant with both hands in front of the shoulder during the catch. Think of vaulting over the extending hand as it holds water—it does not pull back. This posture shifts the center of mass forward to help maintain a horizontal body position.
- The catch with high elbow is central to good swimming efficiency; this is a nonpropulsive posture and position in which the elbow remains close to the surface as the hand, wrist, and forearm (in alignment) move to catch and hold water (not pull).
- In the exit, don't push back toward the hips; exit midtorso.
- Work strokes from the inside deeper core by transferring energy from the pelvis and spine through the body and to the arms.
- Breathe in fully into the abdomen; exhale predominantly through the nose.

Vaulting and Hurdle-Line Exercise

For this exercise, imagine the top of a hurdle horizontally positioned as the left (or right) hand reaches full extension following entry. At this moment, the recovering arm and hand swing to vault over the hurdle. This exercise helps with the front quadrant and early exit to maintain the continuum of the stroke and the holding of water (not pulling). Swim 1,000 meters of 40 × 25 with 15 seconds rest on reps 1 through 10; swim 21 through 30 at very light intensity. For reps 11 through 20 and 31 through 40, include four strokes in the middle with head and torso out of the water. See the line and vault quickly over with the arm and hand.

Hold (Catch) Exercise

In this exercise, the hand, forearm, and underside of the upper arm catch and hold the water in such a way that the body moves over this point. The most efficient swimmers are very proficient, maintaining a fixed position with the hand in the water. Some call this *feel,* and to an extent more swimming volume and increasing the number of workouts does provide a better sensitivity to holding water. The catch is where you take hold, with little or no hand and arm slipping backward through the water. The effective catch holds water by making very small oblique changes in hand pitch to fix a point in the water—this keeps the hand from moving backward.

As you make each catch, find a fixed point in the water, and feel your body moving along its axis over this held position (drawing in the core and maintaining the sternal and pelvic alignment). Do all you can to minimize slipping, sliding, and moving backward via very small changes (less than .5 cm) in the angle of attack with the hand, wrist, and forearm in a vertically positioned alignment. Swim 20 × 50 at light RPE intensity with 20 seconds of rest, as follows:

- Repetitions 1 through 5—work on holding water using your current stroke, counting the number of full strokes for each 50.

- Repetitions 6 through 10—alter the hand and forearm pitch during the downsweep to catch using a downward, backward, and outward motion with very small changes in the angle of the hand and with no more than one centimeter difference from normal (count the number of strokes).

- Repetitions 11 through 15—repeat the previous set breathing bilaterally each third stroke; count the number of strokes.

- Repetitions 16 through 20—return to your normal side breathing working on fixing the hand in a permanent location and transferring energy from the deeper muscles of the core to the hand and forearm; count the number of strokes.

Core, Transversus Abdominis, and Load Transfer

In this exercise you activate the transversus abdominis (TrA) by drawing in to stabilize body alignment, which results in better posture and position for each stroke. The body is more functionally positioned because of the increased activation of the TrA, so the pelvic load transfer amplifies with energy through the torso, shoulders, back, and finally through the arms and hands.

Place two fingers on the hollow areas of the belly on either side of the navel. Draw in as you exhale without any increased lumbar tension; hold this posture fully engaged. If done correctly, you'll be able to speak and breathe freely. Swim 20 × 50 meters at light intensity with 20 seconds rest, as follows: Draw in for 10 seconds at the wall, and then release and rest for 5 seconds (relax the muscle); repeat five times followed by 50 meters working the centerline axis of the body with head, shoulders, torso, and pelvis aligned and hips and feet tapered. Do an open or flip turn, but at the moment that you fully exhale, draw more deeply into the abdomen; hold this posture as you extend from the wall beginning the length. As you breathe out with each stroke, hollow-out by drawing in. This will set the TrA and train the deeper muscles of the core, help body lines and transfer energy to the limbs more effectively.

Soft Catch, High Elbow, and Flattened Scapula

The high-fixed elbow is essential for better freestyle and all-strokes swimming. This posture is not only more effective in helping hold water but also increases the distance per stroke because it places the hand and forearm into the leveraged and stationary position earlier. This posture directs forces backward and thrusts you forward. To do this, the catch must be soft and affected by little downward forces on the hand and forearm during the downstroke. You want to keep the end of the fingertips, wrist, and forearm on the same plane, lined up with one another. With too much downward pressure on the downsweep to the catch, those oblique forces must be overcome, increasing energy and changing the horizontal alignment and posture in the water.

Swim 4 × 100 and then 16 × 25 + 10 seconds + 1 minute between sets at a light intensity, as follows:

- Set 1—gently place into position the high elbow and low (more vertically positioned) hand and forearm using a soft, easy motion.

- Set 2—the elbow is held high just under the water surface and remains fixed (not moving down, out, up, or back).

- Set 3—carry out sets 1 and 2 while thinking of a gently positioned high elbow that does not move as the aligned hand and forearm easily rotate downward and more vertical.

- Set 4—emphasize the soft catch and high elbow by activating and maintaining a flat scapula (shoulder blade) as the hand and forearm move into a more vertical posture. (Note that not everyone can achieve this because of restricted mobility and stability, but most can get into a more vertical placement and use less downward force.)

Motor Units and Mixed Strokes

The central nervous system (CNS) causes muscle fibers to contract via electrical impulses, a process that occurs with phenomenal speed and accuracy. The brain signals the muscle to respond. Each muscle is a collection of thousands of single-cell muscle fibers that connect to bones, normally crossing joints. Force, load, and intensity determine the number of fibers that contract. The contraction occurs via a nerve impulse that stimulates the fiber, releasing energy for movement.

These impulses vary according to demand and determine the number of motor units that contract. Thus easy swimming uses a few units, whereas faster, high-intensity swimming causes a larger number of motor units to be activated. But it's not only intensity that stimulates motor units—movement, technique, and exercise also play a role.

The triathlete with body line training stimulates the CNS responses and through accurate repetition improves efficiency. In swimming, a good way to increase this stimulus is to use different strokes (nonfreestyle) to activate more units—because all four strokes (freestyle, backstroke, breaststroke, and butterfly) share related parts, particularly the high-elbow catch (and the centerline sternum to midpelvis posture).

A good training exercise to activate more motor units while targeting the high elbow is to swim four sets of 200 meters (or yards) freestyle plus 15 seconds of rest at a light intensity to work the high-elbow posture (soft catch) and horizontal body position (front quadrant). This is followed by 8 reps of 50 meters with 15 seconds to 45 seconds of rest, as follows:

- Set 1—200-meter freestyle plus 8 × 50 meters butterfly with 45-second rest
- Set 2—200-meter freestyle plus 8 × 50 meters backstroke with 15-second rest
- Set 3—200-meter freestyle plus 8 × 50 meters breaststroke with 15-second rest
- Set 4—200-meter freestyle plus 2 × 50 meters butterfly, 2 × 50 meters backstroke, 2 × 50 meters breaststroke, and 2 × 50 meters freestyle, all performed with ACES intensity and technique; after each 50 meters is a 30-second rest.

Technique Workouts for Swimming

For each technique-based workout, the first four to six strokes are done with "no breathing" to establish the centerline. Swim with lighter intensity and work on focusing on the body lines with a relaxed but mindful attention to attain the posture and position of each technique. Technique workouts should use ACES movements that are low in intensity with periodic higher-intensity and shorter-duration efforts for neural stimulation.

1500-Meter Technique Workout

This workout (figure 6.28) helps the triathlete train better body posture and four sequenced body lines. The intensity should be light and this workout is effective during recovery, off-season, and in-season easy training days and can be used as a warm-up for any in-season workout. Be sure to swim each set with ACES and work to achieve the correct postures and positions with each stroke.

FIGURE 6.28   1500-meter technique workout.

Set	Body line technique	Description	Distance of set (m)	Distance of repetitions (m)	Repetitions	Rest interval (sec.)
1	Body posture and balance	Level body vertical, lateral, horizontal, or length, depth, and width	300	25	12	10
2	Head	Head, sternum alignment during breath (eye line)	300	50	6	15
3	Entry	Fingertips, hand, wrist, and elbow extend forward in alignment	300	75	4	15
4	Wrist	Slight break preceding the catch phase to trap the water	300	50	6	15
5	Downsweep	Arcing forward and downward with no downward pressure on the water	300	300	1	NA

2000-Meter Technique Workout

The following technique workout (figure 6.29) trains the catch and works on the three sweeps of the stroke. Those are trained as body lines with focus separately and finally putting them all together. Your intensity should be light and work ACES on each movement and posture.

3000-Meter Technique Workout

This longer-distance technique workout (figure 6.30) is excellent for working ACES on the catch, entry, and body streamlines in 50- and 75-meter distances. You'll finish with the sequence of the extension, downsweep, and catch during a straight swim of 400 meters.

Multistroke Swimming Workout

Following is a multistroke 2400-meter workout (figure 6.31) that you can use as described or modify to fit your ability. Soft training fins can be used for all or part of the workout when learning each stroke. The key is to maintain the center posture on all strokes. Technique is the focus, not intensity. Work each swim with ACES. Refer to table 1.2 for the zone intensity levels.

Here are a few options for variation in this workout:

- Do only set 1, 2, or 3.
- Add 50 meters after each set of 4 × 25 or 8 × 25.
- Add 2 × 100 IM after each 8 × 25.

FIGURE 6.29   **2000-meter technique workout.**

Set	Body line technique	Description	Distance of set (m)	Distance of repetitions (m)	Repetitions	Rest interval (sec.)
1	Catch and wing line	Anchor and hold water with and open armpit	400	25	16	10
2	Insweep	Inward rounding diagonally; very slight deflection of water	400	50	8	15
3	Upsweep/ outsweep	Upward and outward motion after insweep	400	1	1	NA
4	Extension to downsweep	Extend the arm fully with the body streamlined; arc forward and downward to the downsweep	400	100	4	20
5	Catch, insweep, upsweep, outsweep	Above together	400	400	1	NA

FIGURE 6.30   3000-meter technique workout.

Set	Body line technique	Description	Distance of set (m)	Distance of repetitions (m)	Repetitions	Rest interval (sec.)
1	Catch	Holding elbow fixed, slowly rotate fingers, wrist, and forearm to a vertical posture.	1000	50	20	10
2	Entry and streamline	Enter the water with no splashing in front of the shoulder extending in a V or Y posture to extension. Keep body narrow and balanced on a center axis.	600	75	8	20
3	Entry, extension, downsweep, and catch	Enter the water and extend fully; slowly arc forward and downward with elbow fixed and near the surface to catch and hold water.	400	1	1	NA
4	Alternate backstroke and freestyle; leveraged and high elbow	Odd swims are backstroke and even freestyle. The elbow is leveraged against the forearm during backstroke; forearm, wrist, and hand are aligned. (Backstroke is upside-down freestyle.) Freestyle is a soft-positioned catch from a high-held elbow.	1000	25	40	10

FIGURE 6.31   Multistroke swimming workout.

Set 1	1. 4 × 25 fly + 15 sec., 25 back + 15 sec. at zone 1-2
	2. 4 × 25 back + 10 sec., 25 breast + 15 sec. at zone 1-2
	3. 4 × 25 breast + 10 sec., 25 free + 15 sec. at zone 1-2
	4. 8 × 25 fly + 30 sec. at zone 1-2
	5. Rest 1 min.
Set 2	6. 4 × 25 back + 10 sec., 25 breast + 15 sec. at zone 1-2
	7. 4 × 25 breast + 10 sec., 25 free + 15 sec. at zone 1-2
	8. 4 × 25 free + 10 sec., 25 fly + 15 sec. at zone 1-2
	9. 8 × 25 back + 30s at zone 1-2
	10. Rest 1 min.
Set 3	11. 4 × 25 breast + 10 sec., 25 free + 15 sec. at zone 1-2
	12. 4 × 25 free + 15 sec., 25 fly + 15 sec. at zone 1-2
	13. 4 × 25 back + 10 sec., 25 breast + 15 sec. at zone 1-2
	14. 8 × 25 breast + 30 sec. at zone 1-2

For many triathletes, swimming is the most challenging discipline to learn. One of the most important parts of the learning process is seeing what postures and positions are used. To reconstruct technique, an initial short video can be of great help. With this in hand, each body line from the beginning of this chapter through the final body regions can be assessed. When technique training is combined with video, ACES, and functional movement and stability exercises, the results are an enormous advantage in acquiring better swimming proficiency.

7 Analyzing and Improving Cycling Technique

Triathlon has shaped extraordinary advancement in cycling technology. Frame geometry, equipment, fitting systems, cycling sciences, aerodynamics, and the physiological approaches to performance have all evolved largely because of the growing popularity of triathlon. That triathlon has emerged as the most state-of-the-art source of so many aspects of contemporary cycling is a testament to the innovative triathletes, coaches, and companies that enhance performance in our sport.

Cycling is advancing all the time, morphing along a continuum of best practices driven primarily by technology and fitting approaches. Both are extremely attractive aspects of triathlon. Here it is sufficient to say that a correct fit of triathlete to bike is significant to performance. The industry and triathletes lean toward the precision of geometry, components, aerodynamics and embrace fitting systems that are well suited for the inherent elegance of cycling. Yet, equally individual functional movements, biomechanics, and movements of the body on and off the bike and technique are without a doubt a major factor in performance.

There needs to be a *coupling* of these features because triathletes are not immutable things, but ever-evolving and adapting. The best practices for bike fitting would be a new approach (some coaches and companies are making this a reality) with thorough movement, stability, posture, and technique analysis combined with the fitting. From here, a series of follow-up evaluations (fitting and movement reassessment) fixed to a set number of training hours on the bike and a protocol for any exercise and technique remedies prescribed (ACES). It is safe to say that one bike fitting is not enough without evaluation of how the triathlete moves and functions in relation to normal postures, controls segments of the body, and applies technique.

In the section that follows, we won't cover bike fitting from the more established norms of geometric angles but from a broader view in fitting the human body to the bike. Focusing on the body first is foremost in importance, but the triathlete needs a system and a starting point, and many fitting systems do provide well-considered means for achieving the best and most functional fit. However, lacking are three important aspects of fitting the rider to the bike. First, there should be an off-the-bike assessment of functional movement and stability. Second, there must be a prefit evaluation of technique in relation to how the body moves. Third, and perhaps most important, there must be ongoing reevaluations of movement, posture, stability, technique, and the fit itself—because changes in functional movement and stability can alter the posture of the triathlete on the bike.

Bike Fitting and Movement Coupling

In this chapter we will not focus as much on fitting the triathlete to the bike as on movement evaluation; stability; foot, shoe, and cleat positions; and technique. As of this writing, triathlon bike fitting is at a junction, a stage of development in which technology and how individuals move—their postures apart from the bike—are beginning to be better understood as equally important. At present, long-standing fitting techniques are now at last coupling state-of-the-art fitting methods and information systems to push the frontiers of technology, with wind tunnels and sophisticated (and some would argue too complicated) fitting methods providing more precise and individualized bike positioning. Simply put, the postures and movement functions of the individual triathlete must be combined with bike fitting.

Rapidly vanishing are the days of a bike fitter in a shop eyeballing or even using a goniometer to do much more than a general fitting for a recreational cyclist. Companies are building systems combining the best bike-fitting minds and methods to deliver better experiences as well as a dynamic and superior functional fit for the triathlete.

We now have state-of-the-art fitting tools, 3-D motion capturing, dynamic fitting systems, analysis software focused on pinpoint landmark measurements, and algorithms with sets of rules that provide more precision to establish the best fit. The level of exactness is skyrocketing in evaluating angles and pathways of limb movements to improve power and aerodynamics. Bike fitting has shifted toward a professional discipline with highly defined, clear-cut fitting systems; fitting is clearly a specialty now, a branch of triathlon more and more built on accepted rules and logic. There are machines that replicate fitting with complex yet elegantly simple apparatuses, technologies, and software that capture the fitting process with incredible accuracy and ease. At the far end of the spectrum of these systems, an emerging trend is the coupling of individual ranges of motion and the

effect of overactive tight muscles on fitting. Some bike practitioners are integrating movement with fitting, but it might be too early to quantify (as many bike fitters like to do) the exact implications of movement limiters and instability in the muscles.

However, as noted later in this chapter when we discuss foot and pedal, there is merit and there are methods for establishing better stability in the bike and body connection sites during the fitting process. To be sure, there will come a time when today's popular fitting systems must begin to couple how the triathlete moves off the bike with the on-bike settings.

When a triathlete compensates during sitting, standing, or walking, his or her postures on the bike very likely place the muscles in underperforming positions. Overactive (tight, inflexible) or underactive (weak, unstable) muscles limit ranges of motion and cause compensations that prevent triathletes from fitting into a community of joint angles for the perfect fit. Expert bike fitters know this and inevitably rely on experience to fit the bike to the triathlete—they couple body measurements and angles, the bike and the human.

It is important to acknowledge and evaluate individual differences in every bike fitting because no single set of geometric angles or positions is equally functional. Even the most sophisticated fitting systems are ranges (although very good starting points) and often based on coordinates of elite athletes. But elite triathletes move differently from most triathletes of their age group; they have different structural alignments and also differ in flexibility, joint mobility, and stability.

The bike frame sets, components, wheel sets, tires, aero bars, clothing, shoes, pedals, helmets, and fueling systems, to name just a few, are extraordinarily efficient. It is difficult to keep pace with all that occurs with cycling technology innovations in bike fitting. When these and other elements are coupled with functional movement and aerodynamic fitting, triathletes are better positioned and postured to use energy more efficiently.

Every triathlete's cycling goal should be to minimize the disturbances of air—the rider's main opponent—and to maximize how the body's muscular capacity best leverages the drive train from the foot, shoe, and pedal spindle. The focus is on forward movement, which is best cultivated by harnessing and improving functional movement and optimizing the motions of pedaling (technique) into the most linear transfer of energy along the rotating arms of the cranks.

Anyone can have misalignments—in fact, most people do. The triathlete and bike fitter should address asymmetries and, when possible, promote corrective solutions not only in adjustments but in exercise remedies. There are useful remedies such as wedging, orthotics, and other modifications, but these might in many instances be needed only temporarily during functional movement and stability development. On the other hand, some triathletes will have genetic misalignments that require permanent adjustments. Whether a temporary or permanent adjustment is required is a key point to consider.

No matter what fitting system you subscribe to, the importance of the foot cannot be overlooked. But strengthening and improving mobility of the foot and ankle alone won't make for a perfect fit, either. The bike fit and foot mechanics assessment must be done in conjunction with fitting corrections and, when necessary, exercises for stretching, strength, stability, balance, and other remedies to bring you as close to neutral as possible. This won't be achievable in every case, but there are ways to improve function; and even the smallest of improvements improves your capacity to produce power, while reducing injury risk caused by misalignments.

When the foot and pedal are connected under moderate rates of intensity, the foot in many instances can remain in a stable posture (because the longitudinal arch and rear foot are sufficient at lower loads). However, once load is increased, more force is directed under the forefoot. When there is instability in the foot, such as forefoot varus, there might also be misalignment in the knee. Corrections to the foot, pedal, and shoe through corrections achieved in stability (via wedges or exercises, or both) can improve power output.

Foot Types

The foot and ankle structures function to provide stability and mobility; when in a neutral position, they also provide support. When the body is in motion, the foot and ankle help to absorb forces and provide stabilization on uneven surfaces; they are also a central lever for movement during the bike and run. The more stable and functional the foot, the less muscular energy required.

A stable foot can readily provide balance and function along the entire body's kinetic chain, resulting in improved mechanics. Foot posture, then, affects the entire body, and making efforts to stabilize and promote as close to neutral motions as possible is a key aspect of bike fitting. For our discussion here, the foot is unstable and might overpronate (roll inward), supinate (roll outward), excessively invert (turn in), or evert (turn out). In contrast, a normal foot has three solid points of contact: the first metatarsal head, fifth metatarsal head, and heel. Additionally, the rear foot is neutral—alignment of the heel with the forefoot makes solid contact from the underside of the big toe.

There are many causes for improper function of the foot, including structural (genetic) causes and strength and flexibility imbalances from immobilization, injury, and even degeneration in the joints of the foot. Because the lower body is weight bearing, many of these problems can be difficult to overcome, and making corrective adjustments (e.g., wedges or alignment) to a cleat and pedal interface might have limited value, both on and off the bike. Thus assessing the mechanics of the feet and ankles is especially important for achieving an optimal bike fit for the triathlete.

The rhythm of pedaling rates and forces are communicated through tactile feedback from the feet. When cycling, you might not think of your feet as being primary contributors to performance, but the nerve endings of the feet, like those of the hands, are particularly sensitive to touch and pressure. This sensitivity is very often undertrained or even unnoticed but can be trained to function proficiently through technique-focused (foot pressure and contact with pedal) training and proper positioning of the foot in relation to the cleat, shoe, and pedal spindle.

Stability of the foot—particularly during weight-bearing activities such as running and, to a lesser degree, cycling—is affected by muscle tension. There can be a difference in how much one foot arches than the other. This affects the symmetry of movements on the bike, and how the foot and pedal interface delivers power.

Medial Arch

Triathletes who have a high or low arch can be less able to apply equal pedal forces across the foot because the foot might have less capacity to produce peak power as a result of compensation (or a weakened position) when the foot is fully loaded during the downstroke.

To assess, the medial longitudinal arch (MLA) should be examined in both weight-bearing and non-weight-bearing postures because it might appear normal when unweighted (some bike-fitting systems use unweighted and are not accurate). A normal MLA has about one centimeter of space under the foot arch during standing. A low arch (pronation) can be genetic, a tendon issue, caused by disease, or result from contraction of the Achilles tendon and posterior tibial tendon. The high-arched foot (supination) has less ability to absorb shock, especially on uneven surfaces, and this places greater stress on the lower limbs and can affect the lumbar spine. A high arch has more than one centimeter of space from the bottom foot to the bed of the shoe, and there might be a clawing of the toes in an attempt to stabilize.

Shape of the Toes

There are generally three types of toe shape. Depending on the length and location of the longest toe, there might be more load at that joint.

1. Egyptian foot. This is the most common toe shape, found in 69 percent of the population. The big toe is the longest and most stable. There is normal foot,

pedal, and shoe posture for this foot shape.

2. Greek foot (Morton's foot). This is the second most common shape (22 percent of the population), in which the second toe is the longest. This condition increases pronation of the foot, and the MLA drops, allowing the ankle to fall inward. There is more loading on the second toe, which might limit transfer of power or cause tingling, numbness, or burning in nerves and increase localized toe pressure. Shoe and pedal interface might require more examination by a sports medicine podiatrist or physical therapist to relieve symptoms and improve functional footpad pressure on the pedal.

3. Asian foot (square toe)—This toe shape is found in about 9 percent of individuals and is identified by the big toe and second toe having the same length. This foot type is typically low arched and slightly broader. There might be some pedal-loading advantage with the first and second toes of equal length, but there must be normal flexibility in both toes and enough room in the shoes.

Forefoot, Cleat, Shoe, and Pedal Connection

The connections of the foot and pedal when functioning optimally provide an important base of support for transferring energy along the kinetic chain to the bicycle. The amount of pressure applied to the pedal is very high, and the foot, especially through the big-toe joint, must be in a position of stability. Thus linking the foot and pedal (shoe comfort and rigidity to harness energy efficiently are equally important) is essential for creating efficient power, and also for reducing musculoskeletal overuse injuries caused by misalignments and compensating motions. Considering toe shape, the load on the toes is highest on the longest toe. The assessment of foot shapes will be covered later, with an emphasis on weight bearing and non-weight bearing. The foot under load (body weight) can be far different from the non-weight-bearing assessments common in popular fitting methods.

Ten muscles in the foot control movement, from rear foot, through forefoot, to the toes. Foot muscles are invertors, evertors, or intrinsic (deep layered). The motion of the foot and the muscular control affect stability and force on the pedals. The foot moves through three key joints that facilitate foot and ankle articulation (figure 7.1). The subtalar joint allows the foot to tilt medially (inversion) and laterally (eversion). The midtarsal joint assists with flattening and recovery of the arch through the pedaling downstroke (the foot is dorsiflexing—movement of foot toward leg). Finally, the metatarsophalangeal joint (MP) is affected more in running, but in cycling the ball of the foot can become hot (burning sensation), numb, and painful. The source of these sensations might be compression caused by restrictions in movement of the joint,

mechanics of the foot (pronation), or shoe fit or pedal placement. Each of these problems can be corrected with foot exercises, correct placement of cleat and pedal, stretching of the lower-leg muscles, and making sure shoes are well fitting and stable.

With good and functional mechanics of the foot and ankle, the entire kinetic chain will connect more functionally and have greater potential for power. The muscles of the foot and ankle function to control supination and inversion (tibialis posterior); support the longitudinal arch (flexor hallucis and digitorum); support the lateral and transverse arches (peroneus longus and brevis); and allow toe extension, dorsiflexion, and ankle inversion (tibialis anterior, extensor hallucis longus, and extensor digitorum longus). Each of these functions collectively and individually provides stability and capability for improving cycling performance.

Foot and Ankle Effect on Posture

The bicycle is powered by muscular power applied to the cranks. The foot, cleat, and cycling shoe connect to the crank arm and have the potential to produce highly efficient movements. The sole of the shoe through the forefoot (notably, the big toe) is where the majority of pedal pressure originates. The foot pressure along the sole of the shoe should be evenly distributed in a way that provides the best use of energy delivery.

Efficient foot, cleat, and shoe positioning and pedaling actions are principally important because they affect the transmission of power through the pedals. Like each of the key fitting components, the foot and pedal interface should not be overlooked. Any misalignments at this critical connection can affect movement patterns and functional performance through the entire kinetic chain.

A functional interconnection of skeletal alignments is a conduit for greater cycling proficiency. Bike fitting at its most fundamental foundation is about the most efficient connection of the human body to the bike. This is a highly professional occupation and triathletes should seek out the most qualified individuals

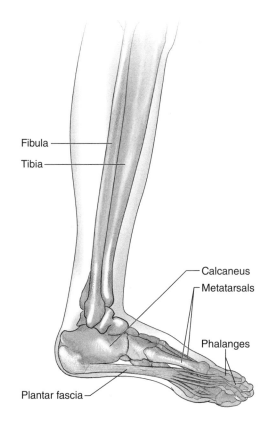

FIGURE 7.1 The foot moves through three joints that facilitate foot and ankle articulation: the subtalar joint, midtarsal joint, and metatarsophalangeal joint.

and systems whenever possible. Many companies are heading in this direction through education and continuing to develop better programs. This integration should begin with assessment of the foot and related joints in providing the best, most efficient foundation of energy transfer to propel the bike forward.

How the forefoot interconnects with the pedal turns out to be one of the most important aspects in bike fitting. Preparing the triathlete for the best kinetic motions begins with assessment of foot biomechanics and the interface among the foot, cleat, shoe, and pedal. A properly positioned foot, cleat, pedal spindle, and shoe alignment establishes the foundation, but positioning alone cannot ensure an optimal placement for any of the following reasons:

- The feet are the contact point of power transfer through the pedals.
- The stability of the foot arch should be assessed both under weight-bearing and non-weight-bearing conditions.
- The body can compensate for misalignments (high or low arches, toe types), and an incorrectly positioned foot, cleat, and pedal interface affects the functional capacity of muscles along the kinetic chain.
- A collapsing arch indicates there might be tissue breakdown where the supporting tissue cannot maintain the structural elevation in the foot. This can cause not only pain and injury (plantar fascia, heel spurs) but a loss of power through lack of stability in the medial arch. If this occurs, there will be a significant lack of efficiency that should be remedied through corrective exercises or temporary (or even permanent) modifications in the pedal, cleat, or shoe (e.g., wedging, foot taping, shims).
- An asymmetrically moving free heel (lateral, medial, looping) might be compensating for structural or soft tissue limitations in the foot.
- A tilting of the forefoot or rear foot (valgus or varus) is a good indication of below-optimal foot stability (caused by

a congenital structural condition or soft tissue compensations).

- The heel, knee, hips, and torso can compensate with lateral and medial oscillating and irregular motions that can result in more upper-body compensations, instability, or overactive or underactive muscle functioning.
- Permanent wedging, pedal spindle modifications, shoe inserts, noncustom orthotics, or canting between the pedal and the cleat might also be correlated to soft tissue limitations (hindered flexibility, joint mobility, or stability) and should be evaluated in connection with exercises to remedy these issues. Thus, attempts to improve, correct, or stabilize the forefoot and pedal interface permanently by using these modifications should be considered temporary retraining of movement unless the issues do not respond to exercises and technique.

Stability of the Ankle and Foot

There are muscles inside and outside the ankle and foot that provide stability and movement. Inside the foot are muscles that control movement in the toes. The muscles on the outside of the foot, such as the gastrocnemius (calf muscle), function to assist the foot in pointing and standing on the toes, whereas the peroneal muscles (also on the outside of the lower legs) provide foot stability and motion control when the foot is turning out.

Muscles also have tendons that are connected to the bones. One of the most important of these is the Achilles tendon. Attached from the calf to the heel bone, this tendon allows you to walk, run, jump, and press down on the pedals. To support the arch (important for full foot pad pressure when pedaling), the posterior (rear) tibial tendon attaches to one of the smaller muscles of the calf on the underside of the foot. On the front of the lower leg, the anterior tibial tendon functions to raise the foot. Figure 7.2 illustrates the tendons and muscles of the lower leg.

The ankle is a hinge-ike joint involved in the stability of the lower limbs. This joint has two work in concert with the ankle joint to propel the foot off the ground. We can speak of three segments of the foot: hind foot, midfoot, and forefoot. The calcaneus and talus make up the hind foot, and the metatarsals and phalanges make up the forefoot. The navicular, cuboid, and cuneiform bones make up the midfoot.

Foot and Ankle Test Exercises

The foot and ankle are the principal interface between the bicycle pedal and the body. As a triathlete, you might have a loss of foot or ankle flexibility or stability for several reasons. Using the following tests to assess basic function is a good place to begin.

Self-Testing Foot and Ankle Function

As we've established, the foot and ankle play important roles in producing power when cycling. Misalignments or instability or too much or too little flexibility can reduce the capacity to deliver peak muscular energy to propel the bike. For this reason, assessing basic functions of the foot and ankles can help establish improved position and posture on the bike, muscular movements, and technique.

In the following tests, video is helpful in self-assessment of the foot and ankle. You need to have front, side, and back views as well as standing, walking, and other views of gait. Your focus here is on the foot's interface with the pedal, but it's also important to look at the posture of the trunk, hips, and knee and alignments that might reveal obvious conditions. For example, knee alignment such as bowlegs or knock-knees can indicate genetic conditions that should be considered during the fitting process. Overcorrecting for such conditions might limit the amount of correction possible. Thus it's important to consider posture off the bike as well as on the bike.

Following are several exercises to assess foot and ankle function.

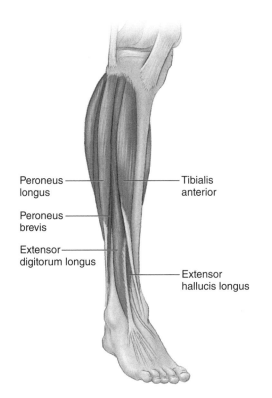

Peroneus longus

Peroneus brevis

Extensor digitorum longus

Tibialis anterior

Extensor hallucis longus

FIGURE 7.2   The tendons and muscles of the lower leg.

key motions: dorsiflexion and plantar flexion. During dorsiflexion, the foot is flexed toward the front of the lower leg. With this capacity for joint movement and the connecting stability, pedaling and energy transfer are enhanced by the leverage of the foot and ankle. During plantar flexion, the toes are pointing down (away from lower leg) with the heel above the toes. This posture is less stable than dorsiflexion but is still important in proper pedaling mechanics (standing on the pedals to climb).

The foot plays an important role in supporting the weight of the body and in locomotion. The bones of the foot are arched longitudinally to facilitate this support. The transverse arch helps with movements of the foot. These movements help keep the sole (plantar surface) in contact with the ground despite the unevenness of the ground surface. They also

Heel Walking Test

This test assesses tibialis anterior (TA) function (ankle dorsiflexion, foot inversion, and longitudinal arch support). To perform this test, walk 15 steps with tips of toes several centimeters (about two inches) off the floor (figure 7.3). Inability to perform this test might indicate muscular weakness in the TA. To progress, first do three sets of 15 steps, then two sets of 30 steps, and finally one set of 60 steps.

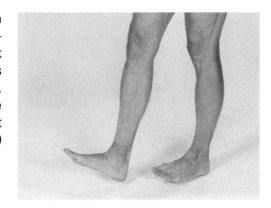

FIGURE 7.3 Heel walking test.

Toe Walking Test

This test assesses plantar flexor strength. To perform this test, walk 15 steps with heels several centimeters (about two inches) off the floor (figure 7.4). Inability to perform this test might indicate muscular weakness in the gastrocnemius and soleus. To progress, do three sets of 15 steps, then two sets of 30 steps, and finally one set of 60 steps before proceeding to the single-leg heel raise test.

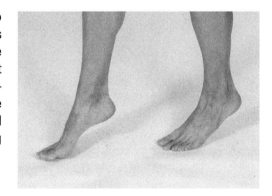

FIGURE 7.4 Toe walking test.

Heel Raise Test

This test assesses plantar flexor strength at the gastrocnemius and soleus (GS) muscles, which control the ankle, foot pointing, and eversion and are assisting muscles for knee flexion; the test also confirms full functional strength for the plantar flexors. To perform this test, place hands on hips and raise heels several centimeters (about two inches) off the floor with balance and control (figure 7.5). Inability to perform this test might indicate muscular weakness in the GS. To progress, do three sets of 15, then two sets of 30, and finally one set of 60.

FIGURE 7.5 Heel raise test.

Lateral Foot Walking Test

This test assesses the inversion strength of the foot and ankle. The tibialis posterior (TP) is a deep muscle on the posterior leg and, when bearing weight, is important in assisting arch support and plantar flexion and in supporting body weight to maintain balance. To perform this test, take 15 steps with the medial arch several centimeters (about two inches) off the floor (figure 7.6). Inability to perform this test might indicate muscular weakness in the TP, weakness in tibial nerve function, or both. To progress, do three sets of 15, then two sets of 30, and finally one set of 60.

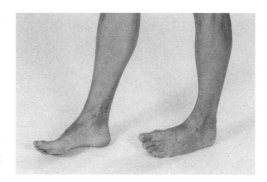

FIGURE 7.6 Lateral foot walking test.

Medial Arch Foot Walking Test

This test assesses walking gait and the ability of the peroneal muscle group to plantar flex the ankle, evert the foot, depress the first metatarsal, and support the transverse and longitudinal arches; all of these functions are important for stability and generation of optimal pedaling forces. To perform this test, take 15 steps with the side of one foot several centimeters (about two inches) off the floor (figure 7.7). To progress, do three sets of 15, then two sets of 30, and finally one set of 60; repeat on other foot.

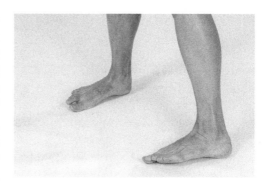

FIGURE 7.7 Medial foot walking test.

Dynamic Exercises for the Foot and Ankle

You might not think about this, but cycling shoes are generally stiff and limit the normal movement that develops strength and preserves foot mobility. In part, that's a very good reason to supplement training with dynamic exercises to develop and maintain foot function. Cycling is not chiefly a weight-bearing activity the way that running is because body weight is supported on the saddle (except when standing), elbow pads, and pedal spindles. This means fewer reactive forces are at play. However, the demands of the foot and ankle are nonetheless important to proper function. You can improve these dynamic motions (contractions with joint and muscle movement) to improve stability, range of motion, and neuromuscular control.

The neuromuscular (brain-to-muscle) component develops sensory and motor systems to engage muscular movement and control these motions with coordinated movements and awareness. By combining better stability and functional movement with technique, you can move with increased efficiency.

To achieve ideal alignments you must maintain, restore, or improve various segments of your cycling motions that are underdeveloped. A bike fit that ignores these important factors is not going to eliminate or correct these underdeveloped motions. In the next section we'll help you determine how to correct or improve these motions.

Dorsiflexion and Plantar Flexion With Inversion: Anterior Tibialis

The anterior tibialis muscle functions to flex the ankle and invert the foot and supports the inside longitudinal arch of the foot. To perform this exercise, sit on the floor with legs outstretched, knees slightly flexed, and hands on floor slightly behind hips. First, flex ankle so foot moves toward shin bone (figure 7.8*a*). Then point toe away from shin bone (figure 7.8*b*). Finally, invert foot (figure 7.8*c*). Contract anterior tibialis muscle during each movement.

FIGURE 7.8   Dorsiflexion and plantar flexion with inversion for the anterior tibialis.

Eversion Exercise: Peroneus

The peroneus muscles function to evert the foot, assist in ankle plantar flexion (point the foot), depress the first metatarsal (bone of the big toe), and support the longitudinal and transverse arches. An exercise for the peroneus involves eversion. To perform this exercise, sit on floor with legs outstretched, knees slightly flexed, hands on floor slightly behind hips. Keeping ankle neutral, evert foot (figure 7.9). Begin with three sets of 15; once movements are accurate and controlled, progress to two sets of 20. Finally, for maintenance, perform one set of 30.

FIGURE 7.9 Eversion for the peroneus.

Medial Longitudinal Arch Raise Exercise

The medial longitudinal arch (MLA) is the highest arch and the most important along the inside of the foot. This arch runs the length of the foot from heel to toe. Soft tissues that have elastic properties provide support and also store energy that can be reused for propulsion. To perform this exercise, sit with feet on floor and forefoot pad (under big and little toes) neutral so toes contact floor throughout. Raise MLA while keeping forefoot on floor (figure 7.10). Tibia (lower leg) will rotate externally, but not hips.

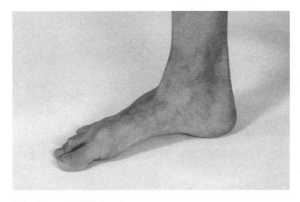

FIGURE 7.10 MLA raise.

Exercises for Stability Based on Foot Type

When your lower body is functioning well, it will stabilize your body's center of gravity via better limb alignment. In cycling, your foot is connected to the pedal spindle and, unlike in running, there are not many changes or reactions necessary to control balance and shock caused by deceleration. However, better lower-body alignment and stability in the foot lend to the specificity of training that is elementally important.

Training movements functionally develops strength, power, endurance, range of motion, and motor learning specific to cycling. This brings together more systems of the body and results in much less compensation of movements on the bike. The interaction of the foot within the shoe and through the pedal and spindle can be improved through the assessment of foot type, exercises to improve mechanics, and adjustment to these interfaces, as needed.

Forefoot and rear foot mechanics are important to assess for foot, pedal, and shoe positioning for the purpose of improving lower- and upper-body alignment. Bike fitting should include an assessment of foot mechanics prior to fitting and positioning the pedal.

Inward Big Toe (Hallux Valgus) The big toe can shift inward toward the second toe or even overlap this toe (figure 7.11). Excessive pronation (inward collapse of the foot and arch) is a frequent cause of this condition, which can be remedied by improving the support of the arch. In this condition, the abductor hallucis muscle is stretched, unstable, and weakened, and the adductor hallucis muscle is restricted. Over time, the flexing and extending muscles can give way and the condition might worsen, become inflamed, and result in bulging bunions, a chronic and painful condition. Severe cases might require surgery.

Often undetected during bike fitting, milder forms of hallux valgus affect the loading capacity through the big toe during the downstroke. There can also be pain and swelling aggravated by shoe wear. For this reason, assessment of the feet is important.

Treatment options for hallux valgus include the following:

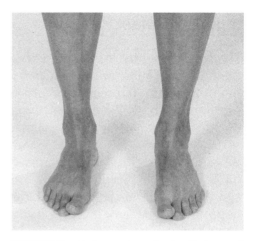

FIGURE 7.11 Hallux valgus foot with inward big toe.

- Shoe modification for mild to moderate deviations of the foot to accommodate space for the forefoot (at the bunion site) by stretching the shoe
- Toe separators (small rubber spacers inserted between the big and second toe) can also be used to alleviate pain and place the big toe into a more functional position. Separators can be used in both bike and running shoes.

Following are two exercises to help accommodate hallux valgus.

Single-Leg Standing With Neutral Foot

This exercise helps move the line of gravity (body weight and alignment) from big toe to second toe. To perform this exercise, stand with feet close together and flex hip and knee while standing on opposite leg (figure 7.12). Draw in the deep abdominals and tighten the quadriceps and gluteals. The supporting foot should be in a full neutral position by maintaining constant the weight on the outside of the foot. Contract and release the gluteal muscles for each repetition (the femurs externally rotate to neutral position). Maintain alignment of the head, trunk, pelvis, and support leg throughout. Do three sets of 15 to begin; progress to two sets of 30 as control improves and to one set of 60 once fully functional.

FIGURE 7.12 Single-leg standing with neutral foot.

Passive Toe Flex

This is a self-stretching and mobility exercise for the toes. Toes that are limited in range of motion can benefit from stretching and mobility exercises. To perform this exercise, sit on floor with knees bent or with one foot crossed onto opposite knee. Grip one toe of foot at the base to stabilize; with other hand, move tip of toe back and forth and sideways, using gentle pressure and motions at first and progressing tension and range of motion as movement increases (figure 7.13). Keep ankle stable. The range of motion in the toe should not fluctuate.

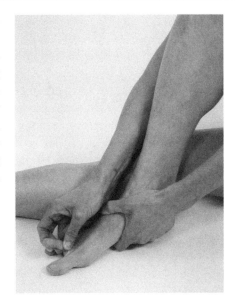

FIGURE 7.13   Passive toe flex.

Toe Abduction and Release

For the inward-shifted big toe, a self-mobilization exercise is necessary. Stand and abduct the big toe outward, separating it from the second toe (figure 7.14) and hold this position for 5 to 10 seconds; do 8 to 12 repetitions.

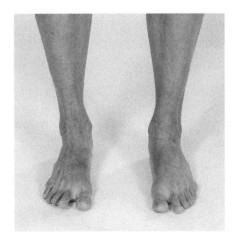

FIGURE 7.14   Toe abduction.

Supinated and Hallux Valgus Foot   A supinated foot is typically associated with a high arch—the reverse of a pronated foot. Much of the weight or force during pedaling is along the outside of the foot. When standing, the foot pad behind the big toe can be off the ground and result in an unbalanced stance. With hallux valgus, however, the toe is angled inward from the first metatarsal joint. Because the big toe is shifted and angled inward by at least 15 degrees, there is usually a bunion that can be progressively painful.

In cycling, hallux valgus foot reduces range of motion and is more rigid, which can contribute to less capacity to produce optimal pedaling forces. In mild to moderate cases, shoe modifications can alleviate this problem. Customized and even off-the-shelf splits between the toes and inserts can help reposition the foot not only for cycling but for running as well. Lateral (outside) wedging or shims might be of benefit for supination. Custom-fitted orthotics might also be beneficial.

Pronated Foot With Flatness of Longitudinal Arch   A pronated foot with a flat inner arch is often accompanied by out-toeing of the forefoot. The inner supporting muscles and ligaments of the foot are stretched and overly tensioned. As a result, the muscles of the lower leg and foot compensate by increasing the control of poor mechanics in an attempt to provide more stability to reduce the excessive mobility. As a temporary solution, an inner wedge or a longitudinal arch support inside the shoe can be used in conjunction with exercise remedies to develop better neuromuscular control and more neutral and accurate movements.

Out-Toeing   Out-toeing is associated with external rotation of the hip or lower leg as part of the mechanics of the foot abducted away from the heel. Out-toeing is also common with tightness in the Achilles tendon and stretching of the gastrocnemius and soleus. During walking or standing, a turning out of the foot is visible. Bike fitters refer to this condition as foot rotation, and common remedies include adjusting the cleat rotation in the direction that the feet point off the bike. For shoe and pedal positioning, relying on pedal float (range of motion between pedal and cleat) or aligning the pedal and shoe in the manner of walking or standing might be only partially helpful because the primary cause—muscular tightness—is ignored.

Mild out-toeing might result from the external rotation of the extremities from hip level, outward rotation of the tibia, foot alignment faults and tightness of the Achilles, weak arches and flatter feet. Remedies include stretching the gastrocnemius and training exercises for the feet for stability and flexibility.

In-Toeing   Inward-facing toes can be caused by an inward rotation of the legs at hip level and can affect the kinetic chain through the femur, knee, or tibia (lower leg). Sometimes the problem lies with the foot being hooked in (with hips, knees, and lower legs not affected). In-toeing is often accompanied by pronation of the feet.

In-toeing might result from tightness of the tensor fasciae latae (TFL) muscle, which lies on the front part of the outer hip and functions to flex the hip and knee, internally rotate the hip, and extend and externally rotate the knee. Moderate toe-in corrections can be made with in-shoe patches or wedges on the lateral base of the small toe (fifth metatarsal); these help with walking (but not with standing) and might also help with stretching.

To remedy in-toeing, the following stretch exercise and the dynamic exercises earlier in the chapter for the foot and ankle are recommended.

Isometric Toe Curls

In a seated position, slowly and isometrically contract the intrinsic muscles of the foot (muscles on top and bottom of foot). Toes should curl and arches rise. Sides of feet remain on the floor (figure 7.15). Perform for 30 seconds, holding the pose for the last 20 seconds. Perform five times up to twice a day.

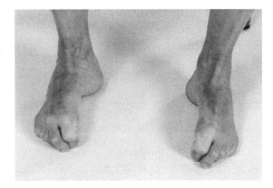

FIGURE 7.15 Isometric toe curl.

TFL Wall Stretch

The tensor fasciae latae, located on the front of the hip along the iliac crest, flexes, medially rotates, and abducts the hip and assists knee flexion. When this muscle is tight, the pelvis can be tilted forward and, in some cases, the knees are inward (knock-kneed). This causes an inward rotation of the femur, resulting in in-toeing.

Stand with side facing wall and hand on wall. Move same-side hip toward wall and externally rotate same-side leg back and across the other leg. With both feet on the floor, shift pelvis toward wall while bending the opposite shoulder downward and bending knees slightly (figure 7.16). Hold this position for 30 to 45 seconds; repeat on other side.

FIGURE 7.16 TFL wall stretch.

Improving Body Position: Isometric Exercises for the Neck

The aero body position when cycling can cause discomfort. Cyclists with cervical symptoms or weakness and tightness might find relief through isometric exercises. Bike fitting and posture play important roles in avoiding discomfort, as does mobility in the neck muscles (levator scapulae, scalenes, sternocleidomastoid), which extend, flex, rotate, and provide stability. Also, elongating the neck places the triathlete into a functional posture (back flattens and power can be delivered more optimally) and the triathlete should learn to use the eyes to look forward instead of extending the neck whenever possible.

To perform these exercises, keep head and neck stationary and place tongue on roof of mouth behind teeth (this helps maintain posture). Place hands on forehead to resist cervical neck flexion (figure 7.17*a*). Place one hand on side of head to resist cervical side flexion (figure 7.17*b*). Repeat on other side. Then place both hands behind head to resist cervical extension (figure 7.17*c*). Hold for five seconds and relax. Perform four to eight reps for each position. As stability increases, increase hold time to 15 seconds for two repetitions.

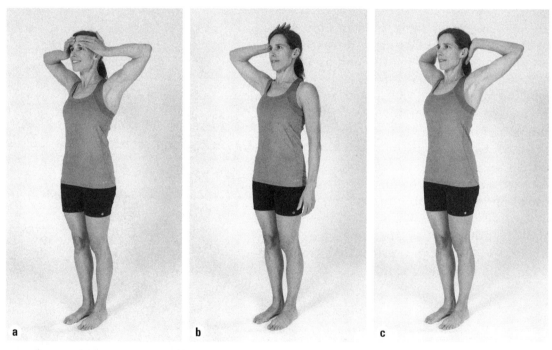

a   b   c

FIGURE 7.17 Isometric exercises for the neck.

Techniques of Pedaling

Pedaling efficiently is connected with many complex functions, including gearing, training status, revolutions (cadence), terrain, bike and crank geometry, bottom-bracket energy storage capacity and materials, pedal, shoe type and foot position, and an almost endless list of fitting variations. Of course the cyclist's movement and stability factors from the foot upward through the kinetic chain also contribute to efficiency.

Fitting a triathlete to a bike should include a comprehensive evaluation of movement and stability as previously examined. This process (bike fitting and functional movement and technique) is in early development, and we hope in this book to inspire coaches, physical therapists, sport scientists, triathlon federations, industry, and a growing field of fitting professionals to contribute to further development. The coupling of movement function and technique evaluations and refinements with fitting is the future of cycling. In the following sections we discuss key aspects for improving pedaling efficiency and technique—a major part of becoming a better triathlete cyclist.

Positioning of the Foot and Pedal

Foot and pedal adjustments can be forward and backward, side to side, up and down, or rotating and tilting (varus and valgus). Some of these required adjustments can be attributed to improper installation of the foot, pedal, or shoe or to overactive soft tissue or structural misalignments in the feet. These issues might be improved through a combination of foot and pedal adjustments and exercise remedies that begin with assessing structural and soft tissue function.

Foot and pedal positioning is a process of temporary adjustments during rehabilitation or retraining technique and changes in fitting and then relearning functional patterns of movement. As with most aspects of bike fitting, this is a process, and continual assessment of movement and fitting is needed. Proper positioning the foot over the pedal will reduce stresses across the knee and maximize mechanical advantages and leverage. Check placement of foot, shoe, and pedal to confirm the best and most functional position that provides most efficient and maximal power.

Forward, Backward, and Side-to-Side Placement

For optimal force and kinetic chain linking, foot and pedal spindle should be positioned with the first metatarsal (ball of big toe) directly centered on pedal spindle (figure 7.18). Some fitting systems use technology to find those points.

The center of the knee joint should align with the second toe during the full pedaling rotation (figure 7.19). The angles of the knee and foot should be biomechanically aligned as much as possible. Excessive medial (inward) or lateral (outward) or an orbiting motion of the knee might be structural or caused by foot, shoe, or pedal misalignments or weakness in soft tissue. The accurate cause must be identified and corrections made to best serve long-term outcome.

FIGURE 7.18 Foot and pedal forward-and-backward spindle position.

FIGURE 7.19 Knee and pedal side-to-side spindle position.

Foot Rotation

Pedal and cleat systems permit float to allow movement and tracking from the foot through the ankle, hip, and knee joints. As noted, some of these motions relate to structural foot mechanics, whereas others result from soft tissue instability that can often be mitigated through exercises and temporary modifications to the foot and pedal interface.

Sometimes the amount of rotation exceeds the pedal floating limits and can change the biomechanics of the pedaling stroke, often causing peaks and valleys in the application of pedaling forces and foot-pad pressures. Some triathletes with increased external out-toeing can experience heel striking against the crank arm on one foot or both. In such circumstances it might be necessary to increase the space or install a wider pedal axle permanently or during retraining of lower limb and feet stability and mobility.

The positioning of the degree of internal and external rotation (toe in and toe out) of the foot and cleat is in some fitting methods mirrored by the triathlete's gait examinations off the bike. Internal and external alignment of the feet can be structural, and in such circumstances augmenting rotation might be the best remedy. This condition might also be caused by weakness, tightness, or too much flexibility, so lower-body foot exercises along with temporary orthotics, shimming, and wedging might be called for. You can relearn to self-correct earlier biomechanical compensations in movement as stability is developed during off-the-bike training and enhanced neuromuscular feedback (motor learning) while training to achieve the more neutral angles of movement. The goal of fitting is to reduce the twisting, turning, and rotating between the tibia and the femur, always doing so within the structural and movement capacity of the triathlete.

Pedaling Tempo and Cadence

There is likely no one ideal cadence (pedaling rate) for triathletes. There are many variations of cadence, depending on slope, body type, gender, hip stability, joint mobility, flexibility, training history (cycling efficiency), fitness level, distance of competition, and other factors, including the triathlete's preferred rate.

Triathletes with lower pedaling rates (less than 80 RPM) are rare, but as Chrissie Wellington (four-time Ironman world champion) demonstrated in her pre–Dave Scott coaching relationship, you can win races with atypical pedaling rates (78 RPM). According to Scott, Wellington's low pedaling rate technique was affecting her marathon performances: "Her quadriceps [were] overloaded . . . combined with weak gluteals." Scott, a six-time Ironman world champion himself, has a well-honed background with strength training for triathletes and, noting Wellington's muscular weaknesses, set on a path for developing more stability. Without this intervention (change of pedaling rate and improved stability), Wellington's running performances might have continued to deteriorate. The result of the intervention was an increase in cadence (84 to 86) and a world record at Challenge Roth (2011 at 8:18:13) that included an evenly split 2:44:35 marathon.

Novice and comparatively inexperienced (cycling) triathletes like Chrissie Wellington (she began triathlon in earnest around 2005 becoming an age-group world champion even before any coaching) will in general pedal at lower pedaling revolutions. Conversely, more experienced athletes will work at 90 to 110 revolutions per minute. This is because of more efficient neuromuscular pattern and power output (higher power results in higher pedaling rates). Interestingly, as pedaling rates increase, there is greater muscle activity in the gluteals (medius and maximus) and other cycling-specific muscles, such as the vastus medialis, medial hamstrings, gastrocnemius, and soleus. Thus stability in these muscles along with training history and coaching can improve (or work to develop) pedaling rates that are closer to norms found in experienced triathletes.

Common faults of low RPM can be a tendency to increase gearing (greater resistance), resulting in more energy use and muscular fatigue on flat to moderate slopes, with RPM below 80 and increased hip and upper body movements. Pedaling rates and motions become less symmetrical, less smooth, and less accurate. Triathletes should strive to find their sweet spot in cadence, which is typically 90 to 105 RPM in training. This sweet spot is the point at which your muscles can absorb the workloads and produce an optimal exchange of energy for the duration of the event, interval, or workout. From there, control the tension on the footpad pressure from medial to lateral forefoot and keep hips, torso, shoulders, arms, hands, and fingertips fully relaxed and tension free.

You should also regularly train at higher RPM to facilitate neuromuscular (motor learning) capacities, doing exercises such as the following:

- Ascending cadence. Four to eight sets of 30 seconds at 95, 30 seconds at 105, 30 seconds at 110, and 30 seconds between 120 and 125 RPM at small chain ring and moderate resistance and intensity

- Single-leg ascending cadence: 6 to 12 sets of 30 seconds with left leg focus and 30 seconds with right leg focus in which:

  o odd-numbered sets begin at 90 RPM and increase by 5 on subsequent odd numbers at small chain ring and moderate resistance and intensity; and

  o even-numbered sets begin at 100 RPM and increase by 5 on subsequent even numbers at small chain ring with very light resistance and intensity.

Phases of the Pedaling Stroke

We will describe four phases (or sectors) of the pedal stroke, but there is only one primary propulsive phase: the downstroke. Over 95 percent of power comes from the downstroke. Each phase overlaps one another and with reduced pedal pressure toward the end and at the beginning of each. The others are transitional phases in which the focus is much less propulsive, but there are still reasons to train them. For the most part, the pedaling stroke should be thought of and practiced as two key motions: the downstroke (power phase) and the upstroke (recovery phase). Those two motions are similar to acceleration and deceleration. One is for power generation, and the other for recovery. It's important to understand the role of each of these strokes because any lifting, pulling, or pressing forward on the pedals during the other phases diminishes the power of the downstroke.

A focus on the power of the downstroke is not to say there are no benefits from the transitional phases (backstroke, upstroke, and overstroke). There are natural tendencies to lift during the upstroke, but these efforts are largely overcome by the acceleration of the opposing leg during the downstroke. Thus this phase, as well as the backstroke and overstroke, should be considered less propulsive and not in terms of increasing the magnitude of power in an attempt to apply continual and equal forces during the pedaling cycle.

As mentioned, there are many pedaling styles, typically depending on foot and ankle range of motion, experience, and how a triathlete has been trained or instructed. However, most elite cyclists and triathletes will over time adopt a pedaling motion that is more fluid (360 degrees of varying pedal pressure in which the footpad remains in contact with the pedal but the tension varies) and very smooth but not overly forceful during the in-between phases.

As we said previously, in the sections soon to follow we'll describe ranges of the pedaling stroke in four phases, or sectors. Note that these are *ranges* because bike geometry, fit, and functional movement abilities will have an effect. For some triathletes, TDC (top dead center) might actually shift forward by as much as 45 degrees (315 degrees becomes TDC), or to the beginning of the downstroke.

For each of the principles of pedaling technique and muscle contributions that we'll discuss, patterns are subject to ranges and change depending on body position, cadence, saddle height, terrain profile, and workload. Of course, these variations couple with joint movement, flexibility, and stability differences, but when riding a bike that is well fitted there are fewer body changes because of the supported postures (saddle, arm rests, pedals). This factor makes fitting and functional movement and stability even more important for the triathlete.

It is accepted that triathletes with more efficient pedaling technique produce higher (effective and functional) forces over those with less efficient or undeveloped pedaling styles. Those with better (normal) stability, joint mobility, and flexibility can deliver force in the best direction to the pedals. Movements away from the path the pedals take reduces the capacity—and for this reason, a professional fit, analysis of foot and body movement, posture, and stability are highly recommended. It is an exciting time in terms of bike fitting, and very soon there will be a more comprehensive and individualized approach to fitting the triathlete to the bike in such a way that distinct differences can be more accurately applied. This has not been the case, as of this writing, no matter the fitting system.

Every triathlete has different muscle mass, limb, and torso proportions, muscle fiber types, skeletal structures, foot function, body weight, fitness status, and competitive and training histories, not to mention functional movement variations of muscle, tendons, and ligaments to move, stabilize, contract, and stretch. Just like some triathletes are better at climbing, rolling, or level terrain, there are also ranges of pedaling technique. That is, the manner in which force is applied to the pedals to produce movement can be slightly different across triathletes.

Studies of pedaling mechanics can be misleading from a standpoint of workload. Scientists in an effort to measure outcomes might standardize instead of customize an individual's intensities. This is important because the workload affects pedal pressure, muscle activation, and body position. Still, there's an adequate amount of information to make recommendations and provide principles that apply to most, if not all, triathletes when cycling.

Cycling and pedaling are much different movements and much less intricate motions with less reliance on proper technique than in running or swimming. Fitting and aerodynamics are the principal considerations in cycling, but so too are the forces and foot compression applied to the pedals. The slightest modifications in bike geometry, rider placement, intensity, pedaling technique, and terrain can significantly change pedal forces.

In the following sections we describe four phases (sectors) for the purpose of improving your ability to work the dominant phase (downstroke) and enhance your ability to reduce forces during the less powerful and transitional phases: the backstroke, upstroke, and overstroke.

Downstroke

When the pedal and foot are near the topmost portion of the stroke (300 degrees, just before the TDC), this is the beginning of the downstroke, by far the most powerful phase of the pedaling cycle. The primary power position during the downstroke occurs when the hip extends the pedal forward and down from 45 to 100 degrees (2 o'clock to 5 o'clock); see figure 7.26.

- Range: 0 to 180 degrees.
- Foot-pad pressure: High-level foot compression on the pedal (medial to lateral forefoot).

- Body lines technique: The center of the knee joint aligns with the second toe; the direction of force is along the centerline of the knee toward the pedal.

For the downstroke, the hip is extended from TDC by the action of the gluteus maximus and about 45 degrees, with the hamstrings combining until about 125 degrees. From this point, the gluteus maximus and hamstring work together until the bottom dead center (BDC) at 180 degrees. There are increased forces, as well, from the gastrocnemius and soleus (calf) muscles. The hip, knee, and ankle joints extend at the same time, producing the push and resulting in peak forces on the pedal.

The force and muscular power increase fluidly by building the acceleration of the foot and leg extension starting at the top of the stroke and maximizing force at approximately 90 to 120 degrees, slowly decreasing toward the end (180 degrees). Efficiency is boosted when you focus on the vertical forces during the downstroke, not by pulling up or back on the opposite pedal.

Backstroke

The backstroke overlaps with the final stage of the downstroke, but the backstroke is a transitional phase during which pedal forces are much reduced. This phase is in between; the goal is fluid, smooth, and even pedaling with no exaggeration or increase of backward pulling, pressing, or lifting (figure 7.20).

- Range: 135 to 225 degrees.
- Foot-pad pressure: Low to very moderate foot compression on the pedal (medial to lateral forefoot).
- Body lines technique: The ankle, arch, and heel should remain stable, with foot (heel) moving along the same path as the pedal.

For the backstroke, another transitional part of pedaling, the tibialis anterior (dorsiflexion of the ankle and arch support) and hamstrings are very active. Training this phase is done by isolating the movement and focusing on improved neuromuscular motor patterns.

FIGURE 7.20 Foot and pedal position for the backstroke.

Upstroke

Beginning with the final phase of the backstroke, the upstroke is another transitional phase with little energy or force applied. In fact, the upstroke is the mirror of the other leg as it enters the powerful downstroke phase. This places the upstroke pedal to be, in effect, lifted by the great forces of the downstroke. Remember that any exaggerated lifting (pulling up) is counterproductive and actually reduces power output.

- Range: 225 to 315 degrees.
- Foot-pad pressure: Low-level (unweighted) foot compression on the pedal (medial to lateral forefoot).
- Body lines technique: The ankle, arch, and heel should remain stable, with the foot (heel) moving along the same pathway as the pedal.

For the upstroke, the biceps femoris (lateral hamstring muscle) is active during the early stages of the upstroke followed by the rectus femoris, vastus lateralis, vastus medius (quadriceps group), which as a group are active to flex the hip.

Overstroke

The overstroke precedes the downstroke and sets the beginning of the extension of the hip. Of the three transitional phases, and depending on ankle mobility, there can be an increase in forward and downward foot pressure applied. The hip is at the beginning of extension at this sector.

- Range: 315 to 45 degrees
- Foot-pad pressure: Moderate to increased foot compression on the pedal (medial to lateral forefoot).
- Body lines technique: The ankle, arch, and heel should remain stable, with foot (heel) moving along the same pathway as the pedal

In the overstroke, the rectus femoris, vastus lateralis, vastus medius (quadriceps group), gluteus medius, gluteus maximus, tibialis anterior, and soleus are all active. The tibialis and rectus femoris are especially active in this stroke.

Technique Training and Testing for Cycling

How a triathlete advances cycling technique is through the practice of better movements, adaptation, and absorption of the improved coordination over time. Some very quick adaptations to technique are possible, but long-term changes that can hold up to high intensity and endurance can take some time. However, reshaping movements through motor learning does enhance performance. The ACES (accurate, controlled, effortless, and smooth) method is particularly effective in helping you mold new and more efficient motions through attention to technique in particular regions of the body at lower intensity and progressive volume training.

In chapter 1 we presented the ACES model of training body lines by regions for three levels of lifestyles (chapter 1; tables 1.1-1.8) and criteria for base testing (tables 1.6-1.8). Within each body line segment recommendations for training and the adaptation workouts are presented as a basis for following the

system, or for fine-tuning your own model and technique principles within the framework of building better movements through deliberate but clear body lines and motions.

As we have mentioned, you need to know you are performing movement correctly, and your coach must be able to communicate this clearly. Referring to the following body lines can help achieve this, but how these positions are assessed can be an imperfect process. The following are the body lines, or regions of the body, triathletes should develop.

Foot-Pad Line

You should feel the same pressure on the inside pad (ball behind big toe) as to the outside (lateral forefoot) during each phase of the stroke (discussed further later). The pressure, tension, compression, and force do change, but the distribution (inside to outside) remains the same. The foot-pad line is fundamental to improving pedaling motions.

Here are common faults of the foot-pad line:

- Asymmetrical medial to lateral pressure (left foot to right foot)—this should be bilaterally the same for each of the four phases of the pedaling stroke.
- Pressure on the medial (inside) ball of the foot is too great.
- Elevated lateral foot results in uneven pressure medial to lateral.
- Pulling back (during backstroke) and pulling up (during upstroke) result in disproportionate pressure distributions.

In proper technique for the foot-pad line, the foot-pad pressure is equal from medial to lateral during each phase of the stroke. A good technique is to initiate force from the gluteals via a subtle activation of this body region during the downstroke. Doing this bilaterally (left to right side) begins the extension of the leg by transferring force from the pelvis through the knee and foot and foot pad equally and symmetrically.

Practice and test the foot-pad line. When you have mastered this, retest by matching your lifestyle level in table 1.3 and your baseline test time in table 1.4 for a Sub-T, as described in the note for figure 7.21.

Knee and Toe Line

The knee and toe line body regions are pivotal and link up the most optimal position for power and efficiency. Deviations in the knee alignment with the second toe that are medial (inward), lateral (outward), or medial and lateral motions while pedaling offset the leverage capacity—the transfer of force is decreased.

In chapter 4 we saw that the deep squat is an exceptional test for evaluating function movement and stability of this important body line. If during the squat the knees move inward or outward, this means there are resulting compensations and much less stability. These asymmetries carry over to the bike and should be addressed.

These are common faults of the knee and toe line:

- Knees move inward toward the top tube.
- Knees move outward away from the top tube.
- Knees move both inward and outward in a looping manner.
- One knee moves inward or outward.

In proper technique for the knee and toe line, the knee and second toe remain aligned throughout the stroke. There should be little difference from left side to right. As indicated earlier, learning to generate forces from the hip (gluteals) helps activate the muscles equally and maintains alignment by working from the core, hip, knee, ankles and foot.

FIGURE 7.21   ACES body lines test: foot-pad line.

*BASELINE TEST TIME: ____	ASSESSMENT				COMMENTS
ACES	Pass		Fail		
Accurate (pass–fail)					
Controlled (pass–fail)					
Effortless (pass–fail)					
Smooth (pass–fail)					
Time of test	1 min.	2 min.	3 min.	4 min.	
**RPM ACES: ____					
**Rating of perceived exertion (RPE)					
**Heart rate (HR)					
**Watts (W)					
**Speed average or distance (SA/D)					

*Sub-T baseline test time (see table 1.4).

**RPM ACES, HR, W, and SA/D: Record each (if applicable) at one-minute intervals.

From M. Evans and J. Cappaert, *Triathletes in motion.* (Champaign, IL: Human Kinetics).

Functional Cycling Lower-Leg Alignment Exercises

These are excellent squatting exercises (bilateral and unilateral) for developing the stability and movement control of the knee and toe-line regions.

- Bilateral short arc squat with vertically placed foam roller (figure 7.22*a*)
- Bilateral short arc squat with horizontally placed foam roller with foot balanced on arch (figure 7.22*b*)
- Unilateral squat with vertically placed foam roller (figure 7.22*c*)
- Unilateral squat with horizontally placed foam roller with foot balanced on arch (figure 7.22*d*)

For each, the motion is the same with the center joint line of knee aligned with second toe. Slowly squat a few inches (the same amount of flexion on your bike at the bottom of the pedal stroke) while drawing in your lower abdominals. The control of downward and upward movement is from the gluteal—this is where you are generating control of the flexing (squatting down) and extension (rising up). An important point is to keep the feet and toes relaxed, with no tension causing curling, flexing, widening, or extending.

FIGURE 7.22   Knee and toe line stability and movement control exercises.

FIGURE 7.23   ACES body lines test: knee and toe line.

*SUB-T BASELINE TEST TIME: ____	ASSESSMENT			COMMENTS
ACES	Pass	Fail		
Accurate (pass–fail)				
Controlled (pass–fail)				
Effortless (pass–fail)				
Smooth (pass–fail)				
Time of test	**1 min.**	**2 min.**	**3 min.**	**4 min.**
**RPM ACES: ____				
**Rating of perceived exertion (RPE)				
**Heart rate (HR)				
**Watts (W)				
**Speed average or distance (SA/D)				

*Sub-T baseline test time (see table 1.4).

**RPM ACES, HR, W, and SA/D: Record each (if applicable) at one-minute intervals.

From M. Evans and J. Cappaert, *Triathletes in motion.* (Champaign, IL: Human Kinetics).

Practice and test the knee and toe line. When you have mastered this, retest by matching your lifestyle level in table 1.3 and your baseline test time in table 1.4 for a Sub-T, as described in the note for figure 7.23.

Arch, Ankle, and Toe Lines

For this body line the region of the foot (arch, ankle, and toe) lines are highlighted. For the arch and ankle, you want to maintain a neutral posture with no excessive collapse in the arch or outward rolling of the ankle during the downstroke. Toes must be relaxed with no curling, widening, tightening, or extending (see previous bilateral and unilateral squatting exercises).

These are common faults of the arch, ankle, and toe line:

- The arch collapses during the downstroke.
- The ankle rolls outward during the downstroke.
- The toes flex, curl, widen, tighten, or extend.

In proper technique for the arch, ankle, and toe line, the longitudinal arch is maintained and the ankle is relaxed but firm. Toes are relaxed with no flexing, curling, widening, tightening, or extending—they are flat and not used to produce power.

Practice and test the arch, ankle, and toe line. When you have mastered this, retest by matching your lifestyle level in table 1.3 and your baseline test time in table 1.4 for a Sub-T, as described in the note for figure 7.24.

FIGURE 7.24   ACES body lines test: arch, ankle, and toe line.

*SUB-T BASELINE TEST TIME: ___	ASSESSMENT				COMMENTS
ACES	**Pass**		**Fail**		
Accurate (pass–fail)					
Controlled (pass–fail)					
Effortless (pass–fail)					
Smooth (pass–fail)					
Time of test	**1 min.**	**2 min.**	**3 min.**	**4 min.**	
**RPM ACES: ___					
**Rating of perceived exertion (RPE)					
**Heart rate (HR)					
**Watts (W)					
**Speed average or distance (SA/D)					

*Sub-T baseline test time (see table 1.4).

**RPM ACES, HR, W, and SA/D: Record each (if applicable) at one-minute intervals.

From M. Evans and J. Cappaert, *Triathletes in motion.* (Champaign, IL: Human Kinetics).

Technique Exercises and Workouts for Cycling

By coupling technique training with intensity, your cycling efficiency will improve. Learning how to apply pedaling forces more accurately results in better initiation and transfer pedaling forces. Cycling by physical and mechanical characteristics is less of a technique discipline than swimming and running, but there are foundations of technique and, as a result, many ways to improve your cycling with the following exercises.

Pedaling Technique Exercises

Technique exercises help you practice motor-learning skills specific to improving pedaling technique. Practiced frequently, these techniques will help to improve the efficiency of your pedaling stroke. Learning how to apply the right type of pressure and tension along the full pedaling stroke cannot be overtrained.

Some key techniques are briefly described here and included in the exercises that follow.

High-RPM Cadence (Low Tension)

These are typically completed in a reduced gear ratio, the small front chain-ring on flat to gently rolling terrain. Cadences range anywhere from 95 to 130 RPM. For higher cadence (110 to 130 RPM), intervals should last 10 to 30 seconds and 5 minutes or more for RPM of 95 to 105. Light pressure from the foot to the pedal (feathering) give the left- and right-side motions the same feel and pedal pressure.

RYAN IGNATZ | Ryan's Five Principles of the Bike-Fit Process

As a fitness instructor and master fitter holding most of the fit certifications, I've learned what it takes to fit riders successfully. I rely on my experience and intuition, not just the science, to maximize the body's potential and decrease the likelihood of injury. Here are some important bike-fit guidelines you can use to understand and reshape your current mindset toward a holistic bike-fit process. (*Note:* These are guidelines, not specific steps to complete a fit.)

1. You can't fit yourself.

This seems obvious, but going by feel takes too long and might mislead you. Even when using mirrors and video, bilateral details are hard to observe. In contrast, if a fitter is using only technology to conduct the fit, walk away. The trained eye and instinct of a certified fitter and his or her interaction with the rider will always yield better results.

2. Body assessments matter.

To determine the cause of an injury or improve efficiency, assess your body structure and function off the bike. A common example is when knee tracking deviates laterally from the sagittal plane, bike fitters are often taught to just widen stance width and add varus shims under the shoe. However, after conducting a body assessment, the symptom might be remedied by increasing range of motion in a tight hip, building strength in a weak hip stabilizer, or simply coaching them to pedal in a more linear fashion.

3. Outliers exist.

Whether the fit is static or dynamic, normative ranges for joint and body angles are used to evaluate the biomechanics of a rider. Understand that these are guidelines, and a proficient fitter will intuitively know when to safely alter your fit out of the range.

4. Be open minded and patient with changes.

The body is dynamic and adaptable. Riding builds stronger muscle memory and movement patterns, which are hard to break instantaneously with a fit. Acutely, altering a rider's movement patterns can be perceived negatively, but with patience you will often gain positive results. For example, you might feel discomfort or soreness in muscles or joints, but those sensations should go away after 10 to 15 hours of riding. Pain should be addressed right away.

5. Multiple fits are needed.

The act of bike fitting involves aligning a dynamic body on a bike in a biomechanically efficient and comfortable way. The human body is constantly in flux as muscles tighten or weaken, adhesions build up, and functional movement patterns are changing. Thus a rider might need a second look after several rides to address the minor issues that might exist after a fit. For long-term success, exercises carried out between fits to gain strength and flexibility might be warranted to allow increased efficiency while decreasing the potential for injury. It might be equally important to check your fit over larger time gaps (6 to 12 months) to address any body, goals, equipment, or fit changes to keep you in good health.

My hope is to see a shift from bike-fit services that are gratification based to a holistic approach with multiple fits. This means the fitter helps facilitate improvements in a rider's functional movement patterns and relate those patterns interactively on the bike for real success. Take a rider who has quad cramping in a tri position. An assessment might find tight and weak hamstrings, shortened hip flexors, and a lack of gluteal function. With some exercises to improve muscular function and tightness, that rider might start to use the muscles around the hip more effectively and significantly reduce cramping.

Low-RPM Cadence (High Tension)

These typically use a heftier gear ratio, the large front chain-ring on flat to gently rolling, with uphill and downhill terrain options. Cadences range anywhere from 45 to 75 RPM. For lower cadences (45 to 55 RPM), intervals should last 15 to 30 seconds and up to 5 minutes for RPM of 55 to 75. Focus on knee and toe lines with dominant muscle activation from the gluteals (keep pelvis stable) with left- and right-side motions with the same feel and pedal pressure.

Isolated Leg Training

These can use either a low- or high-tension gear ratio. To do this technique, both feet remain cleated in, but full pressure is on just one pedal and foot. The other is fully relaxed and directs no pressure on the pedal. To begin this technique, slowly unweight the forces of the opposite (non-targeted) leg. Do not unclip and place this foot back as this puts the pelvis into extensions and alters the stroke mechanics. This exercise keys into the neuromuscular components of pedaling with the targeted side making a near perfect stroke (more downstroke and light transition during back-, up-, and overstroke phases) once the technique can be done with accuracy and controlled smoothness. The ability to unweight the non-targeted

side is central to performing this drill. Your hands, shoulders, neck, and facial muscles should all be relaxed with all of your load and generation of symmetrical movements coming from the central part of your body—the muscles surrounding the pelvis.

Note: Each exercise within a workout can be replicated with indoor training stand or rollers. The road sessions can be a mixture of seated and standing out of the saddle on flat terrain, moderate slopes, rolling terrain, and steep climbing and descents.

- Flat terrain—posture and skill training in steady-state aerobic conditions; sectors pedaling; isolated leg training (ILT); small and large ring; high and low RPM; tension pedaling; ascending and descending pedaling; seated to standing
- Rolling terrain—combine uphill and down slope by integrating the techniques on the basis of the terrain; isolated leg training; seated to standing; high and low RPM
- Moderate grade long climbs—high and low RPM; cadence training; isolated leg training; seated and standing; high and low RPM
- Steep short climbs—seated high RPM
- Descents—less than 3 percent

Normal Stroke Ascending and Descending

The normal stroke was described earlier but is essentially two key and symmetrical parts. The downstroke and recovery phases are the primary elements of pedaling. In the first exercise, concentrate on a normal stroke with high (ascending) pedaling cadences that are typically in the small chain ring. In the second exercise, use a normal stroke at low (descending) pedaling cadences mostly in the large chain ring.

- *Ascending cadence.* Twenty sets (15 seconds each at 90, 95, 100, and 110 RPM) or 30 sets (10 seconds at 110, 20 seconds at 90, 10 seconds at 120, and 20 seconds at 100 RPM).
- *Descending cadence.* Twenty sets (15 seconds each at 65, 75, 60, and 80 RPM) or 15 sets (1 minute at 55, 20 seconds at 60, 20 seconds at 65, and 20 seconds at 70 RPM).

Phase Ascending and Descending

Earlier in this chapter the four phases (or sectors) were described: downstroke, backstroke, upstroke, and overstroke. In this exercise, concentrate on the phases as in the following examples.

- *Low tension sectors (high RPM).* Thirty sets (15 seconds each at downstroke, backstroke, upstroke, and overstroke with odd-number sets starting at 90 RPM and building to 100 RPM and even-number sets at 105 to 115 RPM during each phase) or 20 sets (30 seconds each at downstroke, backstroke, upstroke, and overstroke with odd-number sets starting at 100 RPM and building to 110 RPM and even-number sets at 110 to 125 RPM during each phase).

- *Descending sectors (low RPM).* Fifteen sets (15 seconds each at downstroke, backstroke, upstroke, and overstroke with odd-number sets starting at 55 RPM and building to 60 RPM and even-number sets at 65 to 70 RPM during each phase) or 10 sets (30 seconds each at downstroke, backstroke, upstroke, and overstroke with odd-number sets starting at 50 RPM and building to 55 RPM and even-number sets at 60 to 65 RPM during each phase).

Single-Leg Isolation Ascending and Descending

Single-leg isolations are completed by emphasizing one leg turning the crank with the opposite leg cleated in but applying no pressure at any time. *Note:* Do not unclip because this causes a counterbalance on the saddle and reduces neuromuscular (motor learning), which is the central reason for performing this exercise.

- *Ascending single-leg isolation (high RPM).* Forty sets (15 seconds at 90, 95, 100, and 110 RPM with the left leg, and then repeat with right leg only for 30 sets (10 seconds at 110, 20 seconds at 90, 10 seconds at 120, and 20 seconds at 100 RPM).

- *Descending single-leg isolation (low RPM).* Fifteen sets (30 seconds at 55, 60, 65, and 75 RPM with the left leg, and then repeat with right leg only for 10 sets (15 seconds at 75, 15 seconds at 70, 15 seconds at 65, and 15 seconds at 60 RPM).

Soft Pedaling 360 Degrees

Soft pedaling is a technique in which the pressure on the pedals is light, with no foot pressure to the pedal whatsoever.

- *Soft pedal 360-degree high RPM*—riding in a very light, low-tension gear at 100 to 125 RPM.

- *Soft pedal 360-degree low RPM*—riding in a firmer, high-tension gear at 60 to 75 RPM.

- *Soft pedal 360-degree sectors*—riding in a light, moderate-, or higher-tension gear and isolating each of the sectors (one at a time for a specified time).

- For each of the previous, ride 4 minutes at normal pedaling, 1 minute with downstroke emphasis, 1 minutes with backstroke emphasis, and 1 minute with upstroke emphasis and 1 minute with overstroke emphasis. Concentrate on those sectors one by one.

Seated and Standing

Most triathlon cycling is performed seated and in an aero posture. These exercises place the focus on body position and function for the triathlete. The two sit bones (ischial tuberosity) should be in balanced contact with the saddle. The torso and hips also need to be stable, unmoving. When seated or standing, maintain equal foot-pad pressure and extension of the leg with smooth bilateral timing and posture. Finally, head and neck remain neutral (elongated).

These exercises are low-tension (light resistance), high-tension (heavy resistance), low-RPM (cadence), and high-RPM seated, standing, and seated to standing skills training. There are unlimited ways to construct workouts based on the manipulation of intensity, duration, skill exercises, rest, RPM, and tension. The key is to continue a regular dose of these exercises to promote better efficiency and muscular movement.

Note that for each exercise force and movement are the same for left and right sides, foot-pad pressure on downstroke is balanced left to right, and there's no pitching side to side on the saddle.

Seated Low Tension High RPM

Use a light-tension gear (smallest front chain ring and easy-tension rear gear) and pedal at 105 RPM (110, 115, 120, 125+ for other sets) for the first set for one minute. Continue each RPM for one minute, no matter the slope. Repeat for 30 to 60 minutes.

Seated High Tension Low RPM

Use a high-tension gear (large front chain ring and high-tension rear gear) and pedal at 75 RPM (65, 60, and 55 for other sets) for the first set for one minute. Each RPM is continued for two minutes, no matter the slope. Repeat for 30 to 60 minutes.

Seated to Standing Low Tension High RPM

Use a light-tension gear (smallest front chain ring and light-tension rear gear) and begin seated pedaling at 105 RPM (110 and 115 for other sets) for the first set for one minute; then stand out of the saddle at the same RPM for one minute. Repeat for 8 to 16 minutes.

Seated to Standing High Tension Low RPM

Use a high-tension gear (largest front chain ring and high-tension rear gear) and begin seated pedaling at 75 RPM (65, 60. and 55 for other sets) for the first set for one minute; then stand out of the saddle at the same RPM for one minute. Repeat for 12 to 30 minutes.

Seated High RPM to Standing Low RPM

Use a light-tension gear (smallest front chain ring and light-tension rear gear) and begin seated pedaling at 105 RPM (110 and 115 for other sets) for one minute. Shift to a higher-tension gear (largest front chain ring and higher rear gear) and stand out of the saddle at 75 RPM (65, 60, and 55 for other sets) for one minute. Repeat for 4, 8, 12, or 16 minutes.

Seated Low RPM to Standing High RPM

Use a high-tension gear (largest front chain ring and higher rear gear) and begin seated pedaling at 75 RPM (65, 60, and 55 for other sets) for one minute. Shift to a lower-tension gear (smallest front chain ring and light-tension rear gear) and stand out of the saddle at 105 RPM (110 and 115 for other sets) for one minute. Repeat for 4, 8, 12, or 16 minutes.

Training and Combined Technique Workouts for Cycling

Training time is valuable, and including skill and specific exercises over time will transfer to better riding form. There are, of course, psychological and physiological benefits for training rides that have little or no skills training, but without guidance (even when power and intensity are provided), you might veer from the workout plan's purpose.

Following are three examples (one-, three-, and five-hour training sessions) of incorporating technique, skills, and high-concentration specificity training into your workouts. Tension control and bilateral symmetry (left to right side) with body motions are very important to keep in mind. Use these or develop your own and do them on a regular basis.

One-Hour Cycling Workout

This workout (figure 7.25) prepares you to work on the techniques of relaxation (RLX), sectors (phases of the pedaling stroke), single-leg isolation (SLI), foot-pad (FP) pressures, and using soft-pedal 360 (SPF) pressures during your stroke. This workout is best done indoors on a trainer or on rollers.

Three-Hour Cycling Workout

This three-hour road-training workout (figure 7.26) blends seated high RPM standing with low RPM on flat terrain with focused descending and ascending single-leg isolation that stimulate pedaling neuromuscular patterns, sectors at low tension and high RPM.

Five-Hour Cycling Workout

This five-hour workout (figure 7.27) includes technique and climbing moderate grade (CMG), isolated leg extended (ILE) at high RPM for longer time intervals, a small ring (SR), high RPM TT (time trial) at low gear tension, and finally a low to high RPM set of mixed training.

FIGURE 7.25   One-hour cycling workout.

Begin set at these time intervals	10 min.	20 min.	30 min.	40 min.	50 min.
	4 sets of 30 sec. RLX (select one body area) + 30 seconds all-body RLX; then select another body area.	Sectors: 8 sets (focus 15 sec. on downstroke, backstroke, upstroke, and overstroke); odd-number sets at 90, 95, 100, and 105 RPM in small chain ring and even-number sets at 95, 65, 105, and 70 RPM in large chain ring.	SLI: 10 sets (30 sec. left leg, 30 sec. right); odd-number sets at 105-110 RPM in small ring and even-number sets at 70-80 RPM in large chain ring.	FP: 8 sets (45 seconds foot pad at downstroke plus 15 seconds soft pedal 360); odd-number sets at 65-70 RPM in large chain ring and even-number sets at 105-115 in small chain ring.	SPF: 10 min.

FIGURE 7.26   Three-hour cycling workout.

Begin set at these time intervals	45 min.	90 min.	215 min.
	8 sets (30 sec. seated at 100-105 RPM to 30 sec. standing, 30 sec. soft-pedal seated) on flat terrain; odd-number sets 65-70 at RPM; even-number sets at 75-80 RPM.	20 sets (descending single-leg isolation from 10 to 1 (start with 10 strokes right then 10 left, 9 right, 9 left until 1 stroke right and 1 stroke left); sets 1-5 at 90 RPM, sets 6-10 at 100 RPM, sets 11-15 at 110 RPM, and sets 16-20 at 115-120 RPM in small chain ring.	4 sets (ascending sectors from 1 to 10 (start with 1 stroke right then 1 left, 2 right, 2 left until 10 strokes right and 10 strokes left) with 1 downstroke, 2 backstroke, 3 upstroke, and 4 overstroke +2 min. of soft pedaling between; set 1 at 90 RPM, set 2 at 95-100 RPM, set 3 at 100-105 RPM, and set 4 at 110-115 RPM.

FIGURE 7.27   Five-hour cycling workout.

Begin set at following time intervals	60 min.	120 min.	180 min.	240 min.
	CMG/high RPM: 8 sets (30 sec. CMG + 30 sec. soft pedaling); odd-number sets at 90-95 RPM and 60 RPM soft pedaling and even-number sets at 105-110 RPM and 50 RPM soft pedaling.	ILE/high RPM: 6 sets (3 min. left and 3 min. right leg ILT); odd-number sets at 100 RPM and even-number sets at 105-110 RPM.	SR/high RPM/TT: 20 min. at 105-115 RPM at zone 3-4 (to review intensity zones, see chapter 1).	20 sets of low RPM (20 seconds at 50-65 RPM) to high RPM (40 sec. at 100-115 RPM).

Body Lines Cycling Workouts

Two more sample workouts (see figures 7.28 and 7.29) follow for body line and specific technique training of body regions. Ordinarily, these are best done on indoor trainers or rollers, but they can be adapted to the road. The benefits are training your body to learn by isolating movements over numerous repetitions and sets and intensities and focusing on applying ACES techniques in all movements.

Technique plays a factor in cycling, but it must be combined with fitting. This chapter has addressed those movement, assessment, and technique factors relevant to improving performance with changes in your biomechanics to improve economy. The techniques need to be trained over time to better develop the muscles and recruitment and motor learning. They are slowly programmed and become part of normal movements in training and competition.

Bike fitting is an evolving science and noteworthy profession, but the best fitters know this is as much an art as it is a science. However, triathletes should work with the most experienced fitters and in the future combine movement, muscle function, technique, and a series of fittings over time—the body and bike fit are constantly evolving. There are key businesses, innovative systems, and individuals at the forefront of technology and fitting that are slowly producing methods, education models, and programs for enhancing the standards of competency of bike fitting.

FIGURE 7.28 Body line cycling workout 1.

Set 1	4 sets of 4 (15 seconds at 90, 95, 100, and 105 RPM), working on phases: set 1, downstroke; set 2, backstroke; set 3, upstroke; and set 4, overstroke. No rest.	Chain ring: small
		Cassette: cog 2, 3, or 4
		Intensity: Z1-Z2
		RPM: 90-105
	SET TIME: **0:16:00** *TOTAL TIME:* **0:16:00**	
Set 2	8 sets (10 seconds at each of the following RPM: 85, 95, 105, 110, 115, and 120; light pressure on the pedals; medial and lateral forefoot remain in contact with the pedal throughout. No rest.	Chain ring: small
		Cassette: cog 2, 3, or 4
		Intensity: Z2
		RPM: 85-120
	SET TIME: **0:08:00** *TOTAL TIME:* **0:24:00**	
Set 3	4 sets (2 min. Z3 in large chain ring, 4 × 1 min.; Z2 ILT in small chain ring + 15 sec. soft pedal and 3 min. Z4 in large chain ring) + 30 sec. rest with focus on downstroke and knee lines.	Chain ring: small and large
		Cassette: varied
		Intensity: Z2-Z4
		RPM: 90-100
	SET TIME: **0:38:00** *TOTAL TIME:* **1:02:00**	

FIGURE 7.29 Body line cycling workout 2.

Set 1	20 sets (12 + 12 sec., 10+10 sec, 8+8 sec. of revolutions ILT, alternating left leg and right leg in descending revolutions (both legs cleated in; beginning with only one leg; the opposite leg is unweighted); sets 1-5 at 90 RPM; sets 6-10 at 95-100 RPM; sets 11-15 at 105 RPM; sets 16-20 at 110-115 RPM (low tension, small chain ring).	Chain ring: small
		Cassette: cog 2, 3, or 4
		Intensity: Z2
		RPM: 90-115
	SET TIME: **0:20:00** *TOTAL TIME:* **0:20:00**	
Set 2	12 sets (4 + 4 sec.; 8 + 8 sec.; 6 + 6 sec.; 12 + 12 sec. of revolutions ILT, alternating left and right leg in ascending revolutions; sets 1-4 at 65-70 RPM; sets 5-8 at 75-80 RPM; sets 9-12 at 85-90 RPM (high tension, large chain ring).	Chain ring: large
		Cassette: cog 2, 3, or 4
		Intensity: Z2 to Z2+
		RPM: 65-90
	SET TIME: **0:12:00** *TOTAL TIME:* **0:32:00**	
Set 3	8 sets of 40 sec. arch-line; build for stability and support on longitudinal arch + 20 sec. normal stroke building to 120 RPM; during backstroke and upstroke, focus on ankle stability through the arch and maintaining forefoot at even contact and pressure (inside to outside of the foot pad).	Chain ring: small
		Cassette: cog 2, 3, or 4
		Intensity: Z2
		RPM: 90-120
	SET TIME: **0:12:00** *TOTAL TIME:* **0:44:00**	

Unweighting Your Body Tension

Reducing muscle tension and learning the *feel*, positions, and postures of your body regions and monitoring their movements begin with attention and awareness. To swim, bike, and run better, you must reduce the grip of physical movements and employ accurate, controlled, effortless, and smooth motions—even while working at high intensities. From your head, eyes, jaw, teeth, neck, torso, hips, thighs, lower leg, ankle, feet, and toes, you can regulate tension and improve performance.

Relaxing your muscles to move accurately and efficiently with only the necessary amount of tension is necessary to execute your movements optimally. One of the best ways to do this is to maintain relaxation with the eyes. Do not focus on any specific point or competitor, but instead open, relax, and keep the eyes calm, but aware of where you are and how your body is moving.

During your workouts, practice easing tension in the following body regions. We recommend four sets of one minute for each while calmly and effortlessly relaxing the particular region. Try one body region, then ride normally for a minute; all of your body should now be tension free. Whatever order you choose to do them in doesn't matter.

Forehead: no tension

Head: ears even with shoulders

Eyes: open, relaxed, calm, and viewing a wide range; not focused narrowly

Chin: tucked gently down in neutral posture

Mouth: slightly open with jaw relaxed

Neck: elongated and tension free

Shoulders: low and not rounded, lifted, or extended

Fingers and hands: no tension or pressure

Torso or spine: stable, not flexed or extended

Pelvis: neutral, with no tilt forward or backward; think *stability*

Navel: gently draw in navel toward spine

Knee and second toe: aligned during the downstroke

Quadriceps: muscles relaxed

Gluteals: generate a light, relaxed force during downstroke

Foot: even foot pad contact from medial to lateral; maintain longitudinal arch

Toes: no flexing, extending, or arching

Ankle: relaxed and neutral

8 Analyzing and Improving Running Technique

Running in triathlon can be the difference maker. Yes, to be competitive, triathletes must excel in the water and on the bike, but in the end, the best and most efficient runners typically end up on the podium. Because the run is so decisive in triathlon, each phase of the running stride must be finely tuned and fully functional. The body lines system of training is perfectly suited for the demands of preparing your body and honing your technique for optimal performance in the run.

Improving running performance for triathlon has much to do with maintaining a steady state of effort by delaying the onset of fatigue. You achieve this ability through improvements in posture, balance, and stability. The deep-layered local stabilizer muscles at the joint level might very well hold the key to optimal running performance by maintaining joint postures such as the pelvis, torso, and shoulder in a neutral and stable position. At certain points while you are running, landing forces greater than your body weight fall onto your feet. At these moments, optimal posture is indispensible for maintaining stability and forward propulsion. Learning to position your body in a way that reduces deceleration by preserving posture will generate better muscular movements. Proper posture and stability are by far the most important aspect of effective running.

Running is as complex a discipline to master as swimming but is often underevaluated and undercoached and tends to receive less focus from triathletes in terms of posture and technique. As with swimming and cycling, we have found that baseline assessment and progressive corrections through individualized exercises is the best way to make the most of your athletic skills and abilities as they relate to the run. The goal is to develop the necessary stability and postures that lead to improved capacity to absorb ground forces at foot strike and to reuse those energies with optimal efficiency by anticipating and generating muscular movements and effective positions of the limbs.

There are three predominant foot-strike patterns: rear foot, midfoot, and forefoot. Triathletes should select shoes not so much by foot type but by how the shoe affects landing forces and body posture at foot strike. Regardless of foot type or preferred type of shoe, what's most important is the stability, mobility, and flexibility in the upper body in concert with the posture of the pelvis, torso, and shoulders. Upper-body functional movement very often commands lower-body mechanics, including the foot strike. Although it is important to determine the functionality of the foot and ankle, it is also important to make significant changes, as needed, in how you make foot-to-ground contact, which will be further discussed later in the chapter. To be sure, foot dysfunctions, shoe type, manufacturer, orthotics, and foot-bed alterations all affect foot-to-ground reactivity, but posture, technique, joint mobility, muscle flexibility, and stability are ultimately most important to achieving optimal performance.

In all physical activities, the key tasks the muscles perform are fundamental to performance, and of course this holds true in running. These key tasks include the following:

- The capacity to absorb and control shock and prevent collapse
- The capacity to maintain balance and posture control in the upper body
- The ability of the muscles to generate sufficient propulsion by activating and coordinating the appropriate muscles
- The ability to maintain center of mass posture while moving from one limb to the next and during changes of direction and slope

If you want to run better, you must understand that the body does not function or react effectively from inefficient postures. Event performance and common sense demonstrate how poor, asymmetrical postures and body lines influence results. The last 100 meters and finish in the women's triathlon at the 2012 London Olympics tell the story of posture and performance.

Even at the elite level of triathlon, the smallest of margins at the finish line can demonstrate links in form (technique and body lines) that can be the difference between a gold, silver, and bronze medal. Nicola Spirig of Switzerland, the 2012 Olympic triathlon champion in the final 100 meters, sustained her form and body lines and at no time strayed from the principles of posture during what turned out to be a photo finish.

To be competitive in high-level triathlon, you must have superior running capability. Swim and bike performances depend largely on competition distance and format, but superior running capacity is essential no matter the format. As we have said, it is the running leg of

the triathlon that very often determines who makes the podium and who falls just short.

In future Olympics, the traditional non-drafting rules in triathlon might be added, from sprint to Ironman distance. But, for now, in Olympic triathlon, the draft-legal format requires the highest running potential form and fitness and is a dominant focus of training and racing strategy. The long course (half-Ironman) and Ironman distance also reward the best runners and those who remain balanced and manage intensity and energy levels across the three disciplines.

There is no question that a considerable cardiovascular engine is necessary for elite performance in triathlon. This gift is awarded to individuals by genetics. That said, training volume, intensity, workout specificity, training plan and workouts, recovery, nutrition, psychology, power, and pace are all taken very seriously by elite triathletes and their coaches—and for very good reason. Yes, it helps to be blessed with a strong engine, but this alone does not guarantee success. Much like swimming, running is technique driven, and those who learn to apply the most efficient movements and to correct their movement limitations can largely make up for many genetic deficiencies.

Foundations of Running

Running form and efficiency are related to the interaction and transfer of forces from the ground to the body. The foot adapts to ground reaction forces and terrain through proprioception (sense of limb orientation, alignment, and position in space) in order to balance and maximize leverage for propulsion. Of equal importance is the deep-layered core stability and how the coordination of the core muscles function to maintain posture alignment and control the absorption of forces during foot strikes.

Of course technique has a major effect on efficiency of movement. Postures can be trained to efficiently reuse energy in the form of greater running speed; the reduction of rotating body movements that affect forward propulsion is also important to optimal efficiency. A central theme is your core posture (detailed shortly). You should include the assessments of movement and stability before instructing technique. This shift in learning, coaching, and teaching technique should be a fundamental aspect of every coaching program.

Smart run training combines your functional movement and technique and the transformation of technique can be broken down into four phases (figure 8.1). First, movement and stability limitations are identified through assessment. Second, exercises are selected and performed to correct movement asymmetries and improve stabilization. Third, efficiency and technique workouts in which ACES are achieved pave the way for movement adaptations to take hold. Finally, the stimulation of neural firing (activating muscles via the nervous system) is developed through repeated technique training of body regions and progressions in movement and posture.

Insufficient core stability reduces the ability to absorb and reuse landing energy. This deeper-level stabilization can affect your posture and how the limbs move. One of the keys to better running is to limit movement corrections your body makes as a result of inefficient movements. If you are constantly adjusting and compensating, you will make new and often less effective patterns of movement. Achieving better technique requires specific training but also movement and core stability that provide the greatest ability to

reuse energy most efficiently under training intensities and for various distances of triathlon competitions.

You must build from the innermost stabilizing muscles of the body to develop optimal patterns of movement, technique, and efficiency. Because power and force are chiefly generated from the center of the body, it's important that the core be both stable and mobile. This is what we see in elite runners—stability and mobility with great amounts of force teamed with coordinated and balanced postures and much less compensation. Training programs that work the broader aspects of conditioning (volume, intensity, density and frequency) can boost performance by taking an individualized approach (assessing movement and stability and training the deeper-layered local stabilizers).

Running Efficiency

Some people argue that, left alone, triathletes will learn on their own, through adaptation, the technique that is most efficient for them as individuals. The idea that technique is a self-optimizing process can be accurate to a certain extent. However, if you have plateaued in your performance and are seeking even the smallest edge to help you improve your race time, you'll find that developing your levels of functional movement, stability, neuromuscular firing, and technique will help you get over the hump better than mere training intensity and volume.

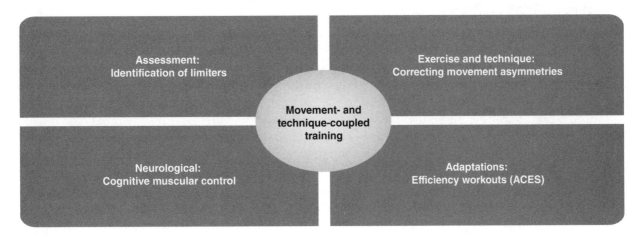

FIGURE 8.1 Movement- and technique-coupled training.

We never want to downplay the importance of a good training program, but it can be reasoned that athletic talent (the cardiovascular engine) is more valuable than any type of intensity, volume, and density-based system of training. Most of of us close to triathlon agree that an extensive and detailed workout plan is absolutely vital for competitive performance, but how do we explain the fact that world and Olympic champions perform at high levels despite changes in coaching, self-coaching, and unorthodox training plans and nutrition strategies?

Most of us need training to attain the level of technique and rarefied movements that we see in champions. But no generic training plan will do. We need to be fully functional, stable, balanced, coordinated, and in complete synchronization. Training at high intensity and volume without matching up functional movements in the joints and muscles and stable postures neglects one of the most crucial areas of triathlon performance success.

The influence of optimal technique on triathlon running performance is so significant because improvements in a runner's economy can increase performance. Running economy that can be measured in a laboratory identifies a triathlete's *total efficiency*. By testing how much oxygen it takes to run a given distance at steady-state speeds, triathlon performances and running efficiency can be somewhat explained. This is not a necessary test by any means, but it does serve to explain why one

TORBJORN SINDBALLE   Mental Toughness

What separates the good from the great? Nature? Nurture? Something else? According to coaches in many sports, the main thing that sets champions apart is neither nature nor nurture but something else deep inside—they call it mental toughness.

What Is Mental Toughness?

In 2002, a team of British scientists asked a group of world-class athletes, their coaches, and sport psychologists this very question. They came up with a two-part answer. Athletes with mental toughness are better at coping with the rigorous routines, pain, discomfort, and sacrifice of a life dedicated to training *and* they are better at remaining determined, focused, and confident under pressure.

In other words, mentally tough athletes train through rain and hail to reach their goals, they are focused and disciplined when optimizing technique, they bounce back quickly from setbacks, and they use razor-sharp focus and those last drops of will to edge themselves in front of opponents at the finish line.

How Do You Develop Mental Toughness?

Developing mental toughness is a complex process involving the ability to cope with prior difficulties; mental skills such as focus, goal setting, and confidence; and a deep inner drive to be the best athlete you can possibly be. Ask yourself, *Am I tough enough? Can I handle the pressure of racing?* If the answer is *No,* or *I'm not sure,* you probably need to work on your training motivation. Motivation is about setting tough goals and then making specific plans to attain them. You must be able to adjust along the way when the road toward achieving your goal unexpectedly veers off in a different direction. Handling pressure is about looking within to separate your thoughts and emotions from the situation and focus on the things that are in your control. Strong and stubborn training in the face of adversity develops mental toughness. If you feel you are not tough enough, challenge yourself to become tougher. Set a goal, and achieve it. Set a slightly tougher goal, and achieve it. Do this time and again, and eventually the possibility of not achieving your goal will never enter your mind. Goal achievement has become habit. You are mentally tough.

central feature of economy—*technique*—is so important for the triathlete.

Improvements in technique cross every phase and spectrum of training and competition. How your body *feels* is the sensory signal from your nervous system to the muscles that amounts to a checklist of how performance is going at any given moment. Technique is one of the first signals. It is the primary ingredient of all forms of energy and determines how energy is used most effectively.

Improving running body posture and technique very likely maximizes efficiency in many areas of performance, including all of the following:

Neuromuscular Efficiency

- How the mind, nervous system, and muscles function and communicate to send movement signals (brain to muscle connection) to the limbs
- Coordination, skill, and movement, through the process of adaptations in technique via the nervous systems expanding ability to move more efficiently and powerfully with more efficient movement

Metabolic Efficiency

- How fuel is used by the muscles
- Metabolic efficiency through pace management
- Aerobic metabolism, a significant source of oxygen

Biomechanical Efficiency

- Mechanically efficient movement patterns and the energy cost of those movements
- The importance of hip range of motion related to speed and stride length
- Muscular performance enhanced by signals from the brain to the nervous system and the efficient recruitment of motor units—training with higher levels of neural recruitment via greater intensity in selected workout to enhance motor recruitment
- Mechanical efficiency, requiring less energy demand to sustain speed

Adaptation and Absorption of Movement

One way triathletes transform running technique is through adaptation and absorption of better movements. As you know by now, every running stride must be executed with the most stable posture from the pelvis, torso, and shoulder region, regardless of running speed, terrain, or fatigue. You must maintain a basic, neutral body posture that limits deceleration and allows optimally efficient forward movement.

Some very quick adaptations to technique are possible, but long-term changes that hold up to high-intensity and high-endurance situations will take time to develop. Remodeling movements through motor learning and improvements in mobility and stability, along with better recruitment training, *will* enhance performance. Training using ACES and body lines is particularly effective in helping you shape new and more efficient regions of the body and motions.

Core Stability and Running Efficiency

Running requires an ample range of motion and muscular stability to absorb and reuse energy generated from one foot strike to the next. Think *posture and form* as you recall one of the most famous battles in triathlon history, between Mark Allen and Dave Scott in the 1989 Ironman. Allen, the ultimate winner, and Scott, the runner-up, ran step for step for all but 24 miles without a word between them.

Allen was a remarkably stable, indefatigable athletic figure with classic posture. Scott—as he often remarked himself—was not a picture of perfect running, though he was one of the best runners in the sport (largely because of excellent pelvic, torso, and shoulder stability). On this occasion, though, Scott's postural shortcomings may have got the best of him. Running with his head (chin) back and neck in extension as he always did, his form may have ultimately demanded more energy. Allen and Scott were running sub-6-minute pace and Scott's compensations were increasing with each stride.

Whether they are efficient or wasteful, running movements are linked to stability, mobility in the joints, and flexibility (range of motion), particularly at the pelvis, shoulders, and torso—the core. Improving and restructuring these important aspects will support technique that over time is self-optimized (i.e., your body adapts to your mechanics) to your movements and by the limits of control and functionality at the core.

This is why maintaining center of gravity is so important during the run. The pelvis, hips, torso, and shoulders each share a principal part in your performance. The central posture and angle of body alignment should never change (figure 8.2). Regardless of speed or terrain, the core alignment and a forward posture must be maintained. When you engage the deep-layered muscles of the core, you activate the transversus abdominis—drawing in ever so slightly while exhaling. This helps to stabilize the pelvis and spine while running and allows for improved movement through the local stabilizers.

Flexibility and Joint Mobility

Contrary to popular thinking, more flexibility is not always better. A hyperflexible triathlete will lose force-generating capacity because of weakness in overelongated muscles. Think of an overstretched and spindly rubber band. Tautness in a muscle (within normal ranges of movement, or even on the outer limits) is more efficient than an overly flexible muscle. Tautness increases the capacity for more substantial forces during running, particularly at toe-off (propulsion). In contrast, restrictions of muscle length (overly inflexible muscles) create the opposite effect by limiting the normal ranges of motions you need to achieve the most productive body positions.

Triathletes and coaches should beware of overly aggressive flexibility routines, or generic movement programs that might result in unintended increases in flexibility and joint mobility. Spine flexion is one key area of mobility, and flexibility training can increase the compression placed on the spine. One exercise that unreasonably loads the spine and

is not recommended is the traditional sit-up. Many positions in yoga are also best avoided.

As discussed in chapter 4, the tension and resulting pressure on tissues when performing certain yoga poses are so great that they place too-high levels of load on the spine. For those with spine issues, this overload can easily cause injury. Another effect of overloading the spine is an overlengthening of muscle tissue, causing too much flexibility and corresponding instability, leading to diminished performance.

We have already cited yoga's deep-rooted history in self-awareness, relaxation, breathing, and equanimity, all of which can benefit everyone, including the triathlete. We are not saying to avoid yoga altogether, but do avoid any complex body position that reduces core mobility and flexibility. If you are not sure a certain position is safe, you are best off to avoid it. Similarly, popular training routines using bands, suspension straps, and stability balls have great potential for enhancing stability and mobility, but too often these routines or exercises fail to teach and establish optimal posture throughout the movement. Such routines might not harm triathlon performance, but they might not help much, either.

Stretch Shortening and Elasticity Efficiency

The effortlessness and stability of elite triathletes' running are largely due to an efficient shortening (contraction) of the muscles followed by a lengthening to provide movement and produce propulsion. When you are about to make foot strike with the ground, your hamstrings are lengthening (stretching). On landing, your energy is now stored elastically, much like a stretched rubber band, and energy is released.

The connective tissues in the muscles act like a corset to resist collapsing. Individual muscles are made up of numerous muscle fibers that lie parallel with one another. A single muscle fiber contains myofibrils made up of smaller structures called sarcomeres. Sarcomeres give the muscle its ability to

FIGURE 8.2 Running posture and alignment.

contract and relax. Here's how the stored energy is used:

- Five to 10 percent of energy is used to absorb foot strike.
- Ten to 15 percent of energy is used to overcome air resistance.
- Eighty percent of energy is used to speed up and slow down leg motion.

When the foot lands correctly under the body, there is decreased ground reaction force (a braking, or slowing, component). The forces acting on the body can be used to stretch the muscles to create a stronger contraction (reusing energy). When your posture, stability, and technique are in good form, the body can use some of these forces for better forward propulsion. The way in which the foot strikes the ground determines the direction of the ground reaction forces (i.e., the amount of braking force), and the angle of the lower leg at foot-strike posture establishes the efficiency with which these forces are used. If the foot is extended too far in front of the hips and knee joint at foot strike, it causes a hard landing, increasing braking forces and decreasing momentum. A foot and lower leg that are flexed (too far back of the hips and knee joint) at foot strike lose landing energy. The desired foot strike is a neutral position (using center of body mass) that promotes the right amount of energy reuse and forward momentum.

All of this means, of course, that combining technique and functional movements are important for the triathlete. Triathletes should listen to the sound and quality of each foot strike, be aware of tempo (contact time and foot position) and tone, and aim for symmetry from one foot strike to the next. Maintaining posture through the pelvis, torso, head, and shoulders is crucial to effective running. Always think of your pelvis as the governor of movement when you run. Focus on holding this core region of your body in neutral position to minimize unnecessary motions.

Elasticity of Muscles

Stored elastic energy in the muscles is used to recoil and produce movement. These elastic elements inside and along the fibers of each muscle form the connective tissues and account for the stability of individual muscles. A key factor in training is to improve your neural productivity, or brain-to-muscle communication and stimulation. Your training should include individually progressed, carefully chosen exercises and running intensities to optimize your nervous system's effectiveness in delivering movement signals to the leg muscles.

Reactive, or plyometric, training that involves short hops, jumps, and bounds with a focus on minimizing the time spent on the ground is excellent for improving the recoil and neural stimulation. Accelerations and exertions to near sprinting for short durations (15 to 45 seconds) along with bounding exercises (single and double leg) can fully engage the energy of the foot strike and unload this force in a very specific way to train reactivity.

Such exercises can be done on uphills or downhills of 3 to 5 percent grade or on flat surfaces using exaggerated (longer time or higher or further distance with each strike) motions or a focus on a body line segment with minimized foot strike. Land on your forefoot to use the forces acting on the body as the stretching of the muscles (e.g., elasticity in the foot and Achilles tendon) becomes reusable energy.

Phases of Running Stride

The ground and your body work together to generate force. Think of each foot strike as an object that collides with the earth. Gravity pulls the body down forcefully into the ground, and the reaction initiates an equal and opposite response. Remember Newton's third law of motion—**for every action, there is an equal and opposite reaction.** When your foot makes contact with the ground, the reaction is energy transfer into, ideally, the core of your body.

The principal phases and divisions of the running gait cycle are shown in figure 8.3. These include the periods of *stance* and *swing* along with the *tasks* of the movements and the *phases*. Each of these relate to the absorption of forces, support, and propulsion. In sequence, the phases are the initial acceptance

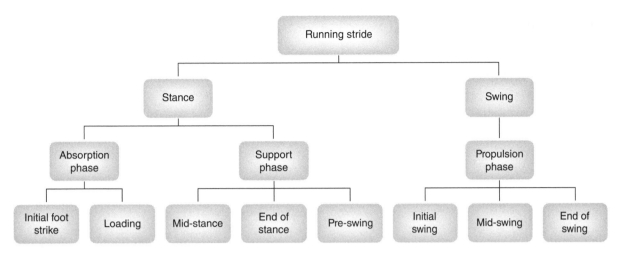

FIGURE 8.3 Running stride and divisions of the gait.

of the body weight, ground forces following one-sided (unilateral) leg support, and finally the advancement (progression and propulsion) of the body into the air.

The foot is always either in stance or swing phase (also called *float*), with the task of absorbing the load, supporting the body, and then propelling the body forward. There is a lot of muscle activity during these phases, with the hip extensors, hamstrings, quadriceps, abductors (gluteus medius and maximus), adductors, and gastrocnemius dominating during the initial foot strike. The adductors are also active during the other phases and play an important role in balance and posture stability. This muscle group also assists with forward and backward flexion and lateral and medial rotation of the legs. As noted earlier, the gluteus medius is a key pelvic postural muscle—a muscle that keeps your hips stable during the single-leg support at foot strike. A weak gluteus medius is demonstrated by a sagging or tilt in the stance limb and perhaps a lateral tilting of the trunk (lateral leaning). Weakness in the gluteus medius affects body posture, technique, and running efficiency and can lead to many injuries, such as iliotibial band syndrome, knee pain, hip pain, and even back pain.

Lower-Body Running Mechanics

The biomechanics of running are largely affected by the lower-limb anatomy, particularly the joints of the ankle and foot. Excessive supination (outward) or pronation (inward) in

the foot causes an associated effect along the entire kinetic chain.

There are 108 ligaments, 26 bones, 33 joints (20 that actively articulate), and more than 100 muscles, tendons, and ligaments as well as 14 phalanges (bones forming toes) that make up the foot and ankle. The foot has two lengthwise (longitudinal) arches and two transverse (crosswise) arches that provide structure and support and can sometimes cause painful conditions caused by faulty positions.

The arches are not generally rigid, but with an overpronating (inward rotation) foot, there is too much laxity. The normal foot is flexible and changes shape to adjust to different demands. During each foot step, there is primarily a flattening of the arch (pronation) followed by an upward and outward (hollowing) of the arch (supination). The foot and ankle joints work together as terrain, intensity, speed, and surges in pace develop in order to provide the best platform for functional performance. The foot and ankle move in many directions, performing countless sensory, balance, and propulsion duties. Thus some emphasis on the assessment and performance of the foot and ankle is important.

In many movements of the foot and ankle, varying degrees of pronation (foot rolls inward through the foot strike and gait cycle) and supination (underpronation, or the outward movement of the foot during the gait cycle) occur in which your body weight tends to be on the outside edge of the foot, which makes for less than optimal energy transfer.

- Stride length is best maximized by a push-off well behind the center of body mass; hip flexibility is important in this movement.
- Technique practice: The push-off is key to running efficiency. A strong and forceful toe-off increases the swing (float) phase; the result is that you cover more ground (figure 8.4).
- Photos of world-class runners during toe-off and float demonstrate the importance of hip mobility and the emphasis on complete extension at toe-off.
- Do not extend the forward swinging leg and knee beyond the center of mass; this reduces stride rate and slows you down because of increased braking forces at foot strike.
- The posterior leg fully extends and allows the forward swinging leg and knee to flex in preparation of initial contact, making a quick, forcefully direct, and light contact with the ground.
- Normal hip extension movement is central to achieving a full and efficient toe-off.
- Faster runners spend less time in the stance phase.
- Stride rates optimize energy use 90 to 97 strides per minute (one left and one right foot strike).

FIGURE 8.4 Running phase at toe-off.

There can be differences in the mechanics of one foot's strike and the other. For example, one foot might pronate more than the other. Such lopsided instability can cause unsteadiness that channels upward to affect the higher-level movements and mechanics. It happens the other way, too—higher-level unbalanced or unstable tightness and joint immobility can affect the biomechanics of the foot and ankle. Your foot-strike forces should be plentiful by allowing the descending leg and foot (arched and dorsiflexed, ready for recoiling and reloading) to strike the ground firmly.

The muscles and tendons of the foot and lower leg play an important role in the kinetic chain. Functional foot mechanics along with mobility and stability of the complex lower leg, ankle, foot, and arch collectively help with absorption, reaction (rebound of stored energy), and efficiency. Asymmetries in the lower leg and feet should be among the first movements assessed. Asymmetry and technique abnormalities result, for example, if one foot or ankle is more pronated or supinated than the other. Correcting imbalances in the strength, mobility, and flexibility of the muscles, including consideration of neutral footwear or orthotic stabilization techniques, might be necessary.

Assessing mechanics of the foot and ankle informs you to what degree you are in or out of normal ranges. Typically, the best position to examine is during the foot midstance (when knees are aligned), which is when much of the loading on the foot takes place. In the following sections we provide an overview of observable foot and ankle positions and recommendations for adjustments.

Foot Alignment

In normal foot alignment when standing, the heel and foot are slightly turned out and no more than two lateral toes (about 5 degrees) are visible when observed from the back. More out-toeing increases the time of foot pronation. Look for strain on the feet (forward, lateral, or back lean) caused by too much weight on the forefoot or heels of the feet; check the alignment of the feet with and without shoes.

- Front view—observe great (big) and lesser (small) toe alignment and balance when standing.
- Inside view—inspect for high-arch or flat-foot postures with both feet (arches) symmetrical.
- Posterior view—look for alignment of the heels.

Foot and Ankle Range of Motion

The foot and ankle are the lower base of support for the body. If there is weakness, improper technique, or inflexibility in the foot or ankle, then foot extension, flexion, inversion, or eversion ranges of motion might compensate. For example, the tibialis anterior muscle dorsiflexes the ankle joint and inverts the foot. If you hold this dorsiflexed foot posture (ankle flexed with foot and toes toward shin), this shifts the center of gravity of the body backward instead of forward but keeps the pelvis, torso, and shoulders forwardly aligned. It's important to have the foot aligned neutral at foot strike with a dorsiflexed ankle for stability and to load energy efficiently as the foot comes under the body and pushes off. The foot and ankle can move through several ranges:

- Flexion (dorsiflexion)—movement of the foot toward the tibia (shinbone).
- Extension (plantar flexion)—movement of the foot away from the tibia (pointed toes).
- Inversion—turning the heel inward. Normal inversion is an ankle that has sufficient, but not excessive, inward mobility and no rigidity.
- Eversion—turning the heel outward. Normal eversion is an ankle that has sufficient, but not excessive, outward mobility and no rigidity.

To improve stability and joint mobility of the feet and ankles, perform the following exercises during warm-up before running or any dryland training. Refer to ACES in chapter 1 for training sets and repetitions:

- *Flexion.* Walk on heels to improve strength of dorsiflexors for extension (toe-up) and to develop strength and stability necessary for loading energy when running (figure 8.5*a*).

- *Extension.* Walk on balls of feet to increase strength of plantar flexors (pointed toe) and to develop strength and stability for unloading energy when running (figure 8.5*b*).

- *Inversion.* Walk on insides of feet to improve stability necessary to maintain a neutral and stable foot and ankle (figure 8.5*c*).

- *Eversion.* Walk on outsides of feet to develop arch stability, especially on uneven surfaces or natural terrain (figure 8.5*d*).

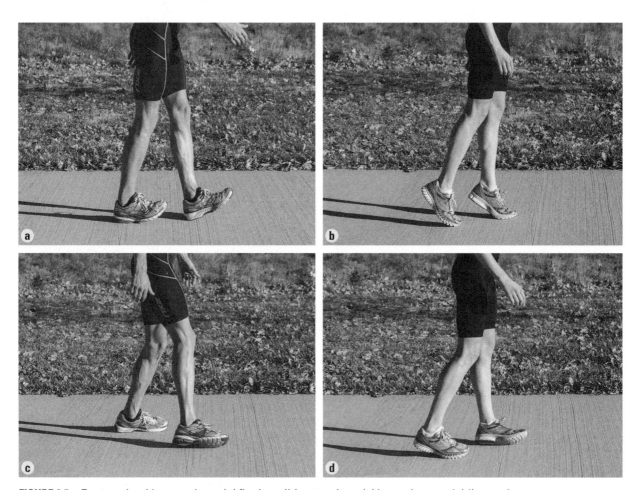

FIGURE 8.5   Foot and ankle exercises: *(a)* flexion; *(b)* extension; *(c)* inversion; and *(d)* eversion.

Foot and Ankle Pronation and Supination

Pronation refers to the extent to which the foot rolls inward as it moves through the gait cycle. Excessive pronation is often caused by loose ligaments or inadequate muscle support. The normal foot pronates (rolls inward) and functions to scatter the loads at foot strike across the intricate muscles, bones, and joints of the foot and ankle. Thus normal pronation is necessary and is how you take on each foot strike, deal effectively with various terrains and fatigue, and maintain best possible propulsion and form.

However, repeated and excessive pronation can place increased stress on the joints in the foot and ankle and along the upper kinetic chain, especially the knee. With excessive foot pronation, the knee can compensate by rolling inward, which can affect performance and possibly lead to other lower- and upper-body problems and injury.

There can be a connection between overpronation and lower-leg injuries, including plantar fasciitis and shin splints. Increased pronation can cause more stress on soft tissue of the foot joints and an overreliance on the foot and ankle muscles. An excessively pro-nated foot during running (stance, midsupport) can cause multiple changes in lower-, mid-, and upper-body motions that are lopsided compensations in technique.

In comparison to the typical low arch of a pronating foot, a supinating foot has a high-arch structure and less surface area when contacting the ground. The oversupinated foot strike (turning the bottom of the sole inward and ankle outward) is important to note because shoes that provide midsole cushioning might not be helpful for this foot type because they can lift the arch higher still. When selecting running shoes, test-run the shoes, if possible, to assess basic body posture, determine any changes in your core, and check how your body lands at the initial foot strike.

- Most effective—neutral posture foot strike. The shoulder, torso, pelvis, knee, shin, and ankle are aligned with a rear-foot-lateral, midfoot-lateral, or forefoot strike at contact (runner on left; figure 8.6).

- Less effective—negative posture foot strike. Pelvis is behind knee and foot at contact with lower leg, ankle, and foot extended in front of pelvis with excessive heel strike (runner on right; figure 8.6).

FIGURE 8.6 Neutral and negative posture foot strike.

Supination is a normal part of running and walking and helps the foot provide a rigid structure during forward propulsion. The supinated foot rolls outward with most of the weight on the outside of the foot, raising the arch. Abnormally high supination can cause increases in external rotation forces on the shin, knee, and thigh and continues to place pressure on the muscles, tendons, and ligaments of the lower limb. A normally pronating foot, however, has better alignment properties and increased capacity for shock absorption, whereas the high arch is less able to absorb shock. Triathletes with high arches (supination) can be more likely to have recurrent injuries such as shin splints, plantar fasciitis, ankle sprains, and stress fractures.

There are of course many factors that cause running injuries and that affect running economy, either positively or negatively. Alignment of the feet and lower limbs is certainly important to consider. There is merit, too, in minimalist ranges of shoes and in foot and ankle mobility and stabilization exercises to awaken inactive and underdeveloped muscles in the foot caused by too much stability in typical running shoes. Running injures are very often the result of continual stress over time combined with faulty foot, ankle, or general running mechanics; training errors; muscle instability; overly tight muscles; hypermobile (too flexible) muscles; or improper assessment and treatment.

Arch, Ankle, and Foot

The arch, ankle, and foot should remain well aligned throughout the running stride. Tendons and ligaments help absorb the forces and support the foot, so they must be strong enough to withstand landing forces. Good alignment helps to use the landing energy generated toward forward momentum. There are two longitudinal arches (medial and lateral) that extend lengthwise from the heel to the ball of the foot. There are also two arches across the foot, rear and front (posterior and anterior). Runners might also be either in-toeing (pigeon-toed) or out-toeing. Either of these conditions can be related to inherited

postures in the feet, knees, or legs, but sometimes muscle tightness is a contributor.

The triathlete can experience overloading in the arches that can diminish speed because of changes in weight distribution. Foot exercises, well-fitting shoes, stability, mobility, the central supporting muscles of the pelvis, and technique can help remedy these issues. Forward momentum is best maintained by a *forward leaning* posture that places the triathlete into an optimal position and posture that reduce landing forces that slow you down. Leaning forward also improves the posture of the ankle joints into a loaded dorsiflexion position and provides a more leveraged foot strike. Simply trying to land mid- or forefoot without coupling posture to alter foot strike is incorrect. Later, in this chapter's section on body lines, you will learn how to better develop a soaring posture and understand the merits of this technique. However, you must have sufficient ankle-joint range of motion; hip extension; proper posture of the hips, torso, and shoulders; and stability in the pelvis to attain and maintain the required posture correctly.

Running Positions and Postures

Running technique training targets the reduction of rotational forces (motions that impede forward propulsion) that can be caused by limitations in functional movement or stability and less than perfect technique. Rotations of the body increase energy use, and triathletes from beginner to elite can have uneven running form.

By now the importance of coupling assessment with corrective exercises and technique work is clear. Every level of triathlete can benefit from body line training technique. Assessment for functional movement and stability combined with technique training are the cornerstone for better running performance. The smallest of irregular-motion corrections can make a great difference in performance.

Good, efficient running looks smooth, with body postures close to structurally perfect. To achieve this, you should first do all you can to develop normal muscle ranges in flexibility,

Key Characteristics of Good Running

How you achieve a proper running position has much to do with the functional performance (flexibility, joint mobility, stability) of your muscles. In its most basic form, good running has the following attributes:

- Stable posture with symmetrical movements of the arms and legs
- Chin level; neck elongated (flattens the scapula and brings the clavicle back so it's aligned)
- Forward and aligned pelvis, torso, and shoulders
- A stable, neutral (not tipping sideways) pelvis (increases load transfer)
- Foot strike under center of body to maximize forward propulsion
- Foot strike cadence of 90 to 97 per foot each minute
- Quick, skillful contact time vaulting from one foot strike to the next
- Reactive posture of the foot strike at midsole to forefoot
- Recovery of the heel (by flexing the knee) during forward swing following toe-off to a point at or above the knee joint
- From midstance, extending the hips through toe-off from big toe (loading and unloading), with *no* exaggeration in leg lengthening (which turns leg into a long lever)
- Recovery during forward swing with a slightly dorsiflexed (toe-up) foot and ankle joint as it comes under the body
- Activation and use of the gluteals, hamstrings, and Achilles for extending the hip backward
- Anticipation of landing with the foot and ankle under center of body and maintaining effective and reactive posture in the longitudinal medial arch

mobility in joints, and the necessary strength and stability in the core muscles. The slightest improvement in efficiency can make meaningful differences in performance, but those changes take focus on form through accurate and controlled repetitions over time.

Postures of the Running Body

To become a better runner, you first need to identify the better postures of your body. In the following sections we'll look at position principles you can work from to build better technique. Every one of your body's regions has a posture; as your functional movements and stability improve, these positions will become more effortless to maintain. These positions are the nucleus of each body line training session described later in the chapter.

Head, Eyes, Chin, Mouth, and Neck

The head is poised neutrally over the shoulders in alignment with the spine; head alignment is forward, vertical, and square when relaxed. The body goes where the head tilts, so keep head level and eyes forward at all times. The eyes' sight line is slightly below the horizon. Eyes are relaxed, open, and calmly taking things in without focusing on any one (narrow) point. Allow eyes to relax and brow (forehead) to completely unfurrow. Do not be overly attached to any other runner. Rather, maintain a connection visually but preserve a calm, relaxed, and broader vision of the circumstances and surroundings. You want to feel *connected* but not *attached* to the situation and competition. Your chin is held forward and slightly below the horizon. Your mouth is open with an uplifted, positive expression. Your neck aligns with your upper spine. Think of this posture as a relaxed, anatomically correct position that you wish to maintain during the entire running stride, step by step.

Shoulders and Scapulae

Shoulders are neutrally positioned over the pelvis. They should remain tension free and low to connect in symmetry with the back, hips, and legs, which are level, square, and low and not elevated, rotated, protracted, or retracted. The clavicle should be back and aligned under the ears with the scapulae (shoulder blades) flat and down toward the hips without arching the back.

Fingers, Hands, and Wrists

The fingers and hands are loosely cupped and unclenched; thumbs rest on middle of index finger. Hands should recover during the forward swing at the middle of the chest (heart). Hands remain generally in the range of the chest to midtorso—just in front of and above the hip, without crossing over the midline. Hands should be cupped lightly, as if holding a small stick in the full hand and fingers. This is the perfect position for the hand and fingers: light and relaxed, with fingertips lightly touching the palms. Wrists are neutral and relaxed (not supinated or pronated) and held in alignment with the forearm. Wrists should not be floppy but more or less in line with the forearm and with no excessive movements.

Elbows

The elbows are central to economical and good running. They should be bent but held relaxed at an angle of 90 degrees. Do not let elbows wrap around the back during the backward swing; keep them moving more or less straight back and forward, close to the body. Moving the elbow in line backward helps increase hip extension during toe-off. Elbows draw back for the propulsive drive and toe-off extension phase of the foot and leg. Note that on steep downhills, winging the elbows helps

maintain stability, like using a balancing pole. The steeper the descent, the higher winging or lifting of the arms and elbows; for ultrasteep downhills, hands are lifted along with elbows. During the forward swing (recovery) of the hand and arm, the elbow finishes about level with the side of the midtorso.

Arms

Arms coordinate contralaterally with opposite leg and hip as your stride pendulums with each foot strike. Focus on a relaxed and compact width (backward swing) and height (forward swing) position. Skillful runners do not overly swing the arms but work within a smaller, economical, and easygoing range of motion. The arms do not provide forward propulsion but are key for maintaining constant horizontal velocity and counterbalancing the rotation of the lower body. The arms stabilize the body by providing angular momentum along the body's axis, which counteracts the momentum of the lower body; you'll run a straighter line because your center of mass is supported by each foot during the stance phase. Arms should be relaxed and held at 90 degrees (bent at the elbow; this angle does not change. Try flexing and extending your arms to find the sweet spot, where there is little to no tension and minimal energy needed to maintain this position. Allow the underside of your forearms to lightly brush your chest during the forward swing. This keeps you compact and symmetrical.

Arms should be straight, high, compact, and relaxed—coupled with the shoulders (held low) and timed at the rate of leg cadence. Arms swing symmetrically with leg movements and assist slightly in forward propulsion.

Torso and Spine

The torso (neck to abdomen) aligns with the neck and is balanced with a very slightly forward torso lean and tilt of the hip (this is referred to as soaring posture and is discussed in more detail later in the chapter). This balances your center of mass neither too far backward, nor upright, nor forward (each of these postures can increase stride-braking forces). The slight forward lean of the torso (chest is pushed forward) uses gravity to sustain forward momentum. Develop this lean by beginning every run in the soaring posture; this will perfect your neutral posture regardless of terrain.

From a standing position, try leaning slowly back and forth, feeling for the most effective position—the soaring position of neutral balance. Or, running on a low to moderate hill, practice moving your torso slightly back and forth until you locate the most economical (least energy used) and balanced body position. Notice how this position changes depending on the level of incline. The key is to remain balanced along the line of the pelvis. A too-upright posture is more common in beginning and recreational runners; this posture results in an excessive forward swing in the arms as well as a foot strike well ahead of the center of mass, thus causing a heel strike and braking force.

The spine arches, generating loading tension throughout the running gait. At support, the spine is more vertical and over the center of mass. At terminal stance (toe-off), there is a reverse-C shape to the spine as hip and leg extend and create loading tension to propel the body forward. Try bringing both hands behind the neck when running to promote a tall, forward-leaning posture. This technique brings the body forward into the soaring posture and places the shoulder blades into the optimal flat-and-down posture that is central to efficient running.

Pelvis and Hip

The pelvis posture is perhaps the most important for maintaining the best base of support. Many running technique and alignment problems are caused by imbalances in muscles supporting the pelvis, and those limiters can affect every part of the body, above and below. At foot strike, the pelvis helps stabilize and absorb load as you alternate from one foot strike, support, and toe-off phase to the other side. Strong deep-layered core muscles help maintain stability and posture of the pelvis. This stability increases load and transfer

potential while the pelvis remains at neutral level with little hip drop. This is why stability (the local stabilizers of the joints) is so vital for optimal running and triathlon performance—these muscles work to hold joints in a neutral posture.

When running, focus on the pelvis to control stability (no up-and-down motion) by feeling the region absorbing, loading, and generating forward propulsion. Train the transversus abdominis and multifidi muscles of your lower back to help maintain a neutral pelvis. Draw in lightly from the lower abdomen (the belly on each side of the navel will hollow out), pulling into a stable low back (no extension of the back).

The hip when running extends (via rotation of the pelvis) and prepares the foot for the best posture during ground contact. This hip extension reduces deceleration that would be caused by a foot strike in front of the center of body mass. Having normal hip extension (and pelvic rotation) flexibility is a requirement of good running. If a line were drawn from shoulder to ankle at toe-off, a runner achieving full extension of the hip and pelvis would have an arched or reverse-C shape (depending on direction) when running. You can preserve and improve hip range of motion through mobility and flexibility training.

From the upper back to the heel, the arch is curved and is demonstrated by the powerful loading of deep-core, back, and leg muscles in preparation for toe-off. Have a photo or video taken of yourself running and freeze the motion at terminal stance (toe-off). You should see the curved C (see figure 8.7 for an example when running uphill, downhill, and on flat land). If you don't, assess hip extension and try combining dryland training with running exercises to improve this essential aspect. Note that the C is observed at faster speeds—5K pace. But remember at toe-off to always extend the hip well behind the gravity of the body, no matter the speed; the C is easiest to see at faster speeds but should always be present and combined with the flat and downward scapulae.

FIGURE 8.7 Forward position with curved C when running *(a)* uphill, *(b)* downhill, and *(c)* on flat land.

Knee and Quadriceps

As the knee flexes and moderately lifts during the forward swing, it leads the ankle and foot. Both the knee and upper leg should be relaxed, with knees moving straight ahead; too much adduction (internal rotation of femur) during the stance phase decreases force production and can lead to overuse injuries. Flex the knee during the forward swing and dorsiflex the ankle to prepare for a quick, reactive, and efficient path from foot strike, toe-off, and forward swing. As thigh moves under pelvis, flex hip gently to increase the tempo of the forward swing.

The quadriceps control the degree of loading and amount of flexion at foot strike (flexion) and then extend the knee toward midstance to increase the degree of flexion following toe-off. Apart from the important role in stabilization, especially during the stance phase, the quadriceps maintain your functional center of mass while your body moves forward and floats up and down (undulates) during each float from foot strike to foot strike. If the quadriceps are limited in mobility or stability, this can result in an excessively forward-leaning trunk.

The knee-flex line is central to maintaining forward symmetry. With normal mobility of the hip and stability of the leg and hip, the knee will travel in line with the second toe.

The foot should be underneath the knee. The knee, hip, and feet work together in a balanced flexing (all together in one motion) with the knee and foot aligned during the entire motion. During the forward swing, the knee should not fully extend the leg but remain somewhat flexed. The intent is to limit the amount of ground-contact time. By attempting to extend the forward swing, the knee and leg reach beyond the center of body mass, which can decelerate the body and increase ground-contact time.

Foot and Lower Leg

In preparation for contact with the ground, the foot and lower-leg muscles are bracing in a functional position for the absorption of impact with the ground and for the regeneration and reuse of elastic energy. You should anticipate ground contact because your foot and lower leg are strong levers for propelling, stabilizing, and maintaining forward momentum. Your foot strike occurs beneath the forward-moving center of mass; the foot contacts the ground midsole to forefoot on the outsides and then rolls inward and off the big toe.

Plant the foot flat to forefoot (heel off the ground) at impact with a somewhat bent knee to absorb the shock of loading. This achieves a loaded and elastic springlike orientation. During forward recovery, the foot dorsiflexes (toes point toward the shin).

Warming the Body for Training

A warm-up is necessary to elevate blood flow to the skeletal muscles. Most capillaries (small blood vessels) are minimally active at rest, but as activity increases so does blood flow to the muscles. After 10 to 15 minutes of warming up, 70 to 75 percent of your blood flow is being directed to the skeletal muscles. A muscle does not reach maximal aerobic capacity until the blood vessels are functional and dilated. The elasticity of muscle is affected by a warm-up because higher muscle temperatures increase the metabolic processes and improves the flexibility of connective tissues, making movement smoother. Cold muscles are more easily injured because the length of the muscle stretch is more restricted and cannot withstand high levels of force. Many exercises can be used as a preevent or training warm-up, or you can warm up by swimming, cycling, or running with light exertion.

FIGURE 8.8 General warm-up exercises: (*a*) walking high-knee gluteal stretch and (*b*) walking hip external joint mobility stretch.

A general exercise warm-up might include one to two sets of four to eight repetitions of the following:

- Walking high-knee gluteal stretch (figure 8.8a)
- Walking hip external and internal joint mobility stretch (figure 8.8, b and c)
- Walking single-leg balance with ground touch (figure 8.8d)
- Foot inversion
- Foot eversion
- Heel elevation
- Toe elevation
- Running backward and sideways on forefoot

FIGURE 8.8 General warm-up exercises: (c) Walking hip internal joint mobility stretch and (d) walking single-leg balance with ground touch.

Running Form Basics: Posture Progressions

When teaching triathletes at any level or when rebuilding running form, it makes sense to start with the principles of body positions. The following posture progressions will help shape running movements by developing the foundations of running technique.

Stationary Posture

This position is fundamental to learning better running form, with posture being absolutely critical for better running. Full-body postures are taught at center of support with the foot directly under the body. All body segments (positions) should line up and be in their respective posture and pose. As you move from the right-side stance to the left side, the positions described are mirrored and rehearsed.

These essential positions and postures should not change; it's most important that the body angle be maintained. The objective is to maintain body lines and prepare during training to preserve form even under demanding circumstances and intensities. These positions are the building blocks for efficient running technique and learning the body line movements. Rehearsing this series of positions is instructive; triathletes at all levels will benefit from including them at the beginning, middle, and end of their lower-intensity workouts.

In an ideal posture, the lobe of the ear lines up with and is centered on the outside of the shoulder, hip, and knee and slightly in front of the ankle. There is a forward-leaning posture (soaring posture) that is maintained throughout the stride. The neck is elongated to elevate the head and chest and to flatten the upper back (this is a key running pose). Last, the pelvis, torso, and shoulders should be forward to distribute body weight in the direction of travel—with a slight fold in the ankle joint (soaring posture).

Every run and every exercise begin with this basic posture: Stand leaning forward, then backward, and to a neutral weighted place. You should feel a sensation of being slightly forward in posture; this slight lean makes the body feel that it could move easily ahead without restraint. This is the ideal posture you want to constantly maintain when running; as you train, you will stay in this posture regardless of technique or slope.

Once you've established the ideal posture, shift weight onto the left leg and elevate (flex) the right leg until the front of that knee is slightly above the top of the left knee. Dorsiflex the ankle of the right foot (bring foot upward). Place the loosely cupped right hand near (and slightly in front of) the right hip, with elbow flexed about 90 degrees. The right forearm is aligned with the right thigh (on the same angle). Place left hand at left of chest (elbow flexes about 90 degrees) while drawing in the navel to activate the deep abdominal muscles (this triggers the transversus abdominis to stabilize hips for better balance). If there is unsteadiness, draw the navel in further. Recheck posture alignment and the drawing in of the navel. This is your basic running posture at the center of foot strike under the body (figure 8.9).

The following exercises progress development from the basic stance posture to walking and running. These are more or less the evolutions from standing to walking to running while maintaining the basic beginning postures and body positions. Some of these exercises will have additional options to vary tempo, height, distance, or practice techniques. We begin with the basic running posture to walking, as shown in figure 8.10.

FIGURE 8.9 Basic running posture at the center of foot strike under the body.

Basic Running Posture to Walking March

Establish the basic running posture shown in figure 8.10. With foot dorsiflexed (toes pointing up), let the right leg fall gently to the ground below the pelvis (figure 8.10a). The foot should land flat to slightly forefoot so the heel does not touch the ground (you want a slight forward tilt of the torso). The left leg and arms now simultaneously change position to assume the beginning running posture (figure 8.10b). Hold this position and go through a quick check of posture by each body region (head, shoulders, torso, arms, knee, and ankle) to ensure positions are accurate. Take another step by marching onto and pausing several seconds with knee flexed and about even with hips. Again, check each posture before taking the next step in a slow walking march. Perform three sets of 10 reps before runs as a warm-up. During runs, perform 10 reps each 10 minutes. Achieve ACES with all movements.

FIGURE 8.10 Basic running posture to walking march.

Basic Walking March to Run

From the walking march stance, progress slowly with knee elevating 30, 45, and finally to 90 degrees; then run 20 meters, maintaining proper body posture (figure 8.11). After 20 meters, slow down, maintaining your posture; then stop, reset your stationary posture, and repeat. Perform three sets of 10 reps with ACES. Follow each 10 reps with a 20- to 50-meter run with proper posture.

FIGURE 8.11 *(a-c)* Walking march to run.

FIGURE 8.11 *(d-f)* Walking march to run.

Walking March, Hop, and Prance to Run

This is an excellent coordination and foot-strike exercise that requires all body lines to be in step. The sequence might take some repetitions to get the timing right for the legs, hips, and arms. Do this exercise only after achieving ACES in the previous progressions.

Begin with a walking march, slowly lifting the knee to 30, 45, and then 90 degrees (figure 8.12*a*). Hop onto the right foot for three reps; then hop on the left foot for three reps (figure 8.12*b*). Maintain a dorsiflexed (stiff foot) for each hop, preserving all body lines—head and neck, arm, elbow, thigh, and feet—with controlled and accurate motions. After the third hop of the left foot, transition into a forefoot-landing run (a prance; figure 8.12*c*). Keep feet rigid and reactively propelling the body forward (prancing). Finish each repetition by ending up in the standing march posture; then begin the next. Begin by doing three to six sets; follow each hop with normal running (not prancing) for 20 meters.

Next, increase the tempo (stride rate, or cadence), maintaining the same increased tempo for the entire set. For example, do three sets of 10 to 15 meters of hopping, 20 meters of prancing, and 30 seconds of walking in which you do the following:

- Set 1—hold a foot-strike tempo of fairly fast.
- Set 2—hold a foot-strike tempo of somewhat faster.
- Set 3—hold a foot-strike tempo of very fast.

Once you have increased the tempo, increase the vertical height of the body during the kickout by directing movement straight up, using elastic energy generated from the force of the foot strike of the stance leg. For example, do three sets of 10 to 15 meters of hopping, 20 meters of prancing, and 30 seconds of walking in which you do the following:

- Set 1—control a foot-strike tempo of somewhat fast.
- Set 2—control a foot-strike tempo of somewhat faster.
- Set 3—control a foot-strike tempo of very fast.

Finally, increase the length of the distance covered during the kickouts (longer distance with less height) by using a powerful bounding action of the stance leg. For example, do three sets of 10 to 15 meters of hopping, 20 meters of prancing, and 30 seconds of walking in which you do the following:

- Set 1—control foot strike for distance somewhat far.
- Set 2—control foot strike for distance somewhat farther.
- Set 3—control foot strike for distance even farther.

FIGURE 8.12 Walking march, hop, and prance to run.

After you have achieved ACES in the walking march to runs, you can add the following variations to stimulate more motor learning and body line adaptations. Maintain the basic posture throughout each technique practice.

Tempo

Fluctuate the rhythm (stride rate) of walking and running by increasing the rate of walking (shorter and speedier steps), and then by increasing the cadence (stride rate; on forefoot) of the running. Perform three sets of four to eight reps of 30 meters, progressing the tempo of walking and cadence of running with a walk or jog as the starting point.

Height

Increase the height of the knee lift when walking; when running, increase the vertical height of the hips by springing from the forefoot with amplified elevation. The purpose here is to increase the height, not the forward distance, while maintaining perfect ACES from head to toe. Do three sets of four to eight reps of 30 meters, progressing the tempo of walking and cadence of running with a walk or jog as the starting point.

Distance

From the walking march through the run, the aim is to increase (by bounding forward) the distance of each stride. For the first several strides (running), take up a long, springing, and reactively energetic stride from one forefoot to the next. Control the same force for each foot strike; the tempo and distance covered are the same (there should be no deceleration in speed or reduction in distance completed) as you seek to maintain ACES. Do three sets of four to eight reps of 30 meters, maintaining tempo and force while running, followed by a recovery walk to the starting point. Rest at least 30 seconds between reps and 60 seconds between sets (jogging okay).

Hurdle Stride

After successful completion of all the exercises described thus far, the hurdle stride guides you to further refinement in running form. Using 8 to 10 hurdles (6-12 inches, or 15-30 cm) positioned in succession (about 2.5 feet [.7 m] apart), maintain and rehearse effective and stable body lines preceding the hurdle, going over, and continuing on to the next.

The height of the hurdles triggers you to step and stride over each hurdle, resulting in less deviation of motion; you want to avoid uncoordinated, asymmetrical, lopsided, or uneven movements. During the lift of the knee and foot over the hurdle, the torso, head, and arms are balanced and symmetrical. Very noticeable running form is shaped into more linear movements, with much reduced foot-to-ground contact force and time.

Hurdle Stride Drill

Start about 10 meters before the first hurdle in the basic beginning ideal posture (figure 8.13*a*). Begin running slowly with body lines (maintaining form) toward the first hurdle; lift the knee and foot by running over the first hurdle with ACES (figure 8.13*b*). The forward swinging knee and foot are aligned, and the recovering knee and foot are aligned. The torso and head are erect and elevated, and the arms and elbow are in ideal postures for perfect ACES as you carry the same movements over each hurdle. Over the last hurdle, try to take the form with you, continuing beyond another 20 to 50 meters with perfect ACES.

FIGURE 8.13   Hurdle stride.

Through body line repetition, you set into motion the motor learning sequences to form and reshape your technique and perfect better proportioned movements. When combined with exercises for stability, mobility, and flexibility, this should significantly improve running efficiency. The hurdle stride helps to improve ACES and is thus highly effective for training greater efficiency in running. It also improves balance, awareness of limb position, stride mechanics, and body lines of the head, torso, hips, knees, and ankle. In addition, it reduces braking forces, promoting shorter foot-to-ground contact time.

Once you have achieved ACES with the basic hurdle stride, you can add higher levels of technique and motor learning to the program. Always maintain the basic posture throughout each technique practice.

Tempo

Reduce foot-strike (contact) time using the same tempo along the 10 hurdles. You are moving off the foot quickly but with the same force over each hurdle. Continue the basic body lines between every hurdle. Perform three sets of four to six hurdles plus 20 meters of ACES body lines. Recover with an easy jog back to the start with at least of 30 seconds between reps.

Height

Following the foot strike, increase the height of the body by springing from the forefoot over the next hurdle. Maintain ACES and keep the same height over each hurdle. Perform three sets of four to six hurdles plus 20 meters of ACES body lines. Height is the goal here, so you can move hurdles slightly closer together.

Distance

Across each hurdle, the objective is to increase horizontal distance following each stride. Perform three sets of four to eight hurdles of 30 meters, maintaining tempo and force running. Follow with a recovery walk to the starting point. Rest at least 30 seconds between reps and 60 seconds between sets (jogging okay).

In the following sections, you can learn parts of the principles of running by using smaller and targeted areas of focused running technique. Coupling these segments with ACES progressions is the pathway for acquiring better technique through training motor skills that link the mind and body, resulting in more coordinated and efficient movements. Over time, you will reach better awareness of limb, joint, and body positions (proprioception) that will improve performance. Because of the considerable ground-to-body forces occurring at foot strikes, you must learn to channel and use that energy via elastic features in the muscles and to reduce wasteful motions caused by ground-to-body contacts.

These workouts should not be so complex that technique is compromised; you are, after all, an endurance athlete. Your goal is to continuously and progressively stimulate a training response that builds threshold endurance and technique together. This won't happen if the training shifts too frequently—there must be an adaption and absorption period. Too much intensity reduces the capacity to maintain body lines by pushing the anaerobic systems. If intensity is too low, stimulus is insufficient for significant adaptation to occur.

Technique Training and Testing for Running

Efficient running is balanced, reactive from foot strike to foot strike, flowing, and controlled. It features coordinated movements of the legs, arms, and body. The forces from the ground during each foot strike can be used to create stronger muscle contractions and requires the best possible posture, functional stability, strength, and coordination. To achieve better efficiency and improved performance, it is important to learn and improve on each running motion. Body lines training can improve running form and efficiency through clear, straightforward practices to achieve a standard of technique. Technique work, however, must always be combined with functional movement and stability. In chapter 4 we presented a comprehensive method for assessing movement and stability, along with

MARK ALLEN Transformation

Transformation is a pact you make with yourself to go from your current state to another one that will be more fulfilling. You know if you reach your goal, you will certainly talk about it with pride. Transformation is a dream, a wish, a desire to shed an old skin that doesn't serve you.

Athletically it can mean shooting for a finish time or placement that has eluded you or that you never had the guts to aim for. It could simply be a desire to take part in a race or event that until now has felt off limits, like something the other half of humanity is capable of. But now it's your time, your chance to pursue something that you know in your current state may be unattainable.

I found myself in those crosshairs in 1982 as a 24-year-old. I was watching the Ironman Triathlon on *ABC's Wide World of Sports*. The event was completely foreign to me. I had no idea what a triathlon was and even less why someone would want to cover 140.6 miles of swimming, cycling, and running all in one day. But it called to me. I had to go to that crazy race and see if I could become one of the seemingly ordinary people who crossed that finish line.

Little did I know that this simple calling would transform my entire life. It became a career born out of passion that lasted 15 seasons. It became a measure of how people would view me as I eventually turned that pivotal moment in 1982 into six victories at an event that some call the most difficult one-day sporting event in the world. I would like to tell you that achieving big dreams is easy. But it is not! If you can surrender to that simple concept, you will be very close to actually fulfilling that ultimate vision you have for yourself.

So let's go to your journey. Think about the big things you want in your life. They could be about athletics. Maybe they are about business. They could be very fundamental changes you are trying to make in how you approach the world. Now here's a question about this journey you are on: What is the one thing you know you need to change about your approach to this dream that you have been avoiding because committing to that change will take you into unfamiliar territory?

You may already know what this change is. Take time to reflect on it. Not the easy change, but the most difficult but necessary change you have to make. Okay, remember that.

I had to go through that process after six "losses" at the Ironman. I had to ask myself what I really needed to do to be prepared to win the biggest race in the sport. The answer was humbling. I saw that I was afraid of the race and that I needed to change that mind-set, to transform how I interacted with a world championship event that took place in some of the harshest conditions on the planet.

Transformation will likely take longer than you thought when you embarked on it. Transformation is digging through your soul until you find the gem hidden beneath self-doubt, fear, uncertainty, and impatience. Transformation works slowly, but with patience its impressive force will let your brilliance shine.

Remember the one thing that you need to change? Make it your goal for the next month to put that change in place. Bring it into action every day. There will be a thousand times when you will want to abandon this crazy pursuit and go back to your old, more familiar approach. But don't give in! Make this key change in behavior so that you bring out your best. Commit and then stick with your new go-to mindset that transforms dreams into a reality!

test exercises to promote continued improvement in basic movements of body function.

Combining functional performance assessment and exercises with technique training is advantageous for triathletes. These benefits interconnect the complex continuum of training, making each marker more efficient. In the following section, we begin with the most foundational and essential aspects of running technique. These movements will serve as models for each of the body line sections following. You should master these movements before advancing to the more specific body line training.

Every runner can improve technique by working on segments of form and movements. However, when coupling technique training with improvement in movements related to weak or immobile muscles and joints, the results are even more beneficial. The learning process begins with sensory information that is processed and converted to movements. One of the challenges in training technique is to self-evaluate your own movement performances, trying to detect your weak areas so you can correct them via targeted training.

Having an awareness of the body's position is one of the key points of relearning, teaching, and improving technique. The ACES training and workout protocols and body line test workouts have been developed to help you learn, feel, and develop the connections between the cognitive and the physical awareness of where the body's limbs are in space (proprioception) and time (tempo). Video is a very good tool, as are the pass–fail principles of teaching and learning.

In the following sections we discuss the body lines, segments, and characteristics that triathletes should strive for and coaches recommend. These should be practiced in sequence with the guidance of the body line training tables that follow the upcoming sections. Recall that in chapter 1 we introduced ACES models of training body lines for three levels of lifestyles and criteria for baseline testing (table 1.4). You will need to refer to these tables, as you did in chapters 6 and 7, to make best use of the tables in this chapter.

Posture and Balance, Head and Neck, and Torso (Soaring) Lines

The purpose of assessing and training to achieve and maintain normal joint flexibility, muscle length (flexibility), and muscle strength (stability) is to improve and sustain the most efficient postures. By repeatedly training patterns of movement (body lines), these areas will eventually develop more economical motions, and technique will be improved. Repetition is the key, and keep in mind that your postures apart from running—your daily postures in everyday activities, such as sitting, walking, picking up the newspaper—are also repeated tasks that affect your movements while running.

Posture and Balance Line

Posture and balance should be taken into account as the foundation of running technique. The essential part of how to practice better technique is to train movements as positions of changing postures—held together from the basic standing posture. Every movement, technique, and body line practice should begin with and maintain the central body posture at all times.

The goal is to achieve an awareness of the positions of your own limbs (proprioception and kinesthetic sense). Through learning how to use your senses to better process information from both inside and outside the body, significant gains can be made. Not only can you learn to move more efficiently, but you can also acquire the skills at the junctions of muscles and tendons that signal information about the forces being applied.

You might consider dividing the body in the sagittal plane and thinking of the body as two parts. A sagittal plane is vertical and extends from front to back, dividing the body into right and left halves from the center of the skull, nose, chest, pelvis, and between the legs (figure 8.14). This is useful in terms of awareness of posture (body lines), but also for perceiving tempo and rhythm and how they compare from one side to the other.

FIGURE 8.14 Posture and balance lines.

Common faults of the posture and balance line include the following:

- Weakness in the gluteus medius (lateral hip stabilizers)
- Poor foot mechanics that affect the movement of and timing from the left to right sides of foot strikes

In proper technique for the posture and body symmetry lines, you work consciously on dividing the body from the center and making each foot strike (on each side) at the same position on the foot and with equal forces. The hips at either side should be extended with precisely the same amount of extension and force (right to left side), and during the forward swing, the hip and knee positions and tempo are equal. The upper body (arms, head, and torso) move or remain stable (elongated neck) when exchanging foot strikes. Ears are aligned over shoulders; chin aligns with sternum and is held forward and slightly below the horizon; and the sight line of the eyes is slightly below the horizon (calm, not fixed).

Practicing posture and balance must include stability training. A central cue is to turn on all of the muscles of the body, particularly the deeper core. Activations at the core can enhance symmetry and stability and create motions that are more equal (mirrored). Much of the ability to achieve posture and balance is based on foot mechanics and stability in the foot and ankle, strength of the Achilles tendon, and the hip and pelvic stabilizers. Try this: Run 20 reps of 50 meters with perfect symmetry and sagittal balance from the left to right foot strike; follow with 20 meters of walking posture.

Head and Neck Line

The head and neck postures are crucial to good running form. Lateral tilting or swaying, flexion (forward bend), and extension (elevated head and extended neck) all affect lower-body mechanics.

Common faults of the head and neck line include the following:

- A flexed (chin-down) neck and head that moves the body's center of mass forward. Practice keeping the upper body in line and rounding the shoulders.
- An extended (chin-up) neck and head increases the extension of the lower back, resulting in an anterior (forward shifting) of the pelvis.
- A lateral (sideways) tilting of the head and neck counterbalances the body in a contrary manner against the forward movements of running.

In proper technique for the head and neck line, the collective torso posture is centered, including arm and leg movements. This provides a balanced base of support—a centering of the body during the foot strike (figure 8.15). The head is poised neutrally over the shoulders, with no compensating movements.

FIGURE 8.15   Head and neck line.

Lengthening (elongating) the neck stabilizes and balances the center of mass of the head over the body. Practice this by raising and lengthening the back of the neck to improve head, upper-back, and scapular posture and performing 20 to 40 reps of 50 to 100 meters while maintaining an elongated neck followed by 20 meters of walking stance posture.

Torso (Soaring) Line

The torso, particularly the chest and upper back, should remain in a balanced posture over the pelvis (figure 8.16). The chest is upright with a slight press forward to maintain this intended and changing balance line with the body's center of gravity. It is important to understand the dynamic (moving) position of the torso when running over varied terrain or at different running speeds. There is continual adjustment of body position and weight distribution to maintain posture and balance. In general, the adjustment is slightly forward because of the forward momentum of running. Being too erect or behind the center of your body's mass places body weight at your back and requires more energy to maintain forward movement.

FIGURE 8.16   Torso (soaring) line.

Common faults of the torso (soaring) line include the following:

- An overly upright posture results in a sitting-in or sitting-back position, increasing heel-strike braking forces.
- Leaning too far forward increases landing forces and energy use.
- Landing with a positive lower leg that is extended in front of the knee and ankle at foot strike.
- A counterbalanced arm swing results from compensations for upright or disproportionate forward lean of the torso.
- There is excessive rotation or lateral movement.

In proper technique of the torso (soaring) line, the body has a slight lean during acceleration, and the pelvis, hips, and back are neutral, with no excessive extension or flexion. The torso is constantly balanced over the pelvis; this position must not deviate during foot strike no matter the pace or terrain. The local stabilizers help to maintain these neutral positions of the joints.

Done correctly, the shoulder, hip, and ankle joints align at toe-off (lifting the heel and not springing off the toes). You should practice running on the forefoot, employing springlike and reactive running, as well as folding into the soaring posture slightly forward from the ankles (figure 8.17). Try to maintain this posture throughout the running movement, regardless of pace or terrain. Awareness of posture and position is central to sustaining forward momentum.

Practice this technique by standing with palms forward and leaning slightly forward from the ankles; then lean slightly backward from the ankles. Find the forward-most posture that advances a neutral body and balance line as you run forward. Then run downhill on a 3 to 5 percent incline with a forward lean that does *not* increase braking at foot strike. Land on the forefoot with a rigid ankle that is balanced and reactive. Turn over the cadence quickly and reactively with linear motions. Begin slowly running, and gradually increase running speed and stride rate, adjusting your body lean to the changes in incline to maintain perfect balance. Do 12 reps of 50 meters with 30 to 60 seconds of recovery. You can also practice uphill running (3 to 5 percent uphill incline) using the same focus as downhill running.

FIGURE 8.17 Soaring posture when running *(a)* uphill, *(b)* downhill, and *(c)* on flat land.

Posture and Balance, Head and Neck, and Torso (Soaring) Lines ACES Test

Practice and test the posture and balance, head and neck, and torso lines together. When you have mastered these, retest by matching your lifestyle level in table 1.3 and your baseline test distance in table 1.4 for a Sub-T, as described in the note for figure 8.18.

Hand and Finger, Shoulder, Forearm, Elbow, and Thigh Lines

The hands, fingers, and shoulders are revealing regions of the body. These areas can indicate posture changes, movement compensations, and high intensities at which running form is breaking down. For example, finger tension (either open or closed) can indicate you are using more muscles away from the core (pelvis, torso, and shoulders) in an attempt to counterbalance compensations caused by overly tight muscles, limited range of joint motion, or instability. These body lines in addition to the forearm, elbow, and thigh make up an important group that with training can lead to more efficient movements and better performance.

Hand and Finger Line

The hands and fingers are important to running form and efficiency because they provide signals of force, tempo, and balance to the entire body.

Common faults of the hand and finger line include the following:

- Fingers are tightly curled, coiled, claw shaped, or tense.
- Fingers are extended, rigid, or exaggeratedly opened.

In proper technique, hands and fingers are relaxed and tension free; each thumb rests alongside a gently curled index finger (figure 8.19). To find this position, place a pencil or similar object between the thumb, forefinger, and palm (figure 8.20). Apply just enough pressure to hold the pencil in place. This is the natural, relaxed, and perfect hand position. Try standing on one leg in basic running posture with this hand position and doing 5 to 15 sets of 20 arm swings (holding elbow at 90 degrees). For odd-numbered sets, swing arms at 90 reps per minute. For even-numbered sets, swing arms at 100 reps per minute. The hand recovers forward in the middle of the chest,

FIGURE 8.18   **ACES body lines test: posture and balance, head and neck, and torso (soaring) lines.**

*SUB-T BASELINE TEST DISTANCE: _____	ASSESSMENT		COMMENTS
ACES	Pass	Fail	
Accurate (pass–fail)			
Controlled (pass–fail)			
Effortless (pass–fail)			
Smooth (pass–fail)			
Rating of perceived exertion	_____		
**Stride rate	_____		

*Sub-T baseline test distance (see table 1.4).

**Stride rate—count number of times the right foot strikes the ground for six seconds and multiply by 10 (e.g., 9 foot strikes equals 9 × 10 seconds = 90).

From M. Evans and J. Cappaert, *Triathletes in motion*. (Champaign, IL: Human Kinetics).

FIGURE 8.19   Relaxed hands and fingers—no tension distal—away from the center of the body.

FIGURE 8.20   Using a pencil to achieve hand and finger line.

hand tension is light, shoulders are low and relaxed, and fingers are slightly cupped.

Shoulder and Scapular Lines

The shoulders support the arms and should be in good position and posture: squared, level, and free of tension, and the clavicle even with the ears. The upper-back muscles support good shoulder position and posture. The shoulder blades as we've discussed as a central running posture must be flat and down. Thoracic exercises can improve these posture body lines.

Common faults of the shoulder and scapular lines include the following:

- Shoulders are rounded forward.
- Shoulders twist, rotating forward and backward.
- Shoulders are sloping or tilted, with one side higher than the other.
- Shoulders slouch.

The scapulae are winging, elevated, and not flat. In proper technique for the shoulder and scapular lines there is very little forward, backward, or sideways shoulder movement. Arms swing below the stable shoulder; shoulders are relaxed, level, square, and low, not elevated or held up. Shoulders are positioned underneath the ears and aligned with the hip joint (figure 8.21).

To practice the proper shoulder-line position, place both hands behind the neck and run 4 to 20 reps of 20 meters; then perform 20 to 50 meters of normal running with square shoulders and flat back. Limit rotation during the drill and carry this technique into the normal run. Another way to practice is to lean your shoulders against a partner's fingers that are lightly touching the points of your shoulders. As you run 20 meters, there should be no deviation in the pressure on both fingers. After the partner steps aside, continue for another 50 meters with the same posture. The upper back (scapulae are flat and down) and the neck are elongated.

FIGURE 8.21 Shoulder line.

Forearm, Elbow, and Thigh Lines

The forearm, elbow and thigh body lines have two elements that can help you maintain balance and posture during the exchange of foot strikes from the left to right sides when running. First, when the right elbow and forearm swing backward, the right knee simultaneously flexes, elevating the right thigh. The forearm and thigh should be close to the same line and angle or very nearly. Second, the inside of the forearm during the forward swing of the arm should be at midtorso height and very close to the chest. Both of these postures and positions help keep rotational motions low and forward propulsion high.

Common faults of the forearm, elbow, and thigh lines include the following:

- Elevating (lifting away from the body) the forearm and elbow results in a backward and outward motion, often a result of instability in the hips (the arms move outward to help balance the body) or restrictions (muscle tightness) in the shoulders.
- The forearm crosses over toward the midline of the body during the forward arm swing.

- The forearm (at back swing) and thigh (during the end of the forward swing of the leg) are not aligned.
- The angle of the forearm and elbow is more or less than 90 degrees.

In proper technique for the forearm, elbow, and thigh line, the forearm and elbow are held at about 90 degrees throughout the forward and backward swings of the arm; there is a neutral position in the joint to hold the arm (figure 8.22). Maintaining proper elbow posture throughout the arm swing (without wrapping around back) reduces body and hip rotation and increases hip extension. At this point, the forearm aligns closely with the elevated thigh of the same side as arm swings and flexes forward and upward.

To practice proper technique, begin in the basic stance posture and assume the posture and positions of the forearm, elbow, and thigh line. Draw in the lower abdomen toward the spine, but continue with normal breathing. Slowly swing arms back and forth with each movement (left to right sides), staying equal in tempo and posture. Keep pelvis neutral (laterally forward and backward) and note the movement and attempts to correct position in

FIGURE 8.22   Forearm, elbow, and thigh lines.

the supporting foot (to maintain arch). Swing arms at a rate of 90 swings per minute, and then switch to the other side. More difficult options are to shift weight onto the forefoot (lifting heel slightly off the ground) and increase the tempo (rate of arm swing) from 100 to 110 to 120 per minute, changing the tempo each 15 seconds.

Forearm, Elbow, and Thigh Lines ACES Test

Practice and test the forearm, elbow, and thigh lines together. When you have mastered these, retest by matching your lifestyle level in table 1.3 and your baseline test distance in table 1.4 for a Sub-T, as described in the note for figure 8.23.

Forward Leg Swing and Knee-Flexion Lines

The next two body lines are important regions for developing your technique. The forward leg swing and knee-flexion lines can improve speed by establishing a more linear, forward-progressing posture.

Forward Leg Swing Line

One of the key points in running is the forward leg swing. When performed correctly, balance, tempo, and timing are improved, and the long leverlike effect of the leg is shortened. What this looks like is having foot, heel, knee, and second toe aligned. At push-off the foot lifts off the ground quickly, coming up and forward toward the gluteal muscles (buttocks). However, this action occurs at the same time as the hip and knee flexion during the forward swing of the leg. This is important because you want to reduce the length of the leg's leverlike action. Too long of an extension following toe-off lengthens the leg and thus requires more energy to bring the leg back under the body. The iliopsoas (iliacus and psoas major) are powerful muscles for flexing the hip and lumbar spine, lateral bending, and rotation of the spine. There is no stronger muscle for flexing the hip.

Common faults of the forward leg swing line include the following:

- There is an elongated extension of the foot, hip, and lower leg during toe-off.
- Back drive of the leg and hip are tense and forced.
- There is an inward or outward angle of the foot or heel (or both) during the forward swing, when the foot is coming under the hips.

FIGURE 8.23   ACES body lines test: shoulder and scapula, forearm, elbow, and thigh lines.

*SUB-T BASELINE TEST DISTANCE: _____	ASSESSMENT		COMMENTS
ACES	Pass	Fail	
Accurate (pass–fail)			
Controlled (pass–fail)			
Effortless (pass–fail)			
Smooth (pass–fail)			
Rating of perceived exertion	_____		
**Stride rate	_____		

*Sub-T baseline test distance (see table 1.4).

**Stride rate—count number of times the right foot strikes the ground for six seconds and multiply by 10 (e.g., 9 foot strikes equals 9 × 10 seconds = 90).

From M. Evans and J. Cappaert, *Triathletes in motion.* (Champaign, IL: Human Kinetics).

In proper technique for the forward swing line the torso is held upright to sustain forces generated by the hip flexors and abdominal muscles, which initiate the forward flexing during the swing (figure 8.24). The forward leg swing and flexion of the knee and hip occurs at the same time, bringing the flexing knee forward in sync with the flexing of the hip. The forward swing is important to maintaining the tempo and extension of the supporting leg, so work to keep the movement on a continuum and balanced. Strive for symmetry of force and tempo from the left to the right side. The center line of the knee and second toe should be closely aligned; knees and feet should drive straight forward and back, with little movement away from the centerline and direction of travel. The foot and ankle should

FIGURE 8.24   Forward leg swing line.

be dorsiflexed during the forward swing. The tension (force generation) from the hips should be active enough to control the joint and the movement of the leg during the forward swing. There should be a relaxed but energetic forward recovery (swing). Energy is important to sustain momentum and tempo of movement from left to right sides. Momentum is continually in a frontward direction.

To practice proper technique, begin skipping relaxed and slowly with a slightly exaggerated (flexing the hip and knee) forward swing of the leg following push-off. Gradually increase the rate (tempo) until posture is all together at flexing of the hip and knee (knee will be higher than normal). The foot and heel comes forward directly behind the center joint of the knee. As the knee flexes, the heel is higher than the knee joint as the swinging leg comes under the body. Practice this by performing 4 to 12 reps of 50 meters of skipping followed by a normal run of 50 meters.

Knee-Flexion Line

The knee-flexion line is central to good running form and begins with the initial forward swing of the leg during toe-off. Skilled runners have this common trait in running biomechanics; less speedy runners do not. This knee-flexion line begins the floating and airborne (both feet off the ground) segment as knee flexes along with hip, and ankle is dorsiflexed under pelvis. As mentioned in the forward swing, the key body line is the posture and position of the knee (how much it flexes during the forward swing). The body moves forward quickly and reactively from the thrust of the foot leaving the ground.

Common faults of the knee-flexion line include the following:

- The knee flexes before the hip (when performed correctly, the movement occurs at the same time).

- The knee flexes too little, leaving heel and foot below the knee joint, lengthening the distance of the leg and foot from the body (this makes for a longer lever that uses energy to bring forward).

- The knee at foot strike lands medially (inside) or laterally (outside) of the center joint line of the knee and second toe.

In proper technique of the knee-flexion line, the foot descends for initial contact (foot strike) as the knee comes forward following the end of stance (toe-off). The knee and hip must flex at the same time during the forward swing, and the heel finishes above the knee (figure 8.25). You land with forefoot underneath the center of the middle inside of the knee. Striking the ground with the center (inside, not the front) of the knee over the forefoot improves joint leverage and capacity to reuse energy more effectively because of the stability of this alignment. This position activates the posterior chain muscles for thrusting backward (gluteus maximus, hamstring. And Achilles line). The knees, ankle, and feet should align during the forward swing and extension (toe-off). As the foot and heel travel forward, they pass through the center of the knee joint and maintain a position over the second toe on foot strike. The hurdle stride exercise (described earlier in the chapter) is an excellent body line drill for perfecting motor learning of this skill to improve the knee-flexion line, hip and knee flexion, and coordination and timing.

FIGURE 8.25   Knee-flexion line.

Forward Leg Swing and Knee-Flexion Lines ACES Test

Practice and test the forward leg swing and knee-flexion lines together. When you have mastered these, retest by matching your lifestyle level in table 1.3 and your baseline test distance in table 1.4 for a Sub-T, as described in the note for figure 8.26.

Gluteus Maximus, Hamstring, Gastrocnemius Soleus, and Achilles Lines

Because these body lines do not have postures or positions, the focus of attention on these regions is in terms of generating force. You must learn how to feel each of these muscle groups activating and generating force, length, and stability. Running technique, as with swimming and cycling, is fundamentally about reducing resistant forces and increasing propulsive forces. These body lines promote learning to better stabilize, anticipate, and generate forces through subtle activations.

Gluteus Maximus and Hamstring Lines

The gluteus maximus is a powerful hip and thigh extender and controls flexion of the trunk and the leg and thigh when they are forward of the hip (during forward swing). The hamstrings are active, controlling the leg and thigh posture as well as slowing the knee before foot landing to increase the muscle stiffness in preparation of loading at foot strike and for most of the support phase. Thus, learning to use stored energy (through stretch shortening and elasticity) in this muscle and others can save energy by making you more economical. You can learn by using subtle generations of movement in specific body regions to gain stability during the support phase and to create more propulsion during hip and leg extension.

Efficient running that uses the storing and then releasing of energy with a balanced posture and attention to muscle generation can be advantageous for triathletes and can minimize energy cost. There should be little deceleration or inertia on foot strike until toe-off from

FIGURE 8.26   ACES body lines test: forward leg swing and knee-flexion lines.

*SUB-T BASELINE TEST DISTANCE: _____	ASSESSMENT		COMMENTS
ACES	Pass	Fail	
Accurate (pass–fail)			
Controlled (pass–fail)			
Effortless (pass–fail)			
Smooth (pass–fail)			
Rating of perceived exertion	_____		
**Stride rate	_____		

*Sub-T baseline test distance (see table 1.4).

**Stride rate—count number of times the right foot strikes the ground for six seconds and multiply by 10 (e.g., 9 foot strikes equals 9 × 10 seconds = 90).

From M. Evans and J. Cappaert, *Triathletes in motion*. (Champaign, IL: Human Kinetics).

foot landing to foot landing. You can learn to continue this efficient exchange of energy largely by generating and engaging muscles that extend and flex the hip and powerfully propel the body forward.

Common faults of the gluteus maximus and hamstring lines include the following:

- Too lengthy of a foot strike results in body deceleration.

- Movement is not actively generated by engaging the hamstrings and gluteus maximus during the stance to extension (toe-off).

- The knee and leg fully extend at toe-off. This increases vertical lift of the body, thus requiring more energy and increasing landing forces that might not be easily overcome. This extension might also increase upper-body rotation, which directs movements diagonally, away from the intended direction of travel. This causes you to overstride, which increases landing forces and depletes stored energy for the thrust.

Proper technique of the gluteus maximus and hamstring lines include better anticipation and control of foot landing (maintaining arch posture) in such a way to minimize the braking forces from the ground and reuse the stored energy. The gluteus maximus and hamstrings fire to control deceleration and increase leg extension. This is achieved by generating and activating these regions through gentle but focused activation of the gluteus maximus and hamstring muscles.

To practice proper technique, as the foot lowers anticipate the landing by feeling the posture and tension and maintaining stability in the foot, hips (no pelvic drop), and gluteal muscles. At contact with the ground, the foot and leg extend back. At this moment, control and produce movement by using and activating the gluteals and hamstrings to extend the leg backward. You are engaging and feeling the muscles assist in extending the leg, giving attention to the body region and how the muscles are firing.

Gastrocnemius and Soleus and Achilles Line

The muscles of the gastrocnemius and soleus (GS) group provide ankle plantar flexion and knee flexion. The GS accelerates the leg from the midstance to later stance, and the soleus provides support for the body by decelerating the downward motion of the trunk at the beginning of the stance phase. At mid- to late stance, the soleus assists powerfully in the acceleration of the trunk and leg upward.

The Achilles is a long and large leverlike tendon that attaches narrowly to the heel and broadens underneath the GS. The capacity of this tendon and the calf complex to stretch and provide energy is an important part of running.

How the foot strikes the ground, posture, and subsequent extension of the hip are all part of running mechanics. Learning to get the most from the stored energy in the back of the leg muscles and tendons will be of benefit. One way to develop this coordination is through reactive training, such as hopping, bounding, form accelerations, jumping techniques, and exercises that include unilateral (single-leg) and bilateral (two-leg) support.

Preactivation (stiffening) of these muscles and tendons (e.g., preparing for impact) is a way to increase the storage of elastic energy. By anticipating the load of impact, you can decrease the stress of the forces while increasing the energy that is reused and released during propulsion.

Common faults of the gastrocnemius and soleus and Achilles line include the following:

- Landing on the heel results in a longer foot strike.
- Body posture is too upright.
- Too much time passes between the storage of energy and release.
- There is overstriding in which the foot lands well ahead of the knee joint.
- There is too much change in vertical elevation from foot strike to the forward float phase.

Activation and Stability Exercises for the Gluteals and Hamstrings

Discovering how to fire muscles is accomplished through learning how to pay closer attention to body regions when training body lines. Some people need a basic lesson in awareness of the function of the gluteals and in how they often fail to use the body's biggest muscle—the gluteus maximus. To evaluate activity in your gluteals, lie on your back with knees bent and feet on floor. Raise pelvis off the floor until level with hips. Holding this posture, extend your right lower leg fully and aligned with the same leg. Do you feel the hamstring firing? If not, that's good. If you do feel the hamstring firing, this means your gluteals are not firing. Try this exercise again, but this time fully engage the gluteals and maintain the holding as you raise the pelvis—don't let up. This time you should not feel the hamstrings firing.

Perform the following exercises to strengthen and practice activating the gluteals. This important muscle is often deactivated through prolonged sitting and needs to be reactivated through both movements of daily living and running.

Unilateral Vertical Squat to Jump

Place your right foot onto a stable platform about midcalf high; hands are on hips. Lower hips with control from the gluteus and hamstring until you feel the muscles fully engaged in the squat (figure 8.27a). The center joint of the knee and second toe are aligned. Rise or jump upward by generating movement from the gluteals and hamstrings through the foot that is fully stable at the arch and planted firmly on the heel and lateral and medial forefoot (figure 8.27b). Do one to three sets of four to six repetitions of jumps plus full recovery, or jog lightly between sets.

FIGURE 8.27 Unilateral squat to jump.

Bilateral Squat to Forward Jump

Lower body by squatting with top of hips above knees (figure 8.28a). Activate gluteal muscles to maintain knee alignment over the second toe. Hands are on hips; head, shoulders, and back are in a functional posture. Thrust upward and forward, generating force from the gluteals and hamstring muscles (figure 8.28b); then land and squat. Rest for several seconds and then start from the beginning. Do one to three sets of 4 to 12 jumps plus full recovery, or jog lightly between sets.

FIGURE 8.28 Bilateral squat to forward jump.

Uphill Bounding with Elongated Movements

On a 3 to 5 percent grade incline on a soft surface, begin with a loping run by slowly bounding and springing lightly onto the forefoot. Increase the thrust and lift (height and distance) of each ensuing foot strike for 20, 40, or 60 meters. Increase the thrust each 20 meters, or run 100 meters and increase the thrust and lift each 25 meters. Perform 20 to 100 meters with full recovery between four repetitions.

In proper technique of the GS and Achilles line, you anticipate the foot landing by slightly stiffening the foot and calf muscles and landing on the forefoot under the knee. You also generate movement (thrust) backward through the gastrocnemius and the push-off of the foot in such a way that there are fewer vertical motions (oscillation) of the body. Slightly more forward fold at the ankle when the foot is underneath the pelvis will help reduce upward motion and increase forward propulsion.

To practice proper technique, perform single-leg hops beginning with a slow 10-meter run followed by 3, 6, 9, and 12 hops onto one foot. The height and distance are moderate, with focus and effort on quick and reactive foot-contact time. Do two or three sets of 3 to 6 hops, followed by one or two sets of 9 to 12 hops. After each series of repetitions, recover with an easy loping jog. You can also perform form accelerations with bounding beginning with light, elastic, and reactive advancing (forward, not upward) strides (foot arch and ankle balanced, stable, and springlike) with picture-perfect body posture. The strides are longer, forward knee lift higher, and arm swing further back, with highly responsive and brief foot-to-ground contact. Perform 20 to 40 meters, increasing acceleration during this distance; or do 60 meters and hold the acceleration level each 20 meters; or do 100 meters, increasing and accelerating during each 25 meters. Perform 12 to 20 reps for distances less than 40 meters, 6 to 12 reps of 60 meters, or 3 to 6 reps of 100 meters. Fully recover with light, reactive jogging between sets.

You can also slowly accelerate running speed for 20 to 100 meters, landing on the forefoot, anticipating the landing by stiffening the foot and lower leg muscles, and quickly transferring weight off the foot by thrusting backward.

Gluteus Maximus, Hamstring, Gastrocnemius Soleus, and Achilles Lines ACES Test

Practice and test the gluteus maximus, hamstring , GS, and Achilles lines together. When you have mastered these, retest by matching your lifestyle level in table 1.3 and your base-line test distance in table 1.4 for a Sub-T, as described in the note for figure 8.29.

Midfoot to Forefoot Strike, D-Flex, Forward Lean, and Knee-Flexion Lines

The foot strike is an important aspect of running, but making too extreme of a change in your inherent strike patterns before, during, and after movement and stability improvement might not be a smart approach. Your posture and stability in the pelvis as well as your trunk and shoulders play a significant role in overall economy. Posture and stability in the pelvis, trunk, and shoulders also affect lower-body mechanics, so it is equally important how the central posture of the pelvis and upper body orients at foot strike. The most efficient triathlon runners are very stable in the pelvis and hips and have exceptional posture in the torso and shoulder lines. Those positions facilitate a more optimal energy-loaded foot strike that reduces deceleration and promotes forward movement; body posture is central, so normal range of motion and joint mobility coupled with exceptional stability endurance are essential.

Though reshaping foot strike might not be the best idea, training for improvements in stability, mobility, and reactivity in the foot and ankle is always a good approach. Even with no designated and measured foot-strike changes, you might face many options in shoe type, and these can also affect the natural inclination of foot-to-ground contact. Thus, learning to improve the body line, stability, and mobility of these regions is a very good way to improve technique and performance.

When the foot is carried as it should be (under the body during the forward leg swing), this can help with balance and energy by creating leverage and stability at and following foot strike. By dorsiflexing (ankle flexes; toes point toward the shins) as the leg swings forward, you can maximize posture, body line, propulsion, and balance.

There are three main types of foot strike (rear foot, midfoot, and forefoot) that influence the economy, efficiency, rate of stride,

FIGURE 8.29   ACES body lines test: gluteus maximus, hamstring, GS, and Achilles lines.

*SUB-T BASELINE TEST DISTANCE: ____ ACES	ASSESSMENT		COMMENTS
	Pass	Fail	
Accurate (pass–fail)			
Controlled (pass–fail)			
Effortless (pass–fail)			
Smooth (pass–fail)			
Rating of perceived exertion	____		
**Stride rate	____		

*Sub-T baseline test distance (see table 1.4).

**Stride rate—count number of times the right foot strikes the ground for six seconds and multiply by 10 (e.g., 9 foot strikes equals 9 × 10 seconds = 90).

From M. Evans and J. Cappaert, *Triathletes in motion.* (Champaign, IL: Human Kinetics).

duration of ground contact, and how the rest of the body reacts. How the foot makes contact influences the ground-reaction forces through the ankle, knee, upper leg (femur), and hip (pelvis). But, as noted, stability, mobility in the joints, and flexibility in the areas above the foot might have more of an influence on economy, speed, and efficiency. The postures and positions of the upper-body regions will affect the foot strikes discussed next.

Triathletes become accustomed to and in some cases adjust (depending on pace, terrain, and fatigue) for their inherent foot-strike patterns. Technique, foot mechanics, foot stability, foot mobility, and shoe types each affect initial ground reaction forces (braking forces), foot and ankle posture and absorption, and stability and reuse of energy. In the following sections we focus on the midfoot, forefoot, arch, and ankle regions that regardless of your foot-strike pattern should help in reducing deceleration at foot-to-ground contact by improving your ability to react. Last, and not the least important, is the posture of the body and the forward-lean line, which is one of the most important body postures through which you can gain significant all-body gains in performance and technique.

Midfoot-to-Forefoot Strike Line

Anticipating the landing and posture of the foot and maintaining arch position can benefit all body movements and increase foot-to-ground reactivity. Where (under the center of gravity) and how the foot accepts the ground and then responds and uses the energy available can be taught. The goal of every runner should be to minimize braking forces at foot strike. Doing so enhances forward velocity by receiving the energy and, through a stable foot and body posture, propelling the body forward more efficiently.

Using a midfoot-to-forefoot strike at the initial contact reduces ground reaction forces in comparison to rear-foot strikers. Midfoot-to-forefoot striking position puts the foot in a reactive and shock-absorbing position in which the calf muscles help reduce the impact loads, and a forefoot strike will significantly increase the loading of the Achilles tendon.

However, to generate the most energy, you should actively prestretch and increase the tension of the tendons around the ankle before the foot strikes the ground. Doing so places the lower leg muscles on alert and increases the neutral position of the ankle. When you achieve this, more energy can be transferred, resulting in faster, more efficient running.

Part of the calf region of the lower leg, the Achilles tendon absorbs, collects, and then takes the stored energy and returns it elastically in a powerful way. During forefoot striking, the tendon elongates during initial contact and support phases, sustaining an immense amount of pulling force.

Running is a bounding activity in which the runner literally springs from foot strike to foot strike; elastic energy in the muscles is stored in each foot strike, returned to the body, and used to produce movement. Learning to use this energy effectively (quickly, using a dorsiflexed foot) and reactively is largely the result of the position of and where the foot and ankle capture the ground and, most important, how quickly those forces are used. It is not the amount of force but how quickly it is used that most influences performance. Landing on either the midfoot or forefoot results in the least amount of contact time compared with rear-foot (heel) striking.

Common faults of the midfoot-to-forefoot strike line include the following:

- Heel striking results in decelerating body speed.
- Unsteady, slow foot strikes from left to right side.
- Lower- and upper-body motions are unbalanced.
- Stride rates are reduced.
- Greater vertical oscillation (upward and downward body motions) occurs.
- The foot lands ahead of the center joint of the knee (overstriding).

In proper technique of the midfoot and forefoot strike line, you land on the forefoot or midfoot to better absorb and collect the energy of forces through the foot strike. Do this with a stable foot (arch and ankle) and move the foot quickly under the body. Maintain a lean or fold as the foot comes under the body. Keep arch stable and strong and ankle firm to increase ground, foot-to-body, and elastic energy and power.

If you are a rear-foot-strike runner, training can help with the lower leg placement; very often, this foot strike in less efficient runners is too far ahead of the knee joint. Rear-foot striking increases ground reaction force, decelerating your forward movement. Techniques that reduce ground-contact time promote better mechanics and improve economy and speed for all runners, regardless of where foot strike occurs.

To practice proper technique, warm up by walking 30, 60, or 90 steps on the rear foot, midfoot, and forefoot. Then walk 90 steps landing on the outside of the rear foot and rolling with good control onto the lateral side of the foot and, finally, off of the forefoot. Proceed slowly with good pelvis, torso, and shoulder posture, making each foot strike as described. Next, begin in the basic standing posture and progress to a walking march. Flex hip, knee, ankle, and arms (held at 90 degrees) at the same time. Take 10 steps with foot falling (lightly) onto the ground, landing on the midfoot; then take 10 steps landing on the forefoot. Slowly progress into a run on the forefoot for 50 meters and then on the midfoot for 50 meters. On each toe-off, lift when the foot plantar-flexes (extending the foot and ankle); at this time, relax the ankle joint to allow a full push-off. Actively pushing off the toes does not increase forward propulsion. At the beginning of the forward swing, the heel is lifted instead of generating movement off the forefoot or toes.

D-Flex Foot Line

The D-Flex (dorsiflexion) line occurs during the forward swing of the leg after the toe-off. The foot is gently flexed (toes and foot up toward the shin) as it passes underneath the pelvis (figure 8.30). The foot and ankle posture is flexed but relaxed with no tension. The foot and ankle remain flexed as the knee, leg, and foot fall effortlessly toward the ground for the foot strike. A foot strike that lands ahead of the knee and center of mass reduces the landing energy because you must suspend propulsion until the foot is underneath the hips. A flexed foot helps the hip and knee flex forward as well and promotes a linear and balanced posture. This position helps establish the rigid, leverlike posture you need to absorb landing underneath the body's center of mass.

Common faults of the D-flex foot line include the following:

- The toe is pointed downward during the forward swing.
- Foot is placed in front of the center of mass (in front of the knee at foot strike).
- The center of gravity of the runner is posterior, causing a prolonged flex in the ankle.
- The heel recoils under body below center of knee joint during the forward swing.

In proper technique of the D-flex foot line, the foot is flexed upward as it comes underneath the pelvis during the forward swing (figure 8.30). Keep the ankle joint firm (as if in a stiff boot) during landing and hopping. Hop forward a moderate distance, maintaining posture lines, foot arch, and ankle posture. After each set of reps, run another 50 meters with a rigid and dorsiflexed ankle (foot and toes flexed toward shin).

To practice technique, begin running moderately with proper posture for 50 meters; then hop for 3, 6, 9, or 12 repetitions of single-leg rigid ankle hops (figure 8.31) onto each leg. Do 8 to 10 reps for 3 sets, 6 to 8 reps for 6 sets, 4 to 6 reps for 9 sets, and 1 to 4 reps for 12 sets. Follow this with another 50 meters of running.

Forward Lean and Knee-Flexion Line

The best techniques in good running can be found in two postures: the forward lean (a soaring forward posture) and knee flexion during the forward swing of the foot as the knee comes under the pelvis. The forward lean is an angle of balance—a neutral, centered body posture that reduces losing speed caused by braking and checking of the foot strike.

A midfoot-to-forefoot strike is often seen in this body posture. This torso posture (forward leaning) advances the runner in a more bounding yet forward fashion that results in higher cadence, less upright and backward torso posture, and shorter heel strike. The torso posture is balanced, rhythmic, symmetrical, and economical.

Combined with this torso angle is the flexion of the recovery leg at the knee during the forward swing. This pendulum motion is seen in good runners—the knee flexes as the forward swinging leg comes under the body. The foot and heel recover above the knee joint.

FIGURE 8.30   D-flex line.

FIGURE 8.31 Single-leg rigid ankle hop to practice D-flex line technique.

Common faults of the forward lean and knee-flexion line include the following:

- Foot strikes result in deceleration, less recoil for energy potential, or poor torso posture.
- Torso body posture is too upright, backward, or frontward.
- There is a low knee-flexion angle during the forward swing.
- The recovering leg is too far back (an extended and long, leverlike leg).
- Cadence is slow.

In proper technique of the forward lean and knee-flexion line, the torso is positioned to limit deceleration of the body at foot strike. The right technique in the knee flexion during the forward leg swing is a quick lifting of the heel that results in proper flexion at the knee (figure 8.32).

Forward lean and knee-flexion postures are combined when running and are positions you must learn to develop. For the torso posture (forward lean), each runner will have a sweet spot depending on mobility in the ankle, foot-strike placement under the body, head posture, and core stability. The posture and

FIGURE 8.32 Forward lean and knee-flexion line.

position of the recovering (forward swinging) leg under the body helps balance the body and improves stride rate by reducing the time it takes from foot strike to foot strike.

To practice proper technique, begin running for 50 meters with basic posture; at the same time, move your center of body mass forward at foot strike and flex the recovering knee so the ankle is slightly above the knee joint. Try to find the most neutral, least-energy-absorbing posture at foot strike, and hold this pace for another 100 meters at a moderate intensity. Then repeat the 50 and 100 meters, but now add to the neutral forward torso posture a prompt lift of the heel up and toward the knee. Repeat these postures and positions on a track, slight incline, and downhill 10, 20, or 30 times.

Midfoot to Forefoot Strike, D-Flex Lines, Forward Lean and Knee Flexion ACES Test

Practice and test the midfoot, forefoot strike, D-flex lines, forward lean, and knee-flexion lines together. When you have mastered these, retest by matching your lifestyle level in table 1.3 and your baseline test distance in table 1.4 for a Sub-T, as described in the note for figure 8.33.

Technique Exercises and Workouts for Running

The training volume (distance), specificity and the right mixture of intensity and recovery during and between workouts is important, but there's a way to mix in technique too. A good coach will include more than time and intensity into workouts. And technique training like the following can go a long way in helping you improve movement while adding attentive body line diversity to workouts in unique and fresh ways. Remember to use the basic characteristics in posture for every run and technique practice.

Technique Exercises for Running

Each of the following exercises can be incorporated into any running workout by focusing attention on body region and technique. On roads, trails, track, or combination of these during a running session, pay close attention to technique. Relax your motions, but in every stride focus on feeling the posture, body line, and muscles at play.

FIGURE 8.33   ACES body lines test: midfoot, forefoot strike, D-flex, forward lean, and knee-flexion lines.

*SUB-T BASELINE TEST DISTANCE: _____	ASSESSMENT		COMMENTS
ACES	Pass	Fail	
Accurate (pass–fail)			
Controlled (pass–fail)			
Effortless (pass–fail)			
Smooth (pass–fail)			
Rating of perceived exertion	_____		
**Stride rate	_____		

*Sub-T baseline test distance (see table 1.4).

**Stride rate—count number of times the right foot strikes the ground for six seconds and multiply by 10 (e.g., 9 foot strikes equals 9 × 10 seconds = 90).

From M. Evans and J. Cappaert, *Triathletes in motion*. (Champaign, IL: Human Kinetics).

Posture Variation Exercise

Over flat, rolling, uphill, or downhill terrain, adjust your posture by changing the position of the torso and shoulders to match the gradient and gravity with the least amount of resistance at each foot strike. The soaring posture is a fundamental position of the running body, no matter the topography. Note how different shoe types affect body posture at foot strike; alterations in foot strike and braking force might be affected by shoe designs that do not best match your foot structure, stability, and mobility. Pay attention to how your shoes feel and how they might be affecting your posture alignment. Sometimes it takes a while to find just the right shoe, but don't ever settle for a shoe that doesn't feel right or doesn't supply the particular kind of support that you need.

At the track, assume the basic standing posture and flex at the ankle forward, with pelvis, torso, and shoulders aligned and frontward in the soaring position. Begin running with no change in posture for 50 meters. Stop. Assume the basic standing posture again. Now lean back and begin running with no change in this poor posture for 50 meters. The idea is to feel the difference in brake time that accompanies this posture. Stop running. Reassume basic standing posture and soaring position; run 10, 20, or 30 reps of 50 meters.

Neutral Arch Foot Strike Exercise

Repeat 20, 30, or 50 reps of 50 meters plus walking 10 to 20 meters while practicing proper landing at foot strike with a neutral arch (maintaining longitudinal and lateral arch posture). The feeling is a supported, reactive, forward-propelling, and noncollapsing arch for each foot strike. After each interval, walk with a firmly held arch and progress into the next distance interval while focusing on quick (low force), responsive (high force), and neutral postures in the foot that do not interfere with forward propulsion. Perform each in basic posture, with pelvis, torso, and shoulder aligned.

Knee Flexion Forward Swing Exercise

Faster triathletes flex their knees during the forward swing; the heel is above the center of the knee joint as the leg recovers and swings forward. Run 10, 20, or 50 meters, bringing heel toward buttocks (slightly above the knee joint); don't push off the toes, but as the stance leg and foot reach full extension, lift the heel up and above the knee. Follow each run with 10 to 20 meters of walking marches, focusing on body posture and dorsiflexing the foot underneath the pelvis—this movement should be initiated from the heel.

Stride Rate Adaptation Exercise

The optimal stride rate has neural, stability, mobility, and flexibility implications; you cannot simply increase stride rate without corresponding functional and neurological training. Good runners have foot-strike rates of 180 to 190 total strikes each minute, and their body postures, stability, and range of hip motion all fit together in a well-coordinated series of movements. Modifying your foot-strike rate should be practiced in an aligned and balanced posture (basic posture) on a variety of slopes and using low-landing forces at foot strike. Run on a flat and gently rolling trail for 60 minutes at a rate no lower than 85 to 90 foot strikes a minute. During the first 15 minutes, include 1 minute of 92 strikes every 4 minutes. After 15 minutes, do two 30-second sets at 94 strikes per minute, plus 30 seconds at no lower than 85 to 90 strikes per minute every 3.5 minutes. After 30 minutes, add three sets of 15 seconds at 96 strikes per minute plus 15 seconds at no lower than 85 to 90 strikes per minute every 3.5 minutes. During the final 15 minutes include 1 minute of 20 seconds at 92, 94, and 96 strikes per minute every 4 minutes.

Foot and Ankle Stability to Bilateral Leaping Exercise

Warm up with basic posture for 12 minutes at low intensity. Form should be relaxed with equal, balanced strides from left to right foot strikes. Walk three to five sets of 20 meters on outside foot, 20 meters on inside foot, 20 meters on heels, and 20 meters on balls of the feet. Perform each with perfect basic posture, drawing in the core, contracting and holding the lower abdomen, and elongating the neck (eyes forward, not down). Maintaining basic posture, put hands on hips and squat down (buttocks pushed back, away) three to six inches, keeping the center of the knee joint aligned with the second toe. Spring upward and forward, initiating the lift from the gluteals; touch down on both feet, squat, and spring up for four to six reps. Jog with basic posture for two to three minutes. Repeat one to four sets. Cool down with one to two sets of walking foot and ankle exercises using a lateral and backward walking direction.

Foreleg (Shin) Angle at Foot Strike Exercise

Good, efficient, economical triathlon runners at foot strike have a foreleg and ankle joint vertically positioned under the knee joint at foot strike. Whether a rear-foot, midfoot, or forefoot strike is used, the better runners have a perpendicular lower leg at the moment of contacting the ground. The foot, ankle, and shin are aligned to minimize resistance and maximize forward propulsion. On the track, begin in the basic march-walking posture. Dorsiflex the foot (toes up) and let the foot and leg fall to the ground; the pelvis, torso, and shoulders will come forward, and the foreleg and ankle are aligned. Walk 10 meters. Repeat 6 to 12 times, following each rep with 50 meters of running.

Change-of-Course Exercise

When racing, triathletes are faced with changes in course direction on flat or rolling slopes and at turn-around points. This exercise alters pace, body direction (going around a cone), and force, and increases energy to restart running. By practicing these changes in training, you prepare for changes in course while racing. Learning to maintain posture by activating the transversus abdominis will help you transition around those change-of-direction points. Perform this exercise by setting up three cones 50 meters, 25 meters, and 100 meters apart on a track or trail. The cones should be at angles, not in a straight line. Run 200 to 400 meters with basic body posture, finishing at the 50-meter cone. Approaching the cone, reduce speed by moving more onto the forefoot, without changing posture. At the apex of the turn, press outside forefoot into the ground while drawing navel toward the spine (activating the core to stabilize the vertebral column and pelvis). Continue on or more toward the forefoot until the 25-meter cone, where you change direction and proceed to the 100-meter cone. Repeat four to eight times.

Hip and Leg Extension to Knee-Flexion Exercise

One of the characteristics of good runners is the range of motion and extension of the hip during the back drive of the leg. Having good hip joint mobility helps maintain natural stride length, and you should consider this as an essential part of supplemental exercise. Normal hip flexibility, mobility in the joint, and stability improve your ability to make balanced, powerful, and faster strides. Note that to produce these desired increases, you must maintain or reshape technique and train joint flexibility, muscle length, and muscle strength in ways that are specific to running. To make use of your hip extension when running, engage muscles to extend the leg and hip backward. Do not make an effort to fully extend the leg because this creates too long of a leverlike leg that results in increasing energy to bring the foot and leg forward. Instead, as the foot moves under the body, drive the hip backward. As the foot leaves the ground, bring the heel up quickly to flex the knee. The gluteals, calf, and hamstring muscles extend the hip and straighten and push the leg backward.

After a 12-minute warm-up, begin running in basic posture at moderate pace. At 50 meters, moderately increase and then hold your tempo level over the next 25 meters with attention to a complete extension of the hip and leg. For the next 50 meters, increase tempo and forward speed, bringing the heel up (after full hip and leg extension) and even with or slightly higher than the knee joint. After each round of 50 meters, 25 meters, and 50 meters, run easily for 275 meters with a focus on extending the hip (activating gluteals and hamstrings) and recovering with the heel lifting up and the knee flexing. Repeat 4 to 12 times.

Low- and High-Loading Speed Exercise

In this exercise you work on synchronizing and controlling body posture and developing forward momentum through better use of landing forces at foot strike. Because the foot is the only part of the body to contact the ground, the skill of controlling foot-strike loading and speed is important. Complete 4 to 10 reps of 300 meters using your natural foot-strike force and speed, 50 meters reducing the force and duration of foot strike, and 50 more meters purposefully increasing the force and duration of foot strike.

Combined Technique Workouts for Running

Following are workouts for training technique by body regions, developing neuromuscular function (stimulating nervous system recruitment of motor units) and proper postures. The entire workout need not be prescribed, but it is of great benefit to regularly mix into running a segment of clear-cut training on technique, stimulating better postures by body region and thus improving economy of movement.

Perform these workouts on trails and track and on both flat roads and roads that feature rolling, climbing, and descending hills of low, moderate, and high slopes. There are many thousands of possibilities for creating workouts and training exercises. No matter which workout you choose, always maintain basic running posture (soaring position).

The following tables show how workouts with technique-driven focus can be incorporated into 30-minute, 60-minute, and 90-minute training sessions.

30-Minute Running Technique Workout

In this 30-minute workout (figure 8.34) you are working on torso posture and the soaring position while running on flats, downhill, and uphill.

60-Minute Running Technique Workout

In this 60-minute workout (figure 8.35) you are targeting torso posture and knee flexion during the forward swing of the leg after toe-off. There are also squatting and bounding exercises to activate motor recruitment.

90-Minute Running Technique Workout

In this 90-minute workout (figure 8.36) you work on body lines for longer durations in combination with short-duration and higher-intensity neural stimulation training. In learning how to initiate and activate specific body regions to enhance neuromuscular patterns of movement under training velocities that will improve the central nervous system, you must stimulate movements via higher intensity to bring about even better movements. Think of this workout as run-specific strength and neural training. You will improve endurance performance by training from time to time at higher velocities. By combining better functional foundations of movement and stability with ongoing body lines and increasing the stimulation of intensity within the framework of technique and movement, you will achieve better performance outcomes.

Begin the workout with neutral arch and torso body line practice to warm up; then do stride-rate work followed by dorsiflexion ankle postures during the forward swing and recovery and foot strike, torso, and soaring. Finally, practice midfoot to forefoot striking with perfect posture and minimal deceleration.

FIGURE 8.34   30-minute running technique workout.

BEGIN SET AT FOLLOWING TIME INTERVALS:	At start	10 min.	20 min.
	Flat terrain: 10 sets of soaring torso posture from the marching-walk position for 30 sec.; each set is followed by 30 sec. of forward leaning while running.	Downhill terrain: on a 3 to 5% downhill grade, assume soaring posture and run for 40 sec. Slowly decelerate, but do *not* brake for 20 sec. Return to starting point or continue from endpoint, repeating for 10 min.	Uphill terrain: on a 3 to 5% uphill grade, assume soaring posture and run for 30 sec. Then march for 30 sec. in the same position. Repeat for 10 min.

FIGURE 8.35 60-minute running technique workout.

BEGIN SET AT FOLLOWING TIME INTERVALS:	At start	20 min.	40 min.	50 min.
	Flat terrain: 1 min. of light running in forward body posture. Then, in 15-sec. intervals for one min., march and unilateral hop for 1 min. Repeat for 10 min.	Downhill knee-flexion exercise: on a 3 to 5% downhill grade, assume soaring posture, leaning down the hill and in balance on forefoot. In 15-sec. intervals for 1 min., progressively increase and maintain knee flexion under the body beginning with 90 degrees (level with knee joint) and finishing with 100-110 degrees of flexion for the last 15 sec. Rest for 30 sec. to 1 min. and repeat for 20 min.	Uphill knee-flexion exercise: on a 3 to 5% uphill grade, assume soaring posture, leaning into the hill and in balance on the forefoot. In 30-sec. intervals for 1 min., increase and maintain knee flexion under the body beginning with 90 degrees (heel level with knee joint) and finishing with 100-110 degrees of flexion for 30 sec. Rest for 30 sec. to 1 min. and repeat for 10 min.	On undulating terrain (flat, uphill, and downhill), work on torso postures by adapting body lean to meet the incline changes; activate knee flexion from 90 degrees on flats, 100 degrees on uphills, and 110 degrees on downhill.

FIGURE 8.36 90-minute running technique workout.

BEGIN SET AT FOLLOWING TIME INTERVALS:	At start	20 min.	40 min.	60 min.	75 min.
	Neutral arch: walk 30 steps with full medial, longitudinal, and lateral arch activation; then run with light, reactive foot strikes, torso forward, and knee flexion at 90 degrees for 2 min. Repeating for 20 min.	Stride-rate neural training: 1 min. normal foot-strike rate of 4 × 30 sec. at 1, 3, 1, and 5 strides a min. higher, followed by 30 sec. at 1 to 2 foot strikes higher than normal. Repeat for 20 min.	Dorsiflexion: flex ankle (foot is held more rigid, flexing toward the ankle) during the forward swing and at foot strike. Continue for 4 sets of 4 min. with 1 min. marching walk postures with a dorsiflexed ankle.	Torso and soaring: 15 min. of perfectly balanced and forward torso soaring with each foot strike reactive and not braking; if done correctly, the knee will flex effectively during forward swing and the feeling when running is forward and efficient.	Midfoot to forefoot striking: focus on the foot and arch posture at foot strike. Maintain the arch and move between 1 min. forefoot and 1 min. midlateral foot strikes for the final section of the workout.

No matter how you are training—in isolated exercises or full workouts—proper posture is important in every stride. Attaining this posture takes more than simply mimicking form. You must also have the right amount of flexibility, mobility, and stability in the joints as well as basic deep-layered core stability. If you observe elite triathletes run, and if you know what to look for, you'll see that posture is the principal characteristic behind optimal technique. Every world champion triathlete has this same posture.

Appendix

The following tables summarize the movement tests and segmental assessment areas for the Overhead Deep-Squat Test, Standing Rotation Test, March Test, Single-Leg Hop Test and Incline Push-Up Test as provided in chapter 4.

Overhead Deep-Squat Test

The overhead deep squat identifies zones of symmetry and asymmetry in the joints, flexibility in the muscles, and stability in the lumbopelvic area and overall body.

Stand with feet hip-width apart and aligned straight forward from heel to toe, with arms straight overhead. Squat as if sitting in a chair (moving buttocks backward) and lower as far as possible while keeping arms as vertical overhead as you can.

Complete three squats filming from the front (anterior), three squats filming from the side (lateral), and three squats filming from the back (posterior).

- Heels are flat with no anterior weight shifting onto balls of feet.
- Feet are straight ahead and parallel from heel to toe with no sliding; longitudinal arch is maintained.
- At the deepest point in the squat, arms and hands are overhead and aligned through the ear, shoulder, torso, and hip joint.
- Torso at the deepest point remains parallel with lower legs (tibia) and does not lean forward more or less than 10 degrees.
- Hips are horizontally aligned with knee (within 10 to 15 degrees above).
- The centers of both knees are aligned over the second toe with no adduction (inward) or abduction (outward) movement during the squat.

Segment	Pass	Fail
Cervical	Head and ears stay in line with arms and shoulders.	Head or chin extends (juts) forward.
Scapulohumeral	Arms stay in line with body and elbows stay straight and do not bend or flex.	Arms bend or lower or shoulder blades elevate or rotate downward.
Thoracic	Upper back and midback stay in neutral position.	Upper back or midback flexes or extends.
Trunk	Low back stays in neutral position.	Low back flexes or extends (arches or flattens).
Pelvis	Pelvis stays neutral and level.	Pelvis rotates, tilts, or hikes to either side.
Femoral	Femur (thigh bone) and patella (knee-cap) stay directly over first two toes.	Varus (outward direction) or valgus (inward direction) of knee is lateral or medial of toes or unable to squat to 90 degrees.
Feet	Toes stay pointed straight forward and arches don't collapse.	Feet turn outward or arches collapse.

Notes:

Standing Rotation Test

The standing rotation test helps to identify zones of symmetry and asymmetry in the joints, flexibility in the muscles and lumbopelvic region, and overall body stability.

Stand with feet together and aligned straight forward from heel to toe, with arms relaxed by sides. Rotate your body as far as possible, keeping arms relaxed. Don't pull with your shoulders.

Complete one rotation on each side (anterior), (lateral), and one (posterior). A perfect standing rotation will have these qualities:

- Big toes and heels stay on the floor.
- Knees remain straight and do not bend.
- Hips and pelvis rotate together without any anterior or posterior tilt.
- Thorax stays erect without any side bending.
- No protraction (forward) or retraction (backward) occurs in the shoulders.
- Head faces forward in line with the sternum.

Segment	Pass	Fail
Cervical	NA	NA
Scapulohumeral	NA	NA
Thoracic	There is 45 degrees of hip rotation combined with 45 degrees of thoracic rotation.	Less than 45 degrees of hip rotation or less than an additional 45 degrees of thoracic rotation.
Trunk	NA	NA
Pelvis	NA	NA
Femoral	NA	NA
Feet	NA	NA

Notes:

March Test

The test assesses the body's ability to control motion at the core (hips, pelvis, and trunk). You are evaluating mobility in active hip flexion.

Stand with feet together and aligned straight forward from heel to toe with arms relaxed at sides. March one knee up to 90 degrees of hip flexion and hold for five seconds. Complete one march on each side while being filmed from the front (anterior) and one march on each side while being filmed from the back (posterior).

- Big toes and heels stay together on the floor.
- Knees remain straight and do not bend; there's no femoral internal rotation, and patella stays forward.
- Hips (femur and thigh bone) remain neutral and do not rotate while lifting knee to 90 degrees.
- Pelvis stays level.
- Thorax stays erect with no side bend.
- No protraction (forward) or retraction (backward) occurs in the shoulders.
- Head faces forward in line with sternum.
- There's minimal weight shift and minimal lateral displacement of pelvis.

Segment	Pass	Fail
Cervical	NA	NA
Scapulohumeral	NA	NA
Thoracic	NA	NA
Trunk	Trunk stays facing forward.	Trunk rotates forward or backward on the standing leg.
Pelvis	Pelvis stays level.	Pelvis opposite to your standing leg hikes up or drops below the level of the pelvis on the standing leg.
Femoral	Foot, kneecap, and pelvis remain facing forward.	Standing leg or pelvis has inward or outward rotation.
Feet	NA	NA

Notes:

Single-Leg Three-Hop Test

The single-leg three-hop test evaluates athletic movement and assesses the body's ability to provide stability and control under heavier loads. This test also provides a means for examining the body's ability to absorb impact from ground reaction forces during high-load activities such as running. This involves movement symmetry from each side and neuromuscular control.

Stand with feet together and aligned straight forward from heel to toe with arms relaxed at sides. March one knee up to 90 degrees of hip flexion and hop in place three times. Your feet must leave the floor with every hop.

Film three hops from the front (anterior), three hops from the side (lateral), and three hops from the back (posterior).

- Feet leave the ground.
- Knee stays at 90 degrees of hip flexion on non-weight-bearing leg.
- No pelvic tilt or rotation; pelvis is level and facing forward.
- No movement in the trunk; lower back stays in neutral position.
- No varus (outward direction) or valgus (inward direction) at the knee; patella stays forward and over first two toes.
- Hip drops vertically over the ankle and does not turn forward over the foot.

Segment	Pass	Fail
Cervical	NA	NA
Scapulohumeral	NA	NA
Thoracic	NA	NA
Trunk	Trunk remains facing forward and low back remains in neutral position.	Trunk turns inward toward standing leg or low back flattens.
Pelvis	Pelvis remains level.	Pelvis on unsupported leg drops below level of pelvis on hopping leg.
Femoral	Patella (center of knee) stays directly over first two toes.	Varus (outward direction) or valgus (inward direction) of knee moves either lateral or medial of first two toes.
Feet	Toes stay pointed straight forward and arches do not collapse.	Feet turn outward or arches collapse.

Notes:

Incline Push-Up Test

The incline push-up test evaluates movement and the body's ability to provide stability and control under higher loads through the upper quadrant.

Stand with feet together and hands on edge of counter, keeping body straight and at a 45-degree angle. Lengthening back of neck so face is in line with sternum, tip shoulder blades up by gently rolling clavicle slightly backward and the inferior angle (lowest part) of shoulder blades forward under armpits. Maintain this alignment as you perform 10 push-ups.

Take one video of 10 push-ups from the back and one video from the side.

- Face and sternum stay in line.
- Chest does not cave in and shoulder blades do not pinch together.
- Body stays straight with no bend in waist.
- Elbows bend down toward sides, not out away from body.

Segment	Pass	Fail
Cervical	Face and sternum stay in line with one another and ears stay in line with shoulders.	Head falls forward of sternum or chin juts forward.
Scapulohumeral	Shoulder blades stay in neutral position.	Shoulder blades shrug toward ears, rotate downward, or pinch together.
Thoracic	Thoracic spine stays in neutral position.	Chest collapses forward or shoulder blades pinch together.
Trunk	Low back stays in neutral position.	Low back arches forward or bends at waist.
Pelvis	NA	NA
Femoral	NA	NA
Feet	NA	NA

Notes:

Index

Note: The italicized *f* and *t* following page numbers refers to figures and tables, respectively.

About the Authors

Marc Evans has been inspiring excellence in endurance athletes and coaches since debuting as triathlon's first professional coach in 1981. Triathletes in Motion, his fourth book, is his most comprehensive work to date and establishes a new standard for coaches and athletes with the Evans assessment principle by stressing the most important precept of coaching: individualization.

Marc has accumulated more than 70 hours of credential-based coursework on movement and technique. He is a respected resource for elite coaches and conducts movement assessment workshops and masters-level education clinics. Marc also has lectured at sport science conferences around the world.

A two-time head coach for USA Triathlon, Marc led the elite 12-member team at the first World Championships in 1989 when Mark Allen won the gold medal for the United States. He was the head coach for the USA Triathlon performance testing at the Olympic Training Center and a founding member of USAT Coaching Commission. Additionally, he was the sports medicine conference coordinator and the director of endurance sports for the Ironman Sports and Endurance Center.

Marc is also the inventor and co-holder of the patent for the Speedo Contoured and Speedo Swim Foil training paddles that have set the standard in swimming design for over a decade. He was presented with the Award of Excellence from the American Medical Association triathlon division and was named the International Coach of the Year.

Marc lives in Boulder County, Colorado.

Jane Cappaert, **PhD**, is a leading expert in the field of biomechanics. Cappaert began her career at the U.S. Olympic Training Center in Colorado Springs. She initially analyzed the biomechanics of athletes competing in a variety of sports. She then spent nine years studying and improving the technique of swimmers and triathletes while working at USA Swimming.

From 1997 to 2000, Cappaert designed, developed, tested, and patented Speedo International's first full-body swimsuit called FastSkin. During its debut at the 2000 Olympics in Sydney, swimmers wearing FastSkin suits won 83 percent of Olympic medals.

After the 2000 Olympics, Cappaert took a position at Reebok International, where she led a team of engineers at Reebok's Human Performance Engineering Lab. While at Reebok, she engineered athletic shoes to meet the specific functional and biomechanical demands of running, power motions, cutting motions, and jumping. After the 2000 Olympics, Cappaert took a position at Reebok International, where she led a team of engineers at Reebok's Human Performance Engineering Lab. While at Reebok, she engineered athletic shoes to meet the specific functional and biomechanical demands of running, power motions, cutting motions, and jumping.

Cappaert is the head of foot care research and development for the Dr. Scholl's brand.

Cappaert lives in Bartlett, TN.